Torn between Empires

Torn between Empires

Economy, Society, and Patterns of Political Thought in the Hispanic Caribbean, 1840–1878

Luis Martínez-Fernández

The University of Georgia Press
Athens & London

Paperback edition, 2012

Athens, Georgia 30602
www.ugapress.org

Designed by Erin Kirk
Set in Palatino by Tseng Information Systems, Inc.
Printed digitally in the United States of America

The Library of Congress has cataloged the hardcover edition of
this book as follows:
Martínez-Fernández, Luis, 1960–
Torn between empires : economy, society, and patterns of political thought
in the Hispanic Caribbean, 1840–1878 / Luis Martínez-Fernández.
ix, 333 p. ; 24 cm.
Includes bibliographical references (p. [301]–322) and index.
ISBN 0-8203-1568-0 (alk. paper)
1. Antilles, Greater—History. 2. Cuba—History—1810–1899. 3. Puerto
Rico —History—To 1898. 4. Dominican Republic—History—1844–1930. 5.
Antilles, Greater—Relations—United States. 6. United States—Relations—
Antilles, Greater. I. Title.
F1741 .M37 1994
972.9—dc20 93-14972

Paperback ISBN-13: 978-0-8203-4165-1
ISBN-10: 0-8203-4165-7

British Library Cataloging-in-Publication Data available

Contents

Acknowledgments

Several persons and institutions deserve recognition for having supported and made possible the preparation of this book. My professors at the University of Puerto Rico and Duke University have been instrumental in my formation as a historian and a Latin Americanist: I wish to acknowledge the late Andrés A. Ramos Mattei, under whose guidance the seed for this project germinated ten years ago, Fernando Picó, whose contagious passion for justice and history continues to have an enormous influence on the way I live and write, Luis Agrait, Guillermo Baralt, Gervasio L. García, Manuel Alvarado, Charles Toth, Aída Caro Costas, Julio Damiani, Blanca Silvestrini, Enrique Lugo Silva, Charles Bergquist, Peter H. Wood, Calvin D. Davis, David Barry Gaspar, Sydney Nathans, Robert Slenes, Arturo Valenzuela, Robert Durden, Colin A. Palmer, and, especially, my mentor, John J. TePaske, whose guidance, high standards, caring, and understanding made the process of researching and writing the dissertation that eventually became this book a challenging and enjoyable experience.

Various institutions and organizations provided support for my research. Duke University awarded me the generous J. B. Duke Fellowship in 1986–87 and 1987–88; the Tinker Foundation and the Program in Atlantic History, Culture, and Society of the Johns Hopkins University granted me a visiting fellowship at Johns Hopkins during the academic year 1988–89; and Bowdoin College awarded me a dissertation fellowship and lectureship in 1989–90 that allowed me to finish the original version of this manuscript in Brunswick, Maine, a town that rightfully prides itself on being a writers' town. Other grants were also important in supporting my research and writing: a Tinker Foundation International Travel Grant allowed me to travel to Spain in the summer of 1987; and two awards by the National Hispanic Scholarship Fund in 1987–88 and 1988–89, a Beveridge Travel Grant from the American Historical Association in 1988, and a Travel to Collections Award from the National Endowment for the Humanities in 1992 allowed me to travel to the Caribbean to conduct research. I am also grateful to the helpful personnel of the depositories, archives, and libraries in which I have worked over the past few years.

I am indebted to the History Department of Bowdoin College for providing support for the typing of the original manuscript and to Virginia Linkovich, who undertook this task with patience and special care. I am also grateful to Peter Miller of Bowdoin College's Academic Computation for helping me with the word processing. The Research Council of Colgate University provided me with support in the final stages of the revision of this book's manuscript that allowed me to revisit the Archivo Histórico Nacional in Madrid and to consult documents at the Public Record Office in Kew, England.

Over the past few years I have benefited from the guidance and friendship of fellow students, colleagues, and professors. Among them I want to acknowledge Carlos Rodríguez Villanueva, Rafael Cabrera, Alex Fernández, Félix Matos, Nicholas Biddle, Herman Bennett, Pablo J. Davis, Rosemary Brana-Shute, Manuel Hernández, Franklin W. Knight, Sidney W. Mintz, Jaime de Jesús Domínguez, Frank Moya Pons, Aarón Gamaliel Ramos, Julius Scott, Chris Bourdouvalis, Raymond Whiting, Ronald Tallman, Tony Kellman, Allen Wells, Tim Hall, Gert J. Oostindie, Francisco A. Scarano, Teresita Martínez-Vergne, and O. Nigel Bolland.

I would also like to acknowledge the role played by the editors of the University of Georgia Press and by the anonymous readers who evaluated an early version of the manuscript. My thanks go to them for treating my work with respect and for helping improve it immeasurably.

An earlier version of chapter 3 was published as "The Sweet and the Bitter: Cuban and Puerto Rican Responses to the Mid-Nineteenth-Century Sugar Challenge" in *New West Indian Guide* 67, nos. 1–2 (1993). Material from several chapters appeared, in different form, as "Caudillos, Annexationism, and the Rivalry between Empires in the Dominican Republic, 1844–1874" in *Diplomatic History,* vol. 17, no. 4 (1993). I would like to thank the editors of these journals for their support.

Finally, I want to express my gratitude for the love and patience that my family displayed while I was working on this project. In researching, writing, and revising the manuscript I used a great deal of time that belonged to them. I am not sure that I can make up for time past, but at least I have something to show for it. This book is dedicated with gratitude and love to my wife, Margie, and my sons, Luis Alberto and Andrés. I am also grateful to God for giving me the strength to go on.

Introduction

This study focuses on the profound economic, social, and political transformations affecting Cuba, Puerto Rico, and the Dominican Republic between 1840 and 1878, a period characterized by waning European control and the consolidation of U.S. hegemony.[1] A number of assumptions underlie this research, the focus of which extends over a period of almost forty years and includes three important components of the Hispanic Caribbean. The first assumption is that an understanding of the international and geopolitical dimensions of the Caribbean is crucial, especially when studying the Hispanic Caribbean, in order to comprehend the major historical developments in the region. As early as the first decades of the sixteenth century the Caribbean became a stage on which the naval powers of Europe played out their rivalries. Well into the nineteenth century the region remained a battleground where the northern Atlantic nations contested for military, political, and commercial hegemony. The structure of this book reflects the importance of interplay between the international and national levels. Chapters 1 and 5 deal with the clash of policies of the northern Atlantic nations that set the stage for the interpretation of developments within the region analyzed in chapters 2, 3, 4, and 6. Despite the attention paid to international developments, the book remains essentially informed by questions pertaining to Latin American and Caribbean history. Developments in the broader Atlantic context are traced here mostly in order to explore developments in the Hispanic Caribbean.

The balance of power in the region shifted dramatically during the mid–nineteenth century. Until 1848–54 the United States stood in a defensive position, while Great Britain, Spain, and France dictated the course of events in the Hispanic Caribbean.[2] After the Mexican War, however, the United States began to assert its commercial and political influence with greater vigor, and by the eventful year 1854, the expansionist thrust of the United States forced the European naval powers to coalesce in order to curb U.S. designs on the Hispanic Caribbean. Thus, an increasingly polarized situation developed between the United States and its European counterparts. This periodization challenges that of most previous studies by North Americanists, which place U.S. dominance in the region at a much later period.[3] A Caribbean perspective on U.S. economic and political expansion and influence produces a picture of greater and earlier domination. This was certainly the view of many of the political actors in Cuba, Puerto Rico, and the Dominican Republic.

During the U.S. Civil War, the geopolitical clock of the northern Atlantic was set back at least ten years, as the war-torn United States reverted to a defensive position. Still, shortly after the Civil War the United States gained even greater political and economic influence over the Hispanic Caribbean. Some crucial realignments also took place during the war. Great Britain toned down its official abolitionism and strengthened its relations with Spain. For their part, liberal and abolitionist Spanish officials in the Spanish colonies sought paradoxically close ties with the Confederate States of America, aiding blockade-running and commerce raiding by Confederate vessels. These wartime realities demonstrated that abolitionist zeal was of secondary importance within Great Britain's foreign policy and that the European naval powers were more concerned about the brewing northern brand of expansionism than about the southern filibustering of the 1850s. The disruptions produced by the U.S. Civil War also provide useful points of comparison in the assessment of trade links between the Hispanic Caribbean and the United States, North and South. Not surprisingly, during this period North American political and commercial influence over the region reached its nadir. Finally, the U.S. Civil War can be considered part of a larger process of liberal, antislavery, anti-European struggles in the hemisphere, of which the Dominican War of Restoration (1863–65), the Mexican struggle against Maximilian's reign (1862–67), and the Cuban Ten Years' War (1868–78) were also part. In this process the European naval powers lost commercial and political preeminence in North and Central America and the Caribbean, while the northeastern and midwestern United States established economic and political hegemony.

A second assumption is that knowledge of the historical developments affecting the United States is critical for understanding the last two centuries of Hispanic Caribbean history. Conversely, the systematic study of the Hispanic Caribbean also provides new and refreshing angles for understanding historical developments in the United States. Throughout the middle decades of the nineteenth century, with the exception of the years of the Civil War in the United States, North American political and economic influence over the region increased tremendously and consistently. Cuba and Puerto Rico became more dependent on their northern neighbor as a market for the region's staples and as a source of foodstuffs, technology, capital, and skilled labor. Politically, members of separatist movements in the region increasingly looked toward the United States as an ideological model and in some cases aspired to solve their colonial problems by promoting annexation to the United States. These circumstances provide the rationale behind the use of a periodization dictated by events in North American history to organize and explain this complicated period in the history of the Hispanic Caribbean. Other students of the Caribbean have applied periodizations based on different criteria, including governorships and colonial legislation, agricultural developments, and technological innovations. All of these have proved valid and useful in their own right and have served well the objectives of those applying them. Nonetheless, focusing on watershed dates such as 1815 or 1873 for Puerto Rico, 1762, 1837, or 1868 for Cuba, and 1844 or 1861 for the Dominican Republic actually creates obstacles to a regional view of the Hispanic Caribbean.[4] The focus of this study is the transformations in the economy, society, and politics in the entire region, and thus the most useful periodization stems from political developments in the northern Atlantic, particularly in the United States. In this study I also make a case for looking at the complexity of the Caribbean policy of the United States, which must be understood as an uneasy compromise worked out among contending sectional, sectoral, and partisan forces.

A third assumption is that understanding the divergent patterns of race and race relations and the ways in which the northern Atlantic powers exploited racial divisions to further their influence in the Hispanic Caribbean is crucial. The historical record demonstrates that a successful application of racial policy by the United States proved instrumental in the process of gaining political influence over the Hispanic Caribbean. Conversely, British abolitionist pressures during the antebellum period and Spain's perceived incapacity to guarantee the subordination of the slave population helped erode the European grip on the region. Analysis of the racial situation offers intriguing possibilities for the study of the different political ideologies developing in the Hispanic Caribbean and also sheds light on the different brands of expansionism and antiexpansionism in the United States.

A distinctive aspect of this study is its regional rather than national focus. The fact that Cuba, Puerto Rico, and the Dominican Republic shared a common heritage of insularity, colonialism, and slavery begins to justify studying them as a whole. Moreover, these three societies shared other elements that separated them from other islands of the Antillean Archipelago: larger size, an original settlement pattern of colonization, late-blooming plantation systems, and racially "whiter" populations. Perhaps their most significant characteristic was their colonial and cultural links with Spain, a weak metropolis that was unable to fulfill the economic role of a modern imperial power.[5] The use of the term *Hispanic Caribbean* throughout this book, indicating Cuba, Puerto Rico, and the Dominican Republic, denotes the relevance of Spain's cultural legacy. The term *Spanish Caribbean*, on the other hand, suggests possession and political ties and is used here only in reference to Cuba and Puerto Rico.[6]

The obstacle remains, though, that only a few historical studies look at the region as a whole. Franklin W. Knight's survey of Caribbean history, Sidney W. Mintz's *Caribbean Transformations*, and Gordon K. Lewis's book on Caribbean thought are exceptions to a fractionalized historical perception of the region.[7] The excellent edited volume *Between Slavery and Free Labor* specifically deals with the Hispanic Caribbean region. These exceptions aside, the fact remains that most Puerto Rican historians study Puerto Rico, most Cuban historians research and write Cuban history, and most Dominican historians engage in the study of their own country.[8] This study, which transcends the country-by-country or island-by-island approach, stresses the commonality of experiences affecting Cuba, Puerto Rico, and the Dominican Republic.

A regional approach allows one to make meaningful comparisons. Different racial compositions, different degrees of integration in the world economy, and different relations with the metropolises of the northern Atlantic are just three of the variables fueling such comparisons. These are extremely helpful in explaining the strength or weakness of movements such as annexationism or abolitionism in the individual components. For example, knowledge of the Dominican case, with its relative underpopulation and the virtual absence of a state apparatus, provides new angles for understanding U.S. expansionist designs in the region. Because of its de jure independent status (except in 1861–65), the Dominican Republic also allows comparisons in which polity stands out as a variable. As the comparative approach prescribes, dissimilarities separating the three countries are underscored throughout the book. Given that the differences have been taken for granted for so long, however, the most important contribution of this comparative approach lies in pointing out the areas of commonality. Focusing on similarities, moreover, strengthens the rationale for including the Dominican case. Despite the obvious differences separating the Dominican Republic from its neighbors, it endured similar political and economic pressures from the northern Atlantic, and its political protagonists responded in strikingly similar ways. As will become evident to the reader, treatment of the three components is at times unequal, a necessary reflection of varying size, population, integration in the world economy, and development of national historiography and the relative wealth and accessibility of documentation.

The chronological scope of this book also warrants an explanation. The year 1840 marks the arrival of British consul David Turnbull in Havana. His presence set in motion revealing and dramatic events marking the erosion of British influence in the Hispanic Caribbean.[9] These changes, of course, would have occurred even if Turnbull had never crossed the Atlantic to play a role in the geopolitical drama. The year 1878 marks the end of the Ten Years' War, the first Cuban war of independence, and also the end of Buenaventura Báez's fifth and last presidential term, which signaled the arrival of a new era in Dominican politics under the aegis of the Blue party. Studies of the region's relations with the United States have mostly centered either on the first stages of the opening of trade and diplomatic relations

(1800–1830) or on the culmination of U.S. expansionism (1890–1900).[10] I was attracted to the study of the relatively ignored middle decades because it was then that the tide shifted toward U.S. hegemony in the Hispanic Caribbean.

Dramatic social and economic transformations also took place in the societies of the Hispanic Caribbean in 1840–78. Increased international competition among the world's sugar producers set in motion a series of changes that transformed the economic, social, and political landscape of those areas with links to the world economy. Hacendados in Cuba and Puerto Rico deemed mechanization as the only road to survival in a world that craved more and more sugar at cheaper and cheaper prices but that was not willing to tolerate slavery much longer. Mechanization, however, eroded the traditional autonomy of the Creole landed elite, as this class was forced to resort to local merchant-bankers as sources of capital. By 1860, for example, an estimated two-thirds of the Cuban sugar industry was in the hands of mortgage holders—most of them Spanish merchants.[11] This loss of economic power further debilitated the political influence of the region's Creole elite within the colonial state. It also pushed many to seek more radical alternatives such as separatism and annexationism.

Finally, I should say a word about the theoretical framework of this book. This study is informed by the dependency approach. The historical record confirmed the adequacy of this perspective, as it became clear that the demands of the core nations of the northern Atlantic not only dictated what, how much, and of what quality the commodities produced in the periphery should be but also the political alternatives open to Creoles in Cuba, Puerto Rico, and the Dominican Republic.[12] I argue that commercial and political influence went hand in hand, and it is with that premise that I trace the changing patterns of trade and navigation, patterns that paralleled changes in political influence over the region. Some critics of dependency have asserted, and sometimes rightly so, that the dependency approach reduces the population of the periphery to mere victims that seem to react subserviently to forces radiating from the core. The pages that follow do emphasize the oftentimes pernicious influence of the northern Atlantic on the part of the world I call home, but they also seek to explore the resilience and originality of the responses that the region has produced, sometimes to its own detriment.

Though not a cold warrior, the author of this book is certainly a creation of the cold war that is thawing even as I write these pages. In writing about nineteenth-century Cubans, Dominicans, and Puerto Ricans who were "torn between empires," I reflect my own experiences and those of millions of fellow *Antillanos* who have also been torn by a struggle between empires and are now scattered throughout the Atlantic Basin wondering what went wrong.

Part One

The Hispanic Caribbean between Empires, 1840–1860

One Clash of Empires

As early as the first decades of the sixteenth century, French, English, and Dutch corsairs and filibusterers began to challenge Spain's exclusivist claims to the New World, turning the hemisphere, the Caribbean in particular, into the arena in which the commercial, ideological, and military forces of Protestant northern Europe and Catholic southern Europe clashed. To use Eric Williams's phrase, the region became the cockpit of Europe. With the passing of time, treaties were signed and broken. The dictates of military strategy, dynastic considerations, and the power of commerce weakened some of the early contenders, while others gained in influence. The United States, even before declaring its independence from Great Britain, began to exert considerable influence over the region as a trading partner. Throughout the nineteenth century the first republic of the New World continued to cast its growing influence over the Hispanic Caribbean, not only commercially but politically as well. The manipulation of matters pertaining to slavery and the exploitation of the fear of racial wars stood at the crux of these geopolitical transformations.

Caribbean Designs of the Northern Atlantic Powers to 1848

U.S. policy in the Hispanic Caribbean during the three decades before 1848 basically aimed at the preservation of the region's status quo. This posture embodied John Quincy Adams's dictum of the "ripe apple": Cuba and other Caribbean islands, Adams believed, would fall naturally into the orbit of the United States once the right conditions arose. This did not mean that U.S. policy in the region was one of inaction. Quite the contrary, the United States sought actively to prevent any situation that would jeopardize its future expansion into the Hispanic Caribbean.

In the 1820s the United States developed a policy toward Cuba and Puerto Rico that differed notably from that applied in the rest of Latin America. Whereas the United States had condoned and even aided the struggles for emancipation in South and Central America, it opposed similar efforts in Cuba.[1] Three factors justified this discrimination. The first was proximity: any disturbance in Cuba, located only ninety miles from Florida, would most certainly have had serious repercussions in the United States.[2] The second was race and slavery: political transformations that could lead to the abolition of slavery in Cuba and Puerto Rico were deemed potentially disastrous for the social stability and labor institutions of the United States, particularly by southern whites.[3] Finally, and perhaps most important, were trade relations. During the 1830s and 1840s the volume of trade between the United States and Cuba surpassed by a considerable margin that between the United States and any other country in Latin America. In 1840, for example, Cuba produced 50 percent of all Latin American exports to the United States and received 43 percent of all U.S. exports to Latin America.[4] Throughout the period Cuba remained the United States's third largest trading partner, behind Great Britain and France. Puerto Rico's role as a trading partner of the United States was proportionately less important, averaging 10 to 20 percent of the volume of Cuba's trade, but still considerable. Thus, commercial and shipping interests in the United States faced the possibility of considerable losses in the event of social and political disturbances affecting Cuba and Puerto Rico. In a recent book John J. Johnson argues that initial sympathies in the United States toward Latin American republicanism subsided, in part, because national attention shifted toward westward expansion and industrial development and because "by 1830 the standard view in the United States was that Latin Americans, despite the rightful pride they took in their independence and in filling the administration gaps left by departing imperial bureaucrats, were on a self-destruct course."[5]

Because Cuba and, to a lesser extent, Puerto Rico were neighboring, slave-based trading partners, the United States sought to preserve the islands' colonial status. As early as 1808 U.S. agents to Mexico and Cuba warned influential local leaders that the United States would be "contented" to see its neighbors "remain under the dominion of the kingdom and family of Spain." U.S. diplomacy also proved instrumental in the failure of the revolutionary conspiracy of Los Soles y Rayos de Bolívar during the early 1820s. This movement and its supporting expeditions, organized in Mexico and Colombia and aimed at liberating Cuba from Spanish domination, were frustrated by U.S. pressure and threats of armed intervention. James Monroe's administration also rejected annexationist overtures by Cuban Creoles in 1822.[6] Two decades later the U.S. Department of State, still adhering to its earlier Cuban policy, relayed confidential information to Spanish minister Pedro de Alcántara Argaíz that proved vital to the violent governmental repression of slaves and free Creoles linked to the conspiracy of La Escalera.[7]

At the heart of U.S. diplomacy in the region was the goal of keeping Cuba and Puerto Rico in the hands of a weak metropolis, Spain. In April 1826 Secretary of State Henry Clay wrote his minister in Spain that the "United States are satisfied with the present condition of these islands in the hands of Spain and with their ports opened to our commerce as they are now open; this government desires no political change of that condition." In favoring continuation of Spanish control over the Hispanic Caribbean, U.S. policymakers also sought to curb British presence in the region. On April 28, 1823, John Quincy Adams communicated to his minister in Spain that "the transfer of Cuba to Great Britain would be an event unpropitious to the interests of this Union."[8]

During the 1840s language behind the U.S. Caribbean policy became tougher. Referring to Cuba, Secretary of State John Forsyth instructed his minister in Madrid "that in case of any attempt from whatever quarter to wrest from Spain this portion of her territory, she may securely depend upon the military and naval resources of the United States to aid her in preserving or regaining it." Robert B. Campbell, the U.S. consul in Havana, echoed this posture in 1843 when he reassured the Spanish captain-general that he could count on

U.S. military assistance in the event of a British intervention in Cuba. A few years later, Secretary of State James Buchanan directed John Slidell to resist encroachments by Great Britain and France in Mexico.[9] U.S. policy in the Hispanic Caribbean during the 1830s and 1840s thus rested on the preservation of Spanish colonialism and slavery in Cuba and Puerto Rico.

While playing neatly into the hands of Spain, this policy clashed with the geopolitical designs of the mightiest of the European naval powers. Great Britain, the nation that once led the world in slave trading activities and that according to Eric Williams owed its industrial takeoff in great measure to capital accumulation linked to slave trading, assumed the role of premier international crusader against the commerce in bonded laborers. Opposition to the slave trade and abolitionism fitted neatly within Britain's foreign policy designs. For one thing, the interruption of the flow of slaves into Cuba and Puerto Rico was deemed necessary to eliminate the edge that the Spanish islands had over the sugar-producing colonies of Great Britain. Also, the end of slave importations and eventually of slavery itself was sought as a barrier against U.S. expansion into Texas and the Caribbean. In Lord Palmerston's words, a free black population "would create a most powerful element of resistance to any scheme for annexing Cuba to the United States, where slavery exists."[10] The rationale was that if slavery was abolished, the United States would no longer covet these territories.

During the late 1830s, particularly after the emancipation of slaves in the British colonies, Great Britain intensified its pressures against the continuing importation of slaves into Cuba, Brazil, and Puerto Rico. Efforts were made to patrol the coasts of Africa as well as the regions receiving the slaves, and institutions like the Mixed Commission for the Suppression of the Slave Trade and the Superintendency of Liberated Africans were created or strengthened to combat the growing smuggling of chattel laborers. A judicial institution composed of Spanish and British judges and arbitrators, the Mixed Commission intended to bring slave traders to justice. In practice, however, this tribunal was virtually inoperative, partly because British and Spanish judges disagreed on most rulings and partly because of endemic corruption.[11]

Between 1838 and 1841 a series of radical abolitionists from Great

Britain filled the positions of the Mixed Commission and the British consular corps. Important among these were Richard Robert Madden, David Turnbull, and Francis Ross Cocking.[12] Because of their staunch abolitionism, these functionaries antagonized those sectors of society seeking the continuation of the slave trade, namely Spanish colonial officials, Creole planters dependent on slave labor, proslavery U.S. consuls, and the slave traders themselves. With a long history of abolitionist activism that included a period of service as agent for the English Anti-Slavery Society, David Turnbull was appointed British consul-general at Havana in 1840. Arriving in Havana late that year, he met a hostile reception by Spanish officials, who refused to recognize his appointment.[13] Despite this, Turnbull and his aide, Francis Ross Cocking, assumed the posts of consul and vice-consul respectively. Their abolitionist activities culminated with the alleged instigation and planning of a slave revolt. Local authorities soon discovered their plans, and both functionaries were forced to flee the island.

There is an ongoing debate about the extent of the slave conspiracies occurring in Cuba between 1841 and 1844. While some historians praise them as examples of overt slave resistance, others maintain that La Escalera and other conspiracies were mere fabrications by colonial authorities, used as pretexts to exercise severe repression against the slave population.[14] There is no disagreement, however, about the fact that David Turnbull and the British government got the blame for these disturbances and their consequences. This situation also favored the dismantling of the anti–slave trade institutions. Spanish officials on more than one occasion ordered that the Mixed Commission be moved to Puerto Rico, where the slave trade was not a controversial issue. Moreover, in 1842 Spanish authorities abolished the post of superintendent of liberated Africans. Robert Louis Paquette, in his recent book on La Escalera, has documented a series of incidents that reflect the strong Anglophobic sentiment among white Cubans following the conspiracy. According to historian Laird W. Bergad, almost all Britons residing in Matanzas and Cárdenas endured the unleashing of Spanish repression in the bloody spring of 1844.[15]

British abolitionist activities of the late 1830s and early 1840s faced strong opposition in the United States, as the slavery issue gained importance there. Richard Robert Madden, the superintendent of liberated Africans, clashed with U.S. consul Nicholas Trist, whom he dubbed "an apologist for slavery."[16] Abel P. Upshur, U.S. secretary of state, went as far as to suggest to Spanish officials that Turnbull and his abolitionist associates be hanged. Reactions were particularly vociferous in the southern United States. Senator James Westcott of Florida asserted that Great Britain sought "to emancipate the slaves in Cuba, and to strike the southern portion of this Confederacy through its domestic institutions." He concluded that this was part of a larger scheme whereby free blacks from Jamaica would be used to expand British influence into the rest of the Caribbean and Mexico. Turnbull's tactics proved to be too extremist even for the taste of the British members of the Mixed Commission, who recommended to the Spanish captain-general of Cuba that he ignore Turnbull on diplomatic matters or issues concerning the slave trade.[17]

Turnbull and Cocking's actions ultimately had deleterious effects both for the standing of Great Britain in Cuba and for the welfare of blacks in Cuba and Puerto Rico. The discovery or fabrication of slave conspiracies in 1842, 1843, and 1844 led to a wave of violent repression not only against the slaves but also against free blacks, mulattoes, and white Creoles.[18] An estimated three hundred slaves died as a direct result of the brutality unleashed against those linked to La Escalera. Furthermore, hundreds of free blacks—six hundred according to one observer—were forced to flee for their lives. The free black and mulatto population suffered the most. Colonial officials blamed this sector with the planning of the conspiracy and executed some of its most prominent members. The mulatto poet Gabriel de la Concepción Valdés, Plácido, was the best-known example. Waves of repression also hit neighboring Puerto Rico, where wholesale slave executions took place in Fajardo and Vega Baja. White Creoles suspected of abolitionist or even anti–slave trade tendencies also endured persecution, and many were forced to leave Cuba.[19]

Repression against blacks was institutionalized by the promulgation of new, more stringent slave codes in Cuba in 1842 and Puerto Rico in 1848. The Cuban slave code restricted the mobility of slaves by requiring them to have licenses to leave their plantations, provided cash incentives for those denouncing conspiracies, and established that blacks had to show respect and obedience to all whites. In Puerto Rico the 1848 code, "Bando Negro de Prim," an immediate reaction to the abolition of slavery in the French colonies of the Caribbean, included provisions for treating violations of the law by slaves and free blacks as military crimes, stipulated severe punishments (death or mutilation) for blacks caught with weapons, and allowed masters to carry out stringent disciplinary measures against their slaves. Interestingly, the spirit and the letter of these codes were directed against blacks and mulattoes in general, regardless of their status. This marked a rupture with traditional Spanish colonial legislation, which formerly had acknowledged and respected the intermediate status of free blacks. These codes must be seen, therefore, as part of a process in which Spanish officials like Leopoldo O'Donnell and Juan Prim sought to secure Creole loyalty by portraying blacks and mulattoes as the common enemies of white Cubans and Puerto Ricans.[20]

The events surrounding the slave conspiracies of the early 1840s injured the standing of Great Britain in the eyes of Spanish officials and Creole planters. In an effort to regain lost territory, the Foreign Office appointed moderate abolitionist Joseph T. Crawford to replace Turnbull. Crawford followed a more pragmatic approach to the issue of slavery and began his tenure as consul-general by firing the radical abolitionist Francis Ross Cocking, whom he said was "up to his neck in the Revolutionary schemes of the Creoles."[21] The impact of the British policies of the late 1830s and early 1840s could not, however, be erased simply by overhauling the diplomatic corps. Turnbull's activities had helped cement the ties between the proslavery parties—Spanish officials, Creole planters, and U.S. consular officials. Furthermore, contrary to British goals, Spain's hold over Cuba, based on the continuation of slavery, was notably strengthened.

Spain's colonial policy in the Caribbean is difficult to assess for two reasons. First, Spain was the weakest of the naval powers, subordinate in foreign affairs to Great Britain. By one estimate, Spain owed 250 million dollars to British lenders in 1847.[22] This standing debt had profound repercussions on Spanish policy, allowing Great Britain to dictate its course on numerous issues. Second, Spanish policy articulated in Madrid changed once it was put into effect in Cuba and Puerto Rico. The anthropologist Marvin Harris wrote, "The Crown could publish all the laws it wanted, but in the lowlands, sugar was king."[23] The transatlantic voyage not only distorted the intentions of Spanish policy but also transformed the character and politics of those instructed to implement it. Miguel Tacón, Leopoldo O'Donnell, Juan

Prim, and others known for their liberalism in Spain turned reactionary and despotic under the glaring sun of Havana and San Juan.

During the 1830s and 1840s, mainly because of British pressure, Spain's policy was one of nominal opposition to the continued importation of slaves into Cuba and Puerto Rico. On March 4, 1845, the Spanish Cortes passed a new law that included harsher penalties for slave smugglers and provisions for the confiscation of their ships and equipment. This piece of colonial legislation, however, met staunch opposition in the Caribbean, where local officials deemed the continuation of slave trading vital to the preservation of the colonies under Spanish rule. In Cuba the new law received little publicity. Despite pressures by the British consul, it appeared only in one issue of one Havana newspaper. The local government prohibited its publication in any other paper in both the capital and the interior.[24]

The distortions Spanish colonial policy suffered in its implementation in Cuba and Puerto Rico helped maintain slavery because Tacón, Gerónimo Valdés, O'Donnell, and most of their successors viewed the preservation of the slave trade as the key to perpetuating colonial domination. In the process, most of these administrators managed to amass huge fortunes derived from bribes related to slave importations. In maintaining the flow of slaves into Cuba they also sustained a twofold strategy aimed at subordinating white Creoles. On the one hand, Creole planters were mollified because they enjoyed a continuous supply of bonded labor. On the other, the expanding number of blacks guaranteed white Creole loyalty to Spain because of growing fears of an islandwide black revolt. O'Donnell once proposed a six-to-four black-white ratio to guarantee submission, and Spanish minister José María Calatrava calculated that the fear of a black revolt was worth one hundred thousand colonial troops.[25] Slavery was also an important weapon against encroachments by other northern Atlantic powers. Emancipation, wrote Captain-General Federico Roncali, "would put an end to the only means for preventing the island's falling to the English or American annexationists."[26]

The foreign policies of the northern Atlantic powers toward the Dominican Republic during the second half of the 1840s were different for three basic reasons. First, Dominicans had gained their independence from Haitian domination in 1844, and thus, unlike Cubans and Puerto Ricans, they were no longer subject to direct foreign control. Second, slavery had been abolished in the Dominican Republic more than two decades earlier, thus eliminating the issue of the abolition of the slave trade. Third, the Dominican Republic, with its subsistence economy, was virtually disconnected from the international commercial system. Despite these differences, Great Britain, France, Spain, and the United States paid close attention to developments in the new Caribbean republic, deploying envoys and secret agents to the Dominican Republic with instructions to check the activities of their rival powers.

Of all the northern Atlantic powers, France was clearly the most aggressive in its Dominican policy. Even before the republic's separation from Haiti, France had demonstrated interest in territorial concessions in the eastern part of the island. In December 1843, for example, the French envoy to Port-au-Prince maneuvered to acquire territorial guarantees around the formidable Samaná Bay in exchange for absolving Haiti of its debt to France. After Dominican independence France insisted on making a portion of the Haitian debt extend to the Dominican Republic. The infant republic resisted this imposition, however, rightly arguing that Haiti had incurred the debt prior to annexing the Dominican Republic in 1822. Undaunted, French agents continued to exert pressure for territorial concessions, withholding diplomatic recognition from the struggling republic until it accepted responsibility for part of the Haitian debt. Later on France became the first European power to establish formal diplomatic relations with the Dominican Republic, a move that forced other nations to follow suit.[27]

Spain also used the prospect of recognition as a means to extort concessions from the emerging nation. In May 1847 the captain-general of Puerto Rico advised Spanish minister of state Antonio de Benavides to use appropriate timing in granting recognition to the Dominican Republic. "It would be desirable," he wrote, "that the Spanish government proceed with great moderation before agreeing to any treaty with Dominican Envoys, in order to secure all possible advantages for Spain." In a later communication he warned of growing British influence in the Dominican Republic and of the injurious consequences of a British loan to the emerging republic. According to his assessment, if the British made the loan, Spain would no longer be able to swap recognition for concessions.[28] If the Spaniards had learned any foreign policy lesson, it was that being indebted to the British meant considerable losses in a nation's autonomy.

For its part, the U.S. Department of State maintained a low-key policy toward the new nation, merely observing the activities of the other naval powers and gathering intelligence about the republic. Early in 1845 Secretary of State John Calhoun sent John Hogan as his agent to the Dominican Republic with instructions to gather information about the island's social and economic conditions. Hogan reported that French and British secret agents and other foreign envoys were active there. Two years later, when President James K. Polk commissioned Francis Harrison as commercial agent in Santo Domingo, he ordered him to monitor the activities of the European agents. In his reports, Harrison continuously mentioned French interest and presence in Samaná.[29]

Thus, despite aggressive and expansionist designs by virtually all the European powers, the Dominicans retained their political and economic autonomy and territorial integrity. The designs of one nation were neutralized by those of others, producing a stalemate. France failed to secure a portion of Samaná, British lenders were unable to force a loan, and neither Spain nor the United States could claim any significant concessions.

The Expansionist Surge of the United States, 1848–1852

The year 1848 stands out as a significant watershed in the course of international rivalries in the Hispanic Caribbean. Up to that point the policy of the United States in the region had been defensive. That year, however, the United States began to put forth a much more aggressive policy, particularly toward Cuba. Several factors explain this shift. First, this was part of a broader antiabolition, anti-British process of expansion in which the Mexican War played a key role. The victory over Mexico in 1847, leading to the absorption of one-half of that nation's territory by the United States, created an expansionist momentum that looked southward to other tropical territories. Colonel William Crittenden, General William Worth, and other veterans of the Mexican War were eager to continue on to Cuba following Mexico's defeat. Also, 1848 was a convulsive year for most European nations. Revolutionary agitation in France, Spain, and other parts of Europe drastically altered the continent's political panorama, and the unity of the European powers against U.S. expansion was seriously, albeit temporarily, undermined. Diplomatic relations between Spain and Britain, for example, deteriorated rapidly, culminating in the dismissal of the British minister to Madrid, Henry Bulwer, and a reciprocal response by the British government.[30]

These circumstances set the stage for the United States to pursue a stronger, more expansionist foreign policy that dissipated both U.S.-based filibuster initiatives and separatist movements originating in Cuba. In June 1848, in response to a series of dispatches warning about an imminent revolt in Cuba, Secretary of State Buchanan cautioned his consul in Havana that an armed insurrection in Cuba would delay, if not destroy, the possibility of U.S. expansion into Cuba. President Polk also instructed Consul Robert B. Campbell that he must remain disconnected from any separatist plot and that he must relay to the Spanish authorities all information regarding such movements. According to Herminio Portell Vilá and other Cuban historians, the Cuban conspiracy of 1848 failed because of Buchanan and Campbell's active interference.[31] Polk's administration also sought to discourage the organization of filibuster groups composed of veterans of the Mexican War.

Official U.S. expansionism was channeled into an attempt to purchase Cuba from Spain in 1848, the first in a series of similar negotiations to take place over the next twelve years. The Polk administration had the support of both northern and southern Democratic elements for this project. In fact, some of the original promoters of the effort were northern Democrats such as Senator Lewis Cass of Michigan and New York editor John L. O'Sullivan, creator of the term *manifest destiny*. Students of U.S. expansionism agree that at this point expansionism had not yet become a sectional issue separating North and South.[32]

Commercial benefits for the different regions of the United States were the primary justification behind the purchase offer. With Spain out of Cuba, free trade could be established, providing unlimited possibilities for commercial growth. In his instructions to the U.S. minister in Madrid, Secretary Buchanan emphasized that "were Cuba a portion of the United States it would be difficult to estimate the amount of bread-stuffs, rice, cotton and other agricultural, as well as manufacturing and mechanical productions;—of lumber, of the products of our fisheries and of other articles, which would find a market in that Island, in exchange for their coffee, sugar, tobacco and other productions." Defensive and military justifications were also a part of the purchase rationale. Protection of standing trade routes was one of the main reasons for acquiring Cuba, the underlying notion being that Spain could no longer keep Cuba under its control and that the island was no longer safe from insurrections or British aggression. Buchanan envisaged a defensive strategy consisting of a series of fortified Caribbean naval stations under the U.S. flag. With such a system in place, the United States would "command the outlet of the Gulf of Mexico between the Peninsula of Florida and that Island. This would afford ample security both to the foreign and coasting trade of the Western and Southern states."[33]

In Madrid, Romulus Saunders received instructions to proceed with the purchase negotiations with extreme secrecy. He was to approach the Spanish minister of state, Pedro José Pidal, in person, not in writing, to avoid the possibility that any document would be made public. Buchanan also stipulated a maximum amount of one hundred million dollars as payment for the island. The approach failed. Saunders proved to be an inept diplomat, who could neither speak nor understand Spanish or French. Moreover, at one point during the negotiations, information leaked, which led to an outcry among the Spanish public. Soon thereafter, the purchase talks ceased altogether. Minister Pidal's final response was that Spain would rather see Cuba sink in the ocean than sell it to the United States.[34]

In November 1848, less than five months after the Cuba purchase fiasco, the U.S. electorate voted the expansionist Democratic administration out of office and elected Whig presidential candidate Zachary Taylor, a southern plantation owner and a hero of the Mexican War. This new administration put in place a different Caribbean policy, spelled out in the instructions to the new U.S. minister to Madrid, Daniel Barringer. Secretary of State John Clayton stated that the United States still adhered to the nontransfer dictum regarding Cuba but that it did "not desire, in future, to utter any threats, or enter into any guaranties, with Spain on that subject." Clayton's successor, Daniel Webster, relayed information regarding Cuban separatist plots to Spanish officials.[35] The Whigs also established more conciliatory policies with Great Britain, agreeing to the Clayton-Bulwer Treaty, which, among other things, restricted future British and U.S. expansion in Central America and prohibited exclusive control by either nation over any Isthmian canals to be built in the future.

The Whig policy no longer provided official support for U.S. expansionism. In fact, the new administration energetically repressed all attempts in that direction. The time thus became favorable for new clandestine brands of expansionism, mainly filibusterism centered in New York City and New Orleans. Between 1849 and 1851 three expeditions left North American soil with the object of overthrowing Spanish rule in Cuba and annexing the island to the United States. Organized under Cuban and U.S. leadership and commanded by Venezuelan-born general Narciso López, the core of the filibusterers was composed of southern veterans of the Mexican War, who were lured into the mercenary projects by prospects of monetary rewards and victory bonuses.[36]

During the years of the Whig interlude, but particularly during and after the debate leading to the Compromise of 1850, the question of territorial expansion ceased to be a national and party issue and became a bitter sectional issue. Many southern statesmen deemed the Compromise of 1850 a serious political setback that threatened to seal the South's minority status and loss of control over the Senate and House of Representatives.[37] California's statehood disturbed the sectional balance of power in the Senate, giving free states a clear majority in the upper house. Southern politicians thus began to look southward for new territories that, once admitted to the Union, would boost slave-state representation. Some white southerners argued that seven new states could be carved out of Cuba and Puerto Rico and as many as twenty-five out of Mexico.[38]

Most of the staunch advocates of expansionism were southern politicians frustrated with their region's impotence in the national political arena. Mississippi and Louisiana produced the core of the expansionists, and New Orleans, a port city with strong Caribbean ties, became the movement's undisputed capital. General López recruited the bulk of his troops and raised most of his funds there. Similar fund-raising efforts in New York had proved fruitless, but in New Orleans, expansionist general John Henderson alone contributed forty thousand dollars to the cause.[39] Violent anti-Spanish demonstrations took place in New Orleans following the execution of López, William Crittenden, and other members of the expedition by Spanish authorities in the summer of 1851.

Alongside the growing sense of sectional political inferiority among southern statesmen were material circumstances favoring southward expansion. The acquisition of territory in the Caribbean appeared to be the solution to the growing need for more land and slaves affecting southern planters in the 1850s.[40] In his study of the South's planter class, James Oaks has asserted that "it is likely that between eighty and ninety percent of the slaveholders did not stay in one place for more than two decades." Migration within the South, Oaks argued, was an integral part of southern elite culture. During the 1850s, however, access to land and slaves became more difficult, forcing expansionist eyes to turn to Cuba and other tropical regions. The Deep South's planter class believed that Cuba, once absorbed into the Union, would become a source of cheaper slaves and cheaper land, land in which to relocate, just as Louisiana and Texas had been for Virginians and South Carolinians a generation before.[41] Some southern planters moved to Cuba in the 1850s, and others were eager to relocate there as soon as Cuba became a territory of the United States.[42] This propensity was particularly evident among cane planters of the lower Mississippi, who struggled under harsher conditions than their Cuban colleagues because they had to pay more for their slaves and because they operated in a climate that made their crops vulnerable to periodic frosts and flooding.

In the 1850s expansionism became a sectional goal of the South. Particularly in the cotton belt, both the white populace and the oligarchy embraced this position. In the North, in contrast, little popular support existed for expansion into the Spanish colonies of the Caribbean. Enthusiasm for expansion in the North was centered in New York City and was linked to commercial, shipping, and financial interests. Prominent among the New York–based proponents of expansion were publicists John L. O'Sullivan and Jane M. Cazneau; Moses Beach, founder of the ardently expansionist New York *Sun;* William Cullen Bryant, editor of the New York *Evening Post;* and capitalist and shipping magnate George Law. Law, who believed that Cuba and the United States would increase their trade ties following Cuba's annexation, even tried to ignite a war with Spain in 1852.[43]

Southern and New York–based filibustering activities faced stringent governmental opposition under the administrations of Zachary Taylor and Millard Fillmore. The Whig governments strictly enforced neutrality laws, prohibiting the arming of expeditions against friendly nations and issuing a series of proclamations prescribing harsh penalties for those connected with filibusterers. In one such document, President Taylor warned of "heavy penalties" and of forfeiture of interference by the government on behalf of the filibusterers. He also equated this type of activity with criminal conduct of the highest degree. In a similar vein, Secretary Clayton delivered orders to district attorneys in New York and New Orleans to arrest those connected with the Cuban expedition. "The honor of the Government," Clayton wrote Logan Hunton, "requires that no just effort be spared to bring [López] to trial and punishment."[44] Fillmore, who succeeded Taylor in July 1850, adhered to the same policy. In a proclamation he said that the expeditions were "adventures for plunder and robbery, and must meet the condemnation of the civilized world."[45] Concrete action gave credibility to the rhetoric of the antifilibuster proclamations. On numerous occasions Federal law enforcement officers arrested López, O'Sullivan, and other expeditionary leaders. The government also mobilized military resources to frustrate expeditions such as the one departing Round Island, Louisiana, in 1849. Such measures, however, were much more effective in New York than in southern cities like New Orleans or Mobile, where popular pressure made the arrest and conviction of filibusterers a difficult task. No judge in these jurisdictions could send a filibusterer to jail without committing political suicide in the process.

Spanish officials in Spain and Cuba, who had welcomed the Whigs' ascent to power in 1849, became increasingly concerned with the inability of the new administration to put an end to filibusterism. Spanish officials were also troubled by the increased militancy of southern expansionism and the importance of that issue among Democrats. Ángel Calderón de la Barca, the Spanish minister in Washington, cautioned his superiors that expansion to Cuba had become one of the pillars of the Democratic party. In another instance, José de la Concha, Cuba's captain-general, asserted that the acquisition of Cuba was a project that combined slave expansionism and economic expansionism.[46]

At this juncture Spanish policy became assertive and challenging. The attitudes of Spanish policymakers were not based on fear of the naval might of the United States. Quite the contrary, the official Spanish rhetoric welcomed a confrontation with the North American power. In an 1852 pamphlet Mariano Torrente bragged that "Spain by herself would destroy the colossus that seems to want to swallow all of America." On another occasion he stated that Spain would have no trouble defeating the United States. Thomas W. Wilson, a U.S. opponent of filibusterism, described this attitude in the following way: "As for Cuba, Spain, now, has no fear; all its inhabitants are Spanish, and no force that the United States can send to the island, could wrest it from her." Another contemporary observer believed that the United States was an inferior naval power and that the Spanish "fleet [was] an overmatch for the whole naval force of America." In 1854 Captain-General de la Pezuela expressed the opinion that in a confrontation between Spain and the United States the latter would stand to lose the most. "If they wish to threaten us with filibuster expeditions," he wrote, "they should send them right away."[47]

During the peak years of filibuster activity, Spain responded by creating a sophisticated, highly effective system of espionage, using Spanish consular offices in New York, New Orleans, Savannah, and other cities in the United States to gather and relay intelligence regarding the schemes of López and his men.[48] In their detailed reports, Spanish consuls included information about proposed dates of expeditions, numbers of troops, and contacts in the United States. The costs of this elaborate intelligence-gathering system and the expenses of the Spanish legation in Washington and other consulates were sustained by funds from the Cuban treasury, the rationale being that these measures were essential for Cuban security and thus should be paid for by the Cubans.[49]

The mightiest weapon in the Spanish antifilibuster arsenal was raising the specter of a racial war, a measure directed to guarantee the docility of the white Cubans. A key ingredient in this strategy was promoting the growth of the black population. In September 1849 Captain-General Roncali wrote to the minister of government, assuring him that wealthy Creoles, because of their material interests, feared the slightest "trace of disturbance or commotion" that might endanger the institution of slavery. He added that as a last resort, Spain could retreat and leave another Haiti in the hands of the victors. Three weeks later he suggested that "the terrible weapon [a decree of emancipation] could, in the last extreme, prevent the loss of the island. . . . if the inhabitants convince themselves that it will be used, they will tremble and renounce every illusion before bringing upon themselves such an anathema." This "Spanish or African" policy toward Cuba was openly proclaimed in the Spanish press and contemporary tracts.[50] In his 1852 volume of *Bosquejo económico* Mariano Torrente advocated measures for the growth of the black population, including government incentives, importation of more female slaves, and better nutrition and prenatal care for pregnant slaves. Torrente stated that even those least favorable to the Spanish government "know well the danger of any attempt to alter the public tranquility." Another publication subsidized by the Spanish government highlighted the horror of a racial war in what it portrayed as an area surrounded by a "multitude of demoralized free blacks." Fears of racial wars were not only used to keep Creoles in line; they were also used to create tensions between Great Britain and the United States. In a revealing document, the president of the Spanish Council of Ministers outlined this strategy: "Although the main threat comes from the Anglo-American Annexationists who desire the Island of Cuba to perpetuate slavery there, I should, however, bring to the attention of your excellency and that of the captain-general the existence of an American Spanish party which aspires to Cuba's independence with abolition of slavery. This party will always receive the support of England, while the annexationist proslavery party will be backed by the United States; it would be convenient for us to wisely take advantage of this rivalry to insure the security of that Province."[51] The Spanish or African policy, however, was a sensitive weapon. Pushing it to a certain point could serve a useful purpose, but its abuse could, as it eventually did, scare the Creoles into taking other extreme measures.

Promoting a coalition of European powers against the United States was yet another strategy in the arsenal of Spanish colonial policy to curb U.S. encroachments in the Caribbean. Torrente believed that all of Europe should be concerned that Cuba not fall into the hands of the United States. As early as July 1849 Minister Pedro José Pidal warned David Barringer that if the United States failed to control the filibusterers, "Spain and the rest of Europe will be obliged to make other arrangements, and combinations." Eventually Spain formally requested British and French support. Great Britain responded by increasing its naval presence in Cuban waters, particularly in August 1851, at the time of López's Bahía Honda expedition. By 1852 a British, Spanish, and French coalition was established to guarantee Cuba for Spain.[52] At that point France and Great Britain took the initiative for a tripartite treaty with the United States, in which all three nations were to "disclaim, both now and for hereafter, all intention to obtain possession of the island of Cuba."[53]

The United States rejected these overtures. Secretary of State Edward Everett responded to Great Britain and France by underscoring his country's traditional aversion to political alliances and presenting Cuba as an American problem, not a European one. He argued that the United States had much more at stake in Cuba defensively and commercially than any of the European nations. In his response to his European counterparts, Everett asked rhetorically how their countries would react if the United States proposed a similar treaty concerning an island that "like Cuba, belonging to the Spanish Crown, guarded the entrance of the Thames and the Seine." Everett also candidly cited domestic politics as an obstacle. No administration, he stated, "could stand a day under the odium of having stipulated with the great powers of Europe, that in no future time . . . should the United States ever make the acquisition of Cuba."[54]

The course of international rivalry over the Dominican Republic was also shaped by the filibuster scares of 1849–51. European statesmen viewed the region as a monolithic unit, fearing that either the U.S. government or the filibusterers would use the emerging republic as an expansionist beachhead. The activities of North American filibusterers were not directed against the Dominican Republic, however, mainly because slavery had been abolished there and because, in their view, it had an unacceptable majority of free blacks and mulattoes. In the southern United States efforts were being made to reduce the free black population, either by closing the roads to manumission or by reenslaving free blacks, so most white southerners deemed a large population of free blacks inadmissible within a southern, slave-based Caribbean empire. Thus, U.S. interests in the Dominican Republic during the 1850s were notably different from interests in Cuba. While most U.S. expansionists coveted the Spanish colony for its potential in the spread of agrarian, slave-based capitalism, other imperialists began to look at the Dominican Republic for its strategic naval possibilities and its prospects for extractive, speculative ventures such as mining and land speculation. Also, because of the island's relatively sparse population, U.S. capitalists planned migration projects to the Dominican Republic.[55] These differences were neatly paralleled in the origins of the consular representatives deployed to the region. Whereas most U.S. consuls and consular agents in Cuba were southerners, many of them plantation owners, those serving in the Dominican Republic were predominantly Northeast-based speculators linked to commercial and shipping interests.

The posture of the United States in the Dominican Republic during the first few years of that country's independence was, at best, a defensive one. Special agent Benjamin Green was dispatched to keep close watch over British and French agents trying to gain concessions in Samaná. Green also received orders to negotiate land cessions in Samaná for the establishment of a coal depot for U.S. steamers and to keep close watch on the activities of Spanish agents.[56]

During the 1850s the European powers continued to check each other's activities in the Dominican Republic, but they became increasingly concerned with the possibility of expansionist activities by the United States. European agents began to signal intensified U.S. presence in Dominican territory as early as 1850. A polarized situation thus emerged, with Europe and the United States on opposite sides. Great Britain, meanwhile, adhered to its policy of not wanting to establish new colonial possessions in the hemisphere while seeking to avoid any disturbances that might hamper British trade in the region. After all, if Great Britain already controlled between half and three-fourths of the Dominican Republic's foreign trade, why should it bother with costly imperial ventures there? In Great Britain a sort of consensus had crystallized around the notion that empires were expensive and even unnecessary, once industrial and naval superiority guaranteed control over neocolonial markets.[57] Also during this period, French policy toward the Dominican Republic became less aggressive and increasingly defensive. Fearing U.S. and British resistance, the French government repeatedly rejected Dominican offers for the establishment of a protectorate. The French envoy to the struggling republic also exchanged intelligence with Spanish authorities concerning alleged schemes by U.S. citizens to bring in troops disguised as immigrant farmers. In one communication to the captain-general of Cuba, a French envoy suggested that their governments use Buenaventura Báez, a caudillo from the Azua region, to curb the growth of U.S. influence.[58]

Of all the European powers, Spain was the most preoccupied with U.S. designs in the Dominican Republic. In the summer of 1852 Spanish agents began to report the details of alleged expansionist schemes by U.S. filibusterers. José M. Pando relayed rumors about a projected immigration of North Americans linked to a filibuster expedition to Cuba. In a similar dispatch, the Spanish consular agent at Turks Islands reported that the migration project was part of a broader scheme, whereby the United States sought to subjugate the Dominican people under a plantation system.[59] By September 1852 the Spanish captain-general of Puerto Rico was recommending armed intervention to stop U.S. expansion, and later that year the president of the Spanish Council of Ministers outlined a drastic strategy, suggesting that secret agents be dispatched and that ties with the Báez party be cultivated for use against the United States. He also recommended troop deployments, adding: "All of this could be achieved without the entanglement of formally recognizing the independence of Santo Domingo, because this is not necessary, and besides, it is convenient to reserve the weapon of recognition for a more propitious and useful moment."[60] In all likelihood Spanish agents purposely exaggerated the seriousness of the filibuster threat. Such reports, their rhetoric notwithstanding, reveal a defensive posture toward a palpable newfound assertiveness in U.S. designs toward the infant republic of the Caribbean.

In 1849 a new variable entered the equation. Faustin Soulouque, the illiterate emperor of Haiti, invaded the Dominican Republic with ten thousand troops in an effort to reunite both parts of the island under his rule. Each of the four naval powers concerned tried to use this situation to its own geopolitical advantage. The two emerging Dominican caudillos also manipulated these circumstances to cement their leadership positions. Pedro Santana, in particular, believed, as did many of his contemporaries, that he was the only Dominican capable of defeating the Haitian foe. Foreign envoys reported details of the developments of the Haitian invasion. In one dispatch, Benjamin Green attested that Emperor Faustin had sworn, "by the soul of his mother, that he [would] not leave a chicken alive on Dominican soil."[61] On April 13, 1849, the U.S. commercial agent in Santo Domingo described the situation in distressing terms: "A great consternation and alarm prevails here due to the fact that Haitian President Soulouque is at two days' distance from this city marching with ten thousand blacks; he has ordered the extermination of all whites and mulattoes, and has thus far defeated the Dominicans in all the battles. My residence is totally filled with frightened women." In the same vein, his French counterpart reported that Soulouque was personally setting villages on fire, leaving a trail of ashes and death on his march to Santo Domingo. Reflecting the same feelings of alarm, the British consul expressed fear that Soulouque's troops would capture Santo Domingo and not "spare either blood, innocence, or property." Spaniards residing in Santo Domingo requested a ship from Puerto Rico's captain-general so that they could flee the besieged capital. Under these pressing circumstances official representatives from Great Britain, France, and the United States, along with delegates from Haiti and the Dominican Republic, negotiated and agreed on a ten-year truce. Within two years, however, multinational mediation collapsed, and the specter of a Haitian invasion reemerged.[62]

The decade leading to 1852 was thus one of profound transitions in the balance of power and the extent of foreign influence over the Hispanic Caribbean. During these years the United States gradually assumed an offensive position in the region, a development that forced the European naval powers to coalesce in order to curb U.S. encroachment. Critical within this transition was the application of policies on race, slavery, and the slave trade. Britain's abolitionist pressures in Cuba and its close links with the Haitian government alienated considerable segments of the region's white Creole population. In the Cuban case, the militant stance against slavery was originally conceived as part of a strategy aimed at weakening the links between the slave-based southern United States and Cuba. Ironically, it resulted in the activation of both U.S. official expansionism and southern filibusterism as movements seeking to maintain the institution of slavery in the neighboring islands. Moreover, U.S. foreign policy regarding slavery and the country's anti-Haitian stance helped establish strategic links with Creoles in Cuba and the Dominican Republic. For their part, Spanish officials on both sides of the Atlantic tried to take advantage of the crisis produced by British abolitionist pressures in the early 1840s and in 1848. On balance, Spain succeeded in using the fears of a sudden emancipation of the slaves to guarantee Creole loyalty. Sometimes, however, this strategy was pushed too far, producing exactly the opposite results. In the Dominican Republic, U.S. influence spread at a much slower pace. Nonetheless, by the early 1850s the European naval powers recognized that there too the United States was the power to be feared and began to work in accord to curb its expansionist designs.

The Africanization Scare

The general trend of growing U.S. influence over the Hispanic Caribbean intensified throughout the 1850s. The year 1854 was of particular importance, because southern and northern antiexpansionisms momentarily canceled each other out as the Franklin Pierce administration embarked on two distinct expansionist projects, one seeking to acquire Cuba, the other seeking territorial concessions in the Dominican Republic. It was indeed a moment of expansionist frenzy that also conceived the purchase of the Gadsden strip from Mexico and an unsuccessful bid to annex Hawaii. Internal divisions in the United States over the issue of the expansion of slavery, also aggravated during the decade, made expansion into Cuba critical for white southerners. Moreover, the exploitation of racial divisions in the region became even more prominent within the international rivalry over the Hispanic Caribbean.

The Cuba "problem" and the government's posture toward the filibusterers became an important issue in the U.S. presidential election of 1852. In fact, Fillmore's chances for his party's nomination were seriously hurt by his attitudes toward filibusterers. In the election the Democrats regained control of the White House under the leadership of Franklin Pierce. He carried all states except Tennessee, Kentucky, Massachusetts, and Vermont, and his administration represented a shift toward a more aggressive posture in the Caribbean and a higher degree of tolerance for the activities of filibusterers. In his inaugural message, Pierce forcefully stated that his administration's policy would "not be controlled by any timid forebodings of evil from expansion."[63]

This new, more expansionist policy was matched by an overhaul of the cabinet and the diplomatic corps. Pierce appointed some of the era's most notorious expansionists to key posts. His own vice-president, William R. King, was sworn in by the U.S. consul in a ceremony conducted at King's estate in Matanzas, Cuba. Expansionists William L. Marcy, Jefferson Davis, and Caleb Cushing were entrusted with the posts of secretary of state, secretary of war, and attorney general respectively. Selection of the diplomatic corps also reinforced the new, more aggressive Caribbean policy. James Buchanan wrote to the newly appointed secretary of state, suggesting, "If you desire to acquire Cuba in a peaceful manner, the President ought to select able and accomplished ministers to Naples, Spain, England and France who would cordially work together."[64] Among the able, accomplished, and expansionist new ministers were Pierre Soulé, minister to Spain; John L. O'Sullivan, minister to Portugal; August Belmont, minister to the Hague; John Y. Mason, minister to France; and Buchanan himself, minister to Great Britain.

With regard to filibuster activities, the Pierce administration tended toward leniency. The days of dubbing filibusterers "criminals" and "pirates" were over; they were now referred to as "a handful of misguided young men . . . persuade[d] . . . to aid an oppressed people in their struggles for freedom."[65] The new administration relied on persuasion rather than force to keep filibusterers under control. Circumstances surrounding the 1853–54 resurgence of filibustering, however, were different from earlier outbreaks in many ways. For one thing, the movement's top military leader was no longer Narciso López, who had been garroted in 1851, but John Quitman, an influential Mississippi planter-politician recruited by a group of Havana planters.[66] For another, this time filibuster activity took place in a more difficult context, with the Africanization scare as a backdrop, a circumstance that generated more popular support, particularly in the South. Basil Rauch, a student of U.S. interest in Cuba, has argued that the Pierce administration favored filibusterers because of a belief that acquiring an independent Cuba would be easier than purchasing it from Spain.[67] It is difficult, however, to prove that Pierce approved of filibustering. The administration opposed such activities in principle but clearly feared the political consequences of showing overt hostility toward them. Furthermore, in 1854 the Pierce administration became engaged in official expansionist projects of its own, to which filibuster activities represented serious obstacles. Nonetheless, filibusterers were given a wide berth, and the administration used to its advantage the pressure that they exerted.

The Caribbean situation was further complicated in 1853–54 by a more active Spanish policy against the slave trade that led to the crisis of the Africanization scare.[68] Historian Arthur F. Corwin has characterized this period as "the high-water mark of British abolitionist pressure." Tensions developed in Cuba between British officials and Spanish administrators who openly allowed the slave trade to flourish. Consul Crawford reported that it was unlikely that the slave trade would stop unless Great Britain adopted "high-handed measures."[69] In Spain the British government pressured for and achieved the dismissal of Cuba's captain-general, Valentín Cañedo, who was notoriously lenient and corrupt with regard to the slave trade. His successor, Captain-General Juan de la Pezuela, became the architect of the measures that led to the Africanization scare.[70] Of an anti–slave trade and moderate abolitionist background, de la Pezuela arrived in Cuba with orders to end the slave trade. He had previously served in Puerto Rico as captain-general, where he issued decrees that eased manumissions, taxed slavery, promoted alternative sources of labor, put an end to the harsh, repressive measures of Juan Prim's black code, and also established harmonious relations with the abolitionist British consul, John Lindegren.[71]

Arriving in Havana in December 1853, de la Pezuela initiated a series of decrees pertaining to slavery that created an unprecedented furor, sending shock waves throughout the northern Atlantic. The first of these set stringent penalties for those caught importing slaves and ordered the liberation of their confiscated cargoes. New laws for *emancipados* (liberated slaves) were also put into effect.[72] Changes in *emancipado* legislation prompted reactions from corrupt bureaucrats and those who rented the liberated slaves. De la Pezuela's New Year's Day present to the slavocracy was equally annoying, because it included provisions for the immediate liberation of all slaves imported after 1835, the year of the second Anglo-Spanish treaty for the suppression of the slave trade.[73] The main weakness of this decree was that it was difficult to prove whether any given slave had been imported or was Cuban-born. On May 3, 1854, de la Pezuela published the most controversial of his decrees, providing for searches into private estates suspected of having imported slaves.[74] In order to settle questions about the origin of the slaves, authorities and slaveholders now had to keep registers. *Bozales*, imported slaves, not appearing in the registers were to be confiscated and set free; unregistered *criollos*, or Cuban-born slaves, would cost their owners fifty-peso fines. This decree soon translated into panic among planters and slave speculators. Once again the royal colonial agenda clashed with local realities and expectations.

To aggravate the already tense situation, later in the month de la Pezuela ordered that free mulattoes and blacks be armed in regiments to protect the colony from foreign and domestic disturbances. Spanish officials were confident that blacks would side with them in the event of an invasion by filibusterers. The same year Mariano Torrente wrote assertively that Cuba would never fall, since Spain "could always resort to recruiting colored volunteers, who have been constant in their loyalty to the Spanish throne. . . . [These troops] under the command of European officers, would terrorize and create confusion in the enemy ranks." Torrente also implied rather overtly the next available alternative: "And there is still another extreme resort which I do not believe prudent to spell out, one that to be defeated would require the invading presence of the entire Republic of the Union." José de la Concha, de la Pezuela's successor, continued to exploit this fear, warning the U.S. consul that if John Quitman's expedition left for Cuba he would arm the blacks.[75]

De la Pezuela's and Spain's racial policies are difficult to grasp because of their apparent contradictions. On the one hand, they sought to end the slave trade, a goal accomplished with unprecedented success during de la Pezuela's tenure as captain-general, when a record of 2,699 slaves were confiscated.[76] Great Britain welcomed this new policy, but it alienated the local propertied classes, since the slave trade was the only viable means of maintaining the plantation economy.[77] On the other hand, Spain adhered to a policy of seeking *ennegrecer* (to darken) the Cuban population by proposing the immigration of free black settlers as apprentices. In January 1854 de la Pezuela's government put in place a series of measures to promote the introduction of large numbers of free black laborers from Africa. A supporter of this policy, Torrente wrote that all previous projects to introduce European laborers had failed because whites could not adapt to the rigors of tropical toil. He proposed the introduction of black settlers as the only alternative to slave trading.[78] Thus, the Spanish policy toward this problem rested on two formulations: the termination of the illegal importation of slaves and the immigration of free blacks, solutions entirely opposed to the aspirations of the Creole planter class. Behind this seemingly ambiguous policy stood the recognition by Spain of the new geopolitical realities, in which the United States was now the mightiest challenger. In such a context, the end of the slave trade leading to the abolition of slavery would debilitate U.S. designs on Cuba and attract the support of the British government. On the other hand, the promotion of a black majority guaranteed Creole loyalty, based on fear, perhaps even beyond the abolition of slavery, as had been the case in the British West Indies. This was, however, a very thin line on which to walk: the black population could be used in scare tactics, but the risks of igniting a Haiti-type revolution were always there. In Puerto Rico, where the slave population was less important in absolute and proportional terms, the Africanization scare was not strongly felt.[79] Nonetheless, the island's captain-general remained watchful, passing a decree prohibiting the entry of blacks from other islands to avoid *el contagio*.[80]

In the United States both the government and the white population reacted negatively and militantly to the Africanization scare of 1853–54. U.S. consuls in Havana and other Cuban ports were the first to sound the alarm. Just days after de la Pezuela's arrival, Consul Alexander M. Clayton called for a broad application of the Monroe Doctrine to keep Cuba from becoming another Jamaica. His successor in the Havana consulate, William H. Robertson, continued to send distressing dispatches on the Africanization scare and the pernicious effects of de la Pezuela's policy. "The natural consequence of this state of things," he wrote Marcy, "would be that the Island would be entirely in the hands of the colored population, the whites would have to abandon it or be sacrificed." In another dispatch Robertson warned: "If a master mind existed among the blacks—a Toussant [*sic*] or a Desalinnes [*sic*], who could read the decrees now being promulgated, and see the encouragement given, ninety days would not elapse, I think, before every white man, woman and child was sacrificed, including the General himself." Ten days after the publication of the decree allowing estate searches, an alarmed Robertson communicated: "We are on the eve of a fearful revolution on this Island."[81]

Marcy dispatched Charles W. Davis, a special agent, to assess the gravity of the Africanization scare. In his briefing to Davis, Marcy explained the dramatic repercussions of emancipation and the implementation of an apprentice system that "would disturb the repose of the Union." He added that "unless . . . our rights are to be [*illegible*] respected and our future completely guarded against influences of bad neighborhood the day of retributive justice must arrive." Davis's reports confirmed previous assessments of the gravity of the scare. He wrote Marcy that emancipation would "undoubtedly" be carried out and that "its inevitable immediate result will be the destruction of the wealth of the Island, a disastrous bloody war of the races, a step backwards in the civilization of America—and, in a commercial view, an immense loss to the United States." Davis blamed all of this on "plans of the British Ministry."[82]

Reactions to the Africanization scare were particularly violent in the South, where discontent raged over the debates leading to the Kansas-Nebraska Act. The Louisiana legislature, for example, issued a strong resolution urging federal action to prevent the Africanization of Cuba.[83] At the peak of the Africanization scare, Consul Robertson brought to Marcy's attention the "pernicious and funest example [of de la Pezuela's decrees] for those states of our Union where slavery exists."[84] In 1854 concern over abolition in Cuba coupled with the effects of the Kansas-Nebraska Act sparked new waves of southern expansionism, whose rhetoric rested on twin pillars: the desire to protect and expand southern slavery and the desire to establish an autonomous southern commercial empire, in which Cuba was to play the key role.

Southern publicists and politicians openly advocated an expansionist route into the Caribbean in order to protect and expand slavery.[85] Mississippi senator Albert Gallatin Brown, referring to the Caribbean islands, explained: "I want them all for the same reason—for the planting or spreading of slavery." The spirit of military expansionism and attachment to slavery was neatly synthesized by George Fitzhugh, when he wrote in the *DeBow's Review:* "It is by war you conquer the barbarian race, and by slavery you reduce them to labor and arts of civilized life. Slavery and war have thus been the two great forerunners of civilization." In a similar vein, Louisiana senator Pierre Soulé called for armed action to take place before Cubans achieved their independence. Building on John Quincy Adams's metaphor of the ripe apple, Soulé argued that the fruit (Cuba) might become spoiled if the United States waited longer to pick it. On another occasion he stated that the time for expansion was right and that if the United States did not act before abolition in Cuba, it would be too late. His colleague John Slidell proposed the suspension of neutrality laws to allow filibusterers to fight Cuba's Africanization. Many influential radical expansionists became disillusioned with the timid Pierce administration. Quitman scorned it as a "humbug administration" that refused to confront the European conspiracy to Africanize Cuba.[86] In this context, filibusterism once again became a respectable option.

Growing sectionalism in the South during this period also brought increased attention to Cuba's commercial capabilities. During the 1850s, and particularly after the passage of the Kansas-Nebraska Act, the South endured political alienation that reinforced sectional sentiments. In its economic manifestations, sectionalism translated into the desire to establish an autonomous commercial system with direct links to European and Caribbean markets and production. A Cuba free of tariffs and trade restrictions was deemed a vital piece in the puzzle of an economically autonomous South. Fitzhugh proposed the development of a southern commercial infrastructure and an independent international trade network. He added that Cuba was the key to this: "The nation that holds Cuba will hold control over the commerce and wealth of this new world." In a similar article, John S. Thrasher underscored the benefits of a liberated Cuba and demonstrated how the volume of trade would increase once Cuba ceased to be Spanish. Meanwhile, Louisiana governor R. C. Wickliffe remarked: "Were Cuba annexed, Havanna [*sic*] would speedily become the great *entrepôt* of southern commerce, and in a few years be the rival of New York itself."[87]

In the North, Whigs, Free Soilers, and considerable segments of the Democratic party and the public at large opposed expansion into

Cuba. This position was linked to the desire to keep the South in a minority status by blocking the addition of new slave states. Influential northern Democrats like Stephen A. Douglas and Lewis Cass continued to favor Cuba's acquisition in the 1850s but became increasingly preoccupied with the political fallout of this proslavery stance. In the 1854 election, northern Democrats suffered serious setbacks that partially reflected the growing North-South sectionalism created by the issue of the expansion of slavery.[88] The Africanization scare, however, did reenergize the New York–based expansionist nucleus. Starting in the spring of 1853, a series of anti-British, anti-Africanization articles flooded the columns of New York's expansionist-annexationist *La Verdad*.[89]

Throughout the period of the Africanization scare the Pierce administration tried to channel expansionism into other avenues, using national instead of sectional justifications and diplomatic pressures rather than filibusterism. In an ironic historical twist, while southern expansionists reacted to what they believed to be the imminent arming of blacks in Cuba, the Pierce administration responded to abuses committed by Spanish authorities against a U.S. ship named *Black Warrior*.[90] The *Black Warrior* grievances became part of the negotiating package in a new attempt to purchase Cuba. In April 1854 William L. Marcy instructed Pierre Soulé to initiate purchase negotiations and to offer up to $130 million for the island. In the event of a Spanish refusal, Soulé was to direct his efforts "to the next most desirable object, which is to detach that Island from the Spanish dominion and from all dependence on any European Power."[91] Whether this was a plausible objective or just a scheme to appease radicals in the South and Cuba and to expand political support for the Pierce administration is not clear. Pierce personally leaned toward the peaceful acquisition of Cuba, but some of his key diplomatic representatives favored more aggressive solutions. In any event, the *Black Warrior* affair gave the administration an extra bargaining chip in its effort to acquire Cuba. A proponent of the radical solution, Soulé demanded immediate redress, an indemnity of three hundred thousand dollars, and the dismissal of those officials responsible for the incident.

Other circumstances also made the mid-1850s a favorable time for the acquisition of Cuba by the United States. The protracted conflict of the Crimean War, for instance, absorbed British and French military resources that could otherwise have been used in the Caribbean. Spain's growing foreign debt also gave the United States the chance to make an attractive offer that would allow Spain to pay off its entire debt and still have millions left to develop its industrial and commercial infrastructure.[92] Moreover, Soulé tried to use rivalries between opposing Spanish political parties to secure the purchase. He negotiated directly with the Spanish Liberal leadership during the convulsive period preceding the revolution of 1854. In a communication to Marcy, a wishful Soulé stated that he had come to an agreement with the Liberal opposition and that he had not "the least doubt that they would get possession of the Government and realize for us what it may not be in our power to effect, at least peaceably, under any other contingency." Soulé publicly supported the Spanish Liberal sector, and when they failed to gain control of the government in July, the purchase negotiations fell apart.[93] In late August the Liberals collapsed, and with them went Soulé's scheme. Soulé was later implicated in the revolutionary conspiracy and was forced to flee Spain. At this point his interim substitute signaled the failure of the purchase plan.[94]

Frustration over the failure of the Cuba purchase negotiation led to a desperate move by Soulé, the minister to Britain, James Buchanan, and the minister to France, John Y. Mason. Between October 11 and 18, 1854, these diplomats met, first in Ostend, Belgium, and later in Aix-la-Chapelle, to produce an aggressive policy document on Cuba that came to be known as the Ostend Manifesto.[95] The manifesto turned out to be an utter failure of foreign policy. Spanish officials were not threatened by its contents, as they chose to reaffirm the Spanish or African policy over Cuba. Soulé, the radical hand behind the document, went into political oblivion after the Ostend episode, while Buchanan, the moderate hand behind it, benefited politically from his participation.

The Haitian Specter

Eighteen-fifty-four was also the high-water mark of U.S. interest in the Dominican Republic. Popular support in the United States for expansion into the Dominican Republic, however, was practically nonexistent. In fact, opposition to such expansion was strong in the South, where the idea of acquiring territories with a free, dark-skinned population was rejected outright. Interest in the Dominican Republic centered mainly on two considerations: first, the acquisition of a coaling station, preferably at Samaná, one of the hemisphere's finest bays; and, second, the creation of extractive enclaves and potential markets that could be developed in an island free from the tariffs and other restrictions affecting Cuba and Puerto Rico.[96] Expansion into the Dominican Republic was arguably an exclusively northern project.

The issue of race was a key determinant of U.S. policy toward the Dominican Republic and for that matter toward the entire Caribbean region. During the 1840s and 1850s the various administrations courted white southern support, being careful not to offend the region's racial sensibilities. White southerners' perception of the Dominican Republic as a struggling nation comprising a lawless, free, dark-skinned population made it difficult for any administration to establish solid diplomatic relations, or even to grant recognition, which was deemed by many the first step toward acquisition. This policy was even clearer with regard to Haiti. The United States consistently adhered to a policy of isolating Haiti both diplomatically and commercially. The first republic of the hemisphere did not establish diplomatic relations with Haiti, the hemisphere's second republic, which had been independent since 1804, and granted its envoys only the credentials of commercial agents. These agents were received only in certain ports of New England, as long as they were "not of African extraction."[97] Haiti was finally recognized only after the outbreak of the U.S. Civil War.

Not surprisingly, the U.S. Department of State exhibited a continuous preoccupation with the racial composition of the Dominican Republic. Virtually all agents dispatched there were instructed to assess the proportion and numbers of the different racial groups and to comment on the relative strength of the white element. The first U.S. agent to the newly independent Dominican Republic, John Hogan, reported to Buchanan that the republic's population consisted "of about two hundred and thirty thousand of whom forty thousand are Blacks and over one hundred thousand are whites." Hogan was applying a very liberal use of the term *white*, obviously including lighter-skinned mulattoes.[98] Interestingly, Hogan's report established a racial polarity: there were blacks and whites, but no groups in between, corresponding to racial perceptions in the United States. A year later, another U.S. citizen entrusted with assessing the republic's racial composition, Commander David D. Porter, produced a more detailed picture. Porter stated that there were only 5,200 pure whites and 20,000 pure Africans in the Dominican Republic. Porter also estimated populations of 75,000 quadroons, 60,000 light-skinned mulattoes, and 14,000 dark mulattoes.[99]

In mid-1849, when the Taylor administration studied the possibility of recognizing the Dominican Republic's independence, special agent Benjamin Green received instructions "to ascertain whether or not the Spanish race has the ascendancy in that government, is likely to maintain it, and whether in [*illegible*] of numbers that race bears as fair a proportion to the others as it does in the other Spanish American states." Green's first impression upon arrival in Santo Domingo was that most Dominicans were black or mulatto. He explained, however, that the proportion of these groups was considerably higher in the capital city than elsewhere. He even argued that Dominican blacks and mulattoes acted and felt like whites. In this report Green sought to make the republic's population less threatening to his fellow white countrymen, using cultural criteria to paint a whiter Dominican Republic. In a dispatch to Secretary of State Clayton, Green calculated that more than half of the Dominicans were white and that three-fourths of the other half were light-skinned people of mixed blood. The remaining eighth of the population (some twenty-five thousand) were dark mulattoes and blacks; even these, Green reported, sided politically with the whites.[100] Later reports by William Cazneau also asserted that whites were the majority and were in control. In a letter to John Quitman, Cazneau sought southern support for the Dominican project, describing the Dominican Republic as "the only free white and republican government" in all of the West Indies. Agents Hogan, Green, Cazneau, and Jonathan Elliot favored a stronger U.S. presence in the Caribbean republic. They also favored the acquisition of the whole island or at least the coal-rich territories around Samaná Bay. A correlation between the perception of race and the desire to acquire the island emerges from their reports: the more ardently expansionist the reporter, the lighter the racial portrayal of the Dominican people. Significantly, several of these envoys were northern entrepreneurs who established exploitative ventures in the island.[101]

A revealing exchange that illustrates the importance of the race issue took place in the New York press between William Cullen Bryant, an opponent of Dominican recognition, and expansionist mouthpiece William Cazneau.[102] On May 24, 1854, writing in his own New York *Evening Post*, Bryant denounced an alleged scheme by Benjamin Green, Robert Walsh, and others to reestablish slavery and to promote U.S. immigration to the Dominican Republic. Bryant also proposed the unification of the island under Haiti. Both governments, he said, were black. Cazneau responded to this attack in a letter to the New York *Herald*, later reprinted in Bryant's newspaper. He wrote: "I charge [the *Evening Post*] with disgraceful ignorance or willful falsehood, in asserting that the Dominican Republic is 'not less a negro government than Hayti.' It ought to know that there is not a negro in the Dominican cabinet or Congress, and that in none of the Spanish American states is a smaller number of colored subofficials." Bryant rebutted a few days later with a racial analysis of his own, stating that "in all Dominica, with a population of from seventy-five to a hundred thousand, there are not two hundred and fifty whites, all told, sailors and diplomats included. What folly to talk of a white republic in such a country!"[103]

Similar discussions were held regarding Cuba, where whites stood separate and dominant, just as in the southern United States. In an 1856 pamphlet Quitman stated redundantly that the people of Cuba belonged to "the pure white Caucasian race, and descended from the best blood of the old Hidalgos." Quitman reiterated that Cubans were "a people of our own race, the white Caucasian man." Another proponent of Cuba's acquisition, John S. Thrasher, stressed that the Cuban population was "composed in a great measure of two unmixed races—the European white and the African black." Yet another vocal expansionist, Senator George E. Pugh of Ohio, while defending the acquisition of Cuba in 1859, tried to neutralize racially based criticism, stating that "the descendants of the Spaniards in America, are like the rest of us." In contrast, opponents of expansion into Cuba argued that Cubans were racially mixed. "Do we want any more mongrel Americans in our Congress?" asked former Virginia governor David Campbell of his expansion-inclined nephew.[104]

Both the United States and the European naval powers promoted and manipulated differences in the racial composition and leadership of the Dominican Republic. In February 1850 Benjamin Green wrote Secretary Clayton that the United States should side with and protect the white element. He added that Great Britain had alienated itself because the Dominicans perceived it as a Negrophile government. Indeed, a year earlier a group of Dominican deputies had stated: "We fear England whose flag is the flag of blackness."[105]

Around 1853 a polarization in Dominican politics became apparent between two caudillos representing different regions of the republic and different economic bases: Pedro Santana, a wealthy rancher from El Seibo, and Buenaventura Báez, a landholder from Azua. Their struggle for power intensified when both sought support from the northern Atlantic powers. This polarization in Dominican politics reflected a growing polarization in international relations. In this process the United States absorbed the Santana party into its camp and repudiated the Báez party, which it associated with the black segment of the Dominican population. This posture was clearly reflected in a report of commercial agent Jonathan Elliot: "The presidential term of Buenaventura Báez, *a mulatto,* expires on February 15. He has been a great enemy of U.S. nationals, his successor being General Pedro Santana, a much better person who I believe has warm feelings towards us, he is considered *a white man,* but I think has a slight mixture with the black race."[106]

William Cazneau relayed information of a similar nature. He cautioned Marcy that an Anglo-Franco-Haitian coalition in accord with Báez's "black party" sought to extinguish the Dominican Republic and turn it into an African dependency. By 1856, when the Santana-Báez polarization had become even sharper, Elliot was scorning Báez as "an ambitious black." Later, Cazneau reported that the black party planned a pro-Báez insurrection that, if successful, would mean the end of white predominance, white property, and white nationality, if not all white people. He added that France and Great Britain were behind this plot. Spanish envoys to the Dominican Republic, for their part, aligned with the Báez faction. "Under the present circumstances," wrote the Spanish commercial agent, Eduardo San Just, "[Báez's] victory would offer us complete protection against the projects of the *Yankees.*" In an earlier report this agent had characterized the Santana administration as being "of poor quality," "ignorant," and "perverse."[107]

A parallel polarization between the United States and Europe emerged with regard to Cuba in the mid-1850s, in conjunction with the de la Pezuela crisis and renewed threats of filibuster activity. Before this, the geopolitical situation had been, primarily, a balance of power. During the disturbances of 1853–55 both France and Great Britain offered their support in order to keep Cuba under Spanish rule. France sent six warships at the height of the Africanization scare, and Great Britain deployed four of its men-of-war when Quitman's expedition was believed to be imminent. In April 1855 a British official reported a continuous presence of British warships in the port of Havana, "sometimes three or four." Spanish officials on both sides of the Atlantic repeatedly expressed confidence in the support and friendship of Great Britain and France in relation to renewed expansionist agitation in the United States.[108]

Tension over the Dominican Republic further increased in 1854, when William Cazneau was appointed U.S. envoy. By the beginning of that year, the most dynamic of the western European commercial powers, Great Britain, France, Denmark, and Holland, had recognized the Dominican Republic's independence. In exchange they received preferential treatment in tariffs and tonnage fees (other nations paid twice as much). Spain, the republic's former metropolis, and the United States remained the only concerned powers that had not recognized Dominican independence. On June 17, 1854, Marcy instructed Cazneau to negotiate a treaty of recognition in exchange for a tract of land, at least one square mile, in Samaná for a coal depot.[109]

Cazneau's arrival in Santo Domingo aboard the USS *Columbia* in July 1854 caused immediate concern among the European consular agents. When Cazneau's intentions became known, the Europeans tried to dissuade the Dominican government from signing any treaty that might yield any portion of its national territory to the United States. The British consul cautioned Juan N. Tejera, Dominican minister of foreign affairs, that the proposed treaty should not be accepted, particularly from a nation that thus far had refused even to recognize the country's independence. The French were even more forceful. According to Cazneau's reports, the French consul at Port-au-Prince instigated the persecution of those elements favorable to the treaty and achieved the closing of a protreaty newspaper, *El Porvenir*. Its editor barely escaped being sent to jail. During the treaty negotiations the European agents also called for increased military presence. Eduardo San Just wrote to the captain-general of Cuba, suggesting the deployment of a ship to join the British *Angus* and French *Mélange*. His desperate communication gave the impression that invading U.S. troops were on their way. Increased U.S. interest in the Dominican Republic further strengthened the European coalition. High British officials manifested their certainty that France would make common cause with Britain in defense of Dominican independence and territorial integrity.[110]

In this struggle against the cession of Samaná, the mightiest weapon was the exploitation of the race issue and the fear of a racial war. Cazneau announced that "Europeans labor incessantly to instill in the Dominicans the belief that native whites will be set aside and blacks enslaved, if Americans gain a foothold on the island." His wife and colleague, Jane M. Cazneau, called for an "armed colonization" to stop Soulouque. For his part, British consul Robert Schomburgk informed Lord Clarendon that he had used his influence with the island's legislators "in order to draw their attention to the humiliating clause of Article 3, by which nine-tenths of their population were rendered liable to arrest and imprisonment, should they, as per example, land in Charleston in South Carolina." In another dispatch he reported that the black population of the Dominican Republic was fearful of the signing of the treaty proposed by Cazneau. The Spanish minister of state sent some revealing instructions to agent Eduardo San Just in which he directed San Just to underscore the negative results that such a treaty would bring, "not only for Dominican independence, but also for the future of their race." Spanish secret agent Juan de Abril also exploited the unreciprocal nature of the treaty. In the end the race issue killed the negotiations, despite Cazneau's efforts to paint his country as one seeking the elevation of the people of color. On December 13, 1854, Juan N. Tejera notified Marcy that Dominicans would not agree to the treaty unless all their people, without racial distinctions, received the same rights and liberties in the United States as would be granted to U.S. citizens in the Dominican Republic. On this matter the United States proved unyielding. Marcy instructed Elliot not even to consider any modifications, which would be contrary to the sentiment of many in the United States. Finally, in December 1854 the Dominican Congress rejected the treaty overwhelmingly. Even then the U.S. government refused to amend the treaty, instead trying to force it on the Dominican executive branch without the approval of the Dominican legislature.[111]

The specter of a Haitian invasion of the Dominican Republic arose once more during the treaty negotiations of 1854–55. Evidence indicates that European agents prodded Haiti into action. Indisputably the European nations stood to gain from Haiti's menacing presence. In November 1854 the Spanish minister of state instructed his envoy to Haiti not to antagonize Soulouque's government and to associate with the French and British envoys, who also opposed U.S. encroachments in the island. San Just received orders to seek the aid of the British and French consuls and to instill the fear of a racial war in the Dominican authorities. According to diplomat-historian Sumner Welles, throughout this period the French and British envoys "lost no opportunity in impressing the Emperor Faustin [Soulouque] with the danger which would threaten his own domain should a slave-holding power such as the United States obtain foothold on the Island." Cazneau complained repeatedly about a French and British plot to Africanize the Dominican Republic under Báez's leadership and Haitian influence. In a letter to Quitman he warned: "Under the specious title of 'the mediating powers,' France and England always hold the negroes in readiness to be let slip like bloodhounds on the whites at the east end of Hayti, if they prove, at any time, refractory to European policy." The renewal of Haitian expansionism in 1854–55 played neatly into the hands of the European powers trying to check the designs of the United States. The British consul, for example, based his campaign on the argument that the Dominican Republic would never achieve peace with Haiti if it granted territorial concessions to the United States.[112]

Given European opposition and interference, the treaty negotiations led by Cazneau resulted in an arduous uphill battle. At one point a frustrated Cazneau scorned the Dominicans as "semicolonial and irresponsible." He also protested against European meddling in direct communications to the British and French consuls. In the end the treaty did not materialize, not only because of foreign interference but also because of popular opposition from a society polarized under two caudillos responding to different international powers. In December, Marcy coldly recalled Cazneau.[113] Like Soulé in Europe, Cazneau had failed to attain any significant goal of the U.S. expansionist Caribbean policy.

Of Great Britain, France, and Spain, the latter remained the most cautious in its policy toward the Dominican Republic. This did not signify any lack of interest, however; on the contrary, Spain stood to lose a great deal if the United States gained a foothold in a territory located between its last two American colonies, Cuba and Puerto Rico. Spain's greatest fear was that the United States would take over Samaná and turn it into "an immense den of filibusterers."[114] The Spanish captain-general of Puerto Rico kept a watchful eye on developments in the neighboring republic. He informed the Spanish minister of state of Cazneau's arrival in Santo Domingo and of his alleged intentions to promote a mass immigration, Texas-style. In later dispatches he described the situation as "extremely complicated and dangerous" and said that Cazneau's activities would lead to "incalculable evils." Also active in checking U.S. encroachment in the Dominican Republic were secret agent Juan de Abril and envoy Eduardo San Just. The latter had instructions before leaving for Santo Domingo "to use all available means to paralyze, if possible, the ambitious projects of the United States." Upon his arrival he reported to the captain-general of Cuba: "I judge that the only way to put an end to so undesirable a situation is to oppose by force with the most rigorous resistance the pretentious designs that the United States have for this country." Two weeks later an alarmed San Just requested the deployment of an infantry division from Puerto Rico.[115]

The tense international rivalry and the imminence of U.S. encroachment in the Dominican Republic in 1854 led Spain to reevaluate its policy toward its former colony. Up to that point the policy had been one of avoiding recognition. "Such a thing as recognition," explained the Spanish minister of state to Dominican envoy Matías Ramón Mella, "could set a bad example before the eyes of the partisans of Cuban independence." Spain remained cautious, not daring to negotiate a protectorate over the Dominican Republic out of concern over U.S. response. In March 1854 the Spanish minister of state warned the president of the Council of Ministers that a protectorate would generate strong opposition, especially within the Democratic party of the United States, which strongly adhered to the Monroe Doctrine. Leading Spanish statesman Mariano Torrente echoed these fears. Cazneau's mission and the prospect of the United States's receiving territorial grants in Samaná moved Spanish officials to reevaluate their position on recognition. Fearing the crystallization of a U.S.-Dominican treaty, Captain-General Fernando de Norzagaray recommended recognition. A few weeks later San Just received instructions to initiate the negotiations. His orders clearly stated that the granting of recognition was a response to the imminent signing of a treaty between the United States and the Dominican Republic. As Sumner Welles ably put it, "The revelation of the ambitions of the United States proved a stronger argument in persuading the Spanish Government to accord official recognition to the Republic than all of General Mella's eloquence."[116]

Once Spain decided that the recognition of the Dominican Republic could no longer be postponed, it sought to gain an advantage from it. Secret agent de Abril began by warning Dominican officials that if they ceded territory to the United States there would be no Spanish recognition. The first Spanish-Dominican treaty was signed by representatives of both countries on February 18, 1855.[117] In the first article the queen of Spain renounced sovereignty over the Spanish part of "Santo Domingo," accepting a reality thirty-three years after the fact. The document also included other provisions, such as the protection of Spanish property, commercial reciprocity, and the mutual assurance of most-favored-nation status. In December 1855, with the Cazneau treaty long dead, the first Spanish consul to the Dominican Republic, Antonio María Segovia, arrived in Santo Domingo.

Frustrated Expansion and Imperial Rapprochement, 1855–1860

Following the failures of its official Caribbean policy in 1854 and 1855, the U.S. government momentarily recoiled from expansionism. Still, extremist and radical expansionists in the South responded with renewed filibustering schemes following the unsuccessful attempt to buy Cuba and the fiasco of the Ostend Manifesto. For their part, Cuban separatist-annexationists, who had grown weary of waiting for help from the Pierce administration, resorted again to López-type expeditions and insurrections from within. They approached Quitman once again, offering him the leadership of the expeditionary forces. After successfully negotiating extraordinary civil powers and an eight hundred thousand–dollar bonus for himself, Quitman accepted the offer.

Relations between Quitman and the Cuban Junta, however, were not smooth. While the Cuban revolutionary leadership sought rapid action, Quitman insisted on more time and money. Furthermore, fundamental differences existed in their visions of a liberated Cuba. While the Cubans had become disenchanted with the annexationist formula, preferring to establish an independent nation (albeit under U.S. protection), Quitman sought to absorb the island into a southern empire. Relations between the Cubans and Quitman were further debilitated when the Pierce administration stepped in to crack down on filibustering. With more diplomacy than his Whig predecessors had employed, Pierce used persuasion rather than force to curb filibusterism. In a series of meetings in April 1855, Secretary of State Marcy and President Pierce advised Quitman to drop his plans. Later that month Quitman resigned his post as commander of the Cuban forces and disbanded his ten-thousand-troop army.[118]

This official U.S. retreat from expansionism was greeted with conciliatory responses from Great Britain and Spain. By 1854–55 it had become clear that the United States would be the hegemonic power in the western Caribbean and that Spain and Great Britain stood to lose more in revenue and trade if they challenged this new geopolitical reality. Spanish colonial officials thus modified their strategies to appease disaffected Creoles by neutralizing some of their political grievances. The architect of Spain's new conciliatory policy in Cuba was Captain-General José de la Concha.[119] Upon his arrival in Havana, de la Concha repealed the controversial de la Pezuela decrees, which had so agitated the proslavery element in Cuba and the United States. A pragmatic administrator, de la Concha accepted that for geographic and commercial reasons the Spanish Caribbean had established special relations with the United States. Mariano Torrente also proposed better relations with the United States, advocating the establishment of a bilingual periodical with the object of "educating" the people of the United States and promoting peace and amity between their government and Spain. In order to curb Cuban annexationist tendencies, de la Concha implemented a series of reforms, among them the extension of some political rights and the opening of state careers to Creoles.[120] Interestingly, the U.S. consul in Havana scorned these measures as "the work of British influence in order to keep Cuba for Spain."[121]

In the meantime, the British public and government began to reevaluate their posture toward the Spanish colonies of the Caribbean. British abolitionist zeal, particularly in 1840–44 and 1853–54, had done little to improve the lot of chattel laborers in the Spanish colonies. On the contrary, slavery was strengthened, since the dispute indirectly solidified the links between proslavery elements in Cuba and the United States. The militant stances of the late 1840s and early 1850s had, moreover, reduced British influence in Cuba, forcing influential Creoles to seek the support of the United States. British visitors to the region during the 1850s questioned the benefits of pursuing aggressive abolitionist policies there. One such traveler, John G. Taylor, argued that annexation to the United States would benefit Cubans, who would flourish under "an enlightened, progressive race." He added that gradual emancipation of the slaves under the United States was preferable to sudden abolition under Spain. Another British visitor, Anthony Trollope, stressed that Cuba's being in the hands of the United States would result in trade benefits for Great Britain. "My best wish for the island," Trollope stated, "is that it may speedily be reckoned among the annexations of the United States." In the mid-1850s yet another British traveler, Amelia Matilda Murray, criticized British policy, arguing that it had been injurious to the planter class and detrimental to the black race because it sparked repressive measures against both sectors.[122]

British foreign policy after 1854 reflected these changing sentiments, namely reduced hostility toward the United States and a less strident abolitionism. Decades of pursuing opposite policies had had negative repercussions for Great Britain. According to historian Christopher J. Bartlett, "The years 1856 to 1860 are normally regarded as the phase when Britain began to recognize that it was perhaps inexpedient to persist in her policy of rivalry with the United States in Central America."[123] Another factor to be considered was the special mercantile relations between the United States and Britain, which the latter could not afford to alter. Cotton from the United States was one of the primary raw materials of British industrialization, an element more important to the British than hegemony over the Spanish sugar islands. As one U.S. expansionist put it, "Cuba for England is worth less than our American cotton at Liverpool prices; with this cotton our might is greater than all of Victoria's fleet. England is forced to maintain peace with us."[124] Changes in official British attitudes were clearly stated in an 1857 dispatch from the British minister in Washington, Lord Napier, to Lord Clarendon. In this document Lord Napier enumerated a series of reasons why Cuba's acquisition by the United States would not be so pernicious after all. According to him, the United States would put in place a less restrictive trade system that would favor British trade, increased and cheaper production of tropical staples would benefit British consumers, increased trade would boost British shipping, the sale of Cuba to the United States would allow Spain to pay off its British debt, possession of Cuba would place the United States in a defensive position, and the slave trade would end. In reducing frictions with the United States, Great Britain also softened its official stance toward slavery. The Havana Mixed Commission remained in place but ceased to be the zealous institution it had been. A British visitor reported that Judge George C. Backhouse, who was later murdered under mysterious circumstances, and Consul-General Joseph T. Crawford were the only Britons in the island who had "abolitionist notions."[125] Also symptomatic of Britain's retreat was its official posture of not risking a confrontation with the United States in defense of the gains produced by the Clayton-Bulwer Treaty.[126]

In 1856 voters in the United States elected Democratic candidate James Buchanan as their fifteenth president. Vital to Buchanan's election were his expansionist credentials, which gained him the southern vote.[127] Once in office, Buchanan initiated the third attempt to purchase Cuba in little more than a decade. Buchanan seemed more serious in his intentions than either Polk or Pierce had been. Both of his predecessors had attempted to buy Cuba during highly convulsive periods, with unofficial efforts under way to separate Cuba from Spain. Thus, it could be argued that the 1848 and 1854 purchase offers were intended simply to neutralize more serious clandestine schemes. In 1858–59, moreover, the situation in the Spanish colonies of the Caribbean was unusually settled. Finally, in contrast to his predecessors, Buchanan demonstrated his seriousness by seeking congressional approval and funding for the Cuba purchase. His attempt to acquire Cuba was also a desperate last effort to unify the Democratic party, to retain its leadership, and to restore sectional equity in the Union.

The movement calling for the purchase of Cuba was sparked by southern legislators and politicians. In January 1859 John Slidell of Louisiana set in motion the southern and Democratic purchase plan when he introduced bill 497, calling for a thirty-million-dollar appropriation to be used in the negotiation of Cuba's purchase. The debate over Slidell's bill developed along clearly defined sectional and partisan lines. This time the purchase plan received strong support from the mainstream southern political leadership and the national Democratic party. Thus, during the Buchanan years the acquisition of Cuba ceased to be solely the project of fanatical expansionist politicians from the Deep South, veterans of the Mexican War, and displaced immigrants. It now received the support of mainstream southern politicians, who had thus far rejected the tactics of López and Quitman. Men like Jefferson Davis, Robert Toombs, and William T. Avery belonged to this new group of converts.

The main objective behind the renewed outburst of expansionism was still the economic-political goal of expanding the slave-based plantation system and boosting slave-state representation in the Senate and House. While defending Slidell's bill, Senator Robert Toombs of Georgia spoke of the necessity of having "all the tropics under our flag" and making a "mare clausum," first of the Gulf of Mexico and eventually of the entire Caribbean Sea. Another supporter of the bill, future president of the Confederacy Jefferson Davis, referred to the project as a road to regaining sectional political equity and attacked Republicans for plotting to keep slave states in a minority. Thomas Bowie of Maryland complained along similar lines, while Senator Albert Gallatin Brown stated that the incapacity to expand slavery using established political means would force the South to secede. Frustration stemming from failed attempts to expand into Cuba was one element—although certainly not the main one—fueling the secessionist movement in the late 1850s. Abraham Lincoln's election made the prospects of expansion into Cuba even more difficult. He rejected outright John Crittenden's proposed compromise to save the Union, arguing that there would be no end to the extension of slavery. "A year will not pass," retorted Lincoln, "till we shall have to take Cuba as a condition upon which they will stay in the Union."[128]

Republican and northern opposition to the purchase bill was as militant and vociferous as was its support among Democrats and white southerners. Again the issue of the expansion of slavery drew the dividing line: Republicans opposed the extension of slavery and the subsequent increase of slave-state representation. John P. Hale, a senator from New Hampshire, complained about the fact that U.S. territorial expansion was "continually in one direction, and for the annexation of countries in which the institution of American slavery exists."[129] William Seward, a senator from New York, also opposed Cuba's acquisition on political and abolitionist grounds.

Arguments against the Cuba purchase bill ranged from the simple "We do not need Cuba" to more sophisticated racial and cultural justifications. Interestingly, many of the racist arguments emanated from the North and were directed against so-called vices and weaknesses of the Hispanic culture and "race." In his antipurchase Senate speech Zachariah Chandler described Cuban whites as "ignorant, vicious, and priest-ridden." He also emphasized the island's high crime rate. Another opponent of the bill, William W. Boyce, characterized white Cubans as inferior and politically radical. "Would Cuba be a stable political community, or, in other words, competent to self-government?" asked Boyce rhetorically. "I doubt it. Self-government involves two considerations—the race, and the training." Boyce continued, "The Spanish Creole race of Cuba are the worst kind of materials with which to build up republican institutions." Chandler stressed deep-rooted traditions of bribery and corruption as obstacles to Cuba's acquisition. In Cuba, he said, "from the judge on the bench, from the priest in the pulpit, to the lowest tide-waiter, bribery is the rule, and there are no exceptions."[130]

One of the most widely used cultural arguments by opponents of the Buchanan policy was the difficulty of absorbing a Catholic population into the predominantly Protestant United States. John P. Hale remarked that "a republican government can only be maintained, and successfully maintained, on the principle of Protestant liberty." He added that the faith of the Cubans would have "a deleterious influence" and that he would not consent to receiving Cuban Catholics into the United States. In the same vein, Chandler stated: "The Catholic religion rules supreme in the Island of Cuba; no other religion is tolerated. Even the rites of a Christian burial are denied to a Protestant upon that island. The people are superstitious and vicious; and they are bigots as well. They are devout Catholics. The Catholic Church is true to Spain; the Catholic Church is true to despotism." Senator

John Perry echoed these concerns, pointing to Catholicism as an obstacle to assimilation. Propurchase senator Stephen R. Mallory, probably the only Catholic in the upper body, energetically rebutted these anti-Catholic attacks.[131]

Spain's official posture toward renewed overtures about purchase remained unchanged: for Spaniards and their government, the island colonies, Cuba in particular, represented an enormous source of revenue and pride, a remnant of their once vast empire. In January 1859, even before the introduction of Slidell's bill, the Spanish Senate voted unanimously against selling Cuba. U.S. prospects for the acquisition of Cuba during the late 1850s were perhaps bleaker than at any earlier time. For Spain this was a period of economic, commercial, and military expansion, in which the Spanish island colonies played vital roles as captive markets, exporters of cheap raw materials, and producers of revenue. The period between 1856 and 1867 was also marked by industrial expansion in Spain, as railroad building and the wool and steel industries developed rapidly, particularly in the northern part of the country. Significantly, during this period in Barcelona, Spain's industrial capital, an association called the Permanent Commission for the Defense of Spanish Interests in Cuba was established. Its primary goal was sustaining colonialism and slavery in the island.[132] Industrial growth during the second half of the 1850s was coupled with an expansionist resurgence and a greater interest in preserving Cuba and Puerto Rico under Spain's aegis. As a sign of its growing nationalism and imperial pretensions, Spain began to give its warships names like *Pizarro* and *Cortés*.[133] Nowhere was this aggressive thrust more evident than in Spain's treatment of the weakest of its former colonies, the Dominican Republic. The precariously established republic was strategically located between Cuba and Puerto Rico, and Spain feared that it might be used as a base for filibustering activities against the remaining colonies.

In late 1855 and 1856 Spanish foreign policymakers and diplomats began to consider seriously the possibility of establishing a protectorate over the Dominican Republic. Mariano Torrente believed that Spain had only three options regarding the Dominican Republic: to reestablish colonial domination, to establish a protectorate, or to recognize its independence. He preferred the protectorate, arguing that either recolonization without slavery or recognition of independence would loosen Spain's grip over Cuba and Puerto Rico. Spanish consul Segovia conceived the protectorate as a República Hispano-Dominicana, in which military and foreign policy matters would be controlled by a Spanish royal commissar, leaving domestic affairs to the Dominicans themselves.[134]

Meddling in the republic's internal politics and creating and promoting rivalries among different groups characterized Spanish policy. Upon his arrival in Santo Domingo in December 1855, Consul Segovia sought the support of Pedro Santana's rival caudillo, Buenaventura Báez, who was in exile at the time.[135] Segovia's strategy consisted of a liberal interpretation of article 7 of the Spanish-Dominican treaty that allowed him to naturalize hundreds of Dominicans as Spanish subjects. The targets of this massive naturalization drive were Baecistas, who thus would avoid service in Santana's army. Jonathan Elliot repeatedly warned Marcy of the consequences of Segovia's naturalization drive. On July 5, 1856, he reported that the officers of two Spanish war vessels had granted Spanish passports to "a great number" of Dominicans, most of them blacks. According to one of Santana's top officials, Segovia succeeded in grouping together the opposition under the pro-Báez party. Spanish officials in the Dominican Republic also sought to re-Hispanicize the country by promoting a massive Spanish immigration from Venezuela.[136]

In 1859 Spanish, French, and British officials found another opportunity to destabilize Santana, whom they deemed too favorable to the United States. From the beginning of its independent existence in 1844, the Dominican Republic endured chronic budgetary deficits that resulted in endemic devaluations of the national currency. One of the republic's political actors humorously commented that his compatriots needed an extra servant just to carry the paper money to buy groceries. In May 1859 Santana passed a decree seeking to stabilize the currency. He fixed the exchange rate for his predecessor's paper money at thirty-two thousand pesos per Spanish gold ounce. This measure injured those engaged in import-export trading, mostly foreigners representing European firms. Unable to continue profiting through speculation in rampant inflation, this sector voiced its opposition through the European consular body. Acting in accord, the consuls of Spain, France, and Great Britain protested and declared the decree void, pointing to extraordinary losses by the merchant class.[137]

After the French, British, and Spanish consuls demanded their passports in protest against Santana's monetary measures, the caudillo reconsidered and reset the exchange rate at its previous level. The consuls then returned.[138]

Despite the growing internal divisions over the issue of the expansion of slavery, which obstructed the expansionist thrust into the Caribbean, the United States increased its influence over the region during the 1850s. Particularly in the aftermath of the Africanization scare, the United States tried to negotiate its way into establishing a Caribbean empire with possession of Cuba, coveted by southern expansionists, and the Dominican Republic, a goal of northern expansionists. Both attempts failed because of opposition within the United States, the European naval powers, and Cuba and the Dominican Republic. After 1854 sectional divisions in the United States continued to increase, making it more difficult for the government to satisfy the expansionist aspirations of the southern elite. Buchanan's 1859 Cuba purchase plan demonstrated the polarization in U.S. politics, as well as the South's incapacity to pursue its sectional goals within the national legislative structures. If internal obstacles did not permit the actual occupation of the islands, still U.S. influence continued to increase in the commercial and political spheres.

The northern Atlantic nations also continued to manipulate racial divisions and fears of racial wars to their advantage. U.S. officials used the Africanization scare as an expansionist pretext to purchase Cuba and later in the vitriolic Ostend Manifesto. For its part, Spain used the fear of a slave revolt, with the object of guaranteeing white Creole loyalty in its colonial possessions. A similar phenomenon took place in the Dominican Republic, where the European naval powers made sure that Haiti's menacing presence served as a deterrent to local pro-U.S. annexationism. During the 1850s, despite the profound changes in the region's geopolitical realities, Cuba and Puerto Rico remained Spanish colonies, and the Dominican Republic managed to retain its independent status and territorial integrity. Although European and Caribbean resistance was definitely a factor behind this outcome, the greatest obstacles for U.S. expansion into the region were by now certainly to be found within the United States itself.

Two | Economic Transformations and the State

The Dominican Republic, Cuba, and Puerto Rico shared similar legacies of Spanish colonialism and slavery. Nonetheless, while Cuba and Puerto Rico remained Spanish colonies throughout the period 1840–60 and managed to establish significant commercial and financial ties with the outside world stemming from their roles as agro-export economies, the Dominican Republic struggled to create a semblance of a national state and failed to develop an export-oriented, exchange-producing economy.

Dual Colonialism in the Spanish Caribbean

The entente whereby the United States agreed that Cuba and Puerto Rico could remain Spanish colonies was part of a broader tacit agreement through which Spain gradually yielded commercial domination over the region to the United States while retaining administrative, military, and fiscal control. Spain, ran the maxim, administers the colonies of the United States. The nineteenth-century Spanish Caribbean thus had to endure two simultaneous, mutually reinforcing forms of foreign domination—Spanish colonialism and U.S. neocolonialism.

During the nineteenth century Spanish colonialism in Cuba and Puerto Rico underwent profound transformations. Cuba and, to a lesser extent, Puerto Rico had flourished during the last quarter of the eighteenth century and the first three decades of the nineteenth century. They became privileged regions in which Bourbon colonial administrators experimented with commercial and administrative reforms. As early as 1765 Havana, San Juan, and other selected Caribbean ports were granted direct trade privileges with several newly opened ports. Later, during the Napoleonic Wars, the colonies received permission to engage in trade with neutral nations, particularly the United States. The city of Havana also enjoyed special privileges. One of these allowed it to become a major ship-building center. A royal decree of 1789 allowed nationals and foreigners to introduce slaves freely in Havana and other Caribbean ports.[1] For its part, Puerto Rico received a generous package of reforms in 1815. The Cédula de Gracias, as the reforms came to be known, relaxed restrictions on the introduction of capital, slaves, and machinery, all of which were essential elements of the takeoff for the island's plantation system. Historian Allan J. Kuethe wrote, "Of all the Spanish colonies in America, Cuba probably enjoyed the broadest commercial privileges under Charles IV." "Cuba," he added, perhaps unjustly, "might well be viewed as a spoiled colony."[2] In political terms, Creoles in Cuba and Puerto Rico held a large degree of control over local institutions and the colonial militia, and sugar barons like Francisco de Arango y Parreño exerted considerable influence within policy-making circles in the Peninsula.[3] To cite another notable example, Ramón Power y Giralt, the Puerto Rican deputy to the Spanish Cortes, was elected the body's first vice-president in 1810. As historian Franklin W. Knight has pointed out, Creole-Peninsular tensions were also milder in Cuba—and in Puerto Rico, one might add—than anywhere else in the Indies because of a smaller bureaucratic and clerical presence. Moreover, taxes levied by the church and state in Cuba were described by contemporaries as "not oppressive."[4] All of these circumstances explain, in part, why Cubans and Puerto Ricans did not join their mainland neighbors in their struggles for independence between 1810 and 1825.[5] While remaining subjects of colonial domination, Creoles in Cuba and Puerto Rico had managed both to flourish economically and to assume partial control over their own governments.[6]

This privileged status, however, ended abruptly in the second half of the 1820s. Having lost its vast imperial domains of Central and South America, Spain shifted its entire colonial focus to Cuba and Puerto Rico, its only remaining colonies in the hemisphere. The sudden shrinking of the Spanish empire translated into the exportation to Cuba and Puerto Rico of a host of displaced bureaucrats, soldiers, and clerics, along with a multitude of Peninsular merchants with their overpriced, overtaxed merchandise. Estimates are that by 1827 both islands absorbed Spanish exports of an amount equal to or greater than that which Spain sent to its entire empire before its collapse.[7]

Despotic Spanish colonialism also grew more intolerable as Creoles lost political rights to which they had become accustomed. A regime marked by press censorship, confiscatory taxes, and political repression emerged. A salient milestone in this process was the proclamation of the *facultades omnímodas* (absolute powers) on May 28, 1825, which granted the highest officers in Cuba and Puerto Rico "all the powers which by the royal ordinances are granted to the governors of cities in a state of siege." That year Cuba's legislative assemblies and municipal legislatures were abolished. Authorities eventually dismantled the Royal Audiencia as well.[8]

Miguel Tacón, captain-general in Cuba from 1834 to 1838, and Miguel de la Torre, his counterpart in Puerto Rico from 1822 to 1837, were key figures in the expansion and centralization of the state and its instruments of coercion. One observer, Richard Robert Madden, described Tacón's legacy in Cuba as a "civilisation of stone and mortar—a military paseo, public markets, a gaol."[9] Repression and public works went hand in hand; criminals and political offenders were forced to work on military constructions and prisons to make more space available for their fellows. The repressive measures of Tacón, de la Torre, and the latter's successor, Miguel López de Baños, reached unprecedented levels of violence, with stringent penalties and gruesome tortures being inflicted upon vagrants, road bandits, political dissidents, and all those who refused to countenance the dual process of expansion of the colonial state and the plantation system.[10]

Perhaps the most far-reaching political change reducing the power of the Cuban and Puerto Rican Creole elites was the law of April 18, 1837, which terminated colonial representation in the Spanish Cortes. According to this law, the Spanish constitution did not apply to "the overseas provinces of America and Asia." It also stipulated that deputies from Cuba, Puerto Rico, and the Philippines would no longer be able to take their seats and that their respective "provinces" would be ruled thereafter by "special laws." These laws never materialized. Instead the so-called Spanish provinces were ruled by the decrees of despotic colonial officials. The Caribbean delegates protested against these measures, but to no avail. Thirty years later Creoles in both islands would still be waiting for the mythical "special laws." One of the unseated deputies said that "Cuba, went from being an integral part of the monarchy to becoming an enslaved colony."[11]

During the middle decades of the nineteenth century Spanish colonial policy in the Caribbean was inspired by the need for increased control and centralization to avoid the repetition of the experiences in Central and South America. One of the early proponents of such policies was Captain-General Tacón, who conducted a vicious campaign to discredit and dismantle any colonial institution that might pose a threat to his absolute rule. The Intendancy, Royal Audiencia, municipal governments, and delegations to the Cortes all endured his onslaught.[12] Mariano Torrente later echoed this posture as he warned: "The loss of our possessions in the American continent, due partially to the untimely declaration of the Cádiz Regency in 1810, and the liberal experiments practiced then and in the 1820s, when the theories of the Peninsula were transplanted to those countries, should make us wary as to not stumble once again." Torrente also stated that the concentration of power was one of the measures leading to a successful colonial administration. He recommended the creation of an Overseas Ministry with centralized authority over the colonies' civil, fiscal, and military affairs. The top officials in each colony, he suggested, should be endowed with similarly broad powers.[13]

The authority of the highest colonial officials in Cuba and Puerto Rico expanded even more in the 1850s. Early in the decade Captain-General de la Concha renewed attacks on the autonomous branches of Cuba's colonial government, including the Intendancy, the Naval Command, municipal governments, and the Development Board. A few years later Captain-General Juan de la Pezuela attained extraordinary powers, which included jurisdiction over fiscal matters previously held by the local intendants. By 1854 the Development Board, a consultative body made up of resident notables appointed by the crown, also ceased to exist. An 1852 broadside signed by Antonio Franchi de Alfaro scornfully equated the mounting powers of Cuba's top official to those of the sultan of Constantinople.[14]

During this period the Spanish colonial state greatly increased its power. While serving as captain-general of Puerto Rico, Fernando de

Norzagaray expanded the island's administrative apparatus and established measures to increase the government's control over commerce. In both Puerto Rico and Cuba the state's budget ballooned to cover new expenditures and the salaries of a bloated bureaucratic corps. The budgets of Cuba's main civil *ramos* (roughly, "departments") skyrocketed between 1840 and 1860: Gracia y Justicia jumped from 68,474 to 924,332 pesos fuertes, Hacienda from 1,894,364 to 9,079,435 pesos fuertes, Gobernación from 89,808 to 1,657,533 pesos fuertes, and Fomento from 42,652 to 1,148,662 pesos fuertes.[15]

The colonial state also expanded through militarization, which took place against the backdrop of fears of slave revolts, insurrection attempts, and filibuster invasions so prevalent in the 1840s and early 1850s. If the budgets of the civil *ramos* rose astronomically, those of the military *ramos* (Guerra y Marina) were not far behind. Defense allocations increased from 6,470,154 pesos fuertes in 1840, reaching a high of 11,247,812 pesos fuertes in 1854 but declining to 7,647,247 pesos fuertes by 1860. During the same years naval expenses went from 1,878,894 to 3,649,362 pesos fuertes, and then fell to 3,446,608 pesos fuertes. As a whole, then, allocations to military *ramos* increased by 78 percent, while those to civil *ramos* shot up by 262 percent, between 1840 and 1854.[16]

Colonial officials in Cuba promoted new military establishments during the peak years of filibuster and insurrectionary activity. In 1849, for example, Captain-General Roncali requested authorization for the creation of a thirty-thousand-troop militia. A few years later Torrente called for the formation of a civil guard to help defend the island of Cuba from filibusterers' aggression. With the same objective, de la Concha organized the infamous volunteer corps (*los voluntarios*) in 1855. Even before this, though, the island of Cuba was militarized to a great extent. In 1853 nineteen thousand soldiers, four thousand sailors, and twenty warships were based on the island.[17] By 1859 troop numbers had reached thirty thousand. This accounts for the fact that so many contemporary visitors commented on Havana's striking martial air. According to one eyewitness, "You can go no where, in Cuba, without meeting soldiers."[18]

The expansion of Spanish control over the Spanish Caribbean did not include the Creole element. Creoles, in fact, were systematically excluded from positions of leadership in the colonial bureaucracy and the military. This discriminatory policy began in the 1830s and became particularly overt in Cuba during Tacón's tenure. A decree of November 1833, for example, barred Creoles from entering the military. Years later Leopoldo O'Donnell advised his superiors not to entrust a single native with the island's public destiny, and Roncali later called for the formation of an all-Spanish militia, arguing that it should include "only Peninsulars because I do not trust the natives enough to give them weapons." Creoles in Puerto Rico were also ousted from the colonial bureaucracy and political establishment. The Puerto Rican historian Fernando Picó has successfully applied the prosopographic method to document this process of displacement in the municipality of Utuado. Olga Jiménez de Wagenheim, a student of Puerto Rican separatism in the 1860s, has noted a parallel process in Lares beginning in the 1840s.[19]

This ouster from colonial offices became one of the principal grievances of the Creole population and fueled Cuban separatism in the late 1840s and 1850s. In an 1848 anti-Spanish pamphlet, Gaspar Betancourt Cisneros estimated that out of twelve thousand government employees and eighteen thousand troops stationed in Cuba, only a few were Cubans. On another occasion he bitterly complained: "To be born in Cuba is a crime. Jobs and appointments are reserved exclusively for Peninsulars, and are sold for gold for immoral and illegal ends to ignorant and corrupt men by the crown's ministers." Spanish officials rebutted such allegations. Torrente, for example, said that the root of discontent among Cubans lay in the excessive number of unemployed lawyers among them who refused to find employment either in agriculture or commerce.[20]

Press censorship and fiscal exploitation also stood high on the list of Spanish abuses. Creoles were not permitted to write freely about controversial topics such as the promotion of European immigration, the abolition of slavery, or the end of the slave trade or about matters that touched on the empire's so-called political and religious unity. Betancourt Cisneros complained repeatedly about his persecution at the hands of the local censors. In 1844 a South Carolina physician, while trying to promote Cuba as a health resort, warned "invalids" not to bring tracts to the island that treated certain banned topics. Another visitor said that censorship was based on "the will and caprice of one individual, who is appointed to scrutinize the most trifling article before it can be presented to the public." Printed materials brought into Cuba were closely monitored. During Tacón's incumbency, for example, customs officials had orders to screen all U.S. and British publications. Wishing to make their censorship practices extend to the United States, Spanish authorities refused to grant a landing permit to William Smith of the *Crescent City*, alleging that he had published "gross lies" about Spain in the New York press. As a special concession, colonial officers in Havana authorized the importation of the Charleston *Courier* on the condition that copies of each edition be sent in advance to the government "in order to judge in the future the paper's editorial doctrines." The few local newspapers that managed to survive the official harassment and confiscatory fines were ultimately shut down by local authorities, and their editors were thrown in jail. This was the case of Cuba's *La Voz del Pueblo* and *El Faro Industrial* in 1852. In Puerto Rico, the editor of *El Ponceño* was fined 393 pesos for publishing an allegorical antigovernment poem. Captain-General de Norzagaray proudly recorded in his diary that the fine money "was *invested* in the purchase of four stone statues that will, of course, be placed on the same number of pedestals."[21]

The Spanish government subjected Cubans and Puerto Ricans to rates of taxation "not elsewhere known in Christendom." One U.S. visitor said that in Cuba everything was taxed "except the air the people breathe, and the light of the sun." Taxes were raised in 1851 to pay for increased military expenses deemed necessary to defend the island from filibuster aggression. Critics of the colonial regime estimated the prevailing rates of taxation and compared them with those of other countries. Ambrosio José González, a Cuban patriot, calculated in 1852 that white Cubans paid over twenty million dollars in taxes and imposts, a per-capita burden of around forty dollars per annum. He contrasted this figure with much lower yearly per-capita rates in Great Britain ($12.33), Spain ($9.00), France ($7.50), and the United States ($2.39). Other contemporary observers produced similarly high estimates of twenty-four dollars per white inhabitant and forty dollars per inhabitant. The rate in Puerto Rico, though lower because of a less significant dependence on imports and a smaller volume of exports, was still high, estimated at eight dollars per head.[22]

The bulk of taxation was indirect, primarily comprising import and export tariffs. Official series of tax totals for the 1854–58 quinquennium reveal that about 62 percent of revenues collected in Cuba came from *ramos marítimos* (duties and shipping fees). Other sources included land taxes (26 percent of revenues), lotteries (9 percent), and court and stamp fees (17 percent).[23] The confiscatory nature of taxation was another grievance of the Creoles. Cuban planter Cristóbal F. Madan complained of the exorbitant tax rates. He estimated that a hacendado owning three hundred slaves and producing four thousand hogsheads of sugar had to pay almost twelve thousand dollars in taxes every year, nearly a quarter of his total expenses. A related criticism concerned the high prices of consumer goods caused by large import tariffs. Pamphleteer Ambrosio José González complained that because of high protective tariffs, bread was "placed entirely beyond the reach of the poorer classes." Heavy taxation was aggravated by the siphoning off of Cuban revenues to Spain as *sobrantes* (leftovers). Between 1847 and 1857 close to 45 percent of all revenue collected in Cuba was remitted to the Peninsula. Furthermore, of the remaining 55 percent, a considerable proportion went toward other foreign expenses, such as sustaining Spanish consulates in the United States and the Spanish legation in Washington, D.C., supporting naval and land forces in the region, paying the expenses of Spain's African penal outpost at Fernando Poo, and paying the interest on Spain's U.S. debt.[24]

Another characteristic of the expanded colonial state was increased coercion. During the early 1840s colonial authorities in Cuba used the fear of slave revolts as a pretext to repress dissident Creoles of all hues. Earlier, José Antonio Saco, deputy-elect to the Cortes at the time of his unseating in 1837, had been banished to Spain for his opposition to the continuation of the slave trade and his vociferous struggle to regain his seat in the Cortes. In 1843 Camagüey planter Joaquín de Agüero fled to Philadelphia, escaping for his life after daring to free his slaves. Around that time, Domingo del Monte, an intellectual related to the Havana oligarchy, was deported by Captain-General Gerónimo Valdés for having sponsored a petition to end the slave trade. Félix Tanco and others of suspected anti-Spanish sentiments were imprisoned. Another prominent member of the Cuban reformist intelligentsia, José de la Luz Caballero, went into forced exile after being implicated in the conspiracy of La Escalera. During Leopoldo O'Donnell's incumbency, planters Juan Montalvo, Rafael O'Farrill, the count of Fernandina, and Benigno Gener, among others, endured systematic political persecution and/or banishment for supporting the termination of the slave trade. The anti-slave trade posture heralded by some Creoles was a direct confrontation to the darkening policy of the island's captains-general. La Escalera and similar scares provided the opportunity to silence the critics of colonialism and allowed the government to strengthen its grip on Cuban society.[25]

New waves of political repression also broke against the backdrop of Narciso López's and John Quitman's conspiracies in the late 1840s and the early 1850s. In 1848 López, the count of Pozos Dulces, Gaspar Betancourt Cisneros, Pedro de Agüero, and other anti-Spanish conspirators had to flee to the United States after officials in the Polk administration informed Spanish authorities of their activities. Two years later, Cristóbal F. Madan, Betancourt Cisneros, Cirilo Villaverde, José Sánchez Iznaga, and Pedro de Agüero were sentenced in absentia to ten years in prison, and their properties in Cuba were confiscated to pay the expenses of fighting López's expeditions. In late 1852 seventy-six Cubans were being processed by the Military Commission for sedition and other political crimes. Meanwhile, an uprising in Camagüey under Joaquín de Agüero's leadership was brutally repressed, and its leaders were executed in the public square. In 1855 another group of suspected conspirators was put down, and its leaders, José Elías Hernández, Francisco Estrampes, and Ramón Pintó, were also executed.[26] Spanish officials in Puerto Rico institutionalized political coercion in 1849 with the issue of "el Bando de Policía y Buen Gobierno," a package of decrees that, among other things, restricted travel in the island, banned public meetings, and closed the streets after midnight. Several Puerto Rican abolitionists, including Julio Vizcarrondo, Ramón Emeterio Betances, and Segundo Ruiz Belvis, were exiled during the following decade. Increased repression was by no means restricted to political elites. The twin developments of state expansion and the growth of the agro-export economy signaled the arrival of harsher times for slaves and free black and mulatto laborers in Cuba and for the peasantry of Puerto Rico's interior.

Commercial and Neocolonial Domination

In the first half of the nineteenth century the United States began to assume the role of a neometropolis over Cuba and Puerto Rico, a role that became evident by its control over the islands' exports, trade, and navigation. During the disruptions of the Napoleonic Wars and the Peninsular war of independence (1793–1812), Cubans and, to a lesser extent, Puerto Ricans began direct trade with the United States. The Spanish government granted licenses to particular Spanish and U.S. firms for the transfer of goods into and out of Cuba and Puerto Rico. This relaxation of Spain's exclusivist trading system established commercial ties between the United States and the Spanish colonies. Yet with peace momentarily restored in 1800 and then again in the second half of the 1810s, Spanish officials aspired to return to exclusivist trading practices. This met strong opposition both in the colonies and in the United States, forcing Spain to yield to the region's geographic and commercial realities. In 1816 Puerto Rico got a license to engage in direct trade with the United States, and two years later *comercio libre* was granted to Cuba. A commercial treaty between Spain and the United States signed in 1819 formalized these new links. In the 1820s tariffs were significantly reduced to facilitate and encourage trade between the Spanish colonies and North America. A new colonial pact further debilitated Spanish economic exclusivism, and Spain began to share with other naval powers the classic metropolitan role of raw material importer and exporter of finished goods. The weakening of the Iberian metropolis and its proven incapacity to supply the needs or to absorb the production of its remaining colonies resulted in the application of a new commercial formula of colonial domination: the exploitation of Cuba and Puerto Rico through import and export tariffs and other customs fees. This arrangement allowed Spain to retain political and fiscal control over the islands, while other northern Atlantic nations, the United States in particular, dominated them commercially.

The United States had obvious advantages over Spain and other European countries in establishing commercial domination over Cuba and Puerto Rico. Geographic proximity made the islands of the Caribbean the "natural" trading partners of the northern republic. While a sea journey from Havana to New Orleans took three days and one from Havana to New York took six, shipping a cargo from Havana to Vigo or Cádiz required twenty-two days. Links between the islands and the mainland of North America had shaped the economic history of the Caribbean for many decades, even before the emergence of the United States as an independent nation. The United States supplied the Spanish Caribbean with cereals, salted meats and fish, butter, lard, wood, hardware, and manufactured goods, and Cuba and Puerto Rico produced tropical staples much in demand in the U.S. market, such as sugar, tobacco, and coffee.[27] Spain, for its part, besides being geographically remote, could not provide its colonies with the necessary elements for the development of large-scale commercial agriculture. Cuban historian Manuel Moreno Fraginals wrote, "[Spain] could not provide the capital, nor the blacks, nor a broad national market, nor an adequate merchant marine, nor an extensive international trade network."[28]

By midcentury a dual system of colonialism and neocolonialism controlling Cuba and Puerto Rico was in full operation. In 1851 the U.S. consul at Havana declared that Cuba was a de facto economic dependency of the United States, despite its being governed by Spain. A year later the newly arrived captain-general of Puerto Rico expressed concern about the considerable edge that foreign nations had over Spain as recipients of Puerto Rico's exports. Less shocked but equally concerned, José de la Concha notified the minister of Development and Overseas that "the commerce carried on by the United States with this Island [Cuba] surely amounts to four-fifths of its imports and exports."[29] These were not simply overreactions by uninformed colonial administrators; they were accurate assessments stemming from the unquestionable fact that profits associated with the commercialization of tropical staples were increasingly gravitating to nations other than Spain. The extent of these ties outside the Spanish empire helps to explain the official policy of the United States toward the region: in keeping Cuba and Puerto Rico under Spanish rule, it preserved its own economic neocolonial domination over the region.

The Spanish Colonies as Exporters

During the 1840s and 1850s, and certainly for decades before that, the Spanish colonies of the Caribbean exported tropical staples to northern Atlantic markets. In 1846–49 Cuba averaged yearly exports of $24,828,988, and Puerto Rico exported an average of $5,563,086 per year.[30] Among the tropical exports for the northern Atlantic markets, sugar dominated both in volume and in value. During the 1850s tobacco was Cuba's second leading export, behind sugar and molasses. Coffee was Puerto Rico's, and the region's, second leading export, although its relative importance dropped steadily. In volume exported, the region's sugar-to-coffee ratio increased from 21:1 in 1846–49 to 35:1 in 1850–54, to 56:1 in 1855–59.[31]

Between 1846 and 1849 Cuba and Puerto Rico exported a yearly average of 6,345,786 quintals of sugar, 85 percent of which was produced in Cuba. During the same period Cuba exported a yearly average of 26,530,000 gallons of molasses and 22,762 gallons of rum to the United States. Puerto Rico's molasses exports averaged 4,031,695 gallons per year. Cuba's share of the region's sugar exports—and, by extension, of all exports—continued to increase at an accelerated pace during the following decade, while Puerto Rico's proportional output declined. By 1859 Cuba produced 92 percent of the two colonies' sugar exports.[32]

The colonies' sugar output represented a considerable proportion of the world market supply. In 1849 Cuba and Puerto Rico produced 23 percent and 5 percent respectively of the world's cane sugar. By 1856 their combined sugar production amounted to more than one-third of world production. The region's importance as sugar supplier for the north Atlantic Basin was even greater, because Cuba and Puerto Rico exported most of their production and enjoyed geographic advantages over more distant sources such as Java, the Philippines, and Mauritius.[33]

Meanwhile, exports of coffee declined. Coffee exports from Cuba and Puerto Rico, which had reached yearly averages of 299,322 quintals in the last four years of the 1840s, decreased to 255,538 quintals during the 1850–54 period and plummeted to 193,465 quintals during the second half of the 1850s, representing a 35-percent decrease from 1846 to 1859. Cuba's coffee output fell drastically, from yearly averages of 193,900 quintals in 1845–49 (almost two-thirds of the region's output), to 77,800 quintals in 1855–59 (a little over four-tenths of the region's output). Puerto Rican coffee exports remained fairly constant, though, registering, in fact, a modest upward trend.[34]

Thus, the 1850s were years of profound transitions in the exporting roles of Cuba and Puerto Rico. For Cuba they represented a period of growth toward a sugar monocrop, with sugarcane displacing not only the other traditional export staples but also subsistence agriculture. On the other hand, Puerto Rico experienced economic stagnation, which forced it to reorient its agricultural output, as sugar fell into a sustained crisis as early as 1840 and coffee gained in relative importance. These contradictory developments are explained, in part, by the different responses of planters in Cuba and Puerto Rico to international sugar demand during the middle decades of the nineteenth century. In chapter 3 we will explore these responses and the political implications of such divergent patterns of agricultural development.

Between 1846 and 1860 the United States was the premier recipient of Cuban and Puerto Rican exports. The share of these islands' exports going to the United States stood at over 40 percent during the 1850s. For the 1851–55 quinquennium, the proportion of Cuban and Puerto Rican exports heading to the United States was 39 and 45 percent respectively. During the second half of the decade, these proportions continued to increase, reaching 44 percent of Cuba's exports and 49 percent of Puerto Rico's exports. In contrast, Spain, the region's de jure metropolis, absorbed only small proportions of its colonies' agricultural output. Spain dominated less than 14 percent of Cuba's export trade in 1846–50, 11 percent in 1851–55, and 19 percent in 1856–59. The Spanish share of Puerto Rico's exports did not pass the 10-percent mark during the 1850s, averaging only 7 percent for the decade.[35] Part of this commercial weakness resulted from Spain's historically limited demand for sugar. Iberia did not have a single sugar refinery, and Spaniards were among the most lackluster consumers of the sweet crystals. While the average Briton consumed 33.4 pounds of sugar a year during the 1860s, the French citizen 11.3 pounds, and the Swiss 17.1 pounds, per-capita sugar consumption in Spain was a mere 1.74 pounds.[36] In 1851 Spain received only 539,387 quintals of sugar from its Caribbean colonies—6.64 percent of Cuba's export output and 0.30 percent of Puerto Rico's.[37] Puerto Rican sugar found itself at a greater disadvantage vis-à-vis Cuban white sugar because Spanish tariffs did not discriminate on the basis of quality. The cheaper Puerto Rican *moscabada* types required as much duty to be exported to Spain as did the finer Cuban categories.[38]

Other important markets for the exports of Cuba and Puerto Rico were Great Britain, Germany, and France. In 1852 Great Britain was Cuba's second largest market, receiving 20 percent of all its exports. Between 1850 and 1860 Great Britain stood as Puerto Rico's second largest market every year, receiving 19 percent of the island's exports during the eleven-year period. Britain's importance as purchaser of Spanish colonial exports was greatly enhanced by the opening of the British sugar market.[39] Per-capita sugar consumption in Great Britain increased steadily throughout the 1840s and 1850s, particularly following the passing of the Sugar Duties Act of 1846. By eliminating the preferential treatment for British colonial sources, this measure drastically reduced the prices of the sweetener. Britain's tariffs for imported sugar, which had remained stable at 24–25*s.* per pound from 1830 to 1844, were slashed to 14*s.* 11*d.* in 1846 and further cut to around 12*s.* in the 1850s. As tariffs plummeted, sugar became more accessible to greater segments of the British population. The cost of a pound of sugar went from 63*s.* 9*d.* before the act to 43*s.* 5*d.* in 1847, and down again to 40*s.* 9*d.* in 1855.[40] These changes turned Great Britain from a limited market for Cuba's sugar to its second largest market. By 1860 Britons were consuming an average of nearly thirty-four pounds of sugar each per year, double the per-capita average of twenty years before. The proportion of Cuban sugar absorbed by Great Britain also nearly doubled, from 8 percent of the island's sugar exports before 1846 to 15 percent in 1856–60. These sweet ties made Cuba and Puerto Rico, combined, Latin America's second largest exporter to Great Britain in 1854–60, close behind Peru.[41]

Not surprisingly, the Anglo-U.S. geopolitical rivalry over Cuba was simultaneously played out in the commercial arena. The notion that sugar tariffs in Great Britain were reduced in the competition for the Cuba trade, however, would be difficult to sustain, because tariff reductions were part of a broader trend in the 1840s and 1850s, when protectionist and exclusivist trade measures were relaxed. Nonetheless, Cuba's sugar and the implications of access to its trade and markets were part of the broader geopolitical equation. Once again, as had been the case with slavery, Great Britain discarded the rules that had helped it achieve its status as a major—the major—commercial power but that now seemed useless.

Closer attention to export patterns further reveals the extent to which the northern Atlantic nations directed the economies of Cuba and Puerto Rico. An obvious link existed between the growing degree of U.S. control over the region's exports and Cuba's transition to monoculture. On the other hand, increased European demand for coffee and the Puerto Rican sugar crisis explain the transition toward coffee there, which began in the 1850s and intensified in subsequent decades. Interestingly, during this crucial period of transformation in the region's economy, Cuba cemented trade and political links with the United States, and Puerto Rico gradually turned toward Europe. These disparate developments had strong implications in the patterns of political thought analyzed in chapter 4.

If the United States dominated the Spanish colonies' export trade, its control over their sugar output was even stronger. Over 60 percent of Puerto Rico's sugar exports and close to 43 percent of Cuba's found their way into the U.S. market. The U.S. market for sugar also expanded geometrically during the 1845–60 period. Not only was the country's population growing at an accelerated pace, but it was also rapidly developing a sweet tooth. Per-capita yearly consumption of sugar in the United States soared from close to thirteen pounds during the 1830s to seventeen pounds in the 1840s and twenty-nine pounds in the 1850s. While the United States produced 54 percent of its sugar needs domestically in 1845–54, it met only 35 percent of national demand during the second half of the 1850s. Moreover, the United States also lowered its tariffs on imported sugar from $6.00 per quintal in 1843–45 to $2.80 in 1846–48 and $1.00 in 1852–54, and then increased them slightly to $1.40 in 1855–60. All these factors combined raised the volume of sugar imports into the United States from 1,140,000 quintals worth five million dollars in 1845 to 4,570,000 quintals and fifteen million dollars in 1852 and further to 6,940,000 quintals and thirty-one million dollars in 1860, a sixfold increase in both volume and value.[42]

The bulk of the expanded demand for sugar in the United States was supplied by exports from Cuba and Puerto Rico. Between 1854 and 1858 approximately 80 percent of all sugar imported by the United States originated in the Spanish Caribbean, representing $86,646,407 worth of sugar from Cuba and around $9 million from Puerto Rico.[43] This trade with the Spanish colonies also represented a considerable slice of the overall U.S. import trade, 7 percent between 1845 and 1854. By the second half of the 1850s this proportion had grown to 9 percent. Cuba was indisputably the third largest supplier to the U.S. market, behind Great Britain and France. Furthermore, during this period Cuba was consistently the biggest single Latin American exporter to the United States, commanding 35, 39, and 47 percent of all Latin American exports to its northern neighbor in 1845, 1855, and 1860.[44]

A different pattern characterized the region's other exports. Coffee, for example, was virtually barred from the U.S. market. It had been singled out as the main target in the tariff wars between the United States and Spain during the 1830s and 1840s. This was a paradoxical development, since the other Caribbean products spared by the tariff wars—sugar and tobacco—were produced in the United States. Coffee, not produced in the United States, nonetheless became the target of prohibitionist tariffs imposed on Cuba. This paradox warrants serious research and reflection. In the meantime, one can only speculate about the motives that led to coffee's demise. Perhaps the U.S. market preferred cheaper, lower-quality coffee beans from Brazil, or perhaps it was in the commercial and geopolitical interest of the United States that Cuba become economically dependent, based on the production of one crop for one market—sugar for the United States.[45]

Between 1845 and 1859 the Spanish colonies exported negligible amounts of coffee to the United States. Puerto Rico exported only 5, 11, and 5 percent of its coffee to the United States during the 1845–49, 1850–54, and 1855–59 quinquennia. In 1859 the United States bought only $7,692 worth of Puerto Rican coffee. Coffee, which had been Cuba's main export to the United States during the early 1830s, rapidly diminished in importance. The share of coffee among Cuban exports to the United States went from 28 percent in the 1830s to 9 percent in the 1840s and 7 percent in the 1850s. Cuban coffee exports to the United States plummeted from yearly averages of $2,717,622 in the 1830s to $844,952 in the 1840s and $155,916 in the 1850s.[46] Only a little over 12 percent of Cuba's coffee exports headed for the United States in 1847. Throughout the next decade the proportion continued to fall. European markets, however, showed more interest in the region's coffee. Germany, Great Britain, Italy, and France became the main customers for Spanish Caribbean coffee, absorbing 72 percent of Puerto Rico's coffee exports between 1845 and 1849. The following decade this share went down but still dominated: 54 percent in 1850–54 and 47 percent in 1855–59. In 1852, 25 percent of Puerto Rico's coffee exports went to Germany, Great Britain received a little less than 25 percent, and Italy received 22 percent.[47] European markets also dominated Cuban coffee exports. In 1847, for example, Germany, France, and Italy received 75 percent of Cuba's exported coffee.[48]

The Spanish Caribbean as a Market

The fact that Cuba and Puerto Rico had export economies also points to their status as importers. Staple production required the importation not only of agricultural equipment and machinery but also of foodstuffs and dry goods to sustain those working on plantations and those servicing the export economy's infrastructure. Despite the region's dependence on imports, historians have paid little attention to their amounts, nature, and origin. Manuel Moreno Fraginals, for example, dedicated forty-three pages of the third volume of *El ingenio* to tables and graphs showing the quantities, types, and destinations of Cuba's exports, but not a single page dealt with imports.

The Spanish Caribbean exhibited an enormous capacity to absorb foreign goods. In fact, throughout the period 1846–60 the colonies maintained negative trade balances. Between 1850 and 1860 Puerto Rico imported 24 percent more than it exported.[49] The Cuban trade imbalance was less, since Cuba imported 9 percent more than it exported during the 1846–50 quinquennium, and 3 percent and 9 percent in 1851 and 1852.[50] During the 1850s, despite a 6.03-percent annual growth in sugar exports, Cuba's trade imbalance grew slightly because imports increased at a sharper yearly rate of 6.56 percent.[51]

The Cuban market imported the most within the region. Between 1850 and 1859 Cuba received $330,566,100 worth of imports, 84 percent of all imports to the Spanish colonies of the Caribbean.[52] Puerto Rico received the remaining 16 percent, a total of $63,043,984 for the decade. When analyzed along with population figures, the region's import data proves to be highly revealing. Cuba had by far the largest per-capita import capacity of all three components of the Hispanic Caribbean, at $31.12 per annum. Puerto Rico followed with $10.58. Not surprisingly, the Dominican Republic had the lowest per-capita import capacity, at $6.26.[53] These numbers suggest a strong correlation between the extent of integration into the world economy and the level of development of the plantation system and the proportional importance of slave labor. At one extreme, with its high per-capita import rate, stood Cuba, which had the most developed plantation system and a slave population of around 40 percent of the total. At the other extreme was the Dominican Republic, with a small per-capita import rate and no plantations or slavery. In Puerto Rico plantations predominated only in specific parts of the island, and slaves represented less than 12 percent of the total population in 1846 and only 7 percent in 1860. Clearly in Cuba, and to a lesser extent in Puerto Rico, the development of an export-oriented economy negatively affected the production of foodstuffs, making their importation necessary. Moreover, the slave populations of both islands, with diminishing access to subsistence plots, came to depend almost exclusively on foreign sources of food. In this sense, slaves in Cuba and Puerto Rico, despite their lack of purchasing power, were more integrated into the world economy than were peasants or dependent peons on any of the three islands. Furthermore, exports produced in Cuba and Puerto Rico provided the foreign exchange necessary for importation.[54]

The origins of imports to the Spanish Caribbean reveal quite a different picture from that of the destinations of the region's exports. Whereas the United States clearly dominated as a market for the region's staples, no single nation controlled imports into the region. Moreover, Spain, which played a marginal role as a recipient of Caribbean exports, actively supplied its Caribbean colonies. Spain generated 24 percent of Cuba's imports between 1846 and 1850, 30 percent during the 1851–55 period, and 22 percent during the last half of the 1850s. Overall, Spanish exports represented around a quarter of all imports to the Spanish colonies of the Caribbean.[55]

The United States was also an important supplier to the region, producing a bit less than a quarter of all imports to Cuba and Puerto Rico. The importation of U.S. goods was proportionately greater in Cuba than in Puerto Rico because the former was geographically closer and had stronger economic ties, based on sugar.[56] Specifically, in 1859, 22 percent of all imports to Puerto Rico originated in the United States, while 26 percent of Cuba's imports did. By 1859 the United States had made considerable headway into the expanding markets of the Spanish Caribbean, particularly in Cuba. The United States was the second largest supplier of the Cuban market, close behind Spain. In Puerto Rico, meanwhile, the United States enjoyed a slight edge over Spain: $1,820,609 worth of goods came from Spain in 1859, and $1,903,779 worth came from the United States.[57] Considering Cuba and Puerto Rico together, the difference only slightly favored Spanish exports. Moreover, considering exports and imports together, by 1859 the United States was clearly the region's dominant commercial power, with a share of $40.0 million against $21.7 million controlled by Spain.[58] Significantly, while Cuba and Puerto Rico had negative trade balances with Spain (in 1852 alone, Cuba imported from Spain $6,329,768 more than it exported there, and Puerto Rico's trade imbalance with Spain was a staggering $1,533,313), both had positive trade balances with the United States, sending a little over two-and-a-half times more than they received.[59]

Most of the remaining half of all imports to the colonies originated among five or six other European and American sources. Great Britain played a significant role within this group as direct exporter to Cuba. A little over 21 percent of all Cuban imports between 1850 and 1853 originated there. Direct British exports to Puerto Rico, however, were much less significant, both in absolute and proportional terms: Britain supplied less than 6 percent of all imports to Puerto Rico during the 1850s. Comparatively, while Cuba imported British goods worth $6,333,067 in 1850–53, Puerto Rico received only $167,014 in direct British exports. Considering both colonies together, British goods constituted 18 percent of all imports.[60]

Of vital importance in Puerto Rico's import trade were the "European" trade depots of the Danish Virgin Islands, St. Thomas in particular. In fact, during the 1850s Puerto Rico received close to a third of its imports through the *Antillas extranjeras*. The bulk of the dry goods and luxury items came from St. Thomas, where European manufacturers had direct commissioners. Puerto Rico's dependence on St. Thomas as a supplier was so strong that when a cholera epidemic struck that island and authorities in Puerto Rico established a quarantine, the prices of consumer goods tripled. Many of the goods imported by Puerto Rico through St. Thomas were British-made, which explains the low volume of goods imported directly from Great Britain. Other suppliers of secondary importance to the Cuban market were Latin America, France, and Germany, each of which provided between 5 and 8 percent of Cuba's imports in 1850–53.[61]

The Spanish colonies' Iberian imports mostly consisted of flour. In 1859, for example, Puerto Rico imported $1,820,609 worth of Spanish goods, and $1,450,000 of that was flour.[62] In contrast, that year the United States only supplied $150,000 worth of flour, barely 9 percent of the island's total flour imports. The predominance of Spanish flour was even greater in Cuba: out of 1,836,706 flour barrels entering the port of Havana in the 1850s, only 51,344 (3 percent) came from the United States. The rest was from Spain. This represented a considerable change from proportions a few years earlier. Foreign suppliers had provided the Cuban market with a quarter of its flour between 1841 and 1844.[63]

Spanish dominance in the flour trade was achieved by Spain's imposing high tariffs in Cuba and Puerto Rico that discriminated against flour produced in other nations or carried in foreign vessels. Whereas coffee had been the Spanish Caribbean's greatest casualty of the trade wars, flour became the primary victim on the U.S. side. Because of the combined influence of the powerful Peninsular grain growers' lobby and the shipping sector, non-Spanish flour incurred prohibitive duties in Cuban and Puerto Rican ports. Following an act passed in 1834, the duty on non-Spanish flour was between $10.50 and $10.81 a barrel (181 to 200 pounds) in Cuba and $12.50 in Puerto Rico; the duty on Spanish flour was only $2.52 per barrel. These measures practically shut off the entry of U.S. flour, causing very high prices for Cuban and Puerto Rican consumers.[64] Flour sold in Cuba for $16.00 per barrel in 1854; two-thirds of that price, if the flour came from the United States, covered the cost of import duties. These prices put flour, and by extension bread, out of the reach of most Cubans and Puerto Ricans. According to an 1853 estimate, the taxes quadrupled the price of bread. One observer noted, "The poor and oppressed Creole whites are compelled to use dry and insipid casava [*sic*] root as a miserable substitute for bread."[65]

In the United States, with its expanding capacity to produce and export wheat more cheaply than any other source, Spanish flour tariffs created great tension and stood high on the list of grievances expounded by opponents of Spanish colonialism. In one of her fire-eating expansionist articles, Jane M. Cazneau estimated that "Cubans import $20,000,000 a year of such commodities as the United States produce, and could sell on better terms than the Island can buy from distant Europe, if they were permitted to compete in open market." Referring primarily to the exclusion of flour from the United States, Cazneau stated that "the Upper Mississippi and the Ohio states are the chief losers." John S. Thrasher blamed Spanish tariffs for reduced U.S. exports to the Spanish Caribbean. If trade between the United States and Cuba was liberated from this burden, he concluded, its volume would double. During the 1859 debate on the Cuba purchase bill, the tariff issue rose once more to prominence. Defending the purchase plan, Senator Stephen R. Mallory explained: "Cuba consumes three hundred thousand barrels of flour per annum, only nine thousand of which are American. . . . Were flour admitted free they [the 1.6 million inhabitants] would consume three fourths of a barrel each per annum, or one million two hundred thousand barrels of American flour, which would sell in Cuba at $5 per barrel, for $6,000,000, instead of the $45,000 of flour we now sell them." This issue was particularly sensitive in New Orleans, the main outlet for midwestern wheat and flour for the Caribbean markets. Of the $1,164,630 worth of flour and grain that left the United States for Cuban ports in 1854–58, $581,748, or close to 50 percent, passed through New Orleans.[66] Thus, the impact of Spanish tariffs was particularly annoying to shipping and commercial interests of the Mississippi Delta. These circumstances help explain the strong anti-Spanish sentiment in New Orleans and the delta region's active support for filibustering in the late 1840s and early 1850s.

Rice, also a southern export, was another victim of the tariff wars between Spain and the United States.[67] During the 1820s and 1830s rice had linked the southern United States and the Spanish Caribbean, but as the 1840s and 1850s wore on, these bonds loosened. In an 1851 report calling for an end to the tariff wars, Senator Mallory asserted that "before the passage of the act of 1834, Cuba obtained her rice almost exclusively from our Southern States. . . . In 1849, the Cuban import of rice was 21,820,167 lbs., worth $1,092,597, of which the value of $799,563 only came from the United States. She now gets rice from Valencia, South America, England, Brazil, Holland." The fact that Mallory was complaining that his country controlled only 73 percent of Cuba's rice imports stands as a revealing indicator of the previous state of affairs. In 1851 Puerto Rico imported 9,400 quintals of U.S. rice, 90 percent of the island's imported rice. By 1855 Cuba bought 337,305 quintals of rice (an increase of 55 percent since 1849); Spain provided 39 percent of the total. Puerto Rico's market for rice was more limited. While Cuba imported rice at the rate of 26 pounds per capita, the smaller island absorbed only 7 pounds per capita.[68] Here again, the larger extent of slave-based plantation agriculture, which absorbed people and land into staple production, explains Cuba's greater dependence on foreign food sources.

Other imported foodstuffs did not meet such severe discrimination in Havana, San Juan, and other Spanish colonial ports as did flour and rice. This was particularly true of goods for which Spain had no national production to protect, such as wood, manufactures, and beef jerky or products like butter and fish, which would spoil during a transatlantic voyage. In the mid-1850s, for example, the duty on beef, butter, ham, and lard did not discriminate on the basis of Spanish or non-Spanish origin. For pork and beef jerky, discrimination was mild: importers from Spanish sources paid 60 to 75 percent of that paid by importers from foreign sources.[69]

Food imports to the Spanish Caribbean dramatize the sharp differences between the economies of Cuba and Puerto Rico.[70] For analytical purposes, major food imports to the region can be broken down into two general and somewhat overlapping categories: imported foodstuffs likely to be consumed by slaves rather than peasants (beef jerky, rice, flour), and imports not likely to be consumed by slaves (soap, butter, cheese).[71] The average Cuban consumed between 0.16 and 0.19 barrels of imported flour, between 16 and 25 pounds of beef jerky, and 8 pounds of rice each year. Puerto Rico exhibited a much lower per-capita rate of consumption of all three items: 0.09 barrels of flour, 0.5 pounds of beef jerky, and 2 pounds of rice. Attention to the second category reveals greater similarities. Each year Cubans consumed between 0.35 and 0.55 pounds of butter, with a slight edge over their Puerto Rican neighbors, who consumed 0.32 pounds. Each year Cubans consumed 0.84 pounds of cheese and 4 pounds of soap, while Puerto Ricans consumed 0.78 pounds and 3.3 pounds of the same goods.[72] These statistics point to the disparate levels of plantation development in Cuba and Puerto Rico and their implications for the colonies' foreign trade.

Other major food items imported to the Cuban and Puerto Rican markets during this period were fish, fish oil, ham, lard, beef, pork, tallow, and bacon, primarily from the United States. In 1854 that country exported $143,691 worth of such goods to Puerto Rico and $1,678,855 to Cuba. In 1851 the United States supplied Puerto Rico with 92 percent of its imported pork, 77 percent of its imported beef, 76 percent of its imported ham, and 97 percent of its imported lard. For Cuba the proportions were either similar or a bit higher.[73]

The Spanish Caribbean colonies also had to import most of the nonfood products that they consumed—textiles, wood, mineral coal, metal and wooden manufactures, and machinery. Cuban purchases of goods and manufactures related to the production and transportation of sugar, such as coal, railroad ties, cooperage, and sugar machinery, increased rapidly during the 1840s and soared even higher during the next decade. By 1860 Cuba was importing 92,000 tons of mineral coal annually to run the island's *ingenios* and locomotives. Moreover, during the second half of the 1850s wood and wood manufactures from the United States became the single largest import category in Cuba, second only to Spanish flour. Cuba received 94 percent of its wood, a vital element for the expansion of the sugar industry, from the United States. Also important among Cuban imports were metal products and machinery, which Spain could not supply. One critic of Spanish colonialism wrote that the garrote was "the only machine . . . that Spain . . . brought to Cuba."[74] The United States found an excellent outlet in Cuba for iron manufactures and machinery. U.S. exports to Cuba in this category soared during the 1850s, when international market pressures forced Cuban planters to mechanize their sugar-producing establishments. Exports of iron manufactures and machines jumped from $649,730 in 1848 to $3,689,137 in 1860, more than a fivefold increase. Because of the stagnation of its sugar industry, Puerto Rico did not absorb these items to the same extent. In 1851 the island imported only $798,921 worth of goods under the broad category of "metals" from all sources. Puerto Rico's proportional share of imported metal manufactures and machines from the United States was also less significant. According to the 1854 *balanza mercantil* (mercantile balance sheet) Puerto Rico imported only $42,438 worth of hardware and machinery, while in the same year Cuba imported $815,116 worth of "iron and iron manufactures."[75] Demand for wood was also lower in Puerto Rico: Cuba imported $3,486,795 worth of wood and wood manufactures in 1854; Puerto Rico received only $254,528 worth.[76]

By the mid-1850s, then, the United States was the single largest trading partner of the Spanish Caribbean. U.S. dominance was more notable in receiving the region's exports, sugar in particular, than in exporting goods to the region. This was owing to the relatively low export duties and extremely high import duties prevailing in the Spanish islands. Just as rivalry existed among the various powers contending in the political sphere, so tensions emerged over the commercial control of the region. The tariff wars between Spain and the United States and the struggle between the United States and Great Britain over Cuba's sugar production and trade are two manifestations of this commercial competition that point to interesting parallels with the political rivalry. The United States gained preponderant political influence over the region as it gained preeminence as the Spanish Caribbean's most important trading partner. This was a critical facet of neocolonial domination. Moreover, the United States was more successful both politically and commercially in Cuba than in Puerto Rico. While the growth of the Cuban sugar industry strengthened Cuba's links with the United States, Puerto Rico's economic reorientation beginning in the 1850s reinvigorated its commercial and political bonds with Europe.

Shipping, Tariffs, and the Transfer of Technology

Shipping and navigation data provide yet another set of indicators to shed light on the Spanish Caribbean's commercial ties and the extent of neocolonialism the region endured in the middle decades of the nineteenth century. The available data confirm Cuba's overwhelming trading superiority. In 1857, 1,454 vessels visited Puerto Rico's ports, with cargoes totaling 176,921 tons. The port of Havana was much busier. In 1857 the number of ships visiting it surpassed those calling in all Puerto Rican ports by 25 percent.[77] One contemporary observer described the port of Havana as "one of the safest, most picturesque, and best frequented in the World." "The arrivals in the month of March," he continued, "frequently amount to 22 vessels in one day." Meanwhile, the U.S. consul estimated that close to one thousand U.S. vessels each year arrived in Cuban ports. The port of Havana was the world's eighth busiest port in 1850.[78]

U.S. shipping predominated in the Spanish colonies of the Caribbean. In 1842 the United States surpassed Spain in shipping in Cuban ports by a two-to-one ratio. By 1855 this ratio had increased to four-to-one, and the ratio of U.S. to British shipping was seven-to-one. In 1857, 53 percent of ships in Cuban waters carried the U.S. flag; Spanish and British ships represented 19 and 4 percent of all vessels entering and leaving Cuban ports. Among the ports outside the United States, Havana was the one most frequented by U.S. ships. In a complaint letter, U.S. consul Charles Helm estimated that the number of U.S. ships departing Havana was 25 percent higher than that of any other port, including Liverpool and London. In Puerto Rico, vessels from the United States also predominated. Figures for 1858 and 1859 reveal that although Spanish shipping was heavier in San Juan, not a staple-exporting port, by more than 4 to 1 in number of vessels and 2.6 to 1 in tonnage, the United States outstripped Spain in all Puerto Rican ports combined, with a hold over 35 percent of all ships entering and exiting, against 32 percent for Spain.[79] This was another way in which trade-related profits gravitated to the United States rather than to the region's de jure metropolis.

Clearly, within the trade networks of the Spanish Caribbean the Iberian metropolis did not play a decisive or dominant role, particularly as recipient of its colonies' exports. Spain had yielded the bulk of trade and shipping into and out of its Caribbean colonies to the United States and Great Britain, while retaining close to a quarter of Cuba's and Puerto Rico's import trade. The United States, Great Britain, and other commercial powers meanwhile gained direct access both to the produce and to the profitable markets of Cuba and Puerto Rico. Spain, for its part, by means of high tariffs and customs fees, managed to control a portion of its remaining American colonial markets and to profit indirectly from the increased trade between its colonies and other nations.

Spain extracted enormous amounts of revenue from maritime taxes collected in Havana, San Juan, and other colonial ports. In Cuba such revenues represented well over half of the island's total income during the late 1840s and 1850s: 55 percent between 1846 and 1850 and 62 percent between 1854 and 1858 stemmed from customs duties and navigational fees. In Puerto Rico these categories also dominated.[80] During the 1846–50 quinquennium, yearly colonial maritime revenues amounted to an average of $7,900,429; by 1854–58 this had risen by over $3 million to $10,931,913. Cuba produced 89 percent of this sum, and Puerto Rico generated the remainder.[81] Considering the two islands' overall volume of trade, Spain managed to tax imports and exports at rates ranging from 11 to 13 percent.[82] The tariff rate on imports—especially those originating in or carried by nations other than Spain—was much higher than on exports leaving Cuba and Puerto Rico. Higher export tariffs on tropical staple crops would have made both colonies uncompetitive in the world market, destroying the islands' economic base and eliminating the source of foreign exchange that made their markets attractive. During the five years 1846–50, for example, import-related revenue in Cuba represented 89 percent of all maritime revenues. Between 1854 and 1858 this proportion was 85 percent. Importers paid customs and tonnage duties ranging between 20 and 25 percent ad valorem, compared with only 3 percent collected on exports.[83]

Within the baroque edifice of Spanish maritime taxation, other measures discriminated against foreign shipping in favor of Spanish vessels.[84] These provided the colonial government with additional revenue while protecting Spanish shipping interests. In 1850, referring to these discriminatory duties, U.S. consul Robert B. Campbell estimated that the protected Cuba trade sustained "more than three-fourths of the whole mercantile marine of Spain." Importers bringing goods to Cuba in the early 1840s paid taxes of 14.25 to 18.25 percent, if the cargo came on Spanish vessels, and 21.25 to 27.25 percent, if it came under a foreign flag. For their part, exporters carrying goods on Spanish vessels paid duties of 4.25 percent, and those hauling products on foreign vessels paid 6.25 percent. Some items required higher duties. Importers of foreign flour, for example, paid duties of $8.50 a barrel on Spanish ships and $9.50 on foreign vessels.[85]

Tariff policies' evolution and their repercussions require further research and careful analysis, but we can conclude that in general the 1820s saw earlier prohibitive customs duties gradually relaxed in Spanish colonial ports. Then, beginning in 1832, Spain and the United States embarked on their tariff wars in which Cuban coffee and U.S. flour and rice became the main casualties. Between 1832 and 1834 the U.S. Congress passed a series of retaliatory navigation and trade acts that increased discriminatory duties against Spanish shipping and certain products originating in the Spanish colonies. Later described by Florida senator Stephen R. Mallory as "suicidal" and "coercive," these acts not only reduced Spanish shipping but also the volume of U.S. flour exports in Spanish vessels. "The annual average of [flour] barrels carried from the United States in Spanish bottoms before the passage of the act [in 1834], was 39,780, whereas but 310 were thus carried in 1843," stated Mallory. He added that the South, in particular, suffered from this exclusion of Spanish shipping because now most tropical imports had to come via northern ports. Moreno Fraginals has pointed out that the navigation act of June 30, 1834, was the first step in establishing U.S. neocolonial control over Cuba, a step that destroyed an emerging Cuban merchant marine by closing U.S. ports to it.[86]

Not surprisingly, the tariff wars escalated further with the passage of higher duties by the Spanish Cortes in 1834. These doubled between 1834 and 1835 the duties for rice, bread, ham, hoops, shooks, staves, shingles, and other U.S. exports. U.S. flour was the big loser that year, since its duty was raised to $9.50 a barrel. In 1846 the tariff war abated somewhat when the United States repealed some of its earlier discriminatory duties and influential sectors in Spain sought to reduce trade frictions as well. Mariano Torrente went to the extreme of proposing the total elimination of export duties and a 33-percent reduction in import duties as measures to stimulate production and curb smuggling. Flour tariffs, he added, should be reduced by one-fifth, and Spanish flour producers must search for other markets.[87]

Another strong link in the neocolonial relations between the United States and the Spanish colonies of the Caribbean consisted of the transfer of technology for sugar production and railroads. By the mid-1840s, for example, the United States had displaced Great Britain as the premier exporter of sugar machinery to Cuba. By 1859 the United States exported $726,591 in products and equipment for Cuban sugar estates, almost half of the island's imported total. Great Britain's share amounted to $557,063 (38 percent), and France's to $167,815 (11 percent). That year Spain supplied only $160 worth of goods in this category, probably some sets of stocks and shackles. The United States also provided locomotives and box and train cars and experts to run them. Cuba's first railroad, established in 1837, was described by Richard Robert Madden as an "American enterprise." U.S. visitors to Cuba in the 1850s recounted pridefully that they had ridden U.S. cars pulled by U.S. engines and driven by U.S. engineers. Sugar-producing machinery from the United States found considerable demand in Cuba: items such as mills made at the West Point Foundry in New York, ovens produced by Philadelphia-based Merrick and Son, and steam engines built in New York's Novelty Iron Works and West Point Foundry were sold there. Cuba's finest mill in 1860 belonged to Juan Poey; it had a splendid steam engine forged at West Point.[88]

North American technology and know-how also made headway in

the area of communications and utilities. Cuba's first telegraph was installed by Samuel A. Kennedy in 1851, just six years after the first successful telegraphic transmission in the United States. Puerto Rico's first was put in place in 1859 by Samuel Morse himself, on the estate of one of his relatives. In the 1850s James Robb of New Orleans established Havana's first gasworks, with an investment of a quarter of a million dollars.[89]

With the machines came those who could run them. When Puerto Rico's first steam engine was installed in Ponce in the early 1820s, William Sinkin, a U.S. citizen, was contracted to operate and maintain it. In Cuba, by the early 1850s an estimated four hundred workers from the United States arrived annually to operate the sugar mills. Estimates for the next two decades put the number at between 1,000 and 1,500 each year. Most of these migratory skilled laborers gravitated to sugar-producing districts, particularly to Cárdenas, described by many as "an American city," and Matanzas, of which one U.S. visitor said, "Our language is more common there than in any other Cuban city, and the customs of the place are more americanized."[90] Most of these migrants settled in Cuba only for the grinding season, six months between late October and late April. The majority of them came from New England and New York State. They returned there each spring suntanned, with their pockets lined with several hundred dollars. Because their skills were in such great demand, engineers and machinists made between $100 and $120 per month, in addition to receiving paid accommodations, meals, and other necessities.[91] This was almost double the salary of a plantation overseer. Carpenters, coopers, rope makers, and other skilled craftsmen from the United States were also in great demand.[92] The flow of their salaries to the United States was yet another form of profit within the emerging neocolonial relation.

Spanish officials in Cuba looked with distrust at the presence of these migratory workers and, for that matter, at any foreign presence. Laws allowing non-Spanish foreigners to settle in Cuba and Puerto Rico had come into existence only in the second decade of the nineteenth century. Even then, immigration was restricted to those willing to swear allegiance to the Spanish monarchy and the Catholic Church. Short-term visitors faced many difficulties from the moment of their arrival: they first had to find someone to put up a *fianza* (bond) to guarantee their adherence to Spanish law.[93] The presence of hundreds of U.S. skilled laborers in Cuba each year irritated colonial authorities, who thought Yankee visitors were vehicles of abolitionist, Protestant, and anti-Spanish ideas. In February 1842 the Spanish vice-consul at Savannah inquired about the character and political inclination of some U.S. citizens who proposed migration to Cuba. He was reassured by B. J. Smith of St. Augustine, Florida, that the participants were mostly Catholic and "without the most remote *taint* of Abolitionism." On another occasion Cuba's captain-general granted permission for the entrance of a hundred railroad workers from the United States, "as long as they are Irish." The truth was, however, that most mechanics and engineers who labored in Cuba were Protestant, New England Yankees, opposed to slavery. A number of them were arrested in relation to the conspiracy of La Escalera in 1844.[94] Their influence was such a concern to Captain-General de la Concha that in March 1851 he reported that U.S. machinists were the best instruments for spreading annexationist ideas. This was reason enough, he continued, to create a Cuban school for the mechanical arts. During his second term de la Concha publicly ordered the island's governors and lieutenant governors to report periodically "on the number and condition of foreign engineers in plantations."[95]

Other Facets of Neocolonial Domination

During the middle decades of the nineteenth century the United States established commercial domination over the Spanish colonies of Cuba and Puerto Rico. This form of control emerged at a time of stagnant sugar prices and increasing prices for sugar technology.[96] The relationship between the United States and the Spanish Caribbean was obviously not one between equals. Sugar producers in Cuba and Puerto Rico struggled to survive in a world market in which they had no control over sugar prices or demand. For their part, the metropolitan nations through a variety of fiscal and regulatory mechanisms exercised enormous control over both price and demand. Moreover, the United States, because of its geographic location, played the role of a virtual monopsony, dictating the course of the Cuban and, to a lesser extent, the Puerto Rican economies. Spain gave its reluctant blessing to this unavoidable takeover in order to secure its own profits from increased tariffs and expanded trade.

The United States and other northern Atlantic nations also exerted control over Cuba and Puerto Rico by allowing their market needs and economic goals to dictate the islands' agricultural activities. Cuba's dependent position forced its economy away from a diversified self-sufficient status into one based on sugar monoproduction, requiring the massive importation of foodstuffs and other products. Moreover, the United States managed to dictate to Cuban planters the specific types of sugar they should produce. Beginning in the early 1840s U.S. sugar tariffs began to discriminate against Cuban semirefined sugar in favor of cruder *moscabada* types. Whereas in 1833 brown sugar required duties in the United States of 3 cents per pound and white sugar required 3.125 cents per pound, by 1846 the duty for the cruder type had dropped to 2.5 cents, and white or semirefined sugar rates had almost doubled, to 6 cents per pound.[97]

These measures had profound repercussions for both sides. High tariffs on refined sugar paved the way for the astonishing growth of the sugar-refining industry in the United States, especially in the Northeast. In 1848 there were only four sugar refineries in the entire United States: three in New York and one in Boston. Eight years later, according to Alfred S. Eichner, "there were twelve refineries in New York City and vicinity, five in Philadelphia, five in New England, two in Baltimore, and one each in St. Louis, Cincinnati, and New Orleans. Together they produced 385 million pounds of refined sugar annually, a fourfold increase since 1850." By 1860 fifteen more refineries were operating in the United States.[98] Cuban planters responded by adapting their technology, as well as their minds, to the market exigencies of the United States. Leví Marrero, a prolific student of Cuban history, has noted that Cuban sugar production in 1847 already showed a significant increase in the production of *moscabada* at the expense of higher-quality sugar; by the early 1850s Cuban planters had voluntarily resigned themselves to raw sugar production. A leading Cuban planter, Miguel Aldama, admitted in the early 1850s that Cuba could not "compete with other countries as a producer of refined sugars." He blamed this on the fact that Cuba had no coal, no bricks, and no lumber, that unskilled labor was too expensive, and that skilled labor had to be imported. Sugar consumed in the United States was thus no longer a purely Caribbean product, since the recipient nation put the final touches on it. More significantly, the role played by U.S. refiners was more highly valued than that played by Cuban planters and sugar manufacturers: the widening gap between the prices of *moscabada* and refined sugar clearly revealed this trend. While the international price of raw sugar went down slightly during the 1847–59 period, refined sugar prices increased almost 21 percent. Put another way, while in 1847 raw sugar was valued at 0.057 cents per pound and refined sugar brought 0.077 cents per pound, in 1855–59 raw sugar was valued at 0.056 cents per pound and refined sugar was worth 0.093 cents per pound.[99]

Interestingly, what Spain could not achieve in two and a half centuries—reducing Cuba to an exporter of raw materials and an importer of finished goods—the United States achieved in two decades. Cuba and Puerto Rico actually suffered the worst of two kinds of colonialism: economic subordination to the powerful, expanding United States and political-fiscal subjection to decadent Spain.

Economy, Trade, and the State During the First Dominican Republic, 1844–1861

Besides having a different polity, four other features differentiated the Dominican Republic from the Spanish colonies nearby. First, slavery had been abolished there in 1822. Second, subsistence agriculture predominated, and therefore the economy was relatively disconnected from the outside world. Third, no plantations to speak of existed in the island. Finally, the state exercised virtually no power over the lives of most Dominicans. In short, the Dominican Republic had not yet embarked on the dual expansion of the state and the export economy that most other Caribbean islands had already undergone.

Most cultivated land in the Dominican Republic was devoted to minor crops for local consumption. Certain regions, however, produced staples for the national market and for export. El Cibao produced tobacco for the markets of Europe; the southern woodlands, particularly Azua, provided mahogany and other precious woods; and El Seibo, a ranching province in the East, produced meat and hides. During the First Republic, lumber and hide production dropped, and tobacco output and exports more than doubled, stimulated by higher international prices. In spite of the growth of the tobacco sector, Dominican production in both quantity and quality still compared unfavorably with Cuban and Puerto Rican production.[100]

Fundamental differences in geography, racial composition, links to the outside world, and political orientation separated the tobacco-producing northern regions and the southern and eastern woods and ranches. The economy of the North was based on small, family-owned, family-run units, producing tobacco for the markets of Hamburg, Bremen, and St. Thomas. Conditions there were favorable for the flourishing of egalitarian and democratic values and institutions. In contrast, the South and East's economy, based on wood cutting and cattle raising, rested on latifundia and dependent peonage and thus favored an authoritarian and oligarchic social arrangement. The South's commercial links were also stronger with Great Britain, Curaçao, and St. Thomas.[101] The republic's two prominent caudillos of the mid–nineteenth century had their roots there: Pedro Santana was a wealthy rancher from El Seibo, and Buenaventura Báez was the proprietor of extensive landholdings in Azua.

Several factors conspired against the development of plantations in the Dominican Republic. The structure of land distribution and ownership carried the imprint of the Spanish colonial legacy and the Haitian occupation. Property in Spanish Santo Domingo was not well defined. During the first three centuries of Spanish colonial domination, colonial authorities had made extensive land grants available to settlers. Over time these overlapping, unsurveyed lands were informally subdivided among the descendants of the original grantees. As a result, the Dominican territory came to be divided into unclearly delimited "common" lands to which the inhabitants had access but did not have legal rights. Between 1822 and 1844 the Haitian occupation government attempted to redefine land ownership structures by partitioning and distributing among the freed slaves the "common" lands, lands of those fleeing Santo Domingo, and church- and state-owned lands. The Haitian state acquired vast tracts of land later inherited by the Dominican government.[102] According to H. Hoetink, as late as 1871 between one-fourth and one-third of the Dominican Republic's territory remained in the hands of the state. One of the results of the Haitian occupation was the formation of an independent peasantry engaged in subsistence agriculture. The population of the republic's North and West thrived untouched either by the coercive arm of the state or by the insatiable demands of commercial agriculture. Moreover, low population density resulted in the easy availability of unoccupied lands, which made regimentation of the labor force a more difficult task. The Dominican Republic had only 10.4 inhabitants per square mile in 1860, compared with 169 persons per square mile in Puerto Rico. Outside the province of Santo Domingo, the population density was even lower—7.2 persons per square mile.[103]

Another factor explaining the absence of plantations in the Dominican Republic was that the country's landed elite fled the island during the Haitian invasions of 1801, 1805, and 1822. Moreover, the lengthy Haitian occupation and Haiti's sporadic expansionism after 1844 discouraged foreign and domestic investment. Foreign merchants, furthermore, shied from investing in commercial agriculture, preferring instead to speculate with paper money and tobacco inventories.[104] Finally, timing was not on the republic's side: the 1840s and 1850s were difficult decades in which to stay competitive in sugar production, let alone to start anew.

During the 1840s and 1850s the Dominican Republic remained on the fringes of the world economy. While Cuba and Puerto Rico averaged yearly export volumes of $24,828,988 and $5,625,933 respectively in 1846–50, Dominican exports amounted to only $681,986 in 1849 and $1,120,349 in 1850.[105] Exports increased only slightly during the balance of the 1850s, averaging $1,152,600 between 1851 and 1855. Exports consisted primarily of tobacco and mahogany for the European markets. Mahogany log exports in 1855 were valued at $321,000; these shipments headed mostly to Great Britain and France.[106] All categories considered, Great Britain was the principal market for Dominican goods. Bremen and Hamburg, however, were the main destinations of the republic's tobacco crop. In 1855 Dominicans exported fifty-five thousand quintals of tobacco. In the following year the Hanseatic port cities received 91 percent of the republic's tobacco export. The role played by the United States as recipient of Dominican exports was not significant. From October 1858 to September 1859 a little over one hundred thousand dollars' worth of Dominican exports reached U.S. ports.[107]

The Dominican Republic produced little sugar and coffee. In 1847, 1851, and 1855 the republic did not export sugar; in 1852 it exported a negligible 257 quintals. According to information appearing in *La Gaceta de La Habana* in 1858, the republic produced barely enough to satisfy national demand. Two years later the Spanish consul, Mariano Álvarez, complained that despite favorable conditions for the production of sugar, coffee, and corn, Dominicans had to import these staples.[108]

As a recipient of foreign goods, the Dominican Republic also had a relatively negligible role. While in 1850 Cuba imported $28,985,227 and Puerto Rico purchased $5,222,031 worth of imports, the Dominican Republic imported only $815,736, or 2.3 percent of all imports to the Hispanic Caribbean. Import data for the republic five years later reflect a further reduction in its capacity to purchase foreign goods: only $561,750 worth was imported in 1855.[109]

Evidence regarding the origins of imports to the Dominican Republic is scanty. Data on values of foreign imports collected by Mariano Torrente in 1849 and 1850 reveal that the three main direct exporters to Cuba (Spain, the United States, and Great Britain) were not as important to the Dominican Republic. In fact, all three combined provided less than 30 percent of all Dominican imports in 1849–50. Great Britain's importance as an exporter to the Dominican Republic increased enormously, however, following the signing of the Anglo-Dominican commercial treaty in 1851. That year Great Britain exported a half million dollars' worth of goods such as textiles, clothing, china, and tools to the Dominican Republic, 78 percent of all Dominican imports. Data for 1855, compiled by the British consul, confirm Britain's grip over the Dominican market. Out of a total of $561,700 worth imported, $321,000 worth originated in Great Britain.[110] Like Puerto Rico, the Dominican Republic received a large proportion of its imports from European colonial entrepôts in the Caribbean. This meant higher prices for goods imported via these ports. In 1849–50 Curaçao was the single largest exporter to Santo Domingo. Likewise, St. Thomas was the chief supplier to the northern port of Puerto Plata. Overall, during these two years imports under the Danish flag averaged $196,005 per year (36 percent of all Dominican imports), and imports under the Dutch flag averaged $101,958 (19 percent). Another 12 percent or so originated in Germany, Sweden, Italy, and France. Because it could not impose trade regulations on the Dominican Republic as it did on Cuba and Puerto Rico, Spain supplied the Dominican Republic with only 9 percent of its imports in 1849–50. This proportion decreased further as the 1850s wore on. The United States was not a significant exporter to the Dominican market either. In 1851 only 12 percent of all Dominican imports came from the United States, which mainly sold flour, salted fish, soap, and candles there. That the Dominican Republic did not export sugar and did not require massive imports of foodstuffs and agricultural equipment explains, in part, the limited extent of its trade with the United States.[111]

Shipping data confirm the Dominican Republic's marginality in international trade. During 1849–50 a yearly average of 251 vessels called in Dominican ports, averaging 82 tons per ship, for a total of 20,582 tons. Puerto Rico's busier ports received 4.8 times as many vessels, weighing 6.8 times as many tons.[112] Shipping in the Dominican Republic's ports was more equally distributed among a larger pool of trading partners. During the early 1850s Great Britain controlled 28 percent of the tonnage of ships in Dominican ports, the United States controlled 20 percent, and Denmark controlled 16 percent. The proportion of British-controlled shipping, however, increased dramatically at the expense of U.S. shipping following the signing of the Anglo-Dominican treaty of 1851. Shipping from France, Holland, and Germany was of secondary importance: each of these nations controlled between 6 and 10 percent. The independent status of the Dominican Republic explains two differences separating it from Cuba and Puerto Rico. The Dominicans had established their own, albeit small, mercantile fleet consisting of vessels averaging thirty tons and representing 5 percent of all tonnage entering and departing their ports. Also in the Dominican Republic, where Spanish ships did not enjoy the preferential status they did in Cuba and Puerto Rico, Spanish shipping amounted to a negligible six vessels and 510 tons per year, only 2.5 percent of all tonnage.[113]

A recognizable national apparatus formed very slowly in the Dominican Republic. Despite the existence of a president, legislature, and courts, the state played a minimal role in the everyday life of the Dominican people. Spanish visitors in the 1850s and early 1860s described the Dominican judicial system as a very simple and casual arrangement whereby local alcaldes administered justice in a paternalistic and arbitrary way and in which court rulings were auctioned publicly. There was no national army either. Instead, personal armies, like Santana's, were composed of dependent peons linked to a caudillo's relatives and friends. There were few funds to pay soldiers, who were often primarily rewarded with titles and commissions. Meanwhile, merchants carried on the operations of the treasury as honorary functionaries.[114] Corruption and ineffectiveness characterized the system: the importer-exporters themselves assessed and collected taxes on their merchandise.

The state's revenues were as limited as its ability to exercise power. In 1845 state income amounted to $281,994, of which $179,057 derived from import taxes and $67,878 from export taxes.[115] Compared with Cuba's revenues, which amounted to $18 million in 1846, Dominican revenues were trifling. In 1860 only $241,347 was spent for the operation of the Dominican state. Later the state sold commercial licenses, or *patentes*, and in 1853 this produced $1,094 in Santo Domingo and $664 in Santiago and Puerto Plata. Military expenses and the maintenance of troops drained the Dominican Republic's budget and produced chronic deficits. In 1845, for example, military expenditures surpassed total revenues by 55 percent. Some have estimated that military expenses absorbed 80 percent of the national budget during the First Republic.[116]

In order to face the endemic budgetary deficits, the various administrations of the First Republic resorted to the irresponsible printing of paper money. This resulted in yearly devaluation rates of around 80 percent between 1847 and 1855.[117] The printing of paper money reached dizzying heights during Buenaventura Báez's second administration, when sixty million pesos were printed in 1857–58. Despite these grave fiscal problems, the Dominican Republic managed to stay free of the burden and political implications of a foreign loan. This was possible because the different northern Atlantic powers checked each other, blocking any one nation from becoming dominant in the Dominican Republic. A British citizen, Herman Hendrick, had approached Pedro Santana's government as early as 1844 with a loan offer: Hendrick required the payment of £13,944,993 over thirty years for a loan of £2,930,000. Santana sent this proposal to the National Congress, where it was repudiated. It was the first of many failed attempts to force a foreign loan on this struggling republic of the Caribbean.[118]

Foreign-born merchants had considerable direct and indirect influence upon the administrations of the First Republic, which they exerted through their consuls. Many in the consular corps were in fact import and export merchants, including Juan de Abril, Spanish agent; John Bothe, consul of Bremen; Federico Finke, consul of Hannover and Oldenburg; Francis Harrison, U.S. vice-consul; and Karl

Newman, consul of Austria and Prussia.[119] These agents pressed to keep import and export duties at a minimum and to obtain rates of exchange favorable to their economic ventures. The extent of their power became quite evident in 1859, when the French, British, and Spanish consuls, acting at the request of foreign merchants, threatened to use force if Santana refused to set the currency exchange rate at a particular level.

Some striking contrasts separated the designs of the United States toward the Dominican Republic from those toward Cuba and Puerto Rico. In the Spanish colonies, colonial legislation thoroughly regulated immigration, shipping, and foreign trade. The Dominican Republic appeared to be an open field, waiting to be populated, exploited, and capitalized. U.S. entrepreneurs and official envoys explored early on the possibilities of promoting massive immigration to the republic from the United States. In 1850 General Duff Green and his son, special envoy Benjamin Green, tried to organize such a colonization project. William Cazneau and his partner, Joseph W. Fabens, tried to organize similar schemes later in the decade. In 1862 they formed the American West India Company to promote migration schemes.[120] These and other U.S. entrepreneurs also sought to establish direct extractive operations in the mining and agricultural sectors. In the late 1840s, in association with Nicolás Juliá, the Greens set up the American-Dominican Mining Company. The agreement stipulated that Juliá would sell mining lands to the company; besides the purchase price he would receive 5 percent of the copper, iron, and other minerals extracted.[121] Cazneau, who at one point wrote of the Dominican Republic that "perhaps no other country in the world exhibits such a broad variety of mineral and agricultural production," also established direct investments there in real estate and mining. Another instance of direct participation of U.S. capital in extractive ventures in the republic was the exploitation of guano deposits on the island of Alta Vela. A mining brigade from Baltimore set up camp there in February 1860 to extract the precious fertilizer, but later that year, at the insistence of the Spanish government, Dominican authorities forced them out.[122] The Dominican Republic's political instability, the threat of Haitian aggression, and the zealous interference of European merchants and consuls blocked such economic endeavors. Báez's administrations, in particular, tended to cancel any concessions made by previous administrations to U.S. investors. During the 1840s and 1850s the Dominican Republic thus remained relatively disconnected from the Atlantic commercial system. Although certain agro-export pockets flourished and the country established trade links with European markets, the bulk of the land and its people remained tied to subsistence activities.

Three | Dual Colonialism in Cuba and Puerto Rico

During the 1840s and 1850s international market exigencies put enormous pressures on the economies of Cuba and Puerto Rico and, in fact, on those of all sugar-exporting countries. Sugar consumption increased tremendously in Great Britain and the United States, as new, lower tariffs for the sweetener were put in place. As Sidney W. Mintz aptly put it: "A rarity in 1650, a luxury in 1750, sugar had been transformed into a virtual necessity by 1850."[1] Increased demand for sugar—an apparently favorable development for sugar producers—was, however, only half the story. The supply of cane sugar from a variety of regions and beet sugar from western and central Europe also increased exponentially during this period, with world beet sugar production jumping from 60,857 metric tons in 1845 to 351,602 metric tons in 1860.[2] Thus, sugar prices fell or at best remained stagnant during the 1840–56 period, shrinking the profit margins of sugar producers around the world.[3] Under such pressing circumstances, sugar planters in the Caribbean had to adjust to the new dictates of the world market. Planters in Cuba and Puerto Rico responded differently to these pressures, reflecting divergent levels of capital resources and adaptability.

The Cuban Response

Cuban planters as a whole responded to the new realities of the world market by accepting the sugar challenge: in the face of diminishing profit rates they sought to expand sugar production. During this critical period Cuba's economy continued to steer away from diversification and relative self-sufficiency toward sugar monoculture and dependency. By 1855 sugar and its byproducts represented 84 percent of Cuba's exports, and by 1862 this category represented 58 percent of Cuba's entire agricultural production.[4] Other traditional staples like coffee, tobacco, and cotton suffered serious setbacks as land, labor, and capital previously linked to these crops were siphoned off to the insatiable world of sugar. The number of coffee farms in Cuba, for example, fell from 2,067 in 1827 to 1,670 in 1846 and to 782 in 1862, representing a 62-percent drop in thirty-five years.[5] By the late 1870s fewer than 200 coffee estates remained on the entire island. In contrast, the number of sugar estates grew considerably, from 1,000 in 1827 to 1,422 in 1846 and to 1,650 in 1850. During the 1850s the number of sugar estates actually declined a bit, to 1,365, but this reduction indicated concentration rather than contraction.[6] Not only did the Cuban economy accept foreign dictates to produce more sugar, but it also responded to pressures concerning what kind of sugar to produce. The core nations with refining sectors to protect, the United States and Britain, shut off their markets to Cuban semirefined sugar and called upon the island to produce more and more of less and less, sugar of a lesser quality for a smaller number of markets.

By the end of the 1850s Cuba was a full-fledged sugar island. Seventy percent of its agricultural production consisted of sugar, close to 50 percent of its slaves worked in sugar plantations, and more than 25 percent of its cultivated land was devoted to sugarcane. These transformations were apparent to contemporary observers. Richard H. Dana wrote in 1859, "There are no manufactures of any consequence; the mineral exports are not great; and, in fact, sugar is the one staple. All Cuba has but one neck—the worst wish of the tyrant." A year later Ramón de la Sagra warned against the island's dependence on a single export crop and coined the phrase *agricultura de rapiña* (preying agriculture).[7] The problem of monoculture was aggravated by the fact that sugar went primarily to one market—the United States.

To stay competitive and to meet the new quantitative and qualitative international demands, Cuba's planter class embarked on expansion, resting on two simultaneous, though seemingly contradictory strategies: the mechanization of the sugar industry and the enlargement of the servile labor force. New machines had always been a symbol of status among Cuban planters. Their mouthpiece of the late eighteenth and early nineteenth centuries, Francisco de Arango y Parreño, had emphasized the necessity of integrating Europe's latest technology into the island's *ingenios*. Steam-powered engines made their debut in Cuba as early as 1796, and the island's first railroad system was in place by 1837, more than a decade before one would appear in Cuba's de jure metropolis.

The mechanization of Cuba's sugar industry in the 1840s and 1850s did not, however, touch upon all aspects of sugar production and transportation. Despite some efforts to introduce steam-powered plows, planting and harvesting remained in their primitive forms, as labor-intensive, manual tasks. Conversely, new technology did dramatically transform most of the manufacturing stages of sugar production. Steam engines to power larger and more sophisticated cane grinders became common in the 1840s and 1850s. Whereas in 1827 only 2.5 percent of the island's sugar mills were run by steam engines, in 1860 close to 70 percent used this type of energy. Some estimates put this proportion near 91 percent by the end of the 1850s.[8] This transition from muscular and hydraulic power to steam increased enormously the grinding capacity and speed of the average *ingenio*.

The next major step in sugar production, the crystallization of the *guarapo* (cane juice), also required improved mechanization in order to keep pace with the greater and faster outputs of the grinding phase. In this area the major technological innovation was the vacuum pan, known in the region as *tacho al vacío*, or *tren* Derosne. In 1844 Wenceslao de Villaurrutia introduced one such device in his *ingenio*, replacing the open pans system (*trenes jamaiquinos*) in which boiling cane juice had to be manually transported through a succession of pans of different sizes. Because of their exorbitant prices, however, Derosnes and similar crystallizing devices made slow inroads into Cuban sugar-making. Only the largest and most financially sound—or the most daring—of the *ingenios* managed to acquire vacuum pans in this period. By 1863 only 4 percent of Cuba's *ingenios* had them. Four years later seventy-five *tachos al vacío* were operating, at a staggering average initial cost of $120,000.[9] The rest of the planters had no option but to multiply the number of open *trenes* in order to keep up with the increased grinding capacity achieved with steam.

The following step, the *purga* or separation of sugar crystals and molasses, was the next phase to be addressed in the mechanization orgy of the midcentury. Bottlenecks now occurred in this slow and simple procedure. Traditionally, the *purga* was achieved through a process of filtration lasting thirty to fifty days, which consisted of pouring the saturated molasses into conical containers, each of which had a cloth-covered hole in the bottom. Most of the molasses covering the crystals dripped out into special containers, leaving behind sugar crystals of various degrees of purity. This stage was revolutionized by yet another innovation of the industrial age—the centrifuge, which pushed the excess molasses out of its inner drum, leaving the dried sugar crystals in the inner chamber. Joaquín de Ayestarán pioneered the use of the centrifuge in Cuba on his *ingenio* La Amistad in 1850. These devices were popularized to such an extent that 116 of them were purchased in 1862 alone.[10]

Students of Cuban agrarian and social history have underscored the importance of yet another aspect of the industry's mechanization: railroads. According to Moreno Fraginals, the establishment of the Güines railroad in 1837 marked "a fundamental mile-stone" in the rapid expansion of the sugar industry in the 1840s and 1850s. Franklin W. Knight later concluded that railroads were instrumental in freeing sugar production from earlier constraints that limited the extension of single *ingenios*. Knight stressed that the introduction of locomotives reduced transportation expenses and liberated a considerable segment of the plantation labor force, which could now be transferred to work in the production stages. Bergad's use of 1837 as a periodization watershed in his recent book on Matanzas indicates the railroad's importance. Twenty-two years after the Güines locomotive puffed its first clouds of smoke, the Cuban railroad network consisted of 378 completed miles, and 184 more miles were under construction. By 1865 the railroad network stretched along 754 operational miles.[11]

In mechanizing the Cuban sugar industry, planters did not simply choose models from the catalogs of the West Point Foundry or Derosne and Cail. Mechanization required enormous amounts of money, which planters often did not have. Since the purchase of new machines had to be coordinated with the acreage, the number of slaves, and the rest of the machines in the complex, one addition in any particular phase usually translated into the necessity of making further investments in machines, land, and slaves. To set up a midsize sugar plantation in Cuba in the 1850s required an original investment of between $300,000 and $350,000, with yearly injections of $40,000 for upkeep and renovation of the slave force.[12] Because of the costs involved, only a small segment of the old Cuban planter class managed to reorganize and expand its sugar operations to meet the challenges of the midcentury. Between 1838 and 1851 Francisco Pedroso y Herrera, Nicolás Peñalvar y Cárdenas, Ignacio Peñalvar y Angulo, Gonzalo de Herrera, Nicolás Martínez de Campos, and José Luis Alfonso and his brother José Eusebio Alfonso either set up new mechanized *ingenios* or reorganized the ones they had. Many others did not have the cash or credit required to buy the expensive machinery and continued to struggle along with what they had for as long as they could. Between 1850 and 1860, 385 *ingenios* stopped operations, representing a 23-percent decrease. According to Moreno Fraginals, the incapacity to purchase vacuum pans ruined the old planter class.[13] One could also argue that the disorderly, yet seemingly unavoidable purchase of sugar-producing equipment paved the road to eventual ruin. Meanwhile, new capital from licit and illicit commercial enterprises moved in to accept the sugar challenge and to establish fully mechanized sugar operations. The Aldamas, the Diagos, and Julián Zulueta were prominent members of this new generation of planters.

Another goal of most planters wishing to mechanize was to reduce the industry's dependence on imported slave labor. The growing number of slaves and their majority status, first revealed by the census of 1841 in 1842, were a constant source of anxiety among the propertied classes, which feared a St. Domingue–style racial war. Moreover, international pressures for the cessation of the slave trade sent clear signals to the Cuban plantocracy that they had better start looking for alternative sources of labor. In 1854 Cristóbal F. Madan estimated that the application of the latest technology could reduce labor demands by seventy-nine men in a medium-sized, four-thousand-hogshead *ingenio*. He continued that it was not possible "to enumerate the changes fostered by the exclusion of ignorant and barbaric hands, substituting them by a higher intelligence, one manifested in machines and inventions as well as direction and rational structuring of the work process."[14]

Since the mechanization of the sugar industry failed to affect the planting and harvesting of sugarcane, the process did not alleviate labor needs; on the contrary, it increased them. The voracious appetite of the flashy new mills had to be satiated, and this required the expansion of the cultivated area and the addition of new hands to do the planting and cutting, to allow the costly new machines to operate at full capacity. Alternative sources to bonded labor were not easily forthcoming. Immigrants from the Peninsula and the Canary Islands tended to avoid plantation labor, and by the 1850s the island's planter class gave up hopes of promoting white colonization, after innumerable failures and frustrations during the previous decade. Attempts were also made to reduce the dependence on black slavery by introducing unskilled laborers from the Orient. During the second half of the 1850s some thirty-seven thousand Chinese coolies arrived in Cuba as contract laborers.[15] An anonymous member of the elite dramatized the labor crisis when he stated in *La Gaceta de La Habana* that he would welcome not only Asian laborers but even "orangutans if these were susceptible to domestication."[16] Thus a paradox arose: the planter class was stepping into the future, embracing the latest technology in sugar manufacturing, while remaining deeply attached to slavery and other forms of servile labor.

The relationship between the industry's mechanization and slave labor has long been a central issue of Cuban historiography. In the late 1940s Raúl Cepero Bonilla put forth the thesis that the continuation of slavery was incompatible with the modernization of Cuba's sugar industry. He argued, rather dogmatically, that the enormous cost of slavery hindered the accumulation of capital necessary for successful mechanization and that slaves were not capable of operating the new, complex machinery. Other Cuban historians have built upon Cepero Bonilla's interpretation, most notably Moreno Fraginals and Fe Iglesias García. Iglesias García recently asserted that slavery constituted a drag on industrialization, estimating that slaves represented between 38 and 40 percent of a mill's investments. The incompatibility thesis was challenged in the early 1970s by Herbert S. Klein. He pointed out that sugar producers in Louisiana had successfully modernized their industry before the abolition of slavery. More recently, Rebecca J. Scott concluded that "during the 1860s and 1870s, when the 'contradictions' within Cuban slavery were in theory becoming most apparent, the major sugar areas were nonetheless holding on to most of their slaves." According to Scott, it was precisely in the most advanced and mechanized sugar regions that slavery persisted. Recent studies by Bergad emphasize both the viability and the profitability of slavery well into the late 1860s. Actually, the Cuban planter class had no alternative but to mechanize and expand if it was to stay in business; this demanded more labor, and since alternative sources failed to provide it, the only reasonable response was to remain attached to slavery. Neither theoretical incompatibilities, which do not affect the course of history, nor slave resistance, which is sometimes romanticized, brought about the institution's eventual demise.[17]

During the 1850s, following four years of sharply reduced slave importation after the conspiracy of La Escalera, slave trading boomed once again.[18] Increased demand and the slave population's inability to reproduce itself spurred the growth of the slave trade. According to estimates reported by the British judges of the Mixed Commission, 67,422 slaves were imported between 1849 and 1858. On October 6, 1855, British consul-general Joseph T. Crawford reported: "This Island seems to be beset with slavers; they are swarming and what is worse, they appear to succeed in landing their Slaves eluding the vigilance of the Spanish authorities always." The high-water mark of slave importation was reached in 1859–61, when the Mixed Commission registered 58,705 importations and ninety-four enslaving expeditions.[19]

Growing demand for labor and the increasing legal difficulty faced by slave traders translated into higher prices for slaves. The average price for an African-born slave jumped from between $300 and $350 in 1845 to between $1,000 and $1,500 in 1860. Commenting on the scarcity and expense of labor and referring to Chinese contract workers, Dana wrote in 1859: "Such is the value of labor in Cuba, that a citizen will give $400, in cash, for the chance of enforcing eight years' labor, at $4 per month, from a man speaking a strange language, worshiping strange gods or none, thinking suicide a virtue." Another indicator of Cuba's desperate demand for labor was recurrent attempts to siphon slaves from Puerto Rico and Brazil.[20] According to a student of Puerto Rico's slave trade, the 1850 epidemic in Cuba, which took a toll of thirty thousand slaves, spurred the flow of slaves from Puerto Rico to Cuba. Nearly six hundred slaves were transferred from Puerto Rico to Cuba between 1848 and 1851. Speculators were accused of buying up entire estates in Puerto Rico just to gain control over their bonded labor force for export to Cuba. This practice continued even after authorities in Puerto Rico established a seventy-five-dollar export tax per slave in 1853. Harsher labor conditions in Cuba made the threat of being sold there one of the most effective disciplinary measures that a planter in Puerto Rico could use. In fact, Cuba was to the Puerto Rican slave what Mississippi and Alabama were to slaves in the Mid-Atlantic region of the United States: hell.[21] In March 1854 Captain-General Fernando de Norzagaray effectively put a stop to this flow of slaves out of Puerto Rico. In his decree's preamble he alluded to constant complaints by Puerto Rico's planter class. Cuba also imported slaves from Brazil, probably from that country's depressed sugar regions of the Northeast.[22]

If planters' labor needs were the main stimulus behind slave trading, bribes and traders' profits insured the continuation of the trade. Captain-General Leopoldo O'Donnell is said to have left Cuba in 1848 with a fortune of over a half million dollars derived from bribes connected with slave importation. His successor, Federico Roncali, true to O'Donnell's precedent, charged a bribe of fifty-one pesos per imported slave. In an 1853 dispatch Consul-General Crawford reported on the extent of official corruption regarding the slave trade: "The Spanish Officers are bribed; the Slave Traders interested commit their offences and repeat them with the most complete impunity; Commissions sent by the Chief Authority of the Island to investigate such offences are baffled, or corrupted; the Masters and Crews are not punished, the Vessels are allowed to escape." In one instance the smugglers of 468 African slaves to the southern coast of Cuba had to pay bribes amounting to 468 ounces of gold to the port's commanding officer, 234 ounces to the captain of the port, and 200 ounces each to the port's collector and tide-surveyor, a total of 1,102 ounces of gold. Rumors circulated that Captain-General José de la Concha received one ounce of gold (worth seventeen dollars) for each slave landing on Cuban shores and that in 1859 alone these fees earned him $680,000.[23]

Despite this high rate of "taxation," slave trading brought enormous profits for traders bringing slaves into Cuba. According to an 1860 report by the British consul, slavers could afford to lose four vessels for every successful expedition and still make a profit. In an 1861 report to Judge Truman Smith of the New York Mixed Commission, U.S. consul Robert W. Shufeldt estimated that a five-hundred-slave expedition could net $236,500. He calculated costs to be $37,500 for the slaves,

$7,000 for the ship, $19,000 for wages, and $100,000 for bribes. Later estimates stated that a slave costing only $40 worth of cheap liquor and rusty rifles in Africa could be sold in Cuba for $600 or more. According to Hiram Fuller of the New York *Mirror*, an individual investor could buy five hundred dollars' worth of stock in a slave trading company and expect to achieve a return of ten thousand dollars in a year or two.[24]

Mechanization and the slave trading orgy of the 1840s and 1850s provided a means for social mobility that eventually led to the subordination of one elite by another. New machines and fresh slaves came at no small cost to Cuban planters. As a class, they soon found themselves indebted to the Spanish-born element, which grew wealthy from speculation in slaves, capital, dry goods, and machines deemed necessary for the expansion of the sugar industry.

The Cuban sugar boom of the late 1700s and early 1800s stands as the deviant case of the Caribbean: it was the only such experience fueled by native capital and native skill. On this matter Knight has written: "The sugar revolution derived its greatest impetus from the entrepreneurial skills of the oldest families in Cuba. These families, having become rich in land and having access to public offices, found themselves strategically positioned to take every advantage of the early economic development." Among the most prominent names of these old families were Arango, Montalvo, Duarte, Peñalvar, Cárdenas, Herrera, Chacón, O'Reilly, Calvo de la Puerta, O'Farrill, Pedroso, and Nuñez del Castillo.[25] The sugar operations of these and other planters had consisted of patriarchal, self-sufficient units, requiring little financing and only primitive technology. According to Moreno Fraginals, the magic number of these units was one hundred slaves, who could produce 115 tons of sugar. Growth beyond that was achieved simply by establishing additional *ingenios*.[26]

Evidence suggests that by the late 1830s most of Cuba's sugar planters lacked the capital needed to expand and reorganize their enterprises. "There are many known cases," wrote one observer, "who while having estates worth 200 or 300,000 pesos, cannot dispose of 2,000 without needing them." Thus, for many Cuban planters willing to accept the challenge of expansion, mechanization meant recourse to outside sources of credit. In a society in which, with few exceptions, there were no banks until the 1850s, merchants played the role of moneylenders, by advancing cash and imported goods in exchange for the guarantee of the planters' next harvests. The recourse to this mechanism, known as *refacción*, represented the subordination of the planters' interests to those of the mercantile class and eventually the takeover of landed wealth by merchants. Interest rates stipulated in *refacción* contracts ranged between 18 and 20 percent. The going rate for credit in Europe was 4 to 5 percent. Aside from earning profits derived from interest, merchants were able to extract profits by forcing planters to buy overpriced hogsheads, by charging excessive sales commissions and storage fees, and by speculating with the sugar inventories that they bought at an agreed price before the harvest.[27]

Many contemporary observers and more recent students of the region's history have blamed these high rates of interest on a specific piece of sixteenth-century Spanish colonial legislation, called *el privilegio de ingenios* (the privilege of the sugar estates). This law protected sugar producers from having their land, slaves, and equipment seized for payment of debt. Arango y Parreño was among the first Cubans to blame the ills of the island's sugar culture on the maligned *privilegio*. In a May 24, 1797, deposition to the Development Board, Arango y Parreño argued that the *privilegio* kept good lands in bad hands and that it favored not only those suffering misfortune but also the "treacherous swindlers." Another critic suggested that such laws favored the debtors: he recounted the anecdote of a merchant who was sentenced to forty years in prison for attempting to collect from a delinquent marquis. In the mid-1800s colonial administrators in Cuba and Puerto Rico stepped in to remedy some of the problems of the sugar industry by attacking the centuries-old *privilegio*. On November 10, 1848, Captain-General Juan de la Pezuela promulgated a decree granting sugar planters in Puerto Rico the dubious right to renounce the *privilegio*. Four years later a royal decree provided that *ingenios* established after that time would no longer enjoy the *privilegio* and that all others would lose it by 1865. It is likely that because of their pressing needs for capital, planters were willing to forfeit their *privilegio* as a precondition to receiving credit, but no documentation supports this contention.[28]

By accepting the challenge of expansion, then, Cuban planters prepared the scenario for their downfall. Having little capital to finance their industry's modernization, the most daring resorted to expensive sources of credit. Others simply backed away from expansion. By the end of the 1850s the planter class had lost financial control over the sugar industry. With the *privilegio* gone or about to expire, the loss of property became a matter of time. The economic and financial crisis of 1857 further aided this process. In that year alone, 250 bankruptcies were registered in Havana. Francisco López Segrera has concluded in his study of the Cuban economy that by 1860 Spanish commercial capital had gained almost complete control of the sugar business. According to Moreno Fraginals, two-thirds of the Cuban sugar industry was mortgaged and consequently in the hands of the mostly foreign merchant class by 1863. At that point 95 percent of the *ingenios* were mortgaged to some degree.[29]

The mechanization of the Cuban sugar industry and the consequent rise in slave importations, the two processes that sealed the fate of Cuban planters, were precisely the circumstances favoring the ascendancy of Spanish commercial capital. During the 1840s and 1850s the Peninsular element gradually moved into territory previously monopolized by the Creole elite. Spaniards seeking a fortune in Cuba usually found it in one or more of three ways: government service through high salaries and access to even higher bribes, usury and speculative trading and lending, and smuggling, particularly of slaves.[30]

Spaniards migrating to Cuba usually carved their niches in the colonial bureaucracy, the church, the military, or the commercial sector. Only on rare occasions would Spanish immigrants engage directly in agricultural ventures. Julián Zulueta was a notable exception to this. "I have not seen during the time I have been in this Island," wrote a visiting traveler, "a single Spaniard cultivating the soil."[31] Many Spaniards started out as *dependientes* (shop clerks) in commercial establishments, perhaps working for a so-called *tío* (a distant relative, called an uncle) or a *paisano* (fellow countryman). Through thrift, cunning, or deceit, or a combination of all three, some *dependientes* managed to amass small fortunes that eventually allowed them to set up their own commercial enterprises.

Made up mostly of Peninsulars, the commercial sector exploited and subordinated the planter class through a multitude of mechanisms. It advanced overpriced goods and cash at exorbitant interest rates. It set the price at which sugar was received as payment. It collected fees, commissions, and other charges for transporting, storing, and selling the sugar. As if this were not enough, some merchants refused to accept sugar not packed in the containers that they sold. Their hogsheads and barrels were thus forced upon indebted planters at prices far above market value. Some merchants collected the molasses that dripped from sugar hogsheads during storage. This dripping molasses was not credited to the planters at the time of shipping; it was retained by greedy merchants as an additional source of profit. For them, it was obvious, every drop counted.[32]

Rather than wait for the drops of molasses to accumulate slowly, some Spaniards opted for quicker ways to make their fortunes. None was quicker than trading in slaves. Roland T. Ely, a student of Cuba's nineteenth-century commercial sector, concluded that a great many of the island's commercial fortunes were made by importing and selling slaves. Another student of nineteenth-century Cuba, Robert Louis Paquette, asserts that slave trading was one of two ways in which newcomers became members of the elite; marrying into it was the other. Julián Zulueta, a poor and illiterate Basque immigrant, started out as a *dependiente,* gradually moving up to become an independent merchant and later a plantation owner as well. By 1857 Zulueta, described by the British consul-general as "one of the [most] notorious slave traders that has ever existed," was Havana's largest slave owner, with 1,475 slaves.[33] To cite another example, José Suárez Argudín arrived penniless from Asturias and within a few decades became one of the island's wealthiest men, elected deputy to Madrid in 1867.[34] Interestingly, contrary to the trend during the eighteenth and early nineteenth centuries, whereby Spanish immigrants soon became "Cubanized" through absorption into older Cuban families, the newer migrants now tended to retain their Spanish identity. They saw themselves as superior, nonpermanent residents of the island. Belonging to Spanish social clubs, such as El Casino Español, and participating in the infamous Volunteer Corps increasingly reinforced this sense of separateness during the later decades of the nineteenth century. The origins of this divide can be found in the anti-Creole policies of Captain-General Tacón and in the midcentury ideological split over the issue of the slave trade. This issue clearly drew the line separating the mostly Creole planter segment, opposed to the continuation of the slave trade, and the mostly foreign import-export sector, intimately linked to slave trading activities. Finally, the colonial state through banishment and confiscation aided in the displacement of the Cuban elite. The coup de grace would come with the Cuban Ten Years' War.[35]

The Puerto Rican Response

Puerto Rico responded quite differently to mid–nineteenth-century world market demands for tropical staples. Whereas Cuban planters attempted to remain competitive by increasing output through expansion and mechanization, in Puerto Rico planters fell victim to a sustained crisis marked by stagnation and decline. Between 1850 and 1859 Puerto Rico's sugar exports declined at an average rate of 26,317 quintals each year; the decade started with exports of 1,121,294 quintals and ended with exports of 884,443 quintals.[36] Because of the crisis, some of the capital backing sugar production was diverted to other agricultural ventures or commerce. Other capital investment simply faded away in the face of a sustained crisis that reached its nadir in the 1870s.

A series of basic differences in economic history and the capacity to meet the challenges of the midcentury separated Cuba and Puerto Rico. Above all, Puerto Rico's sugar boom, which started fifty years later than Cuba's, was fueled, financed, and managed by foreign capital and immigrant entrepreneurs. Interestingly, while the origins of the Cuban sugar revolution are usually traced back to the British occupation of Havana in 1762–63 (an eleven-month period during which the port city received an influx of ten thousand slaves), the boom in Puerto Rico is attributed to the measures of the 1815 Cédula de Gracias, which, among other things, promoted the immigration of foreign capitalists. In short, while Cuba imported its labor force, Puerto Rico began by importing its bourgeoisie.

A prosopographic analysis of Ponce's planter class by Francisco A. Scarano has demonstrated that only between 28 and 30 percent of the municipality's sugar planters were Puerto Rican during the period 1827–45. As Scarano points out, even these percentages do not give the full picture, because the estates owned by Creoles were among the smallest holdings. "By the middle of the century," Scarano writes, "the privileged strata of Ponce's society were primarily composed of first or second generation immigrant families, while only a minority of the sugar estate owners could trace their origins to the old elite of *hateros* and *estancieros*, the patriarchal rural elite of the eighteenth century."[37] One of the drawbacks of having a foreign-born bourgeoisie leading Puerto Rico's transition to an export economy was that the capital behind the process was uncommitted and highly mobile. French, Spanish, or German planters could easily sell their land, slaves, and equipment and retire back to Europe if pressed too hard, or they could shift their capital resources into commerce, from which most of the plantation capital had originated. In contrast, the Cuban planter class had an additional incentive to face the sugar challenge. For them, holding on to their land meant keeping an ancestral symbol of status and prestige: their land, many times linked to titles of nobility, had passed from generation to generation. Land was the most important legacy they could hand to their heirs. Besides, Cuban sugar estates were larger and could resist times of crisis better than their smaller counterparts in Puerto Rico.[38]

If Cuba's sugar boom was a revolution, Puerto Rico's was a revolt. Puerto Rican expansion was shorter, lasting through the 1820s and 1830s, localized, and not as far-reaching in the regions it affected. During the 1840s the island's sugar industry began to show signs of debilitation. The number of sugar estates dropped by two-thirds, from 1,552 in 1830 to 550 in 1860, while sugar output remained stagnant. Puerto Rico's newer planter class did not exhibit the same staying power as its Cuban counterpart. Moreover, mechanization in Puerto Rico lagged decades behind, which meant that modernization to competitive levels required larger sums of money. For example, as late as 1867 vacuum pans had not been adopted in Puerto Rico; that year seventy-five such units were operating in Cuba. Three years later only 120, or 20 percent, of Puerto Rico's sugar estates used steam to run their mills.[39] Significantly, while Cuban planters were downgrading their sugar production to meet the lower quality standards of the U.S. market, Puerto Rico's sugar, with a high content of molasses, was not deemed appropriate for the needs of the United States and other northern Atlantic markets. Moreover, Puerto Rico was geographically farther than Cuba from the United States, which made Puerto Rico's sugar less competitive when transportation expenses were added to the costs. Finally, chronic droughts and declining soil fertility affected the southern coast of Puerto Rico beginning in the 1840s.

Another significant contrast between Puerto Rico and Cuba was that large proportions of the arable land and labor force on the smaller island remained on the fringes of the plantation economy. Sugar plantations had sprung up only in select places of Puerto Rico like Ponce, Guayama, and Mayagüez, while most of the work force and tillable land remained allocated to minor crops and subsistence agriculture. In fact, it could be argued that Puerto Rico was not a plantation society. In the same sense, Cuba's Eastern Department was not a plantation society, although it harbored some plantations in Santiago and Guantánamo. According to 1862 estimates, the amount of land for minor crops, such as plantains, tubers, and corn, in Puerto Rico was still about equivalent to that devoted to the island's chief staples, sugar and coffee. Moreover, Puerto Rico had a massive population of independent or subordinate peasants who remained on the periphery of the plantation economy. In 1844 the British consul at San Juan described this element of the island's population: "The natives who are free surpass by far the slaves, many of them possess small plots in which they live, and since their needs are minimal, they only cultivate that which they find necessary to sustain themselves, they care little about improving their crops or their condition." The availability of land had made this kind of life-style possible for centuries. According to Bergad, unoccupied lands were still plentiful in the first half of the nineteenth century, a circumstance that made controlling labor difficult. The dual expansion of the state and staple agriculture, however, soon pushed this autonomous population into the frontier interior of the island.[40]

During the late 1830s and the 1840s efforts were made to regiment the island's independent work force through antivagrancy laws and other coercive means. In June 1838 Captain-General Miguel López de Baños passed his notorious "Bando contra la Vagancia" (vagrancy law). Antivagrancy tribunals, called Juntas de Vagos y Amancebados, were also set up to punish those who preferred to subsist off officially vacant plots rather than become servile peons in export-oriented units. The crown jewel of Puerto Rico's coercive labor legislation was de la Pezuela's "Ley de la Libreta" of 1849. It stipulated that those without land or a profession either had to become tenants or had to search for employment under a landholder, carrying with them their *libreta de jornalero* (journeyman's passbook) at all times. The *libretas* were used to make annotations about the *jornaleros'* work, wages, debts, and conduct. *Jornaleros* were also forced to remain in one particular municipality and to continue working for the same estate until their debts were cleared. To further control the mobility of the labor force, landowners commonly advanced overpriced goods to their workers from their own estate shops. British consul H. Augustus Cowper praised the results of the *libreta*. "It has been in practice for fifteen years," he wrote in 1866, "and the results have been that every man, without distinction of color, has been forced to work; the productions of the soil have annually increased; and vagrancy, and the higher crimes are almost unknown." The dual expansion of the state and the export economy eventually caught up with the people and the land of Puerto Rico's interior. As Fernando Picó has demonstrated in his studies of the Utuado municipality, the rolls of the *jornalero* class became filled with the names of descendants of the town's founding families and its former local elite.[41]

Perhaps the sharpest contrasts to be drawn between Cuba and Puerto Rico in this period are those relating to slavery and racial patterns. In Puerto Rico slavery never played the crucial role it did in Cuba. According to Philip D. Curtin's estimates, a total of about 702,000 slaves were imported into Cuba, but only 77,000 arrived in the smaller island. Moreover, in Cuba the slave population reached its peak in 1841 at 436,500, or 43 percent of the population; in Puerto Rico it peaked around 1846 at 51,300, or less than 12 percent of the population. Patterns of change in the importation of slaves into Cuba and Puerto Rico further reveal divergent developments, since the crisis of the sugar industry in Puerto Rico had a considerable impact on the demand for slave labor. While an estimated 1,410 slaves entered Puerto Rico yearly between 1830 and 1845, during the following decade and a half only about 700 slaves arrived each year, a decrease of 50 percent. By contrast, in Cuba, where the sugar industry continued to expand, yearly average imports of slaves increased from 10,014 during 1827–47 to 12,330 during 1851–60, a 23-percent increase.[42]

A series of factors explain the crisis of slavery in Puerto Rico. First, the island's economic reorientation away from sugar and toward coffee reduced the demand for slave labor. Second, those who continued to produce sugar were not always in the best position to invest in new slaves. Third, as demonstrated by the studies of José A. Curet, the low technological level of most sugar estates meant that the addition of more slaves in estates that already had fifty or more slaves produced only marginal returns. These factors also help explain the loose attachment of planters in Puerto Rico to the continuation of the slave trade. In 1860, when slave imports were breaking records in Cuba, Consul Charles De Ronceray described the prevailing attitude in Puerto Rico: "The sentiments of the natives, including the planters are opposed to the transportation of slaves from Africa and very little encouragement is therefore given to the slave trade either by the people or Government of the island notwithstanding the want of labor."[43]

The lesser importance of slavery was also reflected in Puerto Rico's racial patterns. The existence of large sectors of society outside the grip of the state and the export economy during three centuries favored the population's miscegenation. Enlightened European visitors to Puerto Rico noted a high degree of race mixture among the population, a characteristic attributed to activities lying outside the sphere of the state and the official economy: piracy, smuggling, illegal immigrations, desertion, and *marronnage*. Census data for San Juan's districts between 1823 and 1833 show that the free population of color in the different barrios ranged between 38 and 59 percent of the entire population. By 1860, according to census figures, Puerto Rico's nonwhite free population was 241,015, out of a total of 583,308 inhabitants, or 41 percent. According to one abolitionist active in Puerto Rican politics, "There is no radical separation of the races in this country, and mulattoes constitute more than 50 percent of the population."[44] In contrast, Cuba, particularly the western districts, where plantations played such a central role, evidenced a far more defined separation of the races and a much stronger correlation between color and status. The Cuban census of 1841, for example, reflected a population consisting of 418,291 whites (41.5 percent) 490,305 blacks (48.7 percent) and 99,028 mulattoes (9.8 percent). In Matanzas, specifically, the census indicated that 31.9 percent of the population were whites, 64.8 percent were black slaves, and only 3.3 percent were mulattoes. Ninety-five percent of the blacks in Matanzas were slaves, compared with only 29 percent of the mulattoes.[45] Racism, the ideology that sought to preserve this kind of stratification and a close association between color and status, was also considerably stronger in Cuba than in Puerto Rico.

The world market demands thus put enormous pressures on the economies of the Spanish colonies of the Caribbean during the middle decades of the nineteenth century. Sugar planters were forced either to accept the sugar challenge, by modernizing the industry and expanding slavery, or to withdraw from the industry altogether. Despite belonging to the same geographic region, sharing similar climatic and geological conditions, and being subjected to the dictates of the same empire, Cuba and Puerto Rico took different economic paths in midcentury. Conditions in Cuba favored the acceptance of the sugar challenge. Planters there resorted to expensive credit in order to modernize and expand sugar production. The result of this was that by 1863 two-thirds of the industry was in the hands of Spanish merchant-bankers, who held mortgages of two hundred million dollars. Meanwhile, in Puerto Rico the mostly foreign planter class had no choice but to continue operating at a reduced level or to back away and diversify into other crops, coffee in particular. Both societies faced similar challenges from the outside world. Both responded to them as best they could, but in the end both floundered, each in its own particular way.

Four | Political Patterns

International rivalry over the Hispanic Caribbean and the manipulation of racial divisions by foreign hands shaped the region's political tendencies to a considerable extent. The formation of a European naval coalition to circumvent the expansionist upsurge in the United States produced a parallel polarization within Cuba and the Dominican Republic, as Creoles in both societies gravitated toward either the United States or Europe. During the middle decades of the nineteenth century, conditions were favorable for the political activation of the Creole elites in the Spanish colonies of the Caribbean, particularly in Cuba, where Spanish commercial capital seriously challenged the Creole elite's hold over the sugar industry. Finding itself in an uncertain position, this class was prone to seek alternative solutions that would guarantee the preeminence of the Creole planters and insure social stability through the preservation of slavery. Tensions existed between these two goals because of the fear that radical political changes might bring about unacceptable radical social transformations. This tension is at the crux of the conservative nature of Cuban political thought during the period 1840–60.

"The history of all countries where slavery has existed has been the same since the most remote times to the present. Always the exercise of rigor has produced the same doleful results as excessive laxness." These statements were part of a protest document produced in May 1854 by hacendados and merchants at the peak of Cuba's Africanization scare.[1] Such statements represented a clear call from the propertied classes for moderation and equilibrium, elements deemed necessary not only for the island's progress but also for the survival of all whites. With Haiti's bloody revolution always in the backs of their minds, Cuba's propertied classes were willing to stand by the established government as long as it guaranteed the conditions that would allow them to maintain control over their slaves and their properties. Thus, generally speaking, social conservatism and loyalty to Spain characterized Cuba's Creole elite.[2] Only when the equilibrium threatened to be disturbed, jeopardizing property and the economic backbone, slavery, was this class willing to consider alternative solutions, but even these were usually of a cautious and conservative brand.

The conservatism of elites operating in contexts of profound racial division and stratification has been a constant throughout the history of Latin America and the Caribbean. Not coincidentally, the last three Iberian colonies of the hemisphere to break their ties with their mother countries—Brazil, Cuba, and Puerto Rico—were also the three in which slavery played the most important role and survived the longest. Furthermore, Peru, a Spanish colony with a large, highly urbanized Indian component, remained throughout most of the independence era (1810–25) a bastion of loyalism into which "revolution" had to be imported, first from the south and later from the north. In Mexico, where social and racial conditions were similar, the white Creole elite played a role in the struggle for independence only when it realized that caste rebellions could get out of hand. Patterns of loyalism and conservatism were perhaps more acute in the Caribbean, where most societies rested on the twin pillars of slavery and sugarcane cultivation. Franklin W. Knight wrote: "As long as slavery existed as a necessary labor component in the sugar enterprise . . . the white groups in the Spanish Antilles supported the metropolis, whose military strength was needed to tip the balance in case of the possible confrontation of the races." Elsa V. Goveia, another student of the Caribbean, has pointed out that similar colonial links in the British Caribbean long survived the abolition of slavery because "the maintenance of the British connection still seemed to offer the best guarantee of the survival of the whites."[3] Conservatism and attachment to the established government among the region's sugar planters can be further explained by their crop's endemic dependence on government protection. From *el privilegio de ingenio* of the sixteenth century to the late twentieth century's heavy subsidization of Cuban sugar by the now defunct Soviet Union, the sugar sector has consistently flourished—or floundered—in the shadow of the state.

In mid-nineteenth-century Cuba, conservatism and loyalty to Spain were the norm. On numerous occasions the island's propertied elite manifested its adherence to and support of Spanish domination.[4] In the wake of La Escalera's upheaval, the Development Board, a consultative but influential body composed of some of the most prominent members of the island's elite, petitioned for the continuation of Captain-General Leopoldo O'Donnell's rule, for he had saved the island from a "far reaching and horrible uprising." The years of the Narciso López expeditions (1849–51) saw further manifestations of adherence to the established order. On June 14, 1850, for example, the members of the Development Board stated that they were "now and always ready with their persons and property to support the flag of Spain and its government in this island." Later that year the board agreed to reward the "heroes" who fought López and presented Captain-General José de la Concha with a six-thousand-dollar sword.[5]

Despite these generally loyalist inclinations, certain elements within the island's propertied and professional classes sporadically embraced other avenues of action, mainly the annexationist route. This essentially conservative response emerged precisely when the desired social equilibrium was threatened either by Spain's inability to provide order or by outside disturbing forces like the López expeditions or British abolitionist agitation.

Filibusterers and Conspirators in Cuba

Narciso López, a Venezuelan-born general who had once fought against Simón Bolívar's troops in South America and held high office in Cuba's colonial administration, led three armed expeditions to overthrow Spanish rule in Cuba between 1849 and 1851. The ultimate objective of López's efforts—annexation of Cuba to the United States or independence—has been a matter of some debate.[6] It is clear, however, that the expeditions ended in utter failure, with López and hundreds of his followers dead.[7]

The tragic outcome of López's expeditions can be explained in a number of ways. Perhaps the soundest explanation is that the expeditions received practically no support from the population at large. Obviously, with only five hundred men López could not have defeated a twenty-thousand-troop army that had an almost unlimited supply of reinforcements and ammunition. His movement had counted on sparking a popular uprising; since he got no such response, the filibuster attempts failed. As the historian Raúl Cepero Bonilla has pointed out, the movement did not appeal to the lower and middle classes. Moreover, López's projects were not seen as Cuban ones, but rather as North American, proslavery, expansionist schemes. In a sense this was true. López's forces had only nominal Cuban representation. Only five men in the second expedition and fewer than fifty in the third were Cubans. More than three-quarters of the filibusterers were U.S. citizens, and another tenth was composed of Germans and Hungarians.[8] Finally, the movement lacked a cohesive ideological backbone. As Basil Rauch has pointed out, López tried to appeal simultaneously to U.S. adventurers and expansionists, European revolutionary exiles, Cuban slave owners, and Cuban reformists.[9] In the end López received little concrete support from any of these groups. They either considered him ideologically incompatible with themselves or felt that victory under his command would be too problematic.

López's movement, at first, did have links with certain prominent elements of Cuba's propertied classes, both resident in Cuba and exiled in the United States. Forced exile, discontent over the loss of political rights, growing anti-Spanish sentiment, and the fear of the island's imminent Africanization spurred some members of Cuba's propertied and professional classes into conspiratorial action in 1848–51, one of the high points of international rivalry over Cuba. The conspirators organized around two main nuclei: the New York–based Cuban Council led by Cristóbal F. Madan, Gaspar Betancourt Cisneros, Victoriano Arrieta, José Aniceto Iznaga, and Pedro Valiente, and the annexationist Havana Club, led by José Antonio Echeverría, Miguel Aldama, José Luis Alfonso, and the count of Pozos Dulces. Fearing the outcome of an ill-directed separatist movement, both groups lured López early on into a unified anti-Spanish front in order to preempt any radical or abrupt measure that could lead to racial war and destruction of property.[10]

Strategic and ideological differences between López and his followers, who were inclined to fast and risky military solutions, and the more conservative and aristocratic annexationists of the Cuban Council and the Havana Club soon produced tensions within the movement. Originally, the wealthy planters of the Havana Club took part in the organization and financing of López's Round Island expedition. After it was aborted in mid-1849, however, internal frictions began to mount. The aristocratic faction insisted on a more carefully planned, larger-scale invasion with at least five thousand troops under the command of a U.S. general. López was unwilling to postpone his next expedition, much less yield leadership over it. He retorted to Echeverría that he would not sacrifice the movement to the interests of the hacendados. By that point the rupture within the Cuban movement was a fait accompli. At its meeting of January 24, 1850, the Cuban Council agreed to relieve López of the command of the expeditionary forces. The council's leadership also demanded that he "suspend all actions for the Cuba cause to avoid tragedy in the island." At the time of the split a prominent member of the council, Victoriano Arrieta, dubbed López's methods "imprudent and irreflective" and his aspirations "criminal" and "murderous."[11]

The differences between the movement's two factions made it impossible for the conspiratorial coalition to function any longer. Because their members had considerable property at stake, the council and the club advocated cautious solutions with the strong backing of the United States. Significantly, in their defense of this posture, they called themselves "the propertied party." Many of them had favored the purchase of the island by the United States in 1848. Later they insisted on diplomatic approaches to the colonial problem. As a last resort, they were willing to accept a filibuster invasion, but only if its leaders could guarantee a rapid victory over the Spanish forces and the submission of the slaves. Moreover, the aristocratic faction feared the mobilization of the popular classes. Madan wrote to John Quitman: "I might add that among the lower classes there is a very strong sentiment in favor of the movement, which should be directed and controlled by the select classes, in order to obtain the blessings of annexation without the perils of insurrection."[12]

Following the split in the movement, López's followers regrouped as the Patriotic Junta and moved their base to New Orleans, where they sought the support of influential southerners such as General John Henderson and Colonel Theodore O'Hara. Meanwhile, the New York–based Cuban Council retained the movement's funds and weapons and began looking for a new military commander. Following López's execution in the summer of 1851, both factions reunited momentarily, only to split again shortly afterward. The class interests and the chronic conservatism of Cuba's propertied classes made it difficult for them to work in accordance with the Lopistas. If Spain had permitted the desired equilibrium to be disturbed in 1848–51, López had threatened to turn their world upside down.

Cuban Annexationism

The topic of nineteenth-century Caribbean annexationism and the broader theme of Latin American annexationism in general have received only superficial attention among historians and other scholars.[13] In Latin America this inattention is explained, in part, by the crucial role that historians play in the formation and preservation of *lo nacional* in their particular countries. Since annexationism is generally viewed as an antinational political project, it does not stand high on the list of priorities of those entrusted with interpreting and/or glorifying their nations' pasts. The reverse is also true, and this fact explains why so much energy and so many resources have been spent studying Simón Bolívar in Venezuela and El Grito de Lares in Puerto Rico, to give but two examples.[14] Annexationism, furthermore, has been generally maligned, seen as some sort of political aberration based purely on material considerations. Gordon K. Lewis, for example, referred to the Cuban annexationist project of the mid–nineteenth century as "nothing more than an ideology crassly based on material interests." Sergio Aguirre, for his part, characterized Cuban annexationism as a "deeply erred policy" that could have destroyed the Cuban nationality and its promoters as "mortgagers of the Cuban nationality in service of the interests of slavery." In a similar vein, Andrés A. Ramos Mattei, a discerning Caribbeanist, characterized midcentury annexationists as "not motivated by ideals, but by calculations such as profit, self-service, the preservation of their properties, control over the slaves, abolition at their convenience, and the acquisition and expansion of political power."[15] Although there is some truth in all these statements, singling out annexationists presents an incomplete and distorted picture.

Some Cuban historians have attempted to characterize Cuban annexationists positively. José Ignacio Rodríguez and Emilio Roig de Leuchsenring, for example, argued that annexationism was a manifestation of "Cuban patriotism" in the struggle against Spanish despotism. Herminio Portell Vilá and Fernando Portuondo defended López and other annexationists by asserting that they were not annexationists and that they used this ideology only to lure U.S. support.[16] In Portuondo's words, mid–nineteenth-century annexationism was "not an offense but a patriotic manifestation."[17]

Annexationism has been—and still is, in the case of Puerto Rico—a recurrent political alternative embraced by diverse segments of society, particularly, but not exclusively, in countries within the U.S. sphere of influence. This desire to become part of another, more powerful state has also flourished in slave societies or in societies with a large nonwhite subordinate element, particularly at times when such subordinate groups present an imminent threat to the social status quo.[18] As Gordon K. Lewis pointed out, during the French Revolution the planter class in St. Domingue sought the support of its "national enemy," Great Britain, when it appeared that France would no longer guarantee the subordination of blacks through slavery. This was also the case in Yucatán, Mexico, during the period of the Caste Wars (1847–57). Then, the state governor, Justo Sierra, offered foreign powers sovereignty over Yucatán in exchange for aid in fighting the Yucatecan Indians, an offer extended not only to the United States but also to France, Spain, and Great Britain. All refused to consider annexation.[19]

Nineteenth-century Hispanic Caribbean annexationism is a complicated phenomenon, on which the study of the broader international context in which such manifestations emerged can shed considerable light.[20] Cuban and Dominican annexationism in the mid–nineteenth century were, to a great extent, the reflection, if not the product, of geopolitical and commercial rivalries among the powers of the northern Atlantic. At times of high anxiety and vulnerability stemming from the fear of racial wars, different segments of these societies gravitated politically to one of two major poles. It was to the advantage of the "polar powers"—the European coalition and the United States—that fears of such events as a slave rebellion in Cuba and a Haitian invasion in the Dominican Republic continue to exist but also that these scenarios be prevented from becoming reality. By promoting and taking advantage of these fears, the concerned powers were also able to subject the societies of the Hispanic Caribbean to a dependence on foreign military assistance.

The ideology of annexation was not a deep-rooted sentiment among Cubans. In fact, Cuban patriots showed many traces of anti–North Americanism.[21] Annexationist sentiment rose and fell in response to foreign stimuli. For the most part, outbursts of annexationism occurred because of perceptions by the planter class, sometimes accurate and sometimes inaccurate, that Spain could not guarantee the subordination of slaves in a state of equilibrium, not too harsh and not too lax. These outbursts peaked particularly at the moments of intensified international rivalry over the region. Annexationism surfaced in Cuba in the early 1840s in connection with the commotion created by David Turnbull's abolitionist agitation. Cuban planters feared then that the British government would force Spain to liberate all the slaves that had been illegally introduced into the island since 1820. In 1842 the Havana Municipal Council bluntly warned local Spanish authorities that British abolitionist pressures would result in rebellion and the separation of Cuba from Spain.[22] Concern intensified owing to the fact that the census of 1841 showed that the island's slave population had numerically surpassed the white population. At this juncture, certain members of Cuba's propertied and professional classes began looking to the United States to guarantee peace and social stability on the island. Cuban Creoles also embraced a paradoxical posture: they stood against the continuation of the slave trade because it was conducive to the dreaded Africanization of the island, but they remained vehemently opposed to the abolition of slavery because it too was conducive to Cuba's Africanization. In short, they were simultaneously anti–slave trade and antiabolition. They felt trapped by a labor system that they feared enough to reject its expansion but one that constituted the economy's backbone and that they could not afford to abolish. To paraphrase an earlier slaveholder, Thomas Jefferson, Cuban planters were holding a wolf by its ears: they did not like it but could not let it go either.

Annexationist fervor cooled after 1842. Gerónimo Valdés's 1842 decree, which promised "to assure the continuation of humane treatment without ceasing to maintain them [the slaves] under a severe discipline and unalterable subordination," and his opposition to the liberation of the slaves reassured many who earlier had sought protection outside the Spanish empire. Captain-General O'Donnell's firm control of the situation between 1843 and 1848 and his handling of the crisis of La Escalera momentarily strengthened loyalist sentiment in Cuba.[23] Moreover, a stricter law against slave trading adopted in 1845 assured many in Cuba that the trend toward a black majority would be reversed. Upon learning about the passing of this law, Domingo del Monte, a prominent Creole, assured the Spanish minister of state: "From now on Spain can count on tranquility, durable security and certainly with the most honest and forceful loyalty in Cuba."[24]

The issue of annexationism arose again in 1848, a year of profound changes in Europe. That year a revolution broke out in France, and subsequently slavery was abolished in the French colonies of the Caribbean. That year also, two different uprisings in Madrid reminded the Cuban planter class of the possibility of similar revolutionary and abolitionist measures being applied in the Spanish colonies. Furthermore, in 1848 Great Britain and Spain came to the brink of war. Had this materialized, it would have certainly led to the island's occupation by the British and to the abolition of slavery there. These circumstances turned the attention of some Cubans toward the United States as a source of the equilibrium that Spain no longer appeared to guarantee. In 1848, in fact, at least three originally unrelated annexationist movements germinated. The Havana Club approached General William Worth, a veteran of the Mexican War, offering him three million dollars to lead a military expedition to separate Cuba from Spain and to annex it to the United States. Meanwhile, a group of landowners from Camagüey, led by Gaspar Betancourt Cisneros, Alonso Betancourt, and José Aniceto Iznaga, conspired to stir up an insurrection. They had a conference with President Polk on June 23 in which they explained their annexationist preference. A similar project took shape in Havana under Narciso López and the count of Pozos Dulces.[25]

Fear of the abolition of slavery and of racial war in its aftermath fueled the annexationist resurgence of 1848–51. In an 1848 letter to

José Antonio Saco, Betancourt Cisneros explained what the annexationist conspirators believed: "The island of Cuba is moving toward a rapid and inevitable destruction, under the aegis of its metropolis; . . . Cuba's fortune is in the hands of those who have determined the fates of St. Domingue, Jamaica, Guadalupe, and the rest of the European island colonies; and . . . the only means to save Cuba is to incorporate it to the great family that is the Confederation of the American Union." Later Betancourt Cisneros asserted that Cuba could be ruined by the stroke of a pen and that salvation was possible only with the United States. In an 1849 annexationist pamphlet he exclaimed that Spain had placed Cuba "on the brink of the precipice where she finds herself" and compared the situation with the "fatal hour . . . sounded for St. Domingue, in 1792." The editors of *La Verdad* in a similar tract remarked: "We annexationists want to give Cuba the Cuban-Anglo-Saxon nationality, instead of the dubious Cuban-African nationality being offered to us."[26]

Cuban annexationist sentiment waned again between 1851 and 1852, a period during which U.S. official expansionism also abated. López had scared off many earlier proponents of annexation, who grew fearful of the consequences of his extremism. José de la Concha's conciliatory measures and his co-opting of some of the earlier conspirators also helped to cool annexationist activities. Moreover, Captain-General de la Concha appeared to be able to guarantee peace and social stability and to protect the institution of slavery.

Annexationist conspiracies and filibuster plans received new life in 1853–54 with the arrival of Captain-General Juan de la Pezuela, which coincided with one of the high points in international rivalry over the region. His measures regarding the search of estates for illegally imported slaves and the creation of black battalions spurred many members of the elite into renewed annexationist activities. The Cuban Junta approached General Quitman, offering him the military command of a separatist expedition.[27] Meanwhile, another separatist conspiracy brewed in Cuba under the leadership of Ramón Pintó. Before the conspiracy was set in motion, however, local authorities arrested Pintó and put him to death. Quitman's resignation as commander and the executions of Pintó, Francisco Estrampes, and other separatists marked the end of an era in Cuba's struggle for independence from Spain.

Other factors, of a more structural nature, perhaps, also favored the development of annexationist tendencies in mid–nineteenth-century Cuba. That the United States had become the region's number one trading partner had obviously helped forge stronger ties between the Spanish colonies and the United States. For Cuba's planter class, annexation represented not only a means to preserve slavery but also the formula by which to achieve complete assimilation into the U.S. economic system on equal footing with other staple-producing states. Such a status would allow Cuban planters not only to sell cheaper sugar without the burden of export and import taxes but, more important, also to import goods, foodstuffs, and machinery from a cheaper source, free of tariffs. U.S. flour would no longer have to go from New Orleans to Spain and thence to Cuba, but could come directly from the mainland at a fraction of the present cost.

Another tie that explains the growth of annexationism in the late 1840s and 1850s lies in the growing preference among the Cuban elite to be educated in the United States. Many in the Cuban propertied classes looked north for higher and professional education. Whether primary, secondary, or professional, education had never been a priority of the Spanish colonial government in Cuba or Puerto Rico. This is how Consul Charles De Ronceray described the state of education in Puerto Rico in 1860: "[It] is bad, there are numerous towns without schools, or, teachers of first letters of the alphabet. A few public schools exist besides one or two seminars but the whole number of pupils hardly exceed three thousand." Betancourt Cisneros estimated that only "one out of 57 among the free population now [in 1849] receives the benefits of education." According to official estimates, only 30 percent of the white population in Cuba could read and write in 1851, and only 20 percent of all whites in Puerto Rico could read in 1860.[28] The state of education continued to deteriorate in Cuba: the ratio of white students to white inhabitants fell during the 1840s and 1850s.[29]

During the 1840s and 1850s many wealthy Cuban families sent their sons to be educated in the United States. By one estimate, the number of Cuban students there was close to two thousand annually. St. John's College and College Hill in New York, the College of Dental Surgery and St. Mary's in Baltimore, and the School of Medicine of the University of Pennsylvania were some of the most popular institutions among Cuban youth. During their college years in the United States, many Cubans experienced what it was like to live in a democratic, more open environment, where the freedoms of speech, the press, and worship were protected by a constitution and where male citizens participated in free elections to choose those who governed them and made their laws. For many of them, returning to Cuba proved difficult, to say the least. As Betancourt Cisneros put it, "It is a Luciferian task" to educate children in the United States and bring them back to live "among slaves and under colonial monarchy."[30] Not surprisingly, some of the most vocal annexationists of the period had been educated in the United States: Cristóbal F. Madan, Juan Manuel Macías, Ambrosio José González, the count of Pozos Dulces, and Joaquín de Agüero. They felt deeply dissatisfied with conditions in their homeland upon returning from the United States and could not help comparing both systems and becoming militant supporters of Cuba's North Americanization.

Like the seasonal influx of U.S. machinists, the choice of many students to go to the United States for an education became a source of anxiety for colonial administrators. On June 21, 1846, officials in Madrid requested that the local government in Puerto Rico furnish information on the reasons that so many youths went to the United States for an education, the possible risks of raising the level of education in the island to avoid this travel to the United States, and the impact that a prohibition on pursuing studies in the United States would have. In his 1851 report on education in Cuba, Captain-General de la Concha complained that "many [families] have sent and continue to send [their children] to schools abroad particularly to the neighboring American Union with serious injury to their sentiments of family and nationality and no less injury to the country to which they return with new and dangerous habits, ideas and affectations." Several months later, Captain-General Valentín Cañedo manifested that the annexationist party was numerous and that most of those who had studied in the United States belonged to it. Mariano Torrente, a zealous defender of Spanish national unity, later criticized "the contagious fad among the wealthiest families of sending their sons to be educated abroad, believing that they will develop more elegant manners and broader knowledge." These students, he continued, "have returned with their hearts full of dreamful ideas and unattainable utopias." Torrente also suggested that the government should declare all those who pursue an education outside the Spanish kingdom to be "bad Spaniards and enemies of the Spanish government." A few years later the editors of the fanatically pro-Spanish organ *La Voz de Cuba* announced that Cuban students in the United States learned "irreligiosity . . . indifference . . . [and] hatred toward Spain."[31]

As early as 1849 Spanish authorities attempted to stanch the flow of Cuban students to the United States. Alleging that these students "return to their country with revolutionary ideas, which they spread among relatives, friends, and acquaintances," de la Concha banned Cubans from studying in the northern republic. Authorities in Puerto Rico implemented similar measures, although fewer families there could afford to send their children to study abroad and those who could still preferred universities in Spain and other European countries. According to Consul De Ronceray, the Spanish government even provided incentives for parents to send their children to study in Europe.[32] Pleading ill health, however, many young men in the Spanish Caribbean obtained passports to the United States, where they suddenly "recuperated" and proceeded to pursue degrees at U.S. institutions.

To curb the flow of students to the United States, de la Concha sought to improve education in Cuba. He recognized that only a small proportion of Cubans had access to an education on the island, a situation that he felt lent itself to unfavorable comparisons of Cuba with the United States. He also advocated allocating better salaries for teachers, recognizing that their meager incomes of four hundred pesos a year were less than what journeymen or hired slaves made. De la Concha's agenda of educational reform and expansion, however, was limited to primary and mechanical instruction. In his view, the University of Havana produced too many lawyers and not enough agronomists, veterinarians, technicians, and machinists. Embarking on the same topic, Torrente proposed the creation of a normal school in Havana to help stop the exodus of students.[33]

Another link between Cubans and the United States helping to explain annexationism was the existence of communities of forced exiles from Cuba in New York, New Orleans, Key West, and other parts of the United States. Many of the period's annexationist leaders endured banishment from Cuba during the mid-1840s and in 1848. Their experience in exile and their interaction with other émigrés strengthened their already deep-seated anti-Spanish sentiment, and some joined the ranks of the filibuster movement in years to come.

Whatever the motivations, Cuban annexationism was not a deep-rooted sentiment based on patriotic love for the United States. For many annexationists, integration into the northern republic was only a necessary or natural consequence imposed by economic and geographic links. As Betancourt Cisneros put it, annexationism was "a calculation." It was more than anything else fueled by anti-Spanish sentiment: separation from Spain was its primary objective. "Death to the Goths!" was the cry of the conspirators and filibusterers of 1848–51, who blamed Cuba's problems on Spanish colonialism. In 1848 Betancourt Cisneros wrote that the only way to save Cuba was "to separate it from Spain." Elsewhere he stated: "If Cuba does not prosper equally with Louisiana and other states of the Union, it is for this simple reason, that it is governed by Spain." Cristóbal F. Madan, for his part, forecasted in 1854: "Cuba is offered the prospect of a precarious existence of backwardness and ruin under Spanish domination." Many of those who joined the annexationist ranks in the 1840s and 1850s had grown disillusioned with Spain and were tired of waiting for the by-then legendary "special laws" and reforms. In a letter to José Antonio Saco, one of the few who was still waiting for reforms, Betancourt Cisneros explained what could be expected of Spain. Spain had failed Cuba over and over again, he stated. To inspire trust in Spain "is like trying to inspire trust in a husband who knows that his wife is a whore." In his *Contestación*, addressed to Saco, Madan asserted that Spain "would never be able to provide liberal and progressive laws."[34]

Another characteristic of Cuban annexationism was its Anglophobia and general anti-Europeanism. Annexationist tracts and correspondence by Betancourt Cisneros, Madan, the editors of *La Verdad*, and others bitterly criticized Great Britain and its influence over the Spanish government. Anti-British sentiment in Cuba ran parallel to the international polarization over the region and the development of annexationism, with its peaks in 1840–41, 1848–51, and 1853–54. In the aftermath of the Turnbull crisis, Betancourt Cisneros wrote to Domingo del Monte that an acquaintance had confided to him the necessity of making public the fact that one hundred thousand Cubans were ready to assassinate every Briton in the island at any moment that

Great Britain decided to strike a blow at slavery. Three months later Betancourt Cisneros compared British policy to that "of a usurer who little by little provides means to a youthful fool until he places him on an unrepayable debt, and then proceeds to embargo his real estate." He later stated that he would not stand to see Cuba go from Spain, "an old, sickly, and impotent master," to Britain, "one who is young, healthy and powerful." He also affirmed that Great Britain could not find a more rebellious subject than him. "My slogan is: Spanish, or Cuban, and Christ with all of us." In 1848 Betancourt Cisneros wrote that he feared that Great Britain would resume its efforts to liberate the slaves, making the annexationist revolution "indispensable." Madan's defense of the annexationist posture was also permeated with anti-British remarks: "It is not necessary to remind Your Illustrious Excellency of the long history of stratagems with which the cunning Great Britain excited Cuba's bondsmen with the establishment of the Mixed Commission, the spectacle of its pontoon in the Havana Bay, guarded by free blacks, and particularly the machinations of Consul Turnbull and his illegal disembarkment in this country." Of Consul-General Joseph T. Crawford, Turnbull's successor, and Captain-General de la Pezuela, Madan scornfully remarked that "they seemed to have been made one for the other."[35]

Because it reflected the polarization of the United States and Europe over the region, the Cuban annexationist discourse was strongly anti-European. In 1851 the editors of *La Verdad* wrote: "We do not adopt European policies but American policies instead; and we do not let ourselves be dazzled by the beautiful and fascinating theories of the abolitionist school, instead we accept things as they are. . . . Only the United States can assure Cuba's physical and political existence, and protect the march of its intellectual and moral progress." In his juxtaposition of the U.S. and the European systems, Madan characterized the former as "one in which intelligence prevails, rational, humanitarian, moral, conservative, and progressive." The European system, he continued, "stimulates the use of brute force, is disconcerted, cruel, demoralizing, revolutionary, and backward."[36]

Cuban annexationism was also fueled by admiration for the political and social institutions of the United States, which were continuously contrasted with those of Spain. *La Verdad* highlighted the progress of "the schools, railroads, steamers, machines, telegraphs, the arts, the wealth and advancements of all sorts" in the United States: "No country in the world has more schools than the United States, no country has more newspapers . . . and nowhere in the world is there more industry and productivity." Betancourt Cisneros and Madan exhibited strong admiration for the political system of the United States. Betancourt Cisneros stressed that within the Union "each state is by itself sovereign. . . . The states are to the Confederation like unto a marriage relation." As a state of the Union, he continued, Cuba would establish civil tribunals and trial by jury, and the *fueros* would be abolished. In a similar vein, Madan emphasized the federal nature of the Union, which allowed "the independence of each member of the Confederation."[37]

Annexationists, particularly the planters, looked toward the southern United States as the paradigm for Cuba. They were fascinated by the South's ability to fuse the elements of slavery, technological progressivism, and free trade within what seemed to be a peaceful and stable society. In one of his speeches, Narciso López commented: "Ancient and modern history demonstrates it and you have the near example of the United States, where three million slaves do not hamper the flourishing of the world's most liberal institutions."[38] Of the U.S. South Madan wrote: "It distinguishes itself for its wisdom, daringness, its anxiety to extend the liberty of its race, and the tenacity, and dexterity with which it struggles within the national fora to defend the right to slave property." Madan also suggested that the value of land and slaves in Cuba would increase within the Union and that "the Pearl of the West Indies, with her thirteen or fifteen representatives in Congress, would be a powerful auxiliary to the South, and her value as an immense outlet for American manufactures, and a source of vast tropical production in exchange, and also as a military post, would surely make the attainment of Cuba a bond of peace and union for all the states."[39]

Another characteristic of Cuban annexationist thought closely related to anti-Spanish sentiment and admiration for the United States was its overt rejection of Catholicism as the island's official religion. The annexationist conspiracies of the late 1840s and 1850s had a strong Masonic component, which was traditionally anti-Catholic. López, Miguel Teurbe Tolón, Cirilo Villaverde, and José Elías Hernández were among the Freemasons who rose against Spanish domination hoisting the Cuban revolutionary flag—a flag with Masonic symbolism, which later became the national flag. Although they were not outright Protestants like many of the Cuban separatists of the 1868–98 period, the annexationists of the 1840s and 1850s strongly criticized official Spanish Catholicism and greatly admired the religious tolerance of the United States. Betancourt Cisneros attacked "the religious fanaticism inherited from Spain," while other critics of antiannexationist Saco dubbed him a "fanatical or backward Catholic." On another occasion Betancourt Cisneros emphasized that religious liberty and political liberty were intimately tied: "There can be no independence, there can be no civil liberty, where there is not religious independence and freedom. Wherever and however the church is connected with the State, and that which is called the religion of the State is established, there and then no other end can be attained than a change in the form of slavery." Another annexationist, Porfirio Valiente, spoke highly of a politico-religious system that if applied in Cuba would allow foreigners in the island to "have their own churches and to be able to worship the Supreme Being differently from us." Protestantism also represented an important link between Cuban annexationists and U.S. filibusterers. Spanish officials referred to filibusterers as "elements of political and religious fanaticism." Significantly, one of López's first acts, had his expeditions proved successful, was to have been the proclamation of freedom of worship.[40]

Cuban annexationists endured attacks from some of Cuba's best pens, those of men like José Antonio Saco, Domingo del Monte, and José Luis Alfonso, who had been an annexationist up to 1849. These proponents of solutions within the Spanish empire based their attacks on annexationism mainly on considerations of culture and heritage. They asserted that annexation would destroy the Cuban nationality and that the Spanish heritage, including language, religion, and race, would be lost through assimilation. (It is interesting to note that these kinds of arguments constitute the core of the antiannexationist discourse in present-day Puerto Rico.) Cuban annexationists in the mid-nineteenth century responded to these attacks with two different lines of argument. On the one hand, they rebutted by saying that the Spanish heritage was nothing to be proud of and that there was no such thing as a Cuban nationality. "Nationality is to us," wrote Porfirio Valiente, "like the livery to the calash driver, like the master's surname to his servant, like the king's brand to his horses: a sign of ownership and domination over ourselves and our property." In a similar vein, Betancourt Cisneros wrote Saco in 1848: "Do not tell me that you want that *nationality* for your country! No, man! Give me Turks, Arabs, Russians, give me demons, but do not give me the product of Spaniards, Congos, and Mandingas."[41]

A less cynical response asserted that annexation would not translate into cultural assimilation. This defense of annexation is strikingly similar to that of present-day prostatehooders in Puerto Rico, who claim the possibility of *estadidad jíbara* (literally, "Puerto Rican peasant statehood"). The Cuban predecessors of the proponents of *estadidad jíbara* argued the improbability of cultural assimilation. They were aware of their distinctively Cuban cultural identity, which allowed them to define themselves as Cuban even while enduring prolonged exile and to conciliate the seemingly antinational annexationist agenda with a profound sense of *cubanidad.*[42] Betancourt Cisneros affirmed that Cuban "population, wealth, religion, occupation, customs, manners, tastes, and habits" would survive even a massive immigration of North Americans and Europeans. Madan also remarked: "Forty-five years have elapsed since the First Consul separated Louisiana. Has the French nationality been lost, its practices and customs?" Meanwhile, Valiente asked whether they should "fear a decree from the President of the American Union, the Senate or any other authority obliging us to eat beef steak instead of *olla,* to be less gallant with our ladies, or to give up the entertainments that we like?"[43] Concerning religion, annexationists argued that the United States was a tolerant society, that Catholics freely practiced their religion there, and that this tolerance would be extended to Cuba.

The Cuban annexationist movement fell into a sustained crisis in the mid-1850s, particularly after the fiasco of the Ostend Manifesto, which led to a retrenchment of U.S. official expansionism. U.S.-Spanish relations regarding Cuba reached a peak of cordiality during the retreat from expansion in the late 1850s, as manifested in numerous consular reports.[44] Even before this rapprochement, at the time of the Narciso López invasions, some Cuban planters had become wary of the possibilities of a racial war. The medicine of filibusterism, they realized, would be far worse than the illness of Spanish colonialism. By 1854 two of the most important anti-Spanish newspapers, *La Verdad* and *El*

Filibustero, explained that Cuba's revolutionary agenda called for independence first and that annexation was but one possibility under consideration.[45] One of the principal factors pushing annexationists into the ranks of separatists or loyalists in the mid-1850s was a growing feeling of disillusionment with the U.S. policy toward Cuba, a sense that Cubans could no longer count on U.S. support after Quitman's resignation from the filibuster enterprise. Furthermore, for most annexationists the purchase of Cuba by the United States represented a humiliating solution. In February 1853 Valiente wrote that "the people of the island reject the idea that it will be bought or conquered by the United States." An editorial in *La Verdad* clearly stated that Cuba "does not ask or desire to be bought."[46] The Cuban Junta also joined in the rejection of Cuba's purchase by the United States.

By 1854–55 the rhetoric of the annexationists of the late 1840s and early 1850s developed an anti–North American coloration, the product of growing disillusion and resentment about the policy of the United States. In an 1854 address delivered at New Orleans, Betancourt Cisneros dubbed the United States—the country that he had so much admired in his earlier writings—"the ravisher that violates and dishonors" Cuba. On June 10, 1855, the previously annexationist Domingo Goicuría manifested that the United States had failed Cuba, that the new path to follow was one leading to independence and emancipation. In another manifesto the Cuban Junta confessed that annexation had been mere bait to appease the fear of the Cubans and a means to flatter the people of the United States. To the junta, "the greatest enemy of the Cuban revolution was always to be found in [the U.S.] Administration, regardless of the political colors in control."[47]

Besides disillusionment with the United States, other significant factors propelled the crisis of Cuban annexationism in the mid-1850s. De la Concha's arrival in 1854 for a second term as captian-general was instrumental in this process. The general's landing sparked a splendid celebration, described by one contemporary observer as "a nuisance to quiet people . . . for, for 3 days you heard nothing but the poppings of small guns of all sorts from morning till late at night." De la Concha orchestrated a more conciliatory policy toward both the United States and Cuban dissidents, co-opting some annexationist leaders and passing liberalizing legislation.[48] More important, de la Concha reestablished confidence among the propertied classes in the colonial state's capacity to protect slavery. These new postures revealed a tragic and persistent consequence of Cuba's relation with, and geographic proximity to, the United States: the harshness of Spanish domination over Cuba responded in direct proportion to the aggressiveness of U.S. policy on Cuba, making the low points of U.S. expansionism also the low points of Spanish despotism. Repression obviously played a crucial role in crushing Cuban annexationism. The earlier executions of López, Joaquín de Agüero, Francisco Estrampes, Ramón Pintó, and other conspirators left important vacuums in the movement's leadership. The death certificate of the separatist-annexationist movement was the Cuban Junta's dissolution in 1855, when Valiente, Betancourt Cisneros, and the count of Pozos Dulces left for Paris. These former annexationists did not even consider the United States as a suitable place for exile at that point.

In sharp contrast with Cuba, Puerto Rico had practically no annexationists among its political actors. The factors behind the outbursts of annexationism in Cuba—international rivalry over the island, commercial and educational links with the United States, and fear of a slave insurrection—were much weaker in Puerto Rico. Moreover, unlike the Cubans, the Puerto Rican separatist minority had virtually no links with U.S. expansionists. Also, for Puerto Ricans the United States was not as attractive a destination for education or for exile.[49] Puerto Rico's most prominent critic of Spanish colonialism, the French-trained physician Ramón Emeterio Betances, strongly opposed annexation. He warned a group of Cuban émigrés in Paris in 1851: "Do not plant a palm tree in Washington nor an apple tree in Havana, for both shall perish."[50]

Cuban Antiannexationism

International polarization in the struggle for hegemony over the Hispanic Caribbean was reflected in a parallel polarization of political thought in Cuba. One segment of the island's elite embraced annexation to the United States, and another responded by seeking stronger political and cultural ties with Europe, reaffirming the Hispanic legacy of monarchy, the Spanish language, Spanish culture, and Catholicism.

Although Saco, del Monte, José Luis Alfonso, Antonio González

Ponce de Llorante, and other militant antiannexationists of mid-century Cuba have often been referred to as liberals, they were in fact moved by the same conservative considerations and fears that motivated their annexationist rivals.[51] Particularly during the early 1840s they became concerned with the growing number and proportion of blacks and the possibility of a racial war that would turn Cuba into another St. Domingue. Del Monte, for example, leaked information on slave conspiracies in 1843, which was later used by Spanish officials to unleash a brutal wave of repression against blacks, mulattoes, and whites suspected of abolitionist ideas. Ironically, del Monte himself endured exile in the surge of repression that he helped initiate. To justify his actions, del Monte stated that his "aim was not, nor has ever been, to see my country reduced to ashes, or my race destroyed in a barbarous manner by a *savage race*, nor to reduce myself and my children to beggary." During his exile in Paris following the conspiracy of La Escalera, he painted a grim picture of prospective destruction, stating that sixty thousand slaves had been ready to rise up in arms. "The Island of Cuba is at present in imminent danger of being irreconcilably lost, not only to Spain, but to the white race and the civilized world." He also highlighted Cuba's dangerous position between the black states of Haiti and the Bahamas. He wrote that these places were "all swarming with blacks, who seem to cover the whole horizon, as if with a dark and ominous cloud."[52]

Another of the period's leading antiannexationists was José Antonio Saco. Like del Monte, he feared that annexationist or separatist conspiracies would lead to racial war and destruction. In 1845 he wrote that Cuba could not achieve independence without being ruined.[53] During the late 1840s, particularly in the eventful year 1848, Saco assumed the role of leading antiannexationist essayist. At the crux of his critique of annexationism was the recurrent fear of a racial war. In a sense, Saco the "enlightened liberal" was more fearful of a racial war than were the Havana planters, who at one point were willing to support radical measures if slavery was guaranteed. "There is no country in the world," wrote Saco, "where a revolutionary movement is more dangerous than in Cuba." He stated that "political revolution must necessarily be accompanied by social revolution; and the social revolution is the complete ruin of the Cuban race." In a letter to annexationist mouthpiece Betancourt Cisneros, Saco prescribed: "Let there be neither war nor conspiracies of any kind in Cuba. In our critical situation either one means the desolation of the country." Saco also advocated the union of all whites, Peninsular and Creole, rich and poor, to curb the increasing presence of the black race. "The day that the thunder of cannon separates them," he warned, "that day we will see renewed in Cuba the horrors of St. Domingue."[54]

The political ideology of the antiannexationist party was loyalism of the most conservative and reactionary brand. In 1845 del Monte described this posture as "union with Spain, imperturbable tranquility, security, order and domestic progress." Five years later del Monte expressed the need for publishing an "*antiannexationist* newspaper." "Its political color," he felt, should be "Spanish . . . monarchical-religious [meaning Catholic] -constitutional; moderate bordering in absolutism. With regard to Cuba it will strongly attack annexation, and will propose the necessary remedies to strengthen forever the union of Cuba to Spain."[55]

Unlike the annexationists, who had lost all faith in accomplishing anything within the Spanish empire, the antiannexationists believed that Spain could provide the necessary conditions for the island's social peace and economic growth. Saco, del Monte, Alfonso, González Ponce de Llorante, and others like them were in a sense annexationists too, because they sought the island's total assimilation to Spain, basing their strategy on trying to regain representation in the Spanish Cortes on an equal footing with the Peninsular provinces. In 1844 del Monte demanded that "the island should be treated by Spain, as she has always treated her kingdoms and provinces in the Indies . . . as an integral part of her territory." A few years later Saco wrote that the Cuban people "expect that, united with Spain, they will enjoy very soon a rational kind of liberty."[56]

The antiannexationist party tended to look to Europe for education, protection, political links, and a place to spend periods of exile. Alfonso, who by mid-1849 had abandoned the annexationists, in the spring of 1852 busily promoted a European treaty that would guarantee Cuba for Spain. Aware of the importance of fostering the international balance of power in the region, Saco wrote Alfonso in January 1853: "Let us pray to heaven for European peace, and above all for peace in England and France, for that way there will be greater probabilities for saving Cuba from turbulence and disaster."[57]

The defense of Cuban nationality was another pillar sustaining the antiannexationist movement. This type of argumentation by Saco, González Ponce de Llorante, and others harmonized with the political goals of assimilation, because it emphasized the Hispanic legacy of the Spanish language, Catholicism, and other aspects of Spanish culture. In 1848 Saco defined a nationality as "a people who inhabit one soil, who share a common origin, a common language, and common usages and habits."[58] Saco's definition of the Cuban nationality, however, excluded the island's numerous black population. In fact, Saco sought to protect the island from what he believed to be two dreadful outcomes: North Americanization and Africanization.

The antiannexationists also feared that annexation to the United States would result in cultural assimilation. Saco warned that a massive U.S. immigration would follow the island's annexation and that "in a few years the Yankees would surpass us numerically." "In the end," Saco added, "this would not be a reunion or annexation, but the absorption of Cuba by the United States."[59] Saco's fear of the island's racial and cultural transformation first emerged, as he admitted, after he traveled to Louisiana, where he witnessed the region's acculturation. Personally, he also disliked the United States and its culture, as attested by a letter he wrote to a friend: "Although I like its institutions very much, neither can I find easy occupation there, nor do I like its people, nor does its climate favor me."[60] Saco, del Monte, and González Ponce de Llorante disliked the South in particular. Saco once prophesied that the South would eventually secede and that if Cuba were annexed to it, "it would remain united to the least civilized part, the least industrious, and unfortunately that which is made up of different races." González Ponce de Llorante exploited similar arguments, asserting that expansionists coveted Cuban lands and would, in the event of annexation, displace the natives. He also manifested profound admiration for the Spanish legacy. "There is justified pride in saying," he remarked once, "that we descend from the Pelayos, the Cids, the Gonzálos de Cordoba, the Corteses, the Leivas, and from thousands of heroes who still fill the world with their famed names."[61]

A salient characteristic of the antiannexationist party was its militant Catholicism, which bordered on anti-Protestantism. Del Monte called for Catholicism to be one of the movement's defining characteristics, and Saco's annexationist critics said he was a "fanatical or backward Catholic." One of González Ponce de Llorante's political tracts gives credence to such attacks. He wrote: "Following Cuba's absorption, the freedom of worship would follow; and this freedom would represent, on the one hand, a humiliation for us, and, on the other hand, a source of disunion and hatred among the people and within the families." He also scorned Protestants as those "who have committed apostasy from the legitimately Christian church."[62]

The Common Ground of Slavery and Racism

Although Cuban annexationists and antiannexationists looked to different sources for solutions to Cuba's problems, for both the issues of slavery and race were at the crux of their political discourse.[63] Not coincidentally, Cuba's political spectrum was energized in the early 1840s, precisely at the time that the island's slave majority became an official, statistical fact and when Great Britain's abolitionist pressures threatened the social equilibrium on the island. While the annexationists looked to the United States to guarantee the permanence of slavery and the end of Spanish weakness and British abolitionist pressures, the antiannexationists rejected U.S. intervention, fearing that it would lead to widespread rebellion and the island's Africanization.

Cuban annexationism was essentially an antiabolitionist movement that sought to strengthen Cuban slavery by incorporating the island into the family of slaveholding states of the southern United States. López admired the South's capacity to maintain slavery while being able to "reinforce the most liberal institutions of the world." The annexationist newspaper *La Verdad* said that slavery was "the most urgent cause, if not the principal which compels the Cubans to shake off the Spanish yoke, and place themselves under the protection of the United States, where the negroes are not an obstacle to the liberty or the political rights of the Americans; where the negroes are not an instrument in the hands of the government to terrify and subjugate its citizens; where the negroes are not an inexhaustible mine of taxes and contributions." Junta leader José Elías Hernández, while calling for monetary support from the planter class in 1853, promised that the annexationist revolution would "keep the slaves calm, preserving almost intact the present wealth." A year later Madan pointed out that the stability of slavery would translate into the stability of wealth in general. *El Filibustero* also advocated the continuation of slavery: "Neither the doctrines of socialism, much less its extremes, nor those of abolitionism under any guise . . . have had any acceptance within our revolutionary program, which deems these matters as premature and as obstacles to the goal of achieving our country's independence." Annexationists were also careful to demonstrate that revolution would not lead to a general slave uprising. In 1851 Ramón de Palma tried to dispel such fears by enumerating reasons that made such an outcome improbable. He assured his readers that avoiding a slave insurrection was a priority within the movement; that there were sufficient white men in Cuba to "keep tranquility in the countryside"; that all whites shared these concerns; that although "some Peninsulars and part of the army" were against annexation, they were whites first and anti-annexationists later; and that U.S. immigrants would come in droves to help curb a slave insurrection.[64]

For Cuban annexationists the United States also represented a source of gradualism and assurance in the eventuality of slavery's being abolished. In 1848 Betancourt Cisneros emphasized that under the United States Cuban abolition, whenever it came, would be peaceful, gradual, and not a source of social disarray. "The gangrenous limb shall be amputated," he wrote, "but it will happen by the hand of an expert surgeon and not by a butcher's axe." Madan contrasted this prospect with abolition under Spain: "Experience has demonstrated," he asserted, "the accuracy of this dictum: violent abolitions have happened or will happen in the various European colonies, and in them the property linked to the institution of slavery endures frequent ups and downs. Contrastingly, in the United States the moral progress of the slave race, and the legislation that regulates it are gradual but certain." Betancourt Cisneros once stated that annexation would provide Cuban slaveholders with the time necessary to apply "safeguarding measures" that would reduce the island's dependence on slavery. Meanwhile, the editors of *La Verdad* asserted that "the problem of the abolition of slavery should be solved only by the great American Confederation with its power, wisdom, and prudence."[65]

The antiannexationists, many of whom were professionals not directly attached to slavery, equally feared the consequences of the institution's destabilization. For them the road to annexation was filled with uncertainties that could trigger a massive slave insurrection.

Their most vocal militant, Saco, in a rebuttal to the annexationists' accusations of abolitionism, stated that his actions were "incompatible not only with abolitionist fanaticism, but also with abolitionism of the most *moderate brand*."[66] Saco and del Monte believed that the issues of slavery could best be solved by regaining Cuban representation in the Cortes and by gradually reducing the island's dependence on slave labor. They were not abolitionists and at best were willing to consider emancipation if it was postponed and gradual and included compensation for the planters. They too were uncertain of what to do with the wolf.

Another common link between the annexationists and the anti-annexationists was their deep-seated racism. The political discourse of both parties was filled with racist statements directed against slaves and blacks in general. Racism became more evident during the eras in which slavery faced the strongest attacks either from outside forces (i.e., British pressure) or internal forces (slave agitation). This ideology sought to preserve the stratification of Cuban society on the basis of a strong correlation between color and status.

Betancourt, Madan, Aldama, Ambrosio José González, and other annexationist leaders were outright racists. In 1841 Betancourt Cisneros, of whose anti-Spanish sentiments there is no doubt, wrote del Monte that he would rather have in Cuba the sons of Spanish friars than those of blacks. "I wish they would send us all their surplus friars," he wrote. In the aftermath of the conspiracy of La Escalera, Aldama referred to blacks and mulattoes as the enemies of Cuban whites. During the 1850s, particularly in the context of the Africanization scare, the annexationist literature grew more intensely racist. The editors of *La Verdad* denounced "the most lamentable spectacle, the most repugnant liaisons to our instincts, the most shocking to our present state of civilization and public opinion, the most degrading and shameful to our race, marriages between white women and blacks, mulattoes, *zambos*, and *mestizos*." The same pamphlet prescribed that "no country-loving Cuban should work for the benefit of the African race, and its liberation in detriment to the whites and their civilization." In an annexationist article published in 1854 Ambrosio José González referred to Cuban slaves as "wild, untutored and ferocious Africans." Madan called them "barbaric Africans" with "animal instincts."[67]

Opponents of Madan and Betancourt Cisneros were no less racist.

Since the mid-1830s Saco had called for the cessation of the slave trade, not out of compassion or abolitionist sentiment but in order to preserve and strengthen the white "Cuban nationality." In 1835 Saco wrote: "There is but one remedy: to whiten, to whiten, and then demand respect." Seven years later he prescribed: "Let there be no more black importations, no more black importations, and this [island] will be saved."[68]

When it became public knowledge in 1842 that slaves had gained majority status among the Cuban population, the island's Creole intelligentsia actively sought to reverse the trend by promoting white colonization. The correspondence and writings of Betancourt Cisneros reveal his expectations, struggles, and frustrations over the issue of white colonization. After a number of failures, Betancourt Cisneros became convinced that white colonization was impossible under Spanish colonial rule. In an annexationist tract he complained: "Now and then it is talked of, and again it is written about; committees are formed, reports are made up, new taxes are imposed, and the Government usurps these, and disposes of them in some other way; and all this time not a single colonist plants his foot there; yet the fields of Cuba are inundated with African slaves." He concluded by stating that annexation would make Cuba attractive for white colonization.[69]

The projects of Betancourt Cisneros were neither the only nor the grandest of the attempts to promote white colonization. In the early 1840s Miguel Estorch tried to set up an all-white labor force of fellow Catalans, but he failed. In 1844 the Development Board established a series of cash incentives to promote white colonization. It promised twelve thousand pesos to planters who could attract fifty white families to their plantations and thirty thousand pesos to anyone establishing a 11,250-quintal *ingenio* with exclusively white labor. In November 1844 Domingo Goicuría left for the Canary Islands to contract five hundred colonists for the junta and another few hundred to be divided among other planters. In 1847 a more desperate Goicuría proposed granting free land to German and Scottish settlers. A year later Joaquín de Agüero traveled to the Canary Islands to encourage immigration. Saco also actively promoted white colonization.[70]

Such projects failed. One reason was that Spain itself was relatively depopulated and Spaniards were trying to restrain the outward flow of laborers. Besides, would-be emigrants were not attracted to areas like Cuba and Puerto Rico, where slavery depreciated the value of all labor. Moreover, mortality rates were high among unacclimated immigrants, who were vulnerable to tropical diseases. That life insurance policies for Galician contract laborers were priced at one peso per month for a two-hundred peso policy graphically reveals the short life expectancy among these laborers.[71] Failure to promote white colonization fueled both the annexationists, who maintained that annexation would make immigration more attractive, and antiannexationists, who insisted that insecurity was the biggest obstacle to white immigration and that closer ties with Spain would solve that problem.

Political Tendencies in the Dominican Republic, 1844–1861

Whereas Cuba was an export-oriented colony where slavery thrived, the Dominican Republic had gained independence, liberated its slaves, and remained practically untouched by international commercial and financial capitalism. Yet despite these dramatic differences, both societies were affected in strikingly similar ways by international rivalries and by interracial tensions inherent to or inherited from slavery. The way these circumstances manifested themselves, of course, differed in each case. In Cuba, Creoles responded by gravitating to one of two poles, embracing annexation to the United States or assimilation to Spain. In the Dominican Republic the two leading parties under Pedro Santana and Buenaventura Báez responded by embracing annexation to the United States in the former case and to France or Spain in the latter case. Moreover, while in Cuba the fear of a massive slave insurrection stimulated and molded political thought, in the Dominican Republic the aggressive presence of neighboring Haiti played a similar role. Finally, the international powers played the Haitian chip in the Dominican Republic in much the same way that they played the slavery chip in Cuba. In Cuba the concerned nations used the fear of a racial war to foster their particular designs, and in the Dominican Republic they exploited—and even prodded—Haiti's expansionist presence.

Like its Cuban counterpart, Dominican annexationist sentiment was not deep-rooted. It was intermittent, based mainly on the belief that the Dominicans by themselves would not be able to thwart a racial war with Haiti. A strong correlation existed between the degree of annexationist fervor in the Dominican Republic and the ebb and flow of the Haitian threat.[72] In the mid-1840s, 1849–51, 1854–55, and 1859–61 both Haitian aggression and Dominican annexationism reached peaks. Interestingly, these were also the high points of international rivalry over the emerging republic.

The inhabitants of Spain's neglected Caribbean colony gained their independence, almost by default, in 1821, during the general Latin American emancipation period. Although easily achieved, Dominican independence was short-lived. Within a few weeks Haitian forces invaded the infant republic and reunified the island under Haitian rule. Later, after the fall of Jean-Pierre Boyer on March 24, 1843, a myriad of Dominican separatist movements coalesced to overthrow Haitian domination.[73]

The Trinitarios, led by Juan Pablo Duarte, Matías Ramón Mella, and Francisco del Rosario Sánchez, represented the most politically liberal of all separatist factions. Their proclamation of independence issued in early 1844 called for political and civil rights for all Dominicans regardless of race and for democratic institutions and the freedoms of worship and the press.[74] Liberal principles, however, were not enough to bring down Haitian domination and preserve national independence; troops, guns, and funds had to stand behind the struggle if it was to succeed. In a conciliatory effort to promote Dominican unity against invading Haitian forces whose divisions were leading a three-pronged attack on Santo Domingo, Santiago, and Azua, the Trinitarios included a number of conservatives in the National Junta and placed the army under a conservative, Santana.

Tensions within the Dominican anti-Haitian coalition mounted in the summer of 1844 over the issue of national sovereignty. The conservatives, the church, Santana and Báez and their troops, and the junta under Tomás de Bobadilla all sought French aid in exchange for a protectorate and/or land concessions in Samaná. Meanwhile, the Trinitarios remained firm in their nationalistic posture. In the light of an impending arrangement with the French government, on June 9, 1844, nationalists Duarte, Mella, and Sánchez staged a coup d'état in Santo Domingo and assumed control over the junta. They failed, however, in their next move to take the army out of Santana's control, as the rank and file refused to recognize the newly imposed Trinitario commander, Esteban Roca. Reassuming leadership, Santana proceeded to march on Santo Domingo with two thousand loyal troops. By mid-July he had gained control over the capital city and reinstated the conservative members of the junta, forcing generals Mella, Sánchez, and Duarte to flee. Soon afterward, the conservatives drew up a constitution. Although it provided for the separation of powers, Santana managed to assume dictatorial attributes by his imposition of the infamous article 210, which allowed him to govern by decree for as long as the Haitian menace remained.[75]

Santana's first presidential term extended through August 1848, when he resigned and retired to his estate. During his incumbency his ministers made numerous attempts to annex the Dominican Republic to a foreign nation or to establish a foreign protectorate over it. Annexationist overtures, in fact, predated the actual achievement of independence: Dominican leaders approached French representatives with offers of territorial concessions in Samaná in return for military aid in the struggle against Haiti.[76] Santana's envoys knocked on the doors of practically every European monarch, making similar offers to Great Britain, Spain, and even the tiny kingdom of Sardinia. During the early years of Dominican independence, however, France continued to be the main target of Dominican annexationist aspirations. Dominican officials and special envoys insistently lobbied French agents in search of support, at one point offering land grants and stipends to prospective French settlers. In order to coerce the French into action, Báez, Juan Esteban Aybar, and other Dominican officials underscored their preference for France but made it clear that they would be forced to approach other nations if the French did not satisfy their aspirations.[77] All of these annexationist maneuvers proved fruitless, because European powers checked one another's designs and because governmental transitions in France and Spain ended negotiations in progress.

Culturally, the endemic annexationism of the Dominican elite manifested itself in profound cultural disorientation and the proclivity to imitate foreign patterns of behavior and material culture.[78] A contemporary poem eloquently describes the extent of this situation:

Yesterday I was born Spanish
In the afternoon I became French,
At night I was Ethiopian,
Today, I am English, they say;
What will become of me![79]

Manuel Jimenes González, who succeeded Santana in the presidency in September 1848, inherited the problems of the previous administration and also created new problems of his own. Following two years of reduced tensions with Haiti, Jimenes González proceeded to dismantle the national army, a move that made the Dominican Republic once again vulnerable to Haitian aggression. Shortly thereafter, Haitian troops mobilized under the command of Faustin Soulouque. Renewed Haitian aggression caused annexationism to resurface with greater splendor than in 1844–46. On April 4, 1849, the Dominican Council of Ministers addressed a desperate letter to Puerto Rico's captain-general, informing him of the invasion by "the usurping antisocial Haitian enemy" and requesting "all the aid that can be spared in favor of the Christian Dominican family." Two weeks later the Dominican Congress passed a resolution offering the French government a protectorate over the country along with land concessions in Samaná. Meanwhile, Jimenes González approached first the British and later the U.S. and French agents, requesting protection and inquiring about the possibilities of annexation. When these overtures failed, a desperate Jimenes González offered his country to the Spanish crown. Congressional president Báez, for his part, remained active in promoting a French protectorate. Despite timid responses from France, Báez ordered the French flag hoisted on April 4, 1849. In September, when the Haitian troops had been momentarily pushed back, a still-worried group of Santiagueños sent Santana a petition calling for their country's annexation to the United States. They emphasized that they belonged to "the great family of American peoples" and that they desired "to enjoy the advantages of the 27 states of the Union."[80] All of these annexationist schemes failed for the same reasons that similar attempts had failed in 1844–46: the concerned powers were actively checking one another's designs.

Haitian aggression also revived Santana politically. Fighting the Haitians came naturally to him. His family had endured economic hardship under Haitian rule and had lost property in Hincha, Santana's birthplace. The National Congress called upon him to reassume command of the army and to mobilize the troops to face the Haitian invaders. On April 21 Soulouque's and Santana's forces met for the bloody battle of Las Carreras. The Haitian army came out badly beaten; Soulouque himself had to jump off a cliff in a desperate retreat.[81] Following this victory Santana regained his status as national hero. A popular song reflected the people's feelings toward Santana and his seemingly magical ability to beat the Haitian foe:

> If Santana retires to El Seibo,
> Mom, I will go with him;
> to avoid facing again
> the black man of Jacomel.[82]

After defeating the Haitian enemy, Santana marched once again on Santo Domingo to reclaim leadership over the national government. This time Santana chose not to participate directly in political affairs, selecting Báez, instead, as his successor. Báez assumed the presidency on September 24, 1849, and immediately initiated talks pursuing annexation to the United States. Meanwhile, Santana, believed to be the only one capable of defeating the Haitians, retained control of the military from his retirement at his El Prado estate. Conflict with Haiti did not abate until 1851, when the mediation of the European powers led to a truce between the two nations. For the balance of his term, Báez, with the support of the Francophile and Hispanophile clergy, maneuvered to establish a European protectorate. He merely alienated the Haitians, who began yet another military mobilization.[83]

At the termination of Báez's term in February 1853, Santana assumed the presidency for a third time. Now he faced the opposition of Báez and his party, who, ironically, had been strengthened when Santana chose Báez as his successor in 1849.[84] Roberto Cassá and other students of Dominican history have stressed personality conflicts and style differences as primary causes for the split between the two caudillos. Plenty of evidence, however, implies that Báez, Félix María del Monte, Juan Esteban Aybar, Pedro Antonio Bobea, David Coen, and other Baecistas broke with Santana in great measure as a response to international pressures. The Dominican political scene for the next eight or nine years would be dominated by the struggle for power between these two caudillos and their partisans. International tensions over the Dominican Republic reinforced and aggravated this rivalry. While Santana's party sought stronger links with, and the protection of, the United States, Báez and his so-called French or clerical party reaffirmed its Europhilia and Catholicism. Before the polarization of international rivalry over the Dominican Republic in 1853–55, annexationism had not been a divisive factor. Santana, Jimenes González, Báez, Bobadilla, and other leaders had been willing to hand over their country to any power wishing to accept it. Báez had said he would favor "whatever Power be it British, French or Anglo-American, whichever offered the best advantages."[85] Now in the mid-1850s, geopolitical shifts forced the caudillos to choose sides: Santana looked westward to the United States; Báez looked east to France and Spain.

Tensions between the two Dominican "parties" became evident early on when Bishop Tomás de Portes refused to appear at Santana's inauguration. Santana then accused Báez and the clergy of conspiring to install Báez as the country's dictator for life and of committing high treason.[86] Tensions escalated over the issue of civil versus church marriages, culminating in the banishment of several pro-Báez clergymen. Later Santana passed a decree whereby prelates and church officials would henceforth be appointed by the state.[87] Interestingly, during the mid-1850s it became clear that the Báez party enjoyed the full support of the Dominican church in part because of Báez's pro-Spanish and pro-European stance. Meanwhile, the relations between Santana and the church deteriorated. This link between politics and religion ran parallel to the postures regarding the Catholic Church embraced by Cuban annexationists and antiannexationists. In both countries the party that gravitated toward the United States was opposed to Catholic exclusivism, and the party that looked to Europe reaffirmed its ties with the Catholic Church.

When Santana returned to power, Báez and many of his partisans were forced into exile abroad, mostly in Curaçao and St. Thomas, where Baecistas had numerous business contacts, particularly with the French. Only nine months into Santana's third term, the U.S. consul at Santo Domingo discovered a French scheme to overthrow Santana and replace him with Báez, who, according to commercial agent Jonathan Elliot, "most cordially hates Americans and all that is American and is purely a Frenchman in his heart."[88] Spain also played a crucial role in this polarization. Spanish consul Antonio María Segovia gave his full support to Báez and worked diligently to reinstate him in the presidential mansion. He even began a naturalization campaign, granting Spanish citizenship and protection to hundreds of Baecistas and setting up an anti-Santana organ, *El Eco del Pueblo*. Popular culture reflected the reach of Segovia's naturalization drive. One contemporary song proclaimed:

I don't fear Santana
Neither do I fear the Alfaus
I only fear Segovia
'Cause I've been naturalized.[89]

Segovia, who deemed Báez the only Dominican capable of restoring peace and progress, was greatly responsible for the caudillo's return to power in October 1856.[90]

In the meantime, the United States was again actively seeking to establish a presence in the republic. The Santana-Cazneau negotiations mobilized the opposition, which sought the support of European envoys. The threat of U.S. encroachment in the Dominican Republic also mobilized the Haitian government, which feared that the United States would try to reestablish slavery throughout the island. Thus, in November 1855 thirty thousand Haitian troops invaded the Dominican Republic, but by January of the following year they were repelled. Haitian aggression and European support behind Báez further fueled Santana's pro–North Americanism. He renewed efforts to cede Samaná to the United States. In fact, the Santana administration offered the United States permission to conduct a naturalization drive, like the one Segovia was carrying on for Spain, in exchange for the protection of four armed vessels. The official press also became ardently pro–United States, and the administration adopted emblems, such as spread eagles, strikingly similar to those of the United States. Spanish envoys, for their part, continued to relay negative assessments of Santana's government. In a letter to the captain-general of Cuba, the Spanish commercial agent stated that Santana was a source of growing hostility against Spanish subjects. The captain-general later requested the deployment of a vessel for protection.[91] Finally, in May 1856 Santana yielded to mounting pressures. He retired once again and left the presidency to Manuel de Regla Mota, who in turn resigned in favor of Báez.

Once in power for a second time, Báez faced strong opposition from the Cibao bourgeoisie. Tensions between this sector and the caudillo dated back to at least 1849, when Báez introduced a bill in the Dominican Congress to establish a tobacco monopoly for himself and his French associates. The pro-U.S. annexationist petition by Santiagueños that year was in part a defensive measure against the threat that Báez posed to their livelihood. During his first incumbency, in 1853, Cibaeños protested once again against Báez's fiscal and monetary measures. In July 1857, in light of renewed efforts by Báez to gain profit at the expense of the tobacco growers, Santiagueño professionals, merchants, and agriculturists responded with outright rebellion.[92] One of the first acts of the revolutionary government set up in Santiago was to call upon the man who had twice defeated the Haitians and had twice marched triumphantly on Santo Domingo: Pedro Santana.

Although in his inaugural proclamation Báez promised "the strictest impartiality" toward all foreign powers to avoid "the predominance of any of them," his short-lived second presidential term developed a strong anti–North American coloration. Just two days after his inauguration, a mob of angry Baecistas gathered in front of the U.S. Commercial Agency in Santo Domingo, threatening to bring down its flag and other emblems. A few weeks later the U.S. interim chargé d'affaires reported that since Báez had taken over, the general cry in the streets was "Down with the Yankees, down with the eagle and the American flag." In the same communication he requested protection for Santana, "who has proven to be a real republican and friend of the United States," and for the other "pro Americans." At one point the U.S. envoy had to request British protection for his quarters.[93]

Báez denounced the Santiago insurrection of 1857 as "pro–North American and filibusterer" and proceeded to request military aid from Puerto Rico's captain-general. For his part, the Baecista minister of foreign relations, Félix María del Monte, complained directly to Secretary of State Lewis Cass about the allegedly antigovernment activities of agent Jonathan Elliot. Del Monte accused Elliot of plotting against Báez, being a partisan of Santana's, and being injurious and insulting to high government officials. He also informed Cass that according to a police report, Elliot had been seen in the streets, apparently "crazed and cheering the enemies of the government." In the meantime, Santana and the Santiagueño revolutionaries put Santo Domingo under siege. Here Báez's troops held firm inside the city walls for a little over a year, until the mediation of the French, British, and Spanish consuls allowed Báez to swap the capital for his life and that of his associates. Before surrendering, a desperate Báez allegedly offered sovereignty over Santo Domingo to the Haitian government.[94] Following the surrender, he fled along with most of the Baecista leaders and Baecista clergy, who went into exile in the neighboring Spanish colonies. Santana, the man with the guns, took power once again. Shortly thereafter, a jubilant Elliot informed Cass: "The time has arrived when we can have a good station for our Navy and depots for our steamers in these waters."[95] The dramatic events of the next few months would prove that Elliot had been hasty in his celebration.

Political developments in the Dominican Republic between 1844 and 1861 demonstrate that despite enormous differences separating the republic from neighboring islands, the entire region was subject to similar foreign forces, contending for commercial and political control. Within both the infant republic and the old Spanish colonies, political polarization occurred. In the Dominican case, the positions of two rival caudillos responded to the growing polarization at the international level. In the colonies, particularly in Cuba, a parallel polarization became evident, separating Creoles into annexationists and antiannexationists. Their differences notwithstanding, the political inclinations of Saco, Betancourt Cisneros, Báez, and Santana were shaped by the same geopolitical circumstances and by race issues aggravated by the intense international rivalry over the region. They all shared the same deep fear of the black man, whether he was a potentially rebellious Cuban slave or an expansionist Haitian general. Thus they also shared a chronic sense of vulnerability that translated into a fatalistic recognition of their incapacity to gain and/or retain political independence. Annexation, whether to Spain, France, the United States, or Sardinia, appeared to them to be the only formula that could guarantee survival.

Part Two

The Impact of the U.S. Civil War and Its Aftermath on the Hispanic Caribbean, 1861–1878

Five The Rearrangement of Political and Commercial Ties

For the historian of the United States, the Civil War represents a pivotal moment, marking a dramatic rupture within the historical development of the republic. It signaled the culmination of tensions between two different societies with conflicting postures regarding slavery and its expansion, tariffs and protectionism, commercial links with Europe, national territorial expansion, states' rights, and the role of the Federal government. More important, the Civil War represented the definite victory of the North and what it stood for and the subordination of the South and its leaders' worldview. Military victory thus gave the commercial, financial, and manufacturing interests of the northeastern United States the opportunity to reconstruct the nation to match its sectional priorities and goals.

For the student of the Hispanic Caribbean, the Civil War in the United States also stands out as an important watershed with far-reaching repercussions for Cuba, Puerto Rico, and the Dominican Republic. The South's defeat marked the end of southern agrarian expansionism, with its vision of establishing a slave-based Caribbean empire. The Reconstruction era brewed a new brand of U.S. expansionism that sought to establish naval bases in strategic locations to protect access to the Caribbean's markets and raw materials—in short, to protect the "new empire." Also of great consequence for the region was the transformation of the United States from a defender of slavery to an active abolitionist power. These changes reverberated throughout the Hispanic Caribbean.[1]

Wartime Diplomacy

During the antebellum years, the United States's apparently undirected Caribbean policy—the word *policy* seems almost inappropriate—was dictated by a tense compromise within a sharply divided nation. Had the southern states had their way, the nation's policy would have been more aggressively expansionist and probably by 1860 the United States would have absorbed Cuba, Puerto Rico, and more of Mexico as slave territories or states. On the other hand, had the northern states been able to shape national policy, U.S. expansionism would have looked northward to British North America; perhaps the free black state of Haiti would have been recognized as well, and protectorates might have been established over Hawaii and the Dominican Republic. Sectional tensions, however, neutralized both northward and southward expansion during the 1850s.

The national division brought about by the secession of eleven of the Union's thirty-three states reoriented U.S. foreign and Caribbean policy. Two different, rival North American nations, the United States and the Confederate States of America, now sought to establish a network of alliances and trade links for support during the war. Both also avoided antagonisms with third parties to avert the participation of foreign nations against them; the last thing that either the Union or the Confederacy wanted was to open another front with a foreign power. While the Confederacy abruptly retreated from the aggressive expansionism characteristic of the South during the antebellum era, the Federal government ignored the European nations' infringement of the Monroe Doctrine and violations of neutrality laws during the war. One basic difference separated the diplomatic agendas of the two warring nations: the Federal Union enjoyed the advantage of having long-standing diplomatic relations with European nations and most of Latin America. Its goal, therefore, was to maintain these relations and to use established channels for negotiation. The Confederacy, in contrast, was a new political entity whose first task was to legitimate its existence in order to be recognized as a belligerent power and eventually as an independent sovereign state.

Yankee Diplomacy

On the eve of the Civil War, the European naval powers embarked on expansionist ventures in Mexico and the Caribbean. Abraham Lincoln's secretary of state, William Seward, originally favored a stern response to these challenges to the Monroe Doctrine as a means of unifying the crumbling Union behind a national war effort. "I would demand explanations from Spain and France, categorically, at once. I would seek explanations from Great Britain and Russia, and send agents into Canada, Mexico, and Central America to rouse a vigorous continental spirit of independence on this continent against European intervention. And, if satisfactory explanations are not received from Spain and France, would convene Congress to declare war against them." When the Civil War broke out and a Confederate-European alliance became plausible, Federal officials reevaluated their stance. Although several of the European naval powers openly sided with the new confederation and pursued recolonization efforts in Mexico and the Caribbean, the United States chose to follow a pragmatic route, using stern rhetoric against such expansionist pretensions while avoiding direct confrontation with Great Britain, Spain, or France. For the time being, U.S. officials had to settle for speaking loudly but carrying a tiny stick.[2]

After having dodged anti–slave trade postures for decades, mainly because of southern pressures, the United States, once at war, finally signed a treaty that granted British vessels the right to search North American vessels suspected of carrying slaves. This treaty also set up a British-U.S. Mixed Commission, similar to the one in Havana, to fight the continuation of the slave trade.[3] Still, British violations of neutrality during the war remained a constant source of friction between the United States and Great Britain. In such a context, Lincoln's able minister to Great Britain, Charles Francis Adams, cunningly employed pressures and outright threats to avoid an armed conflict. The United States's reluctance to engage in any confrontation with Great Britain became evident during the *Trent* crisis, an affair sparked by the decision of Union captain Charles Wilkes to capture Confederate emissaries James M. Mason and John Slidell, who were en route to London on board the *Trent*, a British ship. The British reacted immediately to this affront, deploying several thousand troops to Canada.

The pragmatism of the Union's wartime foreign policy was also evident in its policy toward Spain and its colonies. Although Seward and his envoys to Spain strongly protested the Spanish annexation of the Dominican Republic in 1861, they took no concrete measures against this or similar encroachments. In fact, Lincoln specifically instructed Seward not to present an ultimatum to Spain on this matter. The United States even reassured Spain that it would not pose a threat to the institution of slavery in its Caribbean colonies. In September 1863 Seward clarified this position: "The United States do not want any more territories," stated Seward. "Certainly they do not want any more slaveholding territories." He then underscored his assertion: "The United States govt. is not a forcible propagandist of emancipation even at home."[4]

Indirectly, however, the Federal government established contacts with revolutionary forces seeking to overthrow the Spanish government in the former Dominican Republic and the French-backed emperor Maximilian in Mexico. After the end of the Civil War, U.S. troops were deployed on the Mexican border, and shortly afterward, the French army withdrew from Mexico. Maximilian was deposed and executed, and Benito Juárez assumed political control. Concerning the Dominican colony, the Spanish minister in Washington noted that U.S. citizens participated on the side of the Dominican struggle for independence, complaining that U.S. merchant ships were transporting arms and supplies to the insurrectionary forces via Haiti. Soon thereafter he averred that abolitionist groups in Boston and New York were overtly aiding the Dominicans. A Captain Smith, probably a blockade-runner, reported to the Spanish minister in Paris that James Redfath, a Bostonian, was leading such operations, "aided and supported in his diabolical mission by the Federal government in Washington with its advice and consent, and by the Northern States which have provided the arms and ammunition."[5]

In their attempt to block Spanish recognition of the Confederate States of America, Union diplomats exploited the expansionist record of the Confederate leadership. On June 13, 1861, Horatio Perry, chargé d'affaires in Madrid, wrote Seward: "Yesterday, in a long and very satisfactory interview with [overseas minister] Mr. Calderón, I explained to him the conexion [*sic*] of Mr. Jefferson Davis and other leaders in the southern rebellion with the attempt made in 1854–'55 by the same parties to provoke a war with Spain for the conquest of Cuba." In another dispatch Perry informed Seward that he "traced rapidly for [the overseas minister] the connexion of the principal actors in the present rebellion with former filibustering schemes against Cuba."[6]

The Spanish colony of Santo Domingo and the independent nation of Haiti became particularly important to the United States during the early years of the Civil War because of their potential role as havens for deported liberated slaves. The migration of free blacks to this island had, in fact, begun before the outbreak of the Civil War, when hundreds of former slaves fled Charleston, New Orleans, and other parts of the South out of fear of being reenslaved. Lincoln and many in his administration favored a colonization solution to the "problem" of the liberated slaves, and in 1862 the United States finally recognized Haiti as an independent nation. Shortly afterward a project to send immigrants to Ile à Vache, Haiti, was set in motion.[7] Also in 1862 William Cazneau, Lincoln's envoy to Santo Domingo, established the American West India Company with the object of relocating freed slaves from the United States. Other members of the Federal consular corps in the region also expressed interest in similar projects. Acting Havana consul Thomas Savage and his Matanzas colleague promoted "colonization" efforts to Hispaniola. The U.S. commercial agent at Santo Domingo wrote Seward: "I see that both President Lincoln and Congress, are desirous for some place to locate our unfortunate race of color." "This climate," he continued, "is not adapted for laboring whites but congenial and safe for the persons of color." In Havana consul Robert W. Shufeldt actively promoted a deportation project for liberated slaves into Tehuantepec, Mexico. In the outline of this most Machiavellian scheme, Shufeldt stated that Tehuantepec, a region in which he had financial interests, was ideal because it was depopulated, had good harbors, had good soils for cultivation, and was close to the southern United States. He remarked that the liberated slaves "would settle upon and live off a transit route between the two oceans embodying not only the labor from the construction of this route and affording employment for thousands of them but by these means forming a connecting link between our eastern and western coasts, consisting of a People identified with our interests speaking our language and imbued with our religion & social habits and customs." Shufeldt added that this project, if put in place, would give the United States the additional advantage of having "indirect control in Mexico." Neither Shufeldt's nor Cazneau's schemes materialized, however. Only a few hundred former slaves relocated in Haiti during the war, and by 1864 most of them had either died or returned to the United States.[8]

Confederate Diplomacy

Diplomacy was a critical weapon within the southern arsenal. Through diplomatic negotiation, the Confederacy sought to achieve the international rejection of the Federal blockade, European mediation in the conflict, recognition of the Confederacy's independence, and ultimately intervention on its side. It also aimed to establish a commercial network to assure the inflow of war matériel and the outflow of southern cash crops, cotton in particular. With these objectives, the Confederacy dispatched James M. Mason and John Slidell to Europe and Charles Helm to Havana.

"King Cotton diplomacy" became the backbone of Confederate diplomatic efforts during the early years of the Civil War.[9] This was, in essence, an attempt to exploit Europe's dependence on southern cotton in order to coerce the European nations, Great Britain in particular, first into recognizing the South and then possibly into intervening on its behalf. The strategy consisted of withholding cotton exports until the desperate national markets of Great Britain and France had no choice but to swap recognition for the coveted fiber. A cotton embargo was put in place, cotton brokers and exporters agreed to keep the 1861 harvest in storage, planters substantially reduced their acreage for 1862, and many of the seceded states passed laws and levied taxes to discourage cotton exports. Thousands of cotton bales were also destroyed in southern ports, a flaming holocaust for King Cotton.[10]

In the end this strategy failed to inspire European intervention, mediation, or even recognition. Although Great Britain and France desperately needed southern cotton, they also depended on northern grain. During the war years the United States supplied around one-third of Great Britain's grain imports. Moreover, European markets had large cotton reserves stemming from the South's bumper crop of 1860–61. In the second half of 1862, when the cotton embargo finally made itself felt in Great Britain, the South failed to produce a desperately needed military victory in the North, and the embargo began to fall apart.[11]

The Confederacy's policy toward Spain and its Caribbean colonies was indeed a radical turn from the South's antebellum postures. In the 1850s many influential southern leaders had sought to provoke a conflict with Spain, either by direct filibuster aggression or by official provocations like the Ostend Manifesto. During the Civil War, however, the Confederacy looked to Spain as the only other northern Atlantic power seeking to preserve the institution of slavery. On August 24, 1861, Confederate secretary of state R. M. T. Hunter wrote Confederate envoy Pierre A. Rost: "Of all the great powers of Europe Spain alone is interested through her colonies in the same social system which pervades the Confederate States." In a confidential letter to the Spanish minister of state, Confederate agent Charles Helm asserted that "Now the interest of the South requires a slave power in Europe to cooperate with her in the protection of the peculiar institution of the Confederate States, Cuba, Puerto Rico and Santo Domingo [*sic*]."[12]

Confederate envoys to Spain and the Spanish Caribbean put much effort into dispelling the expansionist reputation that white southerners had earned during the previous decade. In his instructions to Helm, Secretary of State Robert Toombs stated:

> If you should discover that any apprehension exists in the minds of the people of a design on the part of this government to attempt the acquisition of that island [Cuba] in any manner, whether by purchase or otherwise, you will leave no efforts untried to remove such erroneous belief. It is the policy of the Government of the Confederate States that Cuba shall continue to be a colonial possession of Spain. It is true that, during the existence of the late Federal Union, there were persons in the Southern States who favored the acquisition of that island. . . . But it is no less true that, since our separation, the desire thus entertained has given place to a sincere wish that, politically, the two countries may exist separately, but bound together . . . by the most friendly and unlimited commercial intercourse.[13]

The South's Caribbean policy was so conciliatory toward Spain that it even approved Spanish annexation of the Dominican Republic in the spring of 1861.[14]

During the war both the North and the South assumed highly

pacific attitudes toward third nations, particularly toward Spain and its overseas colonies. The war and its diplomatic demands seemed to obliterate the deep differences regarding slavery and its expansion that had led to the Union's rupture in 1861. Paradoxically, Confederate diplomats reassured Spanish officials that they had no territorial pretensions in the Caribbean, while their Yankee counterparts shed the slightest trace of abolitionism.

Europe's Response

Most European governments welcomed the Civil War because it moved back the geopolitical clock ten to twelve years, enabling them once again to take the offensive in the Caribbean and Mexico.[15] At first, European statesmen pursued a cautious policy toward the internal crisis in North America, although Europe's policymakers definitely sympathized with the South. Also, a strong sense of unanimity of action developed among Great Britain, France, and Spain. Thus, one effect of the Civil War was the further strengthening of the European coalition vis-à-vis the United States.

Correspondence between Francisco Muñoz Moncada, the Spanish consul at Charleston, and the chief of the Spanish legation in Washington, Gabriel García Tassara, reveals the development of Spain's policy toward the Confederacy. On December 31, 1860, just eleven days after South Carolina's legislators voted for secession, García Tassara authorized Muñoz Moncada to begin conducting business with officials of the recently seceded state and to "proceed as the other consuls." Two weeks later García Tassara, who was pursuing a wait-and-see course, instructed his consul at Charleston to be polite to South Carolina officials and to protest their actions only if the British and French consuls did so first. García Tassara clearly ordered Muñoz Moncada, however, to avoid "any formula that might imply *de facto* recognition [of the seceded state]."[16]

When war broke out and the Union declared a blockade of southern ports, Muñoz Moncada received instructions to observe the blockade. He was not to allow the departure or arrival of vessels flying the Spanish flag or to permit Confederate ships to depart for Spanish ports.[17] The ineffectiveness of the blockade, however, forced Spanish policymakers to reevaluate this stance. Following the example of Great

Britain and France, Spain, on June 19, 1861, recognized the South's belligerency and declared itself neutral. In late August, García Tassara relayed new orders to Spanish consuls, authorizing the dispatch of vessels through the blockade. Later that year Muñoz Moncada and his colleagues received orders to assist the free flow of navigation in direct challenge to the Federal blockade.[18] Meanwhile, three more southern states had seceded between April 19 and June 19, and Confederate troops won victories at Bull Run and Ball's Bluff in July and October, demonstrating that the Confederacy was a de facto political entity with the potential to assert its independence.

A neutrality policy, but one that incorporated overt sympathy for the South, proved to be commercially profitable while passive enough to avoid a confrontation with the Union. All three European powers pursued this policy for the duration of the war. They never recognized the South. The failure of the Confederate northern offensive in the fall of 1862, Lincoln's Emancipation Proclamation, and a major defeat at Gettysburg in July 1863 laid to rest all hopes of the Confederacy's being recognized. King Cotton diplomacy took the southern nation only halfway through.

The Civil War and the Hispanic Caribbean

The political crisis in the United States and the eventual separation of the North and South cleared the stage for European encroachments into regions of the hemisphere in which the Monroe Doctrine had been in force during the antebellum era. During the war Spain annexed the Dominican Republic; France, Spain, and Great Britain launched a combined attack on Mexico that culminated in the establishment of a European emperor there; and negotiations went on to establish European protectorates over Texas and Ecuador. All of these developments would have been inconceivable before the war.

For some time before the outbreak of the Civil War, France and Spain had considered the idea of reestablishing European control over Mexico and the Dominican Republic. Fear of U.S. reaction, however, had deterred concrete action. The growing political crisis in the United States during the 1860 election year stimulated Spain into action. By the summer of 1860 Spanish officials were clearly working toward the recolonization and annexation of the Dominican Republic. The U.S.

vice-consul in Havana reported that "a scheme is on foot to have the means at hand, under the pretence of assisting the Dominicans against the apprehended attacks of the Haytien Government to bring about the annexation of the country to Spain." Spanish annexation of the Dominican Republic remained in limbo while the United States stood as a unified nation. On December 8, 1860, minister Leopoldo O'Donnell instructed Cuba's captain-general to proceed with prudence and to wait for the final breakup of the Union. He warned: "The reunion of Santo Domingo brought about in such a manner as would give rise to suspicions not destitute of foundation, would not only turn the gaze of the terrified states of Latin America towards the United States, thus destroying the basis of our policy in America, the unity of our race, but also perhaps making the contending parties in America forget their internal discords, might lead them to group themselves under the Monroe Doctrine, a principle accepted without reserve by the slave states no less than by those where free labor prevails."[19] Spain finally annexed the Dominican Republic in the spring of 1861, only when the fighting between North and South had actually begun. Neither France nor Great Britain posed any serious opposition to Spain's move, instead assuming a posture described by the historian Charles C. Hauch as "reluctant acquiescence." British officials were willing to accept the Spanish annexation of the Dominican Republic as well as the French occupation of Mexico because the new European colonies or protectorates represented buffer zones to U.S. expansion.[20] Lord Palmerston went as far as to characterize Maximilian's empire as "a great thing for Mexico."[21]

The successful annexation of the Dominican Republic demonstrated to European statesmen that the government of the United States would not divert its energy, manpower, and resources to oppose European intervention in the hemisphere while it fought a war within its borders. French, Spanish, and British forces landed in Veracruz in January 1862, ostensibly to collect debts from the Mexican government. Within a few months Spanish and British troops withdrew, yielding to the imperial pretensions of Napoleon III, whose forces remained to establish Maximilian as Mexico's emperor. Spanish forces also tried unsuccessfully to seize territories in Peru and Ecuador.

Throughout the Civil War, European representatives and colonial administrators in the Hispanic Caribbean became active supporters of the secessionist cause. One of the wartime paradoxes was that the British consular corps, a former vanguard of abolitionism in the Americas, now became openly partial toward the proslavery side. British officials considerably muted their abolitionist stance and solidified diplomatic links with Spain and its colonial representatives in Cuba and Puerto Rico. In Havana, British consul-general Joseph T. Crawford, Captain-General Francisco Serrano, and Confederate envoy Charles Helm became close allies. This circumstance would have been inconceivable in the antebellum years. Wartime realities demonstrated that abolitionist zeal was of secondary importance within Great Britain's foreign policy and was subordinated to other geopolitical considerations. They also suggest that both Spain and Great Britain were more concerned with the North's capacity to expand into the Caribbean commercially and politically than with the earlier filibustering expansionism. On October 4, 1861, the Union government's acting consul at Havana reported that "Mr. Joseph T. Crawford, the British Consul, and nearly all the German clique, connected by marriage with him strongly sympathize with the South." In a similar vein, Consul Shufeldt complained that Crawford dispensed hospitality "to Every illustrous Exile and fugitive Embassador [*sic*]," adding that Crawford had ambitions of becoming British ambassador at Richmond once his country recognized the Confederacy's independence. For his part, the Confederate envoy to Havana described Crawford as "our warm ardent friend from the beginning of the war, [who] is an old gentleman of great experience and good sense." Among the services that Crawford provided for the Confederate side were registration of southern vessels and the sale of southern cotton. A similar situation occurred in Puerto Rico, where Consul John J. Hyde reported that "all the blockade runners that have visited port, during my sojourn here, can be said to have been consigned to this British consulate, while it has openly & persistently advocated the cause of the secessionists & been covertly hostile to our government & people."[22]

Spanish colonial administrators in Cuba, Puerto Rico, and the Dominican Republic, like their superiors in the Peninsula, were also partial toward the Confederate States of America. Captains-general Francisco Serrano and Domingo Dulce in Cuba and their counterparts in Puerto Rico, Rafael Echagüe and Félix María de Messina, interpreted the crown's neutrality decree as one that allowed Confederate vessels and foreign ships crossing the blockade to enter Cuban and Puerto Rican ports. On numerous occasions Cuban ports harbored and serviced Confederate commerce raiders and bent or violated rules and principles of international law in favor of southern vessels. Union consular representatives complained constantly about this. In late 1861, for example, Shufeldt warned Serrano that his government's actions were "equivalent to a virtual recognition." On another occasion, the U.S. commercial agent at Santo Domingo reported that Spaniards there sympathized with Jefferson Davis and his "bogus" confederation and hoped for the Union's defeat.[23] Spanish officials in the Caribbean rejected such accusations and maintained that they adhered to a strict policy of neutrality.

The Aftermath of the Civil War

The Union victory over the Confederacy in the early months of 1865 and the subsequent military occupation of the vanquished South produced, at least in theory, the conditions for the reconstruction of the United States on the basis of a northern agenda. The nation's foreign and domestic policy no longer had to be the result of conflict and compromise between the North and South, Republicans and Democrats, free and slave states, and importing and exporting regions. In reality, however, the North did not emerge from the war as a unified whole with a clear national policy for reconstruction. Tensions between parties and even within the Republican party became evident even while the war was raging and Lincoln was still president. Lincoln's assassination and the rise to the presidency of a successor of lesser stature and a weak political base aggravated the situation.

Following Lincoln's death, a deep rift occurred between the executive and Congress, which culminated in an attempt to impeach President Andrew Johnson. Besides having serious differences in domestic policy, the executive and Congress clashed over their policy on the Caribbean. The president and the departments of state and the navy sought to expand into the Caribbean to establish coal depots and naval stations. The Civil War had made clear the importance of naval warfare, and such bases could determine the outcome of any future confrontation with any European power in the Caribbean. In his message of December 9, 1868, Johnson said: "Comprehensive, national policy would seem to sanction the acquisition and incorporation into the Federal Union of several adjacent, continental, and insular communities as speedily as it can be done." Regarding the Dominican Republic and Haiti, Johnson affirmed that "the time has arrived when even so direct a proposition for an annexation of the two Republics of the island of St. Domingo would not only receive the consent of the people interested, but would give satisfaction to all other foreign nations."[24]

The new expansionism of the Johnson administration focused on the acquisition of naval stations to service and protect commercial routes, particularly the projected Isthmian route across Central America. To that end, in the winter of 1865–66 Secretary of State Seward personally toured the Caribbean in search of suitable locations for coaling and naval bases. A year later Frederick Seward, the secretary's son and assistant, and Admiral David D. Porter sailed to the once-again-independent Dominican Republic to negotiate the purchase or lease of territory in the much-coveted Samaná Bay. They were instructed to seek sovereignty over Samaná or a second option of a thirty-year lease in exchange for one million dollars in cash and one million dollars in arms. Buenaventura Báez, then serving his third term as Dominican president, proved eager to swap a strip of Samaná for guns and cash, which he needed to fight the insurgent opposition. Meanwhile, the Johnson administration pursued parallel negotiations with Denmark for the acquisition of St. Thomas and St. Croix. Eventually, both efforts failed because of congressional opposition in which Senator Charles Sumner played a key role. The reluctance of Congress to support the imperial pretensions of the administration was not simply a desire to sabotage its designs. This reticence had its roots in the antebellum views of influential northeastern abolitionists such as Sumner, William Cullen Bryant, John Bigelow, and Horace Greeley. The radical opposition viewed these Caribbean societies as free black states in which the United States should not interfere. Racist northern and southern Democrats also opposed the efforts: they sought to keep "turbulent, indolent, unstable and uneducated Spanish Americans" out of the national Union.[25]

A new round of negotiations for the acquisition of territory in the Dominican Republic began during the early years of the Ulysses S.

Grant administration. Grant commissioned General Orville E. Babcock to establish bases for the annexation of the Dominican Republic and to support Báez's regime. In the meantime, Commander E. K. Owen received orders to pursue and capture the *Telégrafo* and its commander, Gregorio Luperón, leader of the insurrection seeking to overthrow Báez. A dozen or so U.S. warships patrolled Dominican waters in support of the Báez regime while the annexation negotiations got under way. Despite the active interference of the U.S. Navy, the Dominican rebellion gained force and succeeded in aiding the overthrow of Haiti's pro-Báez and pro-U.S. president, Silvain Salnave. U.S. officials were quick to warn the new Haitian president, Nissage Saget, that the United States was "ready to make use of all of its might to prevent any intervention in the affairs of the Dominican government." Navy officers in the region were instructed to consider any move on the part of Haiti as a hostile act against the United States and to "destroy" any Haitian vessel attacking Dominican ships. Only after both the Civil War and the Dominican War of Restoration were over did the United States grant recognition to the Dominican Republic, where strongman Báez seemed to provide the best guarantees for social order. Repeatedly, U.S. officials described rebel leaders José María Cabral and Gregorio Luperón as vulgar bandits and petty chiefs.[26]

Racial arguments continued to mark the new debates on expansion to the Dominican Republic as much as they had marked those of the 1850s. Like their antebellum counterparts U.S. envoys to the Dominican Republic in the late 1860s and early 1870s were instructed to report on the country's racial composition: "the number of whites, of pure Africans, of mulattoes and of other mixtures of the African and Caucasian races, of Indians and of crosses between them and whites and Africans, respectively." Samuel G. Howe and the other expansionist members of the 1871 U.S. Commission of Inquiry ascertained that in the republic "white blood predominates." William Cazneau, the perennial envoy to the Dominican Republic, shared these opinions and scorned the anti-U.S., anti-Báez forces as the "Negro party." Opponents to Dominican annexation painted quite a different picture. Congressman Fernando Wood of New York stated on the floor of the House of Representatives that the Dominican race was composed of two-thirds "native African" and one-third "Spanish Creole." This mixture, he continued, "is still more barbaric and savage than the pure African."[27]

President Grant's obsessive desire to acquire territories in the Dominican Republic did not abate following the failure of 1871. His administration proceeded to support the annexationist schemes of the Samaná Bay Company, a private speculative venture that successfully negotiated sovereignty over Samaná under a one-hundred-year lease at $150,000 per year. Beginning on January 1, 1873, Samaná became an unofficial U.S. enclave. Later that year, though, anti-Báez insurrectionaries triumphed and rescinded the lease.[28]

Besides the antagonism between the executive and legislative branches, other deterrents to U.S. expansion into the Caribbean cropped up. Several historians have pointed out that following the Civil War, war weariness curbed any expansionist attempt that could lead the nation into a confrontation with European forces or native populations in the Caribbean.[29] The Civil War not only drained the nation's energies, it also taxed its finances. Many strongly opposed spending over twenty million dollars to purchase coaling stations in the Caribbean. Finally, during Reconstruction national priorities shifted: far more attention was now focused on the internal development of the United States than on external expansion. The age of the tall ships had yielded to the age of railroads.

The failure of the Johnson and Grant administrations to expand into the Caribbean, however, should not be seen as a remnant of antebellum constraints. The Civil War and the resulting transfer of power to the northeastern states ultimately had profound repercussions for the Caribbean policy of the United States and for the balance of power in the region. Three months after the capitulation at Appomattox, not coincidentally, the last Spanish troops withdrew from the Dominican Republic.[30] In February 1866 fifty thousand U.S. troops moved on the Mexican border, and shortly thereafter the French withdrew from Mexico and Maximilian's kingdom collapsed. By mid-1867 Mexico and the Caribbean were clearly within the United State's sphere of influence. The transfer of political and economic power to the northeastern states during and after the Civil War also meant a transformation in the objectives of U.S. expansionism, burying in the scorched battlefields the vision of southern agrarian expansion and the dream of creating a slave-based Caribbean empire.

In the war's aftermath a new brand of U.S. expansionism gained preeminence. It did not seek the absorption of large territories and their enslaved, dark-skinned populations; rather, it sought bastions for the protection of a commercial empire and eventually the establishment of enclaves for the extraction of raw materials and cultivation of tropical staples.[31] Another critical transformation was the emergence of abolitionism as a fundamental element of U.S. foreign policy after 1865. The same William Seward who in 1863 ordered his envoy in Madrid to assure Spanish officials that his government was not a promoter of abolition "even at home" instructed his new minister in Spain to begin pressuring for abolition in 1866.[32] During Reconstruction the United States gave far more attention to the free Dominican Republic and the Danish Virgin Islands than to Cuba and Puerto Rico, where slavery persisted.[33]

The Union victory and northern control over the national government during Reconstruction concerned Spanish officials on both sides of the Atlantic. They had gambled in support of the South and lost. For them the brewing northern-based imperialism represented a more serious threat to Spanish territories than the earlier filibustering schemes of southern radicals. Spanish officials closely monitored Frederick Seward's tour of the Antilles. In January 1867 a Spanish agent in the United States reported on this "mysterious" expedition, which he correctly concluded had the objective of negotiating the purchase of Samaná.[34] Cuba's captain-general also remained vigilant. In mid-1867 he described the ruling Republican party in the United States as having a tendency toward "the expansion of might and power characteristic of young vain nations who believe to be called upon to rule the world."[35] Concerns, in fact, grew, as a new, perhaps more aggressive form of expansionism took shape. The threat of bands of adventurers led by quixotic southern planter-gentlemen gave in to the fear of professional armies responding to the call for a new empire.

The era of Reconstruction saw the development of another thorny Caribbean policy issue for the United States, as Cuban patriots embarked on a ten-year struggle against Spanish domination. Despite obvious ideological affinities with the Cuban cause, the Grant administration failed to recognize the rebels. In fact, it systematically sabotaged the Cubans' efforts while supplying Spain with gunboats and matériel. Grant feared that pushing for Cuban recognition would have jeopardized his efforts at Dominican acquisition. Also, the promise of real reforms in Cuba by Spain's new republican government made U.S. officials wary of supporting what seemed to be at best an unpredictable revolutionary enterprise. Even when several U.S. citizens were executed in 1873 by Spanish soldiers in relation to the *Virginius* affair, the U.S. government refused to antagonize the Spanish government.[36]

Secretary of State Hamilton Fish, viewed by several Cuban historians as the worst enemy of the Cuban cause, was instrumental in implementing a policy of open hostility toward the Cuban insurgents. He had close personal ties with the Spanish lobby in Washington and personally disliked the Cuban leadership in exile, which he deemed incapable of ruling over a liberated Cuba. He characterized the rebels as having evil inclinations and deserving "condemnations of all honest citizens." Fish was also convinced that the "new Spain" would finally bring reforms, which in his view were being blocked by the revolutionary struggle tearing down the island.

The old fears of Cuba's Africanization were at the heart of Fish's position, one shared by many other influential officials. The insurrection's radicalization, the resort to arsonist tactics, and the arming of freed slaves by the revolutionaries reinforced the Grant administration's concerns about the war's outcome. Whatever sympathies Grant had for the revolutionaries dissipated as reports continued to pour out of the island confirming that blacks and Chinese soldiers constituted the bulk of the rebel army. One U.S. official referred to the rebels as "the negro bands of Máximo Gómez," "loathsome and hateful monsters," and "maroon incendiaries." Another opponent of U.S. recognition of the Cubans, Francis L. Norton, employed similar arguments. He described the insurgents as "a few hundred half-naked, poorly-armed and badly officered, negroes, Chinamen and half-breeds." Cuban blacks, he continued, required the discipline of Spanish law, otherwise "the climate being warm, they will wear no clothing, and fruit being abundant, they will not plant."[37]

In accordance with the traditional policy of the United States, Spanish colonialism continued to be tolerated in the Caribbean during the Cuban Ten Years' War insofar as it guaranteed social and political stability.[38] This policy gained further strength after the Civil War, when one of the earlier motivations for U.S. expansion—the threat of European encroachment—virtually disappeared. During the 1868–78 period, the United States openly sided with Spain, proving that it preferred the continuation of the existing colonial system to the establishment of an independent Cuban republic. The rationale behind this policy was that Spain seemed to guarantee the continuation of agricultural productivity, commerce, and navigation and that the laws of political gravitation would continue to pull the region gradually into the political orbit of the United States. The Cuban struggle for independence, despite being ideologically compatible with the aspirations of U.S. officials, was perceived as dangerous to production and trade and conducive to the formation of an unpredictable state headed by blacks and mulattoes. In spite of all the changes brought by the Civil War, the Caribbean policy of the United States was still shaped by the old antebellum fears of the region's Africanization. Spanish colonialism thus continued to be welcomed as the lesser of two evils.

The Federal Blockade, Commerce Raiders, and Their Impact on the Hispanic Caribbean

In the realm of commerce and navigation, the United States endured a wartime setback that paralleled its political retreat from the Caribbean. The disruptions brought about by the war forced U.S. traders to withdraw partially from an area that they had come to dominate. While European trade and navigation quickly moved in to fill this partial vacuum, still wartime disruptions had considerable impact on the economies of Cuba and Puerto Rico. These societies were called upon to play new roles and to accommodate to the wartime demands of the northern Atlantic markets.

One of Lincoln's first military actions after the fall of Fort Sumter was to declare a naval blockade of all the seaports of the seceded states. This strategy was directed toward cutting the outward flow of cotton and other exchange-producing staples and toward preventing the importation of war matériel. The project proved to be extremely ambitious. Blockading 3,549 statute miles of southern coast required a large and efficient navy, and at the time of the blockade's declaration on April 19, 1861, the Federal government lacked an adequate fleet capable of stopping the circulation of vessels into and out of Confederate ports. The Federal forces did some patrolling, but the blockade remained only a token gesture for some time. Reports by Spanish consular representatives commented on the ineffectiveness of Lincoln's naval measure: "In no case has the blockade of the port of Charleston been effective," wrote the Spanish consul at Charleston in June 1861.[39]

Spain's response toward the blockade was cautious at first, but when evidence mounted that the Union could not enforce it, Spanish vessels and Spanish ports began to challenge the blockade openly. Before the declaration of the blockade, minister García Tassara ordered the Spanish vice-consul at Savannah to "delay the clearing" of Confederate vessels and to wait for further instructions. Following the British example, Spain's posture changed in the summer of 1861. Although a royal decree of June 19 did not directly authorize the crossing of the blockade, it ostensibly condoned such actions by establishing exceptions: "the transportation under the Spanish flag of war material, dispatches or communications for the belligerents." Alluding to an old principle of international law, the captain-general of Cuba later argued that "the vessels have a right to clear, for there is no effective force to impede this."[40]

Colonial officials in Cuba and Puerto Rico welcomed blockade-runners. Vessels to and from southern ports began to clear Cuba's ports in greater numbers during the second half of 1861, even though Federal naval patrols increased their strength to 42 vessels in July and further to 160 in December. On August 21 the first Confederate ship arrived in Cuban waters. According to Confederate data, the number of vessels traveling to and from the South calling in Cuban ports jumped from an average of 3.3 per month (May–July) to 7.5 per month (August–December). By November 1861 U.S. consul Robert W. Shufeldt reported that blockade-runners were so numerous that it was "becoming difficult to keep the run of them."[41]

Despite Union patrols and the southern cotton embargo, an estimated five hundred to seven hundred vessels ran the blockade in 1861, and ninety-three of them came from or went to Cuban ports. On September 29, 1861, the Spanish consul at Charleston reported that ships from Cuba figured prominently in blockade-running in and out of the Carolinas. New Orleans, however, was the origin and preferred destination of most blockade-runners in Cuban ports. During 1861 Charleston and other Atlantic southern ports dominated blockade-running activity. A total of 274 vessels entered or cleared Carolina ports that year. Toward the end of the year, however, Federal naval presence in the region increased in both numbers and effectiveness. In

November 1861 Union naval forces under Thomas West Sherman temporarily occupied Port Royal, South Carolina. A month later northern forces sank fifteen ships loaded with stones at the entrance to Charleston harbor, with the objective of obstructing the passage of vessels there. A few days later Muñoz Moncada reported that the blockade was now effective.[42]

In 1862 blockade-running became more sophisticated, as the quality of the vessels improved and the tactics became more refined and the routes more clearly defined. Blockade-runners from Charleston and other Atlantic ports concentrated on the Nassau route: forty out of fifty-six vessels departing Charleston in the first six months of 1862 headed for Nassau. Meanwhile, blockade-runners from New Orleans and other Gulf ports focused on Havana.[43] Despite the fall of New Orleans in the spring of 1862, Cuban-based blockade-running continued to increase, shifting to other Gulf ports in Texas, Alabama, and Florida.

Eighteen-sixty-three was the high-water mark of blockade-running in and out of Cuban and Puerto Rican ports. Consul Shufeldt reported that between May 10 and May 18 eight vessels cleared Havana to run the blockade and two others arrived from Mobile. During July, Shufeldt continued to report arrivals at the rate of one a day. His successor, Thomas Savage, informed his superiors about uninterrupted blockade-running throughout the balance of 1863. That year also saw increased blockade-running in Puerto Rican ports. Consul John J. Hyde reported a total of nine such vessels reaching his consular district. He informed his superiors that San Juan had "become a favorite and frequent place of resort for English steamers bound to blockaded ports in the United States via Nassau & Bermudas." Hyde's predecessor, Charles De Ronceray, who was suspected of being a Confederate sympathizer, did not report a single instance of blockade-running in or out of Puerto Rico the previous year. Despite De Ronceray's questionable political sympathies, the absence of blockade-running data in other sources seems to attest that Puerto Rican ports saw little of this kind of activity before 1863.[44]

In 1864 blockade-runners changed their geographic focus once again. Federal patrolling became more efficient and succeeded in further discouraging navigation into and out of Charleston, Wilmington, and other Atlantic ports. That year the blockading force increased to over 400 vessels, reducing the blockade-runners' rate of success to three out of every four attempts. Only 112 vessels braved the blockade of Carolina ports in 1864. By late February 1865 the occupation of Charleston and Wilmington brought about the collapse of blockade-running into and out of Bermuda and the Bahamas. This activity now shifted to Havana, the port city that became the undisputed center of blockade-running. Route changes also affected blockade-running at Gulf ports. In the summer of 1864 the forts guarding the entrance to Mobile Bay fell to Federal forces, leaving Galveston as the Confederacy's principal Gulf port. Most blockade-runners previously servicing the Mobile-Havana route now transferred their operations to Galveston. This meant a longer trip, requiring a great deal of coal, but it produced huge profits for those who continued running the blockade. In contrast, Puerto Rico's ports lost importance within the blockade-running network during the last year of the war. In mid-1864 Consul Hyde reported no blockade-runners in his district and thought it unlikely that more would appear. His register of blockade-running for 1864 included only two entries, one in September and another in December.[45] Within the next few months blockade-running ended for both Puerto Rico and Cuba. Wilmington fell in February 1865, and Galveston fell in June, signaling the end to this swashbuckling chapter in U.S.-Caribbean trade.

Cuban ports played a prominent role within the Confederacy's trade network, particularly in the final stages of the conflict. Southern cotton, rice, and other staples found their way through the blockade to Havana, where they were sold to European agents. In 1861, with the cotton embargo still in place, rice and naval stores figured prominently in blockade-running trade with Havana. The following year, however, cotton gained a preeminent place. Fifty-three out of fifty-six vessels departing Charleston in the first semester of 1862 were loaded with cotton. On their return to the South, blockade-runners carried consumer goods, arms and ammunition, and other products readily available in the Havana market.[46]

Consular dispatches attested to the extent to which war matériel crossed the blockade. On September 29, 1861, the Spanish vice-consul at Savannah informed his superiors of the arrival of the 1,400-ton HMS *Bermuda* with 5 million rounds of ammunition for carbines, 24 cannons, 36,000 carbines, 72,000 blankets, and an unspecified number of boots. A few months later Muñoz Moncada reported the arrival at Beaufort, South Carolina, of the CSS *Nashville* from Liverpool with war supplies valued at two million dollars. Most of the large ammunition and arms cargoes came from Europe in larger steamers, which made fuel stops in the Caribbean. The British vessel *Giraffe*, for example, called at San Juan for coal, laden with "cannon, shell, shot, small arms, powder etc." Similar reports came from Havana. In April 1863 Thomas Savage informed Seward that José Reyes of M. A. Herrera and Company distributed arms to blockade-runners. William Watson, a blockade-runner, later reminisced in his memoirs that a Havana arms dealer once offered him a package that included "200 Enfield rifles with bayonets and accoutrements, [and] 400 Belgium muskets with bayonets."[47]

Besides arms and ammunition, other goods changed hands in Havana for shipment to southern ports. Charles Helm himself actively purchased foodstuffs and dry goods for the Confederate market. Savage reported that the "rebel agent" was seeking large quantities of "pork, beef, and other necessaries including medicines." Unfortunately for the South, high demand for these products prompted speculation, inflation, and at times the necessity of trading with the enemy. New England cheese and fish and Cuban coffee were sold at markups of around 500 percent to blockade-runners anxious to load their vessels for the west leg of the trip. In San Juan one U.S. merchant allegedly sold coal to a British blockade-runner at twice its regular price.[48] Captains running the blockade did not seem to mind the high prices. They were usually in a hurry to load and refuel and knew that despite the risks and costs the huge profits made it all worthwhile. Sugar purchased at three cents a pound in Cuba sold wholesale for one dollar in Charleston and retailed at four dollars in Charleston and eleven dollars in Richmond.[49]

Union and Confederate officers in Cuba tried to block the trading between enemies, but high demand and hefty profits made this difficult. On most occasions southern money and northern goods, or vice versa, changed hands through Spanish or Cuban intermediary agents. In some instances, northern exporters sold directly to blockade-runners. Robert W. Shufeldt once communicated to Seward that "German or Dutch Jews" had imported ammunition from New York to be sold to Confederate agents in Havana. In another dispatch, Confederate agent Charles Helm expressed pride that only "a few hundred bales of cotton . . . have fallen into the hands of Northern speculators, and been shipped to New York." He added that "the great bulk has, or will go to Europe." Nearly a year later he found that a Mr. Addison Cammack of New Orleans had sold 650 bales of cotton to a New York agent. A Yankee spy who successfully infiltrated the Confederate element in Havana reported other instances of trading with the enemy: he informed his superiors of a suspected cargo of quinine bound for the South disguised in egg cases.[50]

Despite the risks involved in blockade-running, particularly toward the end of the war, many merchants operating out of Havana continued to challenge the Federal blockade. Captains of large steamers shipping cotton to Havana earned commissions of close to five thousand dollars per trip; crew members received one hundred dollars in gold per month plus fifty-dollar bonuses after each successful voyage. Havana proved to be a particularly attractive port of call for captains and sailors running the blockade. One of them said that the city swarmed with a crowd "mostly of the Anglo-Saxon race, consisting of runners and speculators from America, Britain and other places." Blockade-runners found time to relax in the city while their vessels were being unloaded and reloaded. They enjoyed tropical refreshments at the popular Café Louvre and Café Dominica and visited the famous fish market and other tourist spots. Captains and their crews also enjoyed the hospitality of Confederate agent Charles Helm, who aided them in the sale of their cotton and the purchase of provisions and goods. One blockade-runner, Thomas Taylor, wrote: "To us blockade-runners, accustomed to the hard life in the South and the contracted surroundings of Nassau, Havana appeared like Paradise; good hotels and casinos, a capital theatre, magnificent equipages, military bands, handsome women, and last but not least, the lavish and genial hospitality dispensed by our Consul-General, Mr. Crawford and his charming daughters."[51]

Blockade-running and the commercial and navigational activity that came with it became a considerable source of profit not only for the Spanish colonial administration, which collected duties and tariffs, but also for agents, commissioners, merchants, warehouse owners, and others involved in servicing and supplying blockade-runners. Even an old beggar stationed in one of Havana's streets attested that her receipts had doubled since the start of blockade-running. She told Captain William Watson, an occasional contributor to her outstretched hand, that blockade-runners were good people and that she prayed daily for the triumph of the Confederacy.[52]

Puerto Rico played a different and much more limited role within the blockade-running network. At the peak of blockade-running, arrivals to Puerto Rican ports were fewer than one per month. Furthermore, San Juan never became a Confederate entrepôt like Havana. Southern cotton was apparently not sold in Puerto Rico, nor were arms and ammunition purchased there for delivery to southern ports. Puerto Rico served primarily as a coaling station for the larger blockade-runners crossing between Liverpool or Barcelona and Confederate ports.[53] The fast, lean side-wheelers used for shorter trips did not appear in Puerto Rican waters partially for geographic reasons: a trip from New Orleans to San Juan took twice as long as one between New Orleans and Havana. This not only meant higher transportation costs but also more space taken up by coal, leaving less room for cotton and other goods. Moreover, the port of Havana provided more facilities for storing and merchandising a wider variety of cargoes.

The Commerce Raiders

Naval raiders or privateers were the Confederate version of the Federal blockade. These vessels considerably disrupted trade between the Spanish Caribbean and northern ports. One of the commerce raiders' first preys was Captain Meyer's brig *Joseph*, a Yankee vessel captured by the Confederate man-of-war *Savannah* while en route from Cárdenas to Philadelphia. The ship was confiscated. Although Consul Muñoz Moncada pleaded for the restoration of the ship's cargo, forty thousand dollars' worth of sugar, to its alleged proprietor, José María Morales, a Spanish resident of Cárdenas, the judge ruling in the case was strongly influenced by the testimonies of the *Joseph*'s crew. They stated that the cargo belonged to Welch and Company, "one of the biggest Black Republican Houses in Philadelphia." Confederate officials in Charleston eventually auctioned the sugar.[54]

Similar incidents followed. In July 1861 the CSS *Sumter* sank one bark and captured seven other vessels off the coast of Cienfuegos. After causing havoc off Cuba's southern shores, the *Sumter* called at

Havana for coal and provisions. In the same month another northern ship, the schooner *Herbert Mantor,* was seized by a Confederate raider off the coast of Wilmington. Once again Muñoz Moncada asked for restitution for the cargo, but once again it was denied by the presiding Confederate magistrate. A few days later the CSS *Jeff Davis* captured the *John Wesley,* which was bound for Falmouth with Cuban sugar. The same raider intercepted the *Santa Clara,* a vessel laden with sugar and molasses exported by Ramón Pou from Humacao, Puerto Rico, to New York.[55]

Efforts by U.S. envoys in Havana to secure cooperation from Spanish officials to stop the privateering were unsuccessful. In fact, Spanish officials in Cuba continued to be openly friendly toward Confederate raiders. The *Florida,* one of the most devastating of these ships, was repaired in the Cárdenas shipyards in 1862, with the blessing of local authorities. Early the following year the *Florida* returned to Cuba, this time to Havana, where it was welcomed warmly after burning the brig *Estelle,* whose sugar cargo melted into caramel on the high seas, never reaching its intended destination in Boston.[56]

The Confederate raiders also disrupted trade in Puerto Rican waters. As early as May 1861 Puerto Rico's captain-general reported grave consequences resulting from the arming of trade raiders by the Confederacy. "In the island's ports," he stated, "loaded vessels with the American flag remain waiting, for they ignore whether the corzarios [*sic*] authorized by the United States of the South will respect the merchandise that they carry." He added that commerce was paralyzed and that the island was suffering a mercantile and fiscal crisis. A few days later the U.S. consul at San Juan warned Seward about the possible arming of privateers in Puerto Rico "for the purpose of aggression on the commerce of the United States." Soon after, the *Jeff Davis* came to San Juan for coal and provisions. This incident cost De Ronceray his job: he suspiciously left San Juan during the raider's visit, confirming his superiors' doubts about the Baltimorean's loyalty to the Union. In late January and early February 1863 the notorious *Alabama* appeared off the coast of Santo Domingo and in Puerto Rican waters, moving Consul John J. Hyde to report apprehension and complaints among local exporters.[57]

Although trade disruptions and tensions between Spain and the United States never led to any serious confrontation, they showed the important role Caribbean ports could play. The activity in Havana, for example, confirmed how intimately linked that port was with the United States. Havana and other ports in the area played significant roles during the turbulent and disruptive years of the U.S. Civil War.

The Export Economies of the Spanish Caribbean

Cuban historian Herminio Portell Vilá wrote, "The effects of the national crisis of the United States were felt in Cuba with more intensity than in any other country, with the exception of the republic being torn down by the Civil War."[58] A similar assessment could be made for Puerto Rico, particularly its sugar-producing regions. Disruptions in trade and navigation and the shrinking of the U.S. market for tropical staples had profound reverberations for the economies of the Spanish Caribbean.

Even before the beginning of the actual fighting in North America and the establishment of the Federal blockade, the political crisis in the United States could be felt in the region. On January 1, 1861, Consul De Ronceray asserted that the "political and monetary *crisis*, there [in the United States] has seriously affected the business of [Puerto Rico]." He went on to say that demand for sugar had dropped and that planters were "waiting for more cheering news." "It has been well said," added De Ronceray, "that Spain, the mother country, might sink to the bottom of the sea without its affecting the prosperity or business interests of this Island; but the large trade which has grown up between the United States and the West Indies disturbs from centre to circumference, in a crisis like the present, all relations of the commercial character pending with these islands." The Spanish consul at Charleston believed that under the current state of affairs it was highly improbable that trade with Cuba and Spain would return to normal "until the political situation in the United States clears up."[59]

During the first few months of the Civil War, planters and merchants in southern Puerto Rico constantly complained of trade disruptions and of declining productivity, blaming these evils on the war. Ponce planters Juan Prats and Francisco Marich addressed the island's captain-general, asserting that neither during the cholera epidemic (1855–56) nor during the monetary crisis (1857) had their class endured as many troubles and scarcities as it was at present. In a similar communication, three other planters underscored the scarcity of circulating currency and blamed it all on the crisis in the United States and Puerto Rico's "intimate relations" with that country.[60]

Puerto Rico's captain-general relayed some of these complaints and petitions to the Spanish overseas minister. Captain-General Rafael Echagüe painted a grim picture of a "difficult situation that threatens to ruin this country if the political affairs of the United States further complicate." He added that the United States was the island's exclusive market and that events there had virtually closed trade possibilities. According to his assessment, the closing of the U.S. market had led to a scarcity of currency, which made local *refaccionistas* hesitant to lend money. Consequently, some planters had to reduce or even suspend their operations. Another group of planters and merchants from the Ponce region addressed a petition directly to the queen, seeking "remedies for the troubles they endure because of the War in the United States, for that country consumes the majority of this province's products, and is our most important trading partner."[61]

In Cuba the effects of the Civil War were similar, but planters seemed less desperate, despite their numerous requests to delay the payment of tax debts in 1862 and 1863.[62] The strains of the Civil War on the economies of Cuba and Puerto Rico clearly accelerated some of the prewar trends. Puerto Rico's transition away from sugar and into coffee continued during the war as commercial links with Europe were strengthened. In Cuba, where there was less room for diversification, the trend toward sugar monoproduction sharpened.

During the Civil War the overall exports of the Spanish colonies continued to grow at roughly the same pace as in the antebellum period. Exports from Cuba and Puerto Rico jumped from yearly averages of $47.18 million in 1856–60 to $62.64 million in 1861–65, a 33-percent increase. The rate of growth among Cuba's exports was sharper, at 35 percent; Puerto Rico's yearly export output increased by a more modest 13 percent, from $4.98 to $5.64 million. These numbers are indeed striking, given the strong commercial links forged between these colonies and the United States and the extent of the disruptions produced by the Civil War. This paradox is further complicated by the fact that Cuba, which had the stronger links with the United States, apparently suffered less. The continuing growth of exports can be explained by the European markets' ability to absorb the region's exports even beyond the reductions created by the partial closing of the U.S. market. Cuban exports to the United States fell by 13 percent between 1856–60 and 1861–65, and Puerto Rico's dropped by 23 percent. The two colonies together experienced a drop of 14 percent. Meanwhile, the region's exports to Great Britain increased by 43 percent during the same period. This trend was notably sharper in Puerto Rico, where exports to Great Britain nearly doubled from a yearly average of $996,121 in 1856–60 to $1,880,406 in 1861–65.[63]

The U.S. share of Puerto Rican exports fell markedly during this period, from 49 percent during the last five years of the antebellum era to 34 percent during the war. In 1864 it reached its ebb when the United States received less than a quarter of Puerto Rico's exports. Conversely, the shares of Puerto Rican exports destined for European markets increased markedly, from 7 to 10 percent for Spain, from 20 to 33 percent for Great Britain, and from 2 to 4 percent for France. During 1861, 1863, and 1864 Great Britain actually surpassed the United States, becoming Puerto Rico's principal trading partner.[64] Throughout the period Puerto Rico exhibited a greater ability to shift its export output toward Europe, partially because it had begun to do so before the Civil War trend and because it enjoyed stronger links with Old World markets based on the coffee trade.

Sugar and Coffee

During the Civil War years, sugar exports from Cuba and Puerto Rico continued to increase, albeit at a slower rate. During the conflict the two colonies together exported 15 percent more sugar than during 1856–60, representing a jump of 1.5 million quintals. Puerto Rico's export output rose from an average of 1,032,963 quintals to 1,167,826 quintals, while Cuba's increased from 9,596,536 quintals to 11,053,807 quintals.[65] The destinations of the Spanish Caribbean's sugar changed significantly as well. During the war the amount of Cuban sugar going to the United States increased by less than 2 percent, while Puerto Rico's sugar exports to the northern republic declined by 18 percent.[66] While the United States had received 51 percent of Cuba's and 63 percent of Puerto Rico's sugar exports before the war, it only received 45 percent of each island's sugar output in 1861–65. The low point was

1864, when the United States received only 42 percent and 23 percent of Cuban and Puerto Rican sugar exports respectively.[67]

European markets readily absorbed the Spanish Caribbean's output. The volume of sugar exported to Great Britain from Cuba and Puerto Rico rose from 8,581,387 quintals before the war to 15,301,760 quintals during the war, a 78-percent increase. Of the 15,301,760 sugar quintals that left the region for Great Britain during the war years, 84 percent (12,905,485 quintals) originated in Cuba, the remaining 16 percent in Puerto Rico. Sugar exports to France and Spain also expanded during this period in both absolute numbers and percentage shares. Yearly sugar exports to these countries from Cuba and Puerto Rico increased sharply, from an average of 528,109 quintals annually before the war to 1,471,689 quintals during the war. The output absorbed by Spain increased more modestly, from 756,595 to 812,786 quintals. In percentage shares, France went from receiving 5 percent and 3 percent of Cuba's and Puerto Rico's sugar exports respectively to receiving 13 percent and 4 percent.[68] Europe's markets therefore became wide open for the Spanish Caribbean's sugar output not absorbed by the United States during the war.

The Civil War also accentuated prewar trends in coffee production: Cuba's production continued to decline, and Puerto Rico's expanded. By 1862 coffee represented only 2.5 percent of Cuba's agricultural production. There is no record of coffee's being exported from Cuba that year or in 1864, 1865, or 1866. While Cuba exported a yearly average of 91,224 quintals of coffee in 1856–60, an average of only 42,887 quintals was shipped out between 1861 and 1865. Cuban coffee shipments to the United States were insignificant. A total of 214 Cuban coffee estates ceased operations between 1861 and 1862, although this was not necessarily attributable to the Civil War. Meanwhile, in Puerto Rico coffee exports jumped from a yearly average of 120,220 quintals in 1856–60 to a yearly average of 158,020 quintals in 1861–65, an increase of 31 percent. Spain absorbed close to two-thirds of this difference, and its share of the island's coffee exports shot up from less than a quarter to slightly above a third. The shares of Puerto Rican coffee destined for Great Britain, Germany, and France all declined during the Civil War years; all three countries combined had received 47 percent of the island's coffee exports from 1856 to 1860 but absorbed only 32 percent during 1862–65. Puerto Rican coffee exports to the United

States remained low during the first three years of the Civil War but rose moderately in 1864 and 1865. The opening of the U.S. market to duty-free coffee from the Spanish Caribbean in the mid-1870s further stimulated the island's economic reorientation away from sugar and toward coffee.[69]

Cotton

The Civil War in the United States dramatically reduced the South's cotton output. From a bumper crop of close to 4,491,000 bales in 1861, production plummeted 64 percent to 1,597,000 bales in 1862. It dropped a further 72 percent to 449,000 bales in 1863, and then another 33 percent to a mere 299,000 bales in 1864. This abrupt collapse in the supply of southern cotton coupled with the enormous difficulty involved in shipping the available supply inflated the fiber's price to nearly ten times its prewar level, stimulating cotton production in Brazil, the Caribbean, and other parts of the world.[70]

Although attempts had been made in the Hispanic Caribbean to develop cotton cultivation for some time, serious efforts in this direction came only during the war. One of the motivating factors behind the Spanish annexation of the Dominican Republic, in fact, had been the desire to develop cotton cultivation there to reduce Spain's dependence on the United States. Efforts were also made to stimulate cotton production in Cuba during the late 1850s. A study on this subject by Spain's Ministry of State in 1858 underscored the "political and economic advantages that Spain would receive from the cultivation of cotton in the island of Cuba." A royal decree later confirmed previous decrees exempting cotton growers from all tariffs related to the importation of machinery and seeds and the fiber's exportation. Another decree provided further exemptions and established cash prizes for successful cotton estates. Cotton planters in Cuba enjoyed the additional incentive of receiving ten *emancipados* for every thirty-three acres planted in cotton.[71]

Other circumstances besides government incentives favored the development of cotton cultivation in Puerto Rico, Cuba, and the former Dominican Republic. Several émigrés found their way into Cuba during the Civil War, bringing with them capital and the knowledge of cotton cultivation and processing. The Cotton Association of Manchester also distributed free seeds to prospective cotton growers in Puerto Rico. Moreover, soils and climatic conditions in the region proved ideal for cotton cultivation. Finally, in both long-time colonies planters proved willing to take up the cotton challenge, particularly in the south and west of Puerto Rico and in Cienfuegos, Cuba. Among those undertaking cotton cultivation during the Civil War was the Agricultural Association of Plaja, Cortada, and Fornier of Ponce, which in 1864 imported two cotton gins and three cotton presses from New York and cultivated three hundred acres in cotton in the Real and Magueyes sectors of Ponce. The following year Plaja, Cortada, and Fornier received a 1,500-peso prize for successfully running a five-hundred-acre cotton plantation, producing five hundred quintals and employing seventy to eighty workers. Also in Ponce, Luis Toro and Company ventured into cotton cultivation: in 1864 Toro imported 1,280 pounds of cotton seeds. Twenty other cotton growers operated in the municipality that year, producing a total of 725 quintals. Meanwhile in the former Dominican Republic, Francisco de Olazarra cultivated thirty-three acres of cotton on an experimental basis.[72]

The growing interest in Caribbean cotton cultivation soon translated into rising export figures. In Puerto Rico, cotton exports soared from a yearly average of 1,638 quintals in 1859–63 to 13,940 quintals in 1864–66, over an eightfold increase. In mid-1863 the British consul at San Juan estimated that a hundred-thousand-quintal harvest was feasible if additional capital could be found. In its percentage share among Puerto Rican exports, cotton also grew considerably from an insignificant 0.30 percent in 1859–63 to 2.5 percent in 1864–66, edging out tobacco as the island's third largest export staple, behind sugar and coffee. As was the case with coffee, Spain absorbed the bulk of the increase in cotton exports: 42 percent of Puerto Rico's cotton exports between 1861 and 1865 reached Spain. Great Britain and the United States followed with 30 and 9 percent respectively. In 1864 the United States figured prominently as a recipient of the island's cotton, absorbing 2,355 of the 8,794 quintals exported. Cuba embraced cotton cultivation during the Civil War, but proportionately to a lesser extent, barely reviving a crop that had not been an export item since 1857. Official statistics reveal that in 1862, 136,500 pesos' worth of cotton was cultivated in Cuba.[73]

The region's cotton boom was short-lived. As soon as peace was reestablished in the United States and cotton cultivation was renewed there, production began to drop. On November 28, 1865, the U.S. consul at San Juan reported that "the price [of cotton] did not range so high as expected & the news from the United States and England dont promise any advance; many planters are now abandoning that cultivation and it is fully ascertained that the crop next year will fall off to at least one half." By 1866 the Ponce cotton growers dropped their projects, and the amount of cotton exported (13,014 quintals) was only two-thirds of the 1865 total. Output continued to drop, reaching a little over 10,000 quintals in 1867 and 8,413 quintals in 1868. Production continued to dwindle until cotton completely disappeared as an export item in the 1870s.[74]

Navigation

The Federal blockade, northern and Confederate privateers, and the rearrangement of trade priorities in the United States during the Civil War had strong repercussions on the patterns of shipping and navigation in Spanish Caribbean ports. Because the U.S. merchant marine shrank during the war, it lost its earlier hold over the region. Confederate corsairs sank an estimated total of five thousand Union vessels. The *Alabama* alone destroyed or captured sixty vessels. Many ship owners transferred their ships' registrations to Great Britain and other nations for safety, further decimating the Union's merchant fleet.[75]

During the Civil War the overall volume of vessels in Puerto Rican ports fell by 25 to 30 percent, reflecting disruptions in the trade between Puerto Rico and the United States. A yearly average of 440 vessels and 74,324 tons of U.S. shipping had linked Puerto Rico and North America in 1859–60, but this fell to 238 vessels and 38,237 tons in 1861–65. The lowest ebb came in 1864, when only 162 U.S. vessels cleared or arrived in Puerto Rican ports. The share of U.S. shipping in Puerto Rico also fell, from 39 percent in 1859–60 to 24 percent in 1861–64.[76] On March 7, 1863, the U.S. consul at Ponce complained that "only ten American Merchant Vessels have arrived at this Port up to date." Only thirty-nine more U.S. vessels would arrive during the balance of the year. This sum of forty-nine was considerably lower than the totals for 1860, 1861, and 1862 (ninety-four, seventy-eight, and sixty-five vessels). Although all the island's ports endured reductions in U.S. shipping, Ponce and Arroyo, two sugar-exporting ports on the south coast, were hit the hardest. The U.S. consul reported in late 1865 that arrivals of U.S. vessels in San Juan had dropped by more than half.[77]

Spanish vessels in part filled the vacuum left by the retrenchment of U.S. shipping. In 1863 and 1864 a yearly average of 488 Spanish vessels (or 42,533 tons) reached Puerto Rican ports. The share of Spanish vessels rose from 32 percent in 1860 to 37 percent in 1861 and to 46 percent in 1864. The number of British ships calling in Puerto Rico also increased, from 269 in 1859–60 to 287 in 1861–64. Eighteen sixty-three marked the high point of British maritime presence in Puerto Rico, with a total of 332 vessels reaching the island. That year Great Britain dominated over a third of the island's shipping, surpassing both Spain and the United States in tonnage.[78]

Similar changes took place in Cuba, where shipping goods under the U.S. flag became quite problematic. In August 1861 an agent in Havana informed sugar broker Moses Taylor that "no one is interested in loading on United States ships or any other ship heading to the United States." According to navigation information appearing in a January 1863 issue of the Havana *Mercantile Weekly*, a total of 111 sailing vessels lay at anchor in Havana: 61 came from Spain, 36 from the United States, 10 from Britain, 2 from France, 1 from the Confederacy, and 1 from Sardinia. There were also 10 steamers: 4 from Britain, 3 from Spain, 2 from the Confederacy, and 1 from the United States. According to figures produced by Herminio Portell Vilá, the number of U.S. vessels arriving in Havana dropped from 312 during the second trimester of 1861 to 115 during the following trimester, a 63-percent decrease. Four years later only 91 United States vessels called in Havana.[79]

In the aftermath of the Civil War the United States regained and increased its commercial eminence in Cuba and Puerto Rico. In 1868, for example, the United States dominated both imports to and exports from Puerto Rico. By 1877, 82 percent of Cuba's export output went to the United States.[80] During Reconstruction the United States also displaced the European markets to become the Second Dominican Republic's major market, absorbing 32 percent of all Dominican exports in 1877.[81] The economic role of the United States in Cuba and Puerto Rico during this period, however, continued to be essentially limited to import-export trade.[82]

The period of the U.S. Civil War thus represented a watershed affecting not only the nation being torn by it but also the entire circum-Caribbean region. The decimated Union was forced to retrench its political and commercial influence in the Caribbean while it watched a strengthened European coalition violate the Monroe Doctrine and reassume commercial preeminence in the region. Nowhere was this more obvious than in the Dominican Republic and Mexico, where European or European-backed governments were put in place. The North's victory during the fratricidal conflagration produced a new set of circumstances that reverberated throughout the Hispanic Caribbean. First, Europe's military presence in Mexico and the Dominican Republic disappeared. Second, the United States regained the commercial supremacy that it had momentarily lost in Cuba and Puerto Rico and established itself as the Dominican Republic's first trading partner. Third, the Union victory imposed new limits on the political alternatives in the region; the only plausible form of annexationism was now that looking toward the United States. Finally, slavery, now the target of U.S. policy, became an increasingly intolerable institution.

Six Political Change

More than a century ago Carlos de Sedano wrote a political history of Cuba that he periodized before and after January 1, 1863.[1] His recourse to the emancipation of slaves in the United States as a watershed indicates his understanding of the profound consequences that events in North America had for political developments in the island. The Civil War and its outcome also shaped to a considerable extent the course of political events in the Dominican Republic. Indeed, the war and Lincoln's military measure declaring slavery abolished had dramatic reverberations that not only sealed the fate of human bondage in the region but also transformed the political options for the Hispanic Caribbean.

Cuba and Puerto Rico

Like their superiors in the Peninsula, Spanish colonial administrators in the Spanish Caribbean welcomed the political crisis and civil war in the United States. Before the onset of hostilities, the U.S. consul at San Juan complained that in Puerto Rico only the "disunion side" of the question was given. On November 6, 1861, Confederate agent Charles Helm informed his superiors that local authorities in Cuba openly sympathized with the South, and two days later he reported that Captain-General Francisco Serrano had confided to him his grief at not being able to "recognize as 'de jure' the Southern nation that exists 'de facto.'" Helm added that Serrano would gladly meet with him but only unofficially. A year later, when Serrano left office, he told

Helm: "My heart and soul are with your struggle for independence." This paradoxical statement coming from a colonial administrator was followed by a reassurance that Serrano's successor, Domingo Dulce, would have the same views.[2] Indeed, during Dulce's incumbency, Spain's relations with the Confederate States of America improved, while frictions with the Union increased. Serrano, Dulce, and their counterparts in Puerto Rico, Rafael Echagüe and Félix María de Messina, were overtly friendly and helpful to the southern war effort. They opened ports in Cuba and Puerto Rico to blockade-runners and southern commerce raiders, made special concessions to Confederate ship captains, and bent or ignored regulations to accommodate the needs of Confederate shipping and trade.[3]

To assert that the general population in Cuba sided with either the Confederacy or the Union is certainly a distorting oversimplification. Deep divisions existed along class lines, and postures often changed as the war unfolded. Although some Cubans supported each side throughout the conflict, toward the beginning of the war—when the South appeared to be able to assert its independence—most white Cubans apparently leaned toward the Confederacy. Early in the war, southern envoys James M. Mason and John Slidell got a warm reception from the people of Havana while en route to Europe. Their ship's captain, Commander Thomas J. Lockwood, received a Confederate flag from a delegation of Cuban women. Another crowd of cheering Cubans assembled a year later to greet the CSS *Florida*. At one point Helm wrote his superiors in Richmond that "a large majority" of the population in Havana "zealously advocate[d]" the Confederate cause, adding that support extended throughout the island.[4]

U.S. consuls in Puerto Rico relayed similar reports. When Consul Jasper Smith resigned in August 1862, he recommended his interim successor on the grounds that "unlike most persons here his sympathies are with [our] Government." Union consul John J. Hyde reported six months later that in Puerto Rico "the sympathy of the people is almost universally with the enemies of our country." In March 1863 he reiterated this assessment and requested the deployment of "a formidable squadron."[5]

Different signals began to appear in Cuba in the fall of 1862 after the Confederate failure at Antietam. In October 1862 Consul Robert W. Shufeldt reported that "the Cubans even the slaveholders can scarcely refrain from manifesting their sympathy for a govt and a people fighting [*illegible*] for the nationality of America." Toward the end of the war *El Siglo*, the organ of the Cuban reform movement, openly took a pro-Union editorial stand. The November 4, 1863, issue stated that a southern victory—a highly unlikely outcome at that point—would be disastrous because it would close the market for Cuban sugar. *El Siglo*'s editor, the count of Pozos Dulces, wrote a year later that the war would soon end and with it would expire the artificially sustained agricultural production of the South. One day after the capitulation at Appomattox, *El Siglo*'s editor expressed pride in his newspaper's vision and rejoiced at the Union victory.[6]

Raúl Cepero Bonilla and other historians after him have used Pozos Dulces's editorials to conclude that Cubans favored the Union because they desired to see the South's economy, namely the sugar sector, destroyed. Strong evidence suggests, however, that many Cubans sided with the Confederacy. Furthermore, the assertion that Cuban planters saw a northern victory as a means to destroy southern competition has very little substance. The South's sugar industry was destroyed as early as 1862, and victory on either side could not alter that outcome. A southern victory, moreover, would have meant the separation of the Union into two different nations: a South capable of producing its own sugar and a North in need of importing all of its sugar. In such a scenario, the Cuban planter class would have benefited by being placed on at least equal footing with the seceded South as supplier to the United States.

What did happen during the Civil War was that a considerable segment of the Creole elite, in conjunction with colonial administrators, finally realized that slavery was doomed in the hemisphere and that siding with the losing proslavery faction could hurt Cuba in the long run. Thus, toward the end of the Civil War an unholy alliance of reformists, separatists, planters, professionals, abolitionists, and slave owners rallied around the Union cause. They coalesced for different reasons: for sugar producers the northern United States was their market; for the island's few abolitionists the North seemed a natural ally in the struggle against slavery; Cuban separatists, most of them republican and abolitionist, sought the Union's support for their cause; and in an ironic reversal of the Africanization scare, still other Cubans sought links with the North as a guarantee against the disturbing influences of an "Africanized" seceded South. "It is not overlooked here," wrote a contemporary Cuban observer, "that the doctrine of State Rights in accordance with which such a Confederacy must be framed, would involve the constant peril of disunion and anarchy, and in such an event what would be the ultimate fate of Cuba but that of St. Domingo and Jamaica?" Finally, slaves and free blacks in Cuba desired a northern victory for obvious reasons. While the war unfolded, slave work gangs near Havana labored to the tune of "Forward, Lincoln Forward! / You are our Hope!"[7]

Spanish Colonialism Relaxed: Cuba, 1859–1866

President Buchanan's failed attempt to purchase Cuba in 1859, the political crisis culminating in civil war, the end of British abolitionist pressures, and the ascent to power of a liberal regime in Spain produced a favorable context for the liberalizing of colonial administration in the Spanish Caribbean. For the Spanish government, the dual specters of foreign aggression and slave revolts had in previous decades made necessary the establishment of highly repressive, militarized colonial governments with little room for civil liberties. Conditions in the early 1860s differed markedly now that North Americans were fighting each other, Britain no longer was putting pressure on Spain concerning the slavery issue, and a white majority had been reestablished in the Cuban population. Under such circumstances Spain relaxed colonial domination in Cuba, and repression abated.

Responding to these changes, captains-general Serrano and Dulce ruled Cuba between November 1859 and May 1866 through *política de atracción,* namely attempts to garner Creole support for the Spanish colonial regime by granting political and civil rights. Both Serrano and Dulce made a strong case for ending the slave trade, a measure alienating those involved in slave trading but welcomed by most Cubans, even those who owned slaves. They also granted Creoles certain civil liberties and relaxed restrictions on the press. As a result, new newspapers sprang up in the island, most notably *El Siglo* and *La Aurora*. Serrano and Dulce also permitted, even encouraged, Creole political participation. Interestingly, the reformist circle that would eventually become the Reformist party got its start in the halls of the captain-general's palace, absorbing into its leadership some of the most prominent conspirators of the late 1840s and early 1850s: the count of Pozos Dulces, José Antonio Echeverría, Miguel Aldama, and José Luis Alfonso.[8]

Captains-general Serrano and Dulce also cultivated strong personal and familial links with the reformist aristocracy. Married to a wealthy Cuban from Trinidad, Serrano earned the respect and admiration of the Creole elite for his policies, as attested by the warm farewell he received on December 14, 1862. His successor, Dulce, built on Serrano's legacy, and upon Dulce's return to Spain in May 1866, the Creole elite awarded him a diamond-studded cross of Charles III in gratitude for his having led Cuba "through a period of grave difficulties, without the country suffering any shifts in its prosperous and tranquil march." The count of San Esteban de Cañogo asserted on that occasion that during the four years of Dulce's government the population "did not lament any arbitrary act or shed any tears." On the eve of Dulce's departure, four bands played in Havana's main square until one o'clock in the morning. In a dramatic speech that closed the ceremonies, a moved Dulce exclaimed: "Cubans and inhabitants of the Island of Cuba! I say farewell with the fondest memories. Wherever fortune leads me, you will have in Domingo Dulce a fellow Cuban." Not all in Cuba shared warm feelings about the captains-general. Many Peninsular merchants and bureaucrats, in fact, were happy to see Serrano and Dulce depart. During his tenure, Dulce had alienated the conservatives when he banished their mouthpiece, Julián Zulueta, a Peninsular with close ties to slave trading, and when he ousted a number of pro-Spanish extremist officials also linked to the slave trade.[9]

Serrano and Dulce's counterparts in Puerto Rico rejected the methods of *política de atracción*. Captains-general Rafael Echagüe, Félix María de Messina, and José María Marchesi actively repressed Puerto Rico's liberal and reformist element. Echagüe (1860–62) persecuted some of the most vocal of the island's reformists and abolitionists, among them Román Baldorioty de Castro and José Julián Acosta, two natural science professors described by him as "pro-independence" with "*Yankee* ideas."[10] While Cuba's top officials engaged in political discussion even in their mansions, Echagüe prohibited informal public discussions. Messina (1863–65) followed a similar course, leading the Puerto Rican historian Lidio Cruz Monclova to characterize his term in office as "abusive and hurtful." Messina was particularly hard on the press, banning the publication of articles dealing with slavery and other taboo subjects.[11] During his tenure he banished the nationalist abolitionists Ramón Emeterio Betances and Luis Padial Vizcarrondo. He also removed Segundo Ruiz Belvis from his government post in the municipality of Mayagüez for his abolitionist ideas. Repression and wholesale banishments continued during the incumbency of Marchesi (1865–67). In the aftermath of the military mutiny of June 7, 1867, Marchesi expelled some of the island's most vocal reformists.[12]

Several factors help explain the contrasts between the colonial administrations of Cuba and Puerto Rico during the 1860s. First, Puerto Rico's reformists had much less influence than their Cuban counterparts because they were predominantly urban professionals with less economic power than the propertied Cubans advocating reform.[13] Second, the position of the Puerto Rican reformists regarding the issue of slavery was much more radical than that of the Cubans. Spanish authorities found this to be unacceptable not only for what it meant for Puerto Rico but also for the repercussions that abolitionist pressures might have for slave-based Cuba. Finally, unlike Serrano and Dulce, colonial administrators in Puerto Rico did not have personal and familial ties with the Creoles.

The reformist tendency grew stronger during the U.S. Civil War and the era of the *política de atracción*. The retrenchment of U.S. expansionism thus allowed a greater degree of colonial openness that included the toleration of reformist activities, publications, and organizations. Moreover, the United States's wartime retrenchment made difficult the pursuit of radical alternatives such as separatism and annexationism, alternatives that had traditionally depended on U.S. assistance or approval. Like their colonial rulers, Cuban reformists were essentially social conservatives seeking to avoid any radical change in order to guarantee social stability for Cuba through moderate liberalization of the colonial regime. They wanted this process to occur gradually, in an orderly manner, and from the top down. The editors of reformist *El Siglo* wrote emphatically about "evolution as a preventive to revolution," coined the slogan "All for evolution, nothing for revolution," and disapproved of "everything that smells of violence or disorder, everything that can compromise the great interests of society."[14] The general objectives of the Cuban reformists were strikingly attuned to the views of Spanish captains-general Serrano and Dulce.[15] Seldom in the island's history had the rulers and the ruled reached such a harmonious coexistence. The reformist program advocated parity of rights with Spain, representation in the Spanish Cortes, freedom of the press, the end of slave importations, white immigration, the study of the "social question" (the euphemism for slavery), and the application of more liberal municipal laws like those in Spain. Serrano, Dulce, and other Spanish liberals repeatedly expressed their support for such measures.[16]

Cuba's reformists also sought to strengthen the island's political links with Spain on the basis of equality through the assimilationist route, as opposed to the separatist-annexationist solution of the 1850s or the autonomist views now embraced by José Antonio Saco. An editorial in *El Siglo* on March 24, 1865, stated that "far from attacking that [Spanish] nationality [it] aspires to become part of it with all of its rights and benefits."[17] One of the leading reformists of the mid-1860s, Cristóbal F. Madan, whose staunch annexationism in the late 1840s and early 1850s had earned him the nickname Semi Yankee, wrote an elegy to Cuban annexationism in 1864:

> Those days are over in which some of us, moved by an excessively localized patriotism or by the fear of disastrous social experiments in the Antilles, dreamed of an order of things in connection with our powerful northern neighbor. . . . Today, regardless of what reforms are sought, all of us recognize that these have to be found in cooperation with the established metropolitan government and through the exclusive route of persuasion based on a detailed consideration of long-range interests and on the principles of a judicious, enlightened, and skillfull policy.[18]

In just a few years Madan, the count of Pozos Dulces, Miguel Aldama, José Antonio Echeverría, José Luis Alfonso, and other former annexationists shifted radically from the pro–North American, anti-European extreme to the pro-European, anti–North American extreme. While in 1854 Madan had scorned the "European system" as "disconcerted, cruel, demoralizing, revolutionary, and backward," in 1864 he asserted: "We count . . . on the moral and material aid of Europe, and particularly that of England. . . . [We] are disturbed by the terrible events taking place in the United States [namely abolition] which clearly mark the beginning of a new era for them as well as for us.[19]

In their dramatic political shifts, the Cuban annexationists-turned-reformists were responding to major geopolitical transformations in the Hispanic Caribbean. As a result of the Civil War, U.S. political and economic influence diminished enormously. Not only did the annexationist alternative lose viability, but the motivations for seeking annexation also faded as Spanish officials relaxed their colonial grip on Cuba. Annexationism was declared officially dead by Cuba's former captain-general, Serrano, when on May 10, 1867, he asserted that there was no annexationist party in Cuba.[20] Within a year events would prove that the annexationists were temporarily comatose rather than defunct.

The Civil War also had an enormous impact on the status of slavery in the Spanish Caribbean. The abolition of slavery in the United States during the conflict and the emancipation of slaves in the Dutch Caribbean in 1863 left Cuba, Puerto Rico, and Brazil as the last slaveholding countries of the hemisphere. During the antebellum period slaveholding interests in the United States had blocked any attempt by their government to fight slavery and even the slave trade in the region. During and after the Civil War, however, the United States no longer needed to keep compromising with the South to avoid disunion. The North had raised the banner of abolition during the war and did not put it down once the conflict ended.

During the hostilities the United States agreed to aid Great Britain in searching and seizing slavers and in setting up a British-U.S. Mixed Commission to help in this effort. Since U.S. citizens had carried on most slave trading in the antebellum period under the protection of the U.S. flag (90 percent, by one estimate), one effect of the war was the dramatic drop in slave importations in Cuba. As Moreno Fraginals put it, "The first shots on Fort Sumter . . . were the epitaph of the slave trade." An average of 17,862 slaves had arrived in Cuba yearly between 1858 and 1861; this flow dropped 73 percent in 1862–65, when yearly imports averaged only 4,830. After 1867 slave importations practically disappeared.[21]

Panic over the imminent abolition of slavery in the Spanish Caribbean following Lincoln's Emancipation Proclamation coupled with the saturation of the market by record numbers of slave imports between 1858 and 1861 slashed slave prices. In Cuba, the price of a slave, which had reached and surpassed one thousand dollars during the

1850s, plummeted to between six and seven hundred dollars. A parallel trend occurred in Puerto Rico, as reported by a member of the foreign consular corps: "Since the emancipation of the negroes in the United States of America, slaves have greatly lost in value here, and more so yet since the [*illegible*] termination of the American War."[22] This downward trend in slave prices also indicated the realization by planters that slavery was now a doomed institution and slaves no longer represented a safe investment.

Other internal factors favored the cessation of the slave trade in the region. Alternative sources of labor and mechanisms of labor coercion became widely available during the relatively tranquil period of the late 1850s and early 1860s. White immigrants, indentured Chinese workers, and Yucatecan Indians arrived in Cuba in considerable numbers during this period.[23] In Puerto Rico too, the proportion of the slave population continued to drop as the numbers of the free and semifree populations shot up. *Jornaleros*, coerced dependent peons, became one of the primary sources of labor. By the mid-1860s over seventy-five thousand laborers toiled under this label.

Contemporary census figures confirm these demographic shifts. The Cuban censuses of 1859 and 1861 and the Puerto Rican census of 1860 demonstrated for the first time since early colonial times that the white population in both colonies constituted a majority. In Cuba between 1855 and 1859, the nonwhite-to-white ratio was reversed from 1:0.97 to 1:1.09. In Puerto Rico it went from 1:0.93 to 1:1.06. In both islands the numbers and proportions of slaves continued to drop, partly because of manumissions and *coartaciones*, partly because of the slave population's inability to reproduce itself, and partly because the nonslave populations continued to grow.[24] Between 1841 and 1860 the Cuban slave population fell from 436,495 to 370,553 despite massive importations in the 1850s, while in Puerto Rico the number of slaves dropped from 51,265 in 1846 to 41,736 in 1860. In proportional terms, the slave populations fell from 43 to 28 percent in Cuba, and from 12 to 7 percent in Puerto Rico. These demographic shifts had deep political implications, highlighted in a letter addressed to Queen Isabella II by a group of Cubans seeking reforms in mid-1865: "We must say this: the time in which Cuba and Puerto Rico trembled before the thought of becoming African is over."[25]

Throughout the Spanish empire the Union victory in the U.S. Civil

War sounded a grave warning that the days of slavery were running short. On May 6, 1865, Antonio María Fabié stated on the floor of the Spanish Cortes that "the war in the United States is finished, and being finished, slavery in the whole American continent can be taken as finished." Fabié asked rhetorically: "Is it possible to keep the Spanish provinces . . . while keeping this institution in the dominions?" He responded bluntly: "I don't think so." Meanwhile, Isabella II commissioned Eusebio de Salazar y Mazarredo "to examine and study . . . the matter of slavery in those States and the diverse tendencies on the subject in the North and in the South, as well as the influence that these may have on Cuba."[26] Also in the mid-1860s abolitionist societies and antislavery newspapers sprang up in Spain. One of the first victories of the Spanish abolitionists was the passing of a new law for the suppression of the slave trade on July 9, 1866. This legislation prescribed severe punishments, including death in some instances, for those caught introducing slaves into the Spanish colonies.

The next target of the abolitionists was slavery itself. Mounting external pressures and the demands of the Cuban insurrection culminated with the passing of the Moret Law on July 4, 1870, which provided for the liberation of all slaves born after September 1868, all slaves sixty years of age or older, all *emancipados* and state-owned slaves, and all those slaves fighting on the Spanish side in the ongoing Cuban Ten Years' War. Three weeks before presenting his bill in the Spanish Cortes, Segismundo Moret wrote to the captain-general of Cuba. His letter sheds much light on the geopolitical circumstances surrounding the passage of the partial abolition law. "Not another day must pass," said Moret, "without [our] doing something about this. France and England will not help us while we are slaveholders, and this one word [*slavery*] gives North America the right to hold a suspended threat over our heads." Despite its moderate provisions, the Moret Law faced strong opposition in the Spanish Caribbean, particularly in Cuba, where the conservative pro-Spanish extremists had virtually assumed control over the insular government. In fact, two years elapsed before the law was finally published in the Cuban press. Abolitionists in the United States and in the Caribbean were not satisfied with the law either. Hamilton Fish characterized it as falling far short of what his government had expected, while Ramón Emeterio Betances contemptuously referred to it as "the emancipation of death."[27]

These winds of change had other implications for the Spanish Caribbean, where only a few years earlier it had been impossible to write about the cessation of the slave trade, let alone about outright abolition. Cuba's reformist leadership, composed in great measure of slave owners, was forced to consider a directed, gradual, and compensated emancipation of the island's slaves. The Civil War made them accept the fact that the solution of the "social question" could not be postponed any further and that it was to their advantage for the solution to come from the top. Significantly, however, most Cuban reformists were still not abolitionists at this point. They looked at slavery primarily as a property issue but also realized that they could not alienate the United States, the principal market for their sugar.

Thus, while *El Siglo* was filled with advertisements for buying, selling, and renting slaves, its editors began to discuss abolition, albeit reluctantly, toward the end of the Civil War. On August 23, 1864, the count of Pozos Dulces criticized the way in which slaves were emancipated in the United States and prescribed that abolition "should be everywhere the gradual outcome of economic and social progress."[28] Following Lincoln's assassination, *El Siglo* published numerous obituaries and editorial elegies in praise of the fallen leader. These writings conspicuously omitted the emancipation measure among Lincoln's achievements.

On October 11, 1865, an *El Siglo* editorial commented that slavery had been unproductive in the United States. Another reformist, Cristóbal F. Madan, recognized the need "to end slavery gradually in the island, without affecting social sanity, without disturbing industry and without emancipating precipitously those who are neither ready nor prepared for liberty." Another editorial advocated dealing with the "social question," while reiterating concerns about the delicate nature of the institution: "We are heirs to a burdensome legacy, but a legacy that sustains us, we cannot renounce it all of a sudden, for this would lead to a profound social perturbation, cold-blooded suicide." Still another reformist wrote in mid-1865 that the island's destruction should no longer be feared as a consequence of abolition "if we are permitted to apply safeguarding measures."[29]

Following the Union victory in the U.S. Civil War, the links between separatist-abolitionist Cuban exiles and northern abolitionists became more firmly cemented. According to Gerald Eugene Poyo, developments in the Civil War provided "an important psychological breakthrough that opened the door for a political nationalism." In mid-1865 the chief of the Spanish legation in Washington wrote to Dulce, reporting the formation of an alliance between revolutionary Cubans in exile and U.S. abolitionists. Most certainly he was referring to the Republican Society of Cuba and Puerto Rico, organized that year in New York City. The society's organ, *La Voz de América*, openly embraced abolitionism and the inclusion of Cubans of all races in the struggle for national liberation. The Republican Society was also highly critical of Cuban reformists and their strategy of seeking concessions within the Spanish empire. An 1866 propaganda leaflet by the society dubbed reformists "vile, ungrateful, traitors; revolutionaries when they had no other choice turned into reptiles who today are slapped in the face by their despot." Publications of the Republican Society accused the reformist party of being a club for rich landholders and slave owners brought together by the fear of the loss of their property. One of the basic differences separating the Republican Society from the reformists was that its members advocated armed struggle against Spain. The authors concluded one of their leaflets with the following harangue: "Cubans, whites, blacks, mulattoes, those of you who are real men, take up arms, burn, destroy, kill, make things happen; do not fear: the hour of struggle, sacrifice, and pride has come." Another group of abolitionist-separatist exiles emerging in the aftermath of the Civil War was the Sociedad Democrática de Amigos de América. One of its founders, Juan Manuel Macías, denounced the raising of the specter of Haiti as a conservative antiabolitionist ploy and called Cubans and Puerto Ricans to arms. This was also a period of revolutionary ferment in certain places in Puerto Rico, where in 1865 the island's first underground separatist junta emerged. A year later the U.S. consul at San Juan relayed information to Secretary of State Seward about a "considerable" movement for independence seeking annexation to the United States without slavery.[30]

Agricultural Reform in Cuba

Cuban reformists' new willingness to consider abolition and their sympathies for the Union during the latter part of the Civil War were intimately linked to the agricultural agenda of the Cuban planter class. This agenda rested on two pillars: the promotion of white labor immigration and the breakdown of the sugar industry into internal and international divisions of labor. These divisions of labor were conceived so that small, independent white farmers would grow the sugarcane, specialized *centrales* operators would manufacture the sugar up to an unrefined state, and U.S. refiners would turn the Cuban raw material into table sugar. An extreme version of this division of labor suggested that Cubans drop manufacturing altogether and ship sugarcane stalks to be processed in the United States. All of these propositions dovetailed neatly: the internal division of labor would attract white immigrants, a larger nonslave population would make feasible the eventual abolition of slavery, and the international division of labor and the abolition of slavery would strengthen the island's commercial links with the United States.

El Siglo, the best source on the reformists' agricultural agenda, criticized the existing agrarian system, in which the same units conducted both the agricultural and industrial phases of production. "This agriculture cannot continue to prevail," exclaimed *El Siglo*'s editor, "because it is composed of elements and conditions leading to the systematic devastation of the country's surface." *El Siglo* repeatedly argued that the present system repelled white laborers and promoted "the continuation of labor by extraneous races." The editors of *El Siglo* prescribed: "Small-scale agriculture, small landholdings, these are the true pillars upon which the edifice of our agricultural future shall rest." Another editorial asserted: "The ideal to which we aspire is to see Cuba covered with cane fields, not forming a horizon, boundless and aggravating the present system, but conveniently scattered and alternated . . . within the sphere of the small rural landholding, which is the richest base for wealth and population growth." On January 16, 1867, *El Siglo* again called for the division of labor in sugar production, arguing that "the *agricultural ingenios*, relieved from the burden of manufacturing, will dispose of more time to invest in their particular phase, and thus improve cultivation."[31]

Clearly, one of the main goals behind the proposed system was to promote white immigration to the island. The traditional system, asserted the editors of *El Siglo*, had driven white laborers away. The same piece announced that the agro-industrial *ingenios* represented, "because of their constitution and magnitude, the death of the workers' aspirations." A system based on a division of labor, continued the editorialist, "would produce a flow of immigration similar to that which yearly increases the population of the United States." This and similar articles also stressed that productivity would increase under the *central-colono* system. Another advantage often pointed out was the political and social stability that the white *colono* population could provide.[32]

An extreme version of the division of labor strategy was also explored. During the Civil War, blockade-runners had demonstrated that it was feasible to transport freshly cut cane stalks to U.S. ports before they fermented or lost their sucrose content. Moreover, the new machines of the industrial age had proved disastrous for the Cuban planter class, which had responded to their lure by taking out burdensome loans. The technological fever evident in the works of Francisco de Arango y Parreño in the early years of the nineteenth century had already cooled by the 1860s, as evidenced in one editorial: "The net sum of productivity is higher in Cuba's [sugar] industry in the agricultural phase than in the manufacturing phase, and it is toward the former that our efforts and capital should lean." On the same topic, the editorialist later wrote: "If both countries [Cuba and the United States] would realize their own true interests, they would yield to us the exclusive production of the raw material to the point that we can ship it, and we would yield to them the exclusive task of fabrication or refining."[33] Thus, in a sense the landed elite's agricultural agenda responded to new regional realities, namely the growing rejection of slavery and the tightening of the grip of the United States on the economies and trade of the Spanish Caribbean.

Caribbean Delegates in Madrid: La Junta de Información, 1866–1867

Almost three decades had elapsed since the unseating of colonial delegates in the Spanish Cortes and the promise of rule through special legislation, when a royal decree of November 25, 1865, convoked Creole representation to examine the bases for the long-awaited "special laws." The "social question," tax reform, and political reform were the items on the agenda of the so-called Junta de Información. The junta was designed to include twenty-two Creoles and twenty-two Peninsulars. Electors satisfying high property qualifications elected delegates in Cuba and Puerto Rico, while the Spanish overseas minister designated the Iberian representatives. Puerto Rico elected six delegates: three reformists, two moderate conservatives, and one conservative. Of these, only the three reformists, José Julián Acosta, Segundo Ruiz Belvis, and Francisco Mariano Quiñones, and the conservative Manuel de Jesús Zeno actually participated in the Junta de Información.[34] Cubans elected sixteen delegates: twelve reformists, three conservatives, and one autonomist, José Antonio Saco. In all, according to the assessment of one of the Cuban delegates, the junta had fifteen reformists and five conservatives.[35] This reformist-conservative dichotomy, however, can be misleading, because within the reformist ranks one finds radical separatist-abolitionists like Ruiz Belvis and timid reformists like most of the Cuban delegates.

The sessions of the Junta de Información began in the fall of 1866, a few months after the collapse of Leopoldo O'Donnell's government in Spain. Although the new regime of Ramón Narváez was not committed to reform in the Antilles, it agreed to honor the previous government's convocation. In order to obstruct any radical changes, however, Narváez rigged the junta with conservative appointees and banned discussion of topics pertaining to "national unity, religious unity, and the monarchy." The "social question" was the most crucial issue in the junta's discussions. In a sense it had to be, because at the time of the unseating of colonial delegates in 1837, Spanish officials argued that Caribbean delegates represented an unfree constituency and therefore had no right to assume their seats. Slavery and political rights thus were intimately linked. The issue of slavery also proved to be highly divisive: the Spaniards, three Cubans, and one Puerto Rican favored its continuation; eleven Cubans were willing to consider gradual, compensated abolition; and the three Puerto Rican abolitionists sought immediate emancipation.

The Puerto Rican reformist delegates, Ruiz Belvis, Quiñones, and Acosta, introduced a project calling for the immediate emancipation of slaves with compensation for the master class.[36] The fact that these delegates underscored the peculiar conditions in Puerto Rico that made abolition there easy and nondisruptive suggests that they had no intention of extending their project to Cuba, where slavery played a far more significant role. Trying to downplay criticisms of the project's impact on agriculture, Acosta pointed out that in Puerto Rico only 10,164 slaves worked in sugarcane, 1,832 in coffee, and 1,450 in other agricultural ventures. The proposal emphasized that because of "benign laws, sweeter customs, and habits of good treatment," slaves in Puerto Rico were not vindictive and would not revolt. The project's sponsors also added that the island's slaves were not numerous and were mostly Puerto Rican, not African-born.[37]

The Puerto Rican project put the Cuban delegates on the spot. The motion, wrote delegate José Morales Lemus to Miguel Aldama, "placed us in a compromising situation." "If we remained silent," he said, "we would have exposed ourselves to criticisms that we acquiesced to instantaneous abolition, which for Cuba would be more than a mistake, a cruelty, a direct attack on civilization and nationality." Referring to the Puerto Rican project, another Cuban reformist, José Antonio Echeverría, asserted: "There is no motion more radical than this one; there is no greater cry of alarm for Cuba; I believe that we must soften it." In response to the project, the Cubans stated that under the present circumstances their island could not survive "the consequences of sudden innovations in its means of production." A contemporary observer justified the posture of the Cubans, characterizing them as "abolitionists, but moderate, practical, and reflective." Not only were many of the Cuban delegates slaveholders, but they were also under strong antiabolition pressures from their constituents. Conservative antiabolitionist reaction had begun to mount in light of Serrano's and Dulce's opposition to the slave trade, and in June 1865 conservatives expressed their concerns directly to the queen. They applauded Dulce's recall to Spain in 1866, not knowing that they had not yet seen the last of him.[38]

Two members of the Cuban delegation, Luis Pastor and Domingo Sterling, vocally sympathized with the Puerto Rican plan, while Manuel de Jesús Zeno, a delegate from Puerto Rico, embraced the antiabolitionist posture. Pastor clarified his position when he stated that it was "impossible to harbor the illusion that the solution to this problem can be further delayed." Meanwhile, Zeno asserted what even the Cubans dared not say: "I understand that the degree of civilization of this century demands its abolition; but seeking the welfare of my nation, and because I know the black race, I fear, I am horrified by the idea, that if the solution is not paused, well meditated, it may cause in my beloved country an economic and social dislocation whose consequences will place us at the brink of a precipice." He concluded by predicting that the day of the slaves' liberation would be "a *black* day" that would lead to racial war. Zeno's conservative counterparts in the Cuban delegation also vehemently defended slavery. In an anti-abolitionist speech, Manuel de Armas, a conservative delegate from Havana, argued that the right to own slaves was sanctioned by the Bible and the Catholic Church.[39]

Attention to the voting record of the Cuban reformists reveals how uncommitted they were even to the mildest forms of amelioration. Only eight Cubans, for example, appeared on record in favor of the banning of whipping to punish slaves. Interestingly, the most reform-oriented of the Cubans opposed the establishment of religious missions in *ingenios*. Their lame retort to such a proposal was that the newly imported *bozales* would not understand the teachings of the curates.[40]

Intimately linked to the issue of slavery were the old aspirations of white immigration. The Cuban delegates called for the relaxation of immigration laws, recommending that the waiting period for the naturalization of immigrants be reduced from five years to one. The Puerto Rican delegates also came dangerously close to violating one of the taboo topics when they pointed out that religious intolerance was one of the obstacles to white immigration.[41] Another topic actively discussed in the Junta de Información was taxation. Reformists on both sides of the Atlantic favored reductions or outright elimination of duties and a shift toward direct rather than indirect taxation.

The last session, which one contemporary critic dubbed a comedy, of the Junta de Información took place on April 27, 1867. The overseas minister came to the closing ceremonies, making his first appearance since the inaugural session six months earlier. He politely thanked the participants and bid them farewell. The junta had made a mockery of Creole expectations. The delegates exercised no real decision-making power; they simply received a series of questionnaires to complete. Some of the questions were outright ridiculous: "Which type of immigration do you consider the most convenient?" "White immigration," answered the Caribbean delegates unanimously, but to no avail.[42]

Participation in the Junta de Información was the last exercise in patience for many reformists. Shortly after the junta was disbanded, José Manuel Mestre, one of the key leaders in the Cuban reformist movement, wrote to a friend: "The Reformist Party has ceased to exist. . . . And if you ask me now, what do Cubans think? I will tell you: nothing. Maybe they will start thinking of annexation again." Miguel Aldama and other prominent reformists began to show clear indications of a renewed annexationist preference.[43]

The greatest testimony to the junta's utter failure was the fact that it called for lower taxes and tariffs and in response the government increased the colonies' fiscal burden. If the *política de atracción* had succeeded in granting certain political and civil liberties to Cubans, it had failed to produce a more just structure of taxation. In fact, Spanish fiscal exploitation of Cuba and Puerto Rico became even more unbearable after the mid-1860s, as the two island colonies were forced to foot the bill for Spain's adventures in the Dominican Republic and Mexico.[44] Before 1864 Cuba did not have a foreign debt. That year the Spanish government issued the first Cuban colonial bonds in the amount of three million pesos. During the Ten Years' War (1868–78), Cuba's foreign debt grew exponentially, with bond debts reaching fifty-five million pesos.[45]

During the 1860s Spain extracted revenues from its Caribbean colonies in greater proportions than ever before. Revenues collected in Cuba in 1866 amounted to 26.8 million pesos, twice the sum collected in 1855.[46] In 1868–69 revenues reached 31.2 million pesos in Cuba and 3.7 million pesos in Puerto Rico. Of these funds, 5.7 million pesos and 200,000 pesos were remitted to Spain as *sobrantes*, or surpluses. Taxation through state lotteries also increased sharply. In 1863–64, for example, the colonial government collected 8.3 million pesos in lotteries in Cuba, an amount that represented 27 percent of all revenues. Only customs duties surpassed lotteries as a source of revenue that year, at 11.9 million pesos, or 39 percent of total receipts. José Antonio Saco calculated that the average Cuban annually paid 30.90 pesos in tax, compared with only 6.80 in Spain, 11.60 in Great Britain, 6.00 in France, 5.00 in the British Antilles, and 4.42 in Canada.[47]

The enormity of the tax burden was further aggravated by the arbitrary ways in which revenues were spent. Cubans often protested that so much of what was collected in the island was shipped abroad. *Sobrantes* to Spain almost quadrupled between 1854 and 1864, from 2.7 to 9.8 million pesos, and an additional yearly average of 200,000 pesos left Cuba's treasury to cover the expenses of Spain's African penal colony of Fernando Poo. The inflated salaries of the island's bureaucrats were another source of grievance. V. de Roches complained that the island's captain-general earned a yearly salary of 50,000 pesos plus living expenses and the governors of the departments had salaries of 25,000 pesos in addition to houses and other perks.[48] In contrast, only negligible amounts were spent on education and other domestic needs. In 1862, for example, only 84,233 pesos went to education, and in 1866 only 194,571 pesos were spent on public works. Saco commented at the time that while millions of pesos were shipped abroad, "not one single *maravedí*" was spent on teaching Cubans to read and write.[49]

Not only did the Spanish government fail to listen to the plight of the Creoles during the 1866 depression, but it also ignored the recommendations of Spanish colonial administrators who were sending signals of local discontent with the burdensome tax structure.[50] The results of this inattentiveness proved grave.

Challenge to Colonialism, 1868–1878

In the fall of 1868 two unrelated separatist groups revolted in Cuba and Puerto Rico. In both cases, the new tax system was a major grievance.[51] The Puerto Rican insurrection, known as El Grito de Lares, lasted only a few hours and was limited to the west central municipalities of Lares and San Sebastián. Its Cuban counterpart also had modest beginnings, but it evolved into an all-out separatist struggle, the Ten Years' War, which extended throughout all but Cuba's westernmost districts. While only a handful died in the Puerto Rican revolt, 50,000 Cubans and between 150,000 and 210,000 Spaniards lost their lives during the Cuban Ten Years' War.[52]

El Grito de Lares was Puerto Rico's only indigenous separatist revolt of the nineteenth century. Ramón Emeterio Betances, who helped organize but did not participate in the revolt, was later referred to by Rafael María de Labra y Cadrana as the island's only separatist.[53] On numerous occasions Betances manifested his frustration and disgust over the docile conduct of his fellow countrymen. On December 16, 1868, for example, he expressed grief over the fact that only three hundred pesos had been collected among the population to support the imprisoned participants of El Grito de Lares. In order to liberate the country, he said, his countrymen must "sacrifice their money, their comfort, and their lives." A few months later he wrote to a friend that Cuba had an abundance of courageous people, but they were lacking in Puerto Rico.[54] Betances's frustration increased in the early 1870s, when the island's Creole elite opted to seek solutions to Puerto Rico's problems within the imperial system, by sending delegates to the Spanish Cortes. On April 10, 1871, he complained to Eugenio María de Hostos: "Puerto Rico is in a state of total drunkenness. They are drunk with the reforms that have not been delivered. The fumes have intoxicated them. It is the strangest and saddest spectacle, an entire population—young and old—celebrating the liberties that they think they have but which they do not have. . . . It looks like a meeting of madmen who dance without music." Hostos shared these frustrations, later jotting in his diary: "How tranquil, how conformed, how patient, how peaceful, how loyal this meek island is! Not one conspirator, not one separatist, not even a reformist. Not one single shout, no aspirations, no motion within this tomb. Everybody sleeps silently. The portentous Governor Sanz in the Fortress; the cannons lay idle in the forts; the Spaniards in their dry goods stores; the improvised nobility with its titles; Spain in its full confidence." Puerto Rico's reformists were highly critical of the Cuban situation and sought to capitalize on the fact that their Cuban neighbors were staging an all-out war. De Labra y Cadrana, a Cuban-born reformist active in Puerto Rican politics, openly criticized the Cuban route, which he blamed for blocking the implementation of reforms in Puerto Rico.[55] In 1873, amid high tension stemming from the events surrounding the *Virginius* affair and an alleged anti-Spanish plot organized in Camuy, Puerto Rico, reformists from Humacao, Lares, Camuy, Utuado, and other municipalities publicly announced their loyalty to colonial authorities and the queen of Spain. By this point even some of the veterans of El Grito de Lares had recanted their separatist actions of the late 1860s and joined the ranks of the island's pro-Spanish conservative party.[56]

Meanwhile, Cuba's Ten Years' War continued to escalate, profoundly shaped in its aims and strategies by direct and indirect pressures exerted by the United States. From the beginning the Cuban separatist leadership, both in the island and in exile, realized that their struggle's success depended on the support, or at least the sanction, of the United States. Thus, once again an important segment of the Cuban leadership embraced the annexationist route for strategic purposes.[57] A few days into the insurrection, Carlos Manuel de Céspedes, the movement's first leader, addressed William Seward, requesting "aid" and "influence" and manifesting the possibility of Cuba's seeking annexation to the United States after gaining independence from Spain. Three months later Céspedes instructed his agents in New York to promote the idea of Cuba's annexation to the United States.[58] The revolutionaries of the central districts, where slavery was less important, displayed even more enthusiasm for an annexationist solution. In Camagüey, significantly, Cuban rebels wore ribbons of intertwined Cuban and U.S. flags.[59] It is interesting to note that some of the most ardent annexationists of the late 1860s and early 1870s also embraced abolitionism, while some of those who openly attacked the annexationist route expressed concerns about measures that could "undermine the social basis" (i.e., abolition).[60] Cuban annexationism in the 1860s and 1870s, like that in the 1840s and early 1850s, continued to be sparked and molded by issues pertaining to race and slavery and by the position assumed by the United States on such matters.

Many of the leading Cuban reformists of the mid-1860s also embraced annexationism during the early stages of the Ten Years' War, when they assumed key positions in the revolutionary government in exile. For some this shift represented the completion of a full circle: annexationism in the late 1840s and early 1850s, reformism in the early to mid-1860s, and annexationism again in the late 1860s and early 1870s. José Morales Lemus, José Manuel Mestre, Miguel Aldama, José Antonio Echeverría, and other wealthy reformists joined the anti-Spanish struggle in 1869.[61] They fled Cuba because of the government's failure to stop the brutal acts of terror of the militarized pro-Spanish party.[62] These representatives of the most conservative segments of the revolutionary constituency looked to the United States as a moderating variable within the Cuban separatist equation. They became the agents of the Cuban revolutionary government and actively promoted the island's annexation to the United States. Cuban annexationism, however, waned after 1870, in part because of the Grant administration's hostility toward the Cuban cause. By mid-1871 Aldama, Mestre, Echeverría, and other moderate annexationists resigned from their "diplomatic" posts, allowing a proindependence group of leaders to assume control of the Cuban Junta in the United States.[63]

Because the Cuban struggle came to depend on the stance of the United States, its leadership also embraced abolitionist postures. Although Raúl Cepero Bonilla and other historians have tried to discredit the Cuban leadership by questioning its commitment to abolition, there is strong evidence to suggest that the Cuban government-in-arms viewed the emancipation of the slaves as one of its main goals. One of the first acts of the revolutionary leaders following El Grito de Yara was to set their slaves free. A few weeks later Céspedes issued a proclamation, stating: "A free Cuba is incompatible with a Cuba with slaves, and the abolition of Spanish institutions must include by reason of need and of the highest justice the abolition of slavery, the most evil of them all." On another occasion Céspedes pronounced that abolition was necessary and that it should be "gradual and with indemnification." The revolutionary leadership of Camagüey was even more committed to emancipation. On February 26, 1869, the revolutionary congress of the central districts declared slavery abolished and promised to compensate the master class eventually. By 1870 even the most conservative of the exiles assumed a proabolitionist stance.[64]

The revolutionaries' annexationism and abolitionism were both responses to geopolitical realities that dictated to a great extent the ideological course of the Cuban struggle against Spain. The reassertion of U.S. hegemony in the region after the Civil War and the proximity of the northern republic to Cuba forced the revolutionary leaders to look to the United States for moral and material support.[65] They realized that abolitionism was a prerequisite for recognition and therefore embraced it from the onset of the Ten Years' War. Abolitionism persisted and gained strength within the movement. It could not have been any other way; it was a dictate of the mighty abolitionist power to the north. On the other hand, because of the United States' systematic sabotage of the Cuban struggle, annexationist sentiment abated after mid-1869.

The Dominican Republic

Like their Cuban counterparts, Dominican annexationists have not fared well in the eyes of most historians, past and present. Pedro Santana, under whose direction Spain reincorporated the Dominican

Republic into its overseas empire, endured the vitriolic attack of some of the republic's best pens. His contemporaries dubbed him "monster," "cannibal," "hyena," "butcher," and "assassin," said he was "thirsty for human blood," and compared him to Attila, Nero, and Satan himself.[66] Doubtless Santana also enjoyed the support of some contemporary writers, but on balance the early portrayals of him were overwhelmingly negative. The works of José Gabriel García and other exponents of the first generation of Dominican nationalist historiography built upon this hostile characterization of Santana, Buenaventura Báez, and other annexationists. In García's estimation, Santana was a "mediocre soldier" guilty of the "crime" of annexation, and Báez was nothing more than an "unskilled diplomat and vulgar politician."[67] This negative assessment of the two most visible nineteenth-century Dominican annexationists prevails to the present day, both in the popular mind and in the works of professional historians. Monuments in honor of Santana or Báez are not to be found anywhere in the Dominican Republic, nor are streets and parks named in their honor. Contemporary historians prefix Santana's name with "traitor," "despot," and similar epithets.[68] One Caribbeanist recently described Báez's annexationism as a "political, social and cultural aberration" and said that it was "incubated in the tiny feverish brain of a leader who was as corrupt as he was evil." Another student of the period characterized Báez as "one of the worst politicians in all of Latin American history."[69]

Not surprisingly, Santana enjoyed a moment of positive reevaluation during the years of the Trujillo dictatorship (1930–61). Rafael Leónidas Trujillo promoted and personally subsidized a reinterpretation of his fellow dictator, and out of this effort came a number of laudatory publications. One year after the infamous massacre of thousands of Haitians under Trujillo's orders, Rafael Senior published a Trujillo-subsidized biography of Santana. As one reads Senior's book, the parallels between the two dictators become uncomfortably obvious. Senior went to great lengths to justify Santana's annexationism as necessary "to save the fatherland from the Haitians." He also rationalized Santana's authoritarianism as "the most necessary and energetic medicine to combat the profound illness that the Republic suffered."[70] Later works by Rufino Martínez, Emilio Rodríguez Demorizi, and other scholars with ties to the Trujillo regime also produced favorable pictures of the controversial caudillo. Martínez described Santana as upright, proud, firm, and sincere. Rodríguez Demorizi, referring to Santana's rule by decrees, concluded that "discipline and subordination, indispensable in time of war, are also necessary to preserve peace." Rodríguez Demorizi argued that Santana's annexationist tendencies were "an imperative necessity" that only a handful opposed.[71]

The passionate and highly politicized tone of the debate over Santana and Báez and their annexationist maneuvers has shed little light on the true motivations of nineteenth-century annexationism and the external and internal forces acting upon this phenomenon. More recent works by students of Dominican history have begun to provide sounder explanations for the historical problem of annexationism, the most recurrent political tendency of the First Republic and early years of the Second Republic. While Detlev Julio K. Peukert sees nineteenth-century Dominican annexationism as a result of the state's endemic weakness, William J. Nelson stresses the difficult relations between the Dominican Republic and Haiti. Jaime de Jesús Domínguez underscores that the growing economic and political power of the Cibao bourgeoisie pushed Santana to seek annexation to Spain. Frank Moya Pons, for his part, interprets the Baecista party's annexationism during the Second Republic as a result of its dwindling economic base and its leaders' desperate need for foreign economic support. The Blue antiannexationist party, in contrast, could count on the expanding financial resources of the northern tobacco bourgeoisie. Roberto Cassá's interpretation of the period's annexationism and antiannexationism rests on class analysis and asserts that the annexationism of the Baecista party was an expression of the class interests of dominant groups, in opposition to the nationalism of the petty bourgeoisie.[72]

The political crisis in the United States and the civil war that momentarily reduced that nation's political and military might in the hemisphere set the stage for the Spanish annexation of the Dominican Republic. Earlier, during the 1840s and 1850s, at least a dozen different attempts were made either by the various Dominican administrations or by the governments of Spain, France, and the United States to incorporate all or part of the infant republic into one of the northern Atlantic naval powers. All failed. In this earlier period the northern Atlantic powers had checked each other to block any foreign encroachment in Dominican territory. Not coincidentally, the Spanish annexation of the Dominican Republic took place when the balance of power in the region was momentarily upset because of the U.S. Civil War.

The annexation of the Dominican Republic was a combined project of Spain and Pedro Santana's government. Events may give the impression that a desperate Santana forced his country's annexation on Spain. The truth is, however, that Dominican statesmen have never to this day been able to force anything on the world powers. Spain had been seeking to establish control over the Dominican Republic for almost a decade, but Caribbean geopolitical realities and the presence of the United States made that impossible. Santana's role was simply to legitimate Spain's occupation.

Spain carried out the annexation for several reasons. First was the fear that the struggling Dominican Republic would fall victim to either U.S. or Haitian expansionism. "Santo Domingo will be Haitian or Yankee," predicted Antonio Peláez Campomanes, a Spanish envoy entrusted with assessing conditions in the republic on the eve of its occupation. In a similar report, Consul Mariano Álvarez warned: "Two different enemy races of the Dominicans covet this precious Antille." For obvious reasons Spain feared U.S. encroachments in the Dominican Republic. The republic was strategically located between Spain's last colonies of the hemisphere, and a U.S. presence there could provide a base for filibustering operations against Cuba and Puerto Rico. As Consul Álvarez put it, possession over Samaná would turn the United States into "the owners of the Gulf of Mexico, [a situation] that would hang like the sword of Damocles over our rich possessions." In a statement defending annexation and control over Samaná, another Spanish official, José Varela, referred to the United States as "our crudest enemies," adding that "Cuba and Puerto Rico would shortly and fatally feel the consequences of their nearby presence." Spanish policymakers also feared the possibility of Haiti's conquering the Hispanic part of Hispaniola, an outcome perceived as a serious threat to both Cuba and Puerto Rico, where slavery still thrived. Thus, Spanish control over Samaná Bay was deemed strategically vital for the preservation of both colonies. Consul Álvarez exclaimed grandiloquently that possession of the Dominican Republic would give Spain "greater importance as a maritime nation with control over the three Greater Antilles." "From these," he added, "we would dominate not only the

Gulf of Mexico but also Central and South America; [and] would have an edge over the Union greater than we now have."[73]

For the Spanish government the Dominican Republic also appeared to provide endless resources to supply and complement the export economies of Cuba and Puerto Rico. Spain and its Caribbean colonies had come to depend too heavily on British and U.S. products, and control over the Dominican Republic could reduce this dependence. In 1860 Álvarez wrote that the Dominican Republic had the potential to supply the needs of the Cuban market with cheaper and better cattle than that imported from Florida. He also stated that Dominican timber would likewise be better than the "excessively high priced" Florida pines. If cotton were to be produced in the Dominican Republic, he continued, the Spanish empire's dependence on U.S. cotton would end. For his part, the Spanish vice-consul at Santo Domingo reported that Dominican coal and other minerals would supplant British sources.[74]

Santana and his partisans had their own reasons for desiring annexation to Spain. Above all else, Santana sought to strengthen his position by wiping out internal opposition to his regime with the backing of Spanish troops. Santana had also come under attack from insurgent movements with strong Haitian ties. On the eve of annexation, a high officer in his administration produced distressing reports about Haitian presence in Azua, while Santana spread rumors that the Haitian government was building up a navy.[75] Thus, prior to his country's annexation by Spain, Santana cried "Haitians" and "Yankees" to accelerate the process under way and to avoid coups against him, such as those that had occurred in 1848 and 1856. At this critical juncture, Santana once again proved to be an indiscriminate annexationist. Up to the late 1850s he had been an ardent promoter of annexation and making concessions to the United States. When this was no longer plausible, Santana turned his attention to Spain.

Santana's administration began to plan for annexation to Spain in 1859, when the caudillo sent Felipe Alfau, one of the founding members of La Trinitaria, to Madrid to convince Spanish officials of the benefits of annexation. A year later Santana personally addressed Isabella II, emphasizing cultural affinities between the two countries: "Our origin, our language, our religion, our customs, our sympathies." Interestingly, Santana at the same time sought a rapprochement with the Catholic clergy, his former foes. He issued a number of decrees favoring the church in the areas of control over marriages and state financial support.[76] In an obvious allusion to the political crisis in the United States, Santana stressed that "perhaps we will not have a better opportunity than the one offered by the current circumstances." He also explained that the Dominican Republic lived in fear of Haiti and of "a powerful nation to the North, that does not take its eagle eyes off from this coveted nation."[77]

By the summer of 1860 the Spanish government had already devised a project for the gradual reincorporation of the former colony of Santo Domingo. On June 27 the Spanish minister of state wrote to Cuba's captain-general, Francisco Serrano, spelling out a strategy that included deployment of military supplies and troops, the promotion of Spanish immigration to the Dominican Republic from Venezuela and Cuba, and increased naval presence around the island of Hispaniola.[78] Spanish troops, immigrants, and warships began to arrive soon after.

Meanwhile, Santana continued pressing for de jure annexation. Lincoln's election in the United States and the worsening of the political crisis there increased Santana's chances of succeeding in his quest. In November 1860 Santana's secretary of state approached Cuba's captain-general with a list of conditions under which his country would welcome annexation: he insisted that slavery not be reestablished, that the Dominican Republic be treated as a Spanish province, that Dominicans be employed in the colonial bureaucracy and militia, and that the laws and acts of the Dominican government since 1844 be considered valid. Santana's administration also sought to give the impression that the Dominican people welcomed annexation. Petitions were signed, and pro-Spanish demonstrations were organized. In October 1860 U.S. envoy William Cazneau reported that in a matter of days the Santana government had shifted its sympathies from the United States to Spain. Meanwhile, his Spanish counterpart, Antonio Peláez Campomanes, said that his contact with Dominicans of all classes and all races convinced him "that if a consultation of the *universal vote* were carried out on the topic of the incorporation of the island to Spain, there would not be 1,500 opposing votes."[79] He also noted widespread pro-Spanish sentiment, the flying of the Spanish flag on holidays, and the public celebration of Spanish victories in northern Africa.

Finally, on March 18, 1861, Santana, the former ally of the United States and the caudillo who once promised to "look out for the conservation of independence," declared his nation's annexation to Spain. "Our anxieties and dangers are over!" he exclaimed, adding that his country had gone from being "a weak nation whose independence was a vain title repeatedly blown around by powerful winds" to being "the robust child of a mighty power." Within the next two months, with an all-out war raging in the United States, Spain formally annexed the Dominican Republic. More soldiers, priests, and bureaucrats continued to arrive. Meanwhile, Santana was rewarded: he became the colony's governor, received the titles of La Gran Cruz de la Real Orden de Isabel la Católica and Orden de Carlos III, was named marquis of Las Carreras, and was appointed to the Spanish Senate. He was paid in his own currency—titles and promotions.[80]

A Colony Once Again

The Dominican Republic that reentered the Spanish empire in 1861 as the colony of Santo Domingo was quite different from its sister colonies to the east and west. The Dominican Republic had no structured state apparatus and no plantations. Santana openly prided himself on having delivered to Spain a country without lawyers and newspapers. But under Spanish rule the state grew in size and influence. The national budget increased almost nineteen times, going from $241,000 in 1860 to $4,476,000 in 1863. José de la Gándara y Navarro, a Spanish official who participated in the annexation but later became critical of it, described the expansion of the Dominican state: "The children of this island incorporated by Spain witnessed the transformation of an administration composed of a scarce and cheap personnel, sustained with modest allotments, into a luxurious administration, requiring three and a half million pesos to operate." Funds from Cuba and Puerto Rico and locally collected revenue helped support the bloated colonial bureaucracy. Taxes and duties similar to those of the other colonies were now levied. These became a source of great irritation for the Dominicans, particularly those active in international trade.[81]

With the Spanish state came its church. Like the Dominican state, the church had not touched the lives of most people during the First Republic. Most Dominicans were nominally Catholic, but few attended mass or participated in the basic sacraments of baptism and marriage. According to de la Gándara y Navarro, "illegitimate unions" were more common in the colony of Santo Domingo than anywhere in Latin America. Another contemporary observer noted that Dominicans "do not attend mass, do not go to confession, and skip the sacrament of baptism to avoid traveling a few miles." Annexation and the strengthening of Catholicism went hand in hand. Thus Spanish officials promoted the spread of Catholicism as a political and a religious strategy. On September 5, 1861, Francisco Serrano stated that Catholic sentiments were "inseparable from pro-Spanish sentiment." Serrano also requested the appointment of a prelate "to fix" the Dominican church. The arrival of Bienvenido Monzón in May 1861 fulfilled this request.[82] A zealous prelate, Archbishop Monzón was determined to purify the Dominican church and to reestablish "religious unity" in the colony. His crusade had three principal targets: common law marriages, Freemasonry, and Protestantism. Monzón first ordered parish priests to excommunicate those living outside Catholic marriage and declared Protestant marriages invalid. Monzón also persecuted Freemasons, whose activities had been widespread before annexation, barring from communion all Freemasons until they recanted their vows and gave up their practices. Protestants endured persecution as well: some of their churches were burned or confiscated for military purposes.[83] These intolerant practices alienated many in the colony of Santo Domingo, igniting opposition to the Spanish colonial regime. Protestants, Freemasons, and poor peasants who now had to pay for their marriages, burials, and children's baptisms became active opponents of the regime. Monzón also lost the support of the native clergy. With the notable exception of Father Fernando Arturo Meriño, the Dominican clergy had initially welcomed annexation as a way to increase the economic and political power of the church and to restore religious unity and orthodoxy.[84] The pro-Spanish annexationism of the Dominican clergy, however, was short-lived. Monzón and his prelates outraged the local clergy by discriminating against it and by cutting off some of its traditional sources of income. By 1863 the Dominican clergy opposed the new Spanish colonial government.[85]

In violation of one of Santana's conditions for annexation, Spanish authorities excluded Dominicans from the expanded state apparatus and from leadership positions in the military. Spanish officials rationalized this exclusion by arguing that Dominicans had "an innate incapacity to govern themselves" and lacked "morality." On one occasion Serrano asserted that he had difficulties organizing the government because of a lack of competent native personnel.[86] Discriminating against Dominicans because of their darker skin, Spanish officials incorporated only a few natives into the colonial government, and these people performed only low-paying menial tasks. Many Spanish officials earned eight hundred pesos or more annually, and a number were in the two-to-three-thousand-peso range. In contrast, only one native earned more than eight hundred pesos.[87] Santana himself was forced to resign his governorship in January 1862. As a result he went on to do what he did best—lead armies. This time he led an army against his own people, who soon revolted against the new colonial regime.

Another goal of Spanish annexation was to turn the Dominican Republic into a productive colony to service the export colonies of Cuba and Puerto Rico and to become a market for Spanish and Spanish-carried goods. One plan in that direction, the Varela project, included land reform, whereby uncultivated land would be taken away from Dominicans and given to immigrants from the Canary Islands, who in return would pay back to the state one-fourth of their income. Difficulties in attracting settlers and an all-out rebellion after mid-1863 made this and other projects impossible. A few months into annexation, U.S. agent Jonathan Elliot reported that annexation had brought the republic's economy to a virtual standstill: "There are no exports worth naming—no person will work the soil and [there is] no prospect, (at least at present) of there being any commerce, or trade." According to one Dominican historian, all eight ships clearing the port of Santo Domingo between February 16 and 20, 1864, left laden with ballast for lack of export products. New shipping taxes discriminating against non-Spanish vessels made the trade crisis worse.[88]

William Cazneau and Joseph W. Fabens, the perennial U.S. speculators in the Dominican Republic, welcomed Spanish annexation, which they saw as a source of stability conducive to the economic exploitation and population of the extinct republic. During the previous decade, political instability and the shifts in power between Santana and Báez had had deleterious effects on investment prospects because the concessions and policies of one administration were not honored by the next one. Following the Spanish occupation, Fabens wrote that the Hispanic part of Hispaniola was "now under an established government, which affords strong guarantees."[89] According to William Cazneau's wife, Jane, in late 1862 Spain was exhibiting its "best behavior." In May 1863 another of William Cazneau's associates presented Spain in very favorable terms. The Dominicans, he asserted, "had heard with 'lively pleasure' of the regeneration of Spain. They had heard of her 'railways and steamships, and of her encouragement of popular education, of her repeal or relaxation of her old oppressive laws regulating commerce and industry,' and 'they asked to be participants in the benefits of her liberal enlightened policy.' With 'very natural feelings of pride' Young Spain had accepted the responsibility of raising the Dominicans to higher levels."[90]

With the new colonial regime in place, Cazneau, Fabens, and a handful of New York–based capitalists established a new enterprise in Dominican territory, the American West India Company, a company with two faces. In the United States it purported to promote the colonization of North American free blacks in the Caribbean. Meanwhile, in the Spanish colony of Santo Domingo, the company presented itself as one promoting white immigration. In 1863 Fabens issued a pamphlet to lure prospective immigrants to Santo Domingo. It included an account of an obviously fictitious settler from Boston. According to Fabens, the settler bought forty acres of mahogany woodland for $150, and in just one year he was able to pay off his debt by selling mahogany to the land's original proprietor. In reality, however, the company was a fiasco. It failed to colonize blacks from the United States or to bring whites to Santo Domingo. Even Cazneau's own estate was destroyed by Spanish troops.[91]

The annexation of the Dominican Republic thus alienated many within Dominican society, even those who originally advocated such a measure. Intolerance, arbitrary government, and discrimination against Dominicans, coupled with a sustained agricultural and commercial crisis, fueled an all-out rebellion against Spanish rule. Spain had gotten itself into a profound foreign policy labyrinth. The question, now, was how to get out of it gracefully.

The War of Restoration

Only six weeks into the new colonial era, rebellion began. On May 2, 1861, Dominican general José Contreras and his followers, "most of whom were colored," rose up in arms.[92] Spanish troops quickly suffocated the uprising and executed its leaders. Opponents to Dominican annexation, some of whom had been in exile for many years in St. Thomas and Curaçao, also began to conspire against the Spanish government. In St. Thomas, Francisco del Rosario Sánchez, one of the patriots of the 1844 Dominican struggle for independence, organized the antiannexationist exiles. Soon after his forces invaded Dominican territory in June 1861, he was captured and shot. Meanwhile, Baecista exiles in Curaçao coalesced under José María Cabral to form the Revolutionary Party of Dominican Regeneration.

Even before the arrival of Spanish forces, wide segments of society plotted against Santana and his annexationist agenda. It became obvious that the majority of the population disagreed with his scheme. As early as May 1, 1861, one of the Spanish army's highest officers admitted that the "public sentiment in this country is contrary to the annexation that has taken place, a certain contemptuous coldness against our soldiers is evident." A few weeks earlier the U.S. commercial agent at Santo Domingo had reported that annexation was not the popular will. Báez and his partisans, for obvious reasons, were anti-Santana and antiannexation, not out of principle—for most had been and would again be annexationists themselves—but for reasons of political rivalry. Báez, in fact, became an accomplice of annexation: while his followers and relatives conspired against Spanish colonialism, he accepted a commission as field marshal in the Spanish army. Another sector vehemently opposing annexation was the black and mulatto peasantry, which feared that Spain would try to reestablish slavery.[93]

In order to be fully understood, the Dominican struggle for independence between 1861 and 1865 must be seen within its broader context. The Dominican War of Restoration was certainly not merely a reflection of the Civil War in the United States. Dominican patriots would have fought the Spanish regardless of events to the north. The nature of the fratricidal war in North America, however, to a great extent determined the configuration, alliances, objectives, and outcome of the Dominican struggle. Like the Civil War, the Dominican War of Restoration was an antislavery, anti-European struggle. Dominican patriots looked for support in Haiti and among U.S. abolitionists and the Union government. Meanwhile, Spain sought the support, or at least the sanction, of Great Britain and France.

For strategic reasons, Sánchez, José María Cabral, and other revolutionaries entered Dominican territory via the Haitian border. Such actions had dangerous implications because they could suggest that the insurgents had connections with the traditional enemies of the Dominican Republic. In a revolutionary proclamation, Sánchez had to explain apologetically that he "had set foot on Haitian territory because [he] could not enter any other way." A Dominican tradition of setting aside anti-Haitianism for strategic purposes dated back to 1821. Santana still invoked anti-Haitianism, referring to the revolutionaries as "a handful of nonconformists, who without conscience of their actions allied themselves with the enemies of the Dominican people, with Haiti." Meanwhile, a proannexation publication in Madrid dubbed revolutionary leader Cabral as one who "labored incessantly to gather a body of Haitians, that is, the irreconcilable enemies of his nation, to penetrate the Dominican territory and raise the banner of opposition to annexation."[94]

The Haitian government of Fabre Geffrard, indeed, supported Cabral's war effort with supplies and also allowed Dominican revolutionaries to cross the Haitian border at will.[95] Geffrard had good reasons for backing the revolutionaries in their struggle against Spanish colonialism. First, Haitians feared that Spanish presence would strengthen slavery in the region and be used against the free black societies of the Caribbean. Some even believed that Spaniards would reenslave the Dominicans. Second, the Spanish occupation of Dominican territory not only blocked Haiti's historical aspirations to unify the island but also threatened the black republic's territorial integrity. Spanish forces mobilized in an attempt to impose on Haiti the old Dominican-Haitian border agreed upon in Aranjuez in 1777.[96]

Geffrard reacted to the Spanish move on Dominican territory with a fire-eating proclamation, denouncing the hoisting of the flag "that authorizes and protects the enslaving of the children of Africa." He added that the "degraded banner" of Spain foretold the end of Haitian liberty and concluded by calling his people to arms. "To the battle field!" he exclaimed. "It is necessary that Spanish domination come to an end in America. We shall force them out of St. Domingo." Black solidarity with the revolt was also evident in other parts of the Caribbean. Shortly after Dominican annexation, 3,700 Jamaicans signed a petition demanding that Great Britain not recognize Spanish domination over Dominican territory. Free blacks in the Turks Islands later played an important role, supplying war matériel to Dominican insurgents. Aware of these racial links, the Spanish government prohibited the entrance of free blacks into the new Spanish colony of the Caribbean.[97]

A second wave of insurrectionary activity crested in mid-1863, this time in El Cibao, in Santiago. Increased taxes, arbitrary currency exchange policies, and an attempt to establish a state-run tobacco monopoly ignited a revolt among many of those who had risen against Báez in 1857 for similar reasons. Annexation proved particularly detrimental to the interests of the tobacco sector.[98] Insurrectionary forces soon captured Santiago and set up a provisional government. Meanwhile, Cabral, a Baecista and therefore theoretically a rival of the Santiago bourgeoisie, aided in the struggle against Spanish domination. This revolutionary coalition made considerable progress toward the overthrow of the colonial government. After August 1863 continuous reports of rebel victories began to pour out of the island.[99] Sympathies in the United States were with the rebels, partly because they were antislavery and anti-European. Private organizations in New England gave the rebels some aid, but the U.S. government was reluctant to openly support the anti-Spanish struggle.[100]

By the end of 1863 it was clear that Dominicans were serious about their intentions to force out the Spaniards, and they seemed likely to succeed. Meanwhile, on the other side of the Atlantic criticism of annexation was mounting. This culminated in January 1865, with the introduction of a bill in the Spanish Cortes for the abandonment of Santo Domingo.[101] Spanish critics of Dominican annexation argued that annexation had not been a spontaneous act of the majority but an imposition of Santana's to which the Spanish government had acceded. The strongest argument against remaining in Dominican territory was the enormous cost in human lives. Death estimates within the ranks of the Spanish army ranged between 6,000 and 18,000, with 7,500 being perhaps an accurate assessment.[102] According to calculations by de la Gándara y Navarro, a little over 6 percent of the deaths stemmed from actual battle wounds. The remaining 94 percent were caused by the greatest ally of the Dominicans, yellow fever. Although most Spanish envoys to the Dominican Republic had reported that it was a healthy country and that yellow fever was practically nonexistent, in the end this disease forced the Spanish army out.[103]

Added to the enormous human toll was the financial strain imposed on the Spanish empire, particularly on Cuba and Puerto Rico. The Spanish overseas minister, a critic of annexation, estimated that the administration of Santo Domingo cost 5.3 million pesos during the first four years and 2.5 million pesos during the last year. Cuba footed most of the bill, while Puerto Rico contributed 1 million pesos. The rationale for making the two islands pay the costs was that the annexation had occurred for the defense of the entire Spanish Caribbean and, therefore, Cuba and Puerto Rico should pay for it.[104]

Opponents of annexation also employed racist arguments. Whereas the proponents of annexation before 1861 had painted a picture of a republic in which more than half the population was white, those favoring Spanish withdrawal began to speak of a "degraded race," of a "colored population," and of a "black state." In his speech of March 30, 1865, Senator Manuel Seijas Lozano stated contemptuously: "It is known that the Caucasian Race can never be in the fraternal concord to form an homogeneous whole with the Ethiopian Race, and that people in its greater part are negroes and mulattoes."[105]

For their part, advocates of staying in Santo Domingo argued that the enormous human and material costs were necessary for the protection of Cuba and Puerto Rico.[106] Commander Manuel Buceta, one of the campaign's military chiefs, admitted that economically the Dominican annexation had been a disaster, but this disaster, he explained, was necessary for the conservation of the two long-time colonies. National honor was also hailed as a justification to stay and to deploy more troops to vanquish the insurrection. In the end, antiannexation forces won both on the battlefields and in the Spanish Cortes. On May 1, 1865, three weeks after the Confederacy's surrender, the bill for the abandonment of Santo Domingo became law. Within three months all Spanish troops withdrew.

The First Years of the Second Republic, 1865–1878

The Civil War in the United States and the War of Dominican Restoration created new geopolitical realities. First, the Union victory signaled the end of European political domination of the Dominican Republic. Dominican politics could no longer be based on the rivalry between those seeking annexation to the United States and those looking to Europe for protection.[107] Moreover, Santana's death in 1864 left one of the parties of the First Republic without a leader. During the first years of the Second Republic, two barely distinguishable parties emerged: the Reds and the Blues. The Reds were essentially the Baecistas, a more autocratic, more agriculturally based party, while the Blues were former Santanistas and liberals, a party with a stronger urban composition and links with the northern commercial sector. Interestingly, the Red party attracted not only the traditional oligarchy but the nation's peasantry as well. In considering annexation, after 1865 the United States became the only viable option for both the Reds and the Blues. While in power, leaders of both parties sought protection, annexation, or U.S. presence in Samaná in exchange for cash and arms in order to stay in control and curb Haitian hostility. When not in power, both became extremely nationalistic and critical of annexation.[108] Some Blue leaders, like Luperón and Meriño, however, remained firmly nationalistic throughout this period.

The War of Restoration had provided the context for the temporary unification of different segments of Dominican society under a common antiannexation banner. Baecistas and Cibaeños, tobacco growers and cattle ranchers, independent peasants and subordinate peons, blacks, mulattoes, and whites, rose as one to free their country from Spanish domination. After their victory, however, this informal coalition collapsed just as it had following the declaration of Dominican independence in 1844. A similarly broad coalition of Santanistas and elements of the Cibaeño bourgeoisie had also collapsed after fulfilling its goal of overthrowing Báez in 1858. In all three instances, the northern liberal intelligentsia played a major role. In all three cases the men with military power (Santana in 1844 and 1858, and Cabral in 1865) refused to hand control over to the Cibaeños. In all three cases, furthermore, the most economically dynamic region, El Cibao and its capital, Santiago, failed to assume control over the central government. The Trinitario government of Juan Pablo Duarte, Francisco del Rosario Sánchez, and Ramón Matías Mella had lasted only a few months before Santana and the conservatives established control in July 1844. In 1858, again, Santana refused to yield power to the Cibaeños. In August 1865, in a third attempt to dominate Santo Domingo, Santiageño forces under Pedro Antonio Pimentel were stopped cold by Cabral's Baecista forces. Patron-client relations between the caudillos and the republic's subordinate peonage continued to be at the crux of military and, therefore, political power.

The political divisions between the Santiagueños and the men on horseback of the South and West reflected deep-seated socioeconomic divisions separating the different regions of the Dominican Republic. El Cibao was an increasingly export-oriented region composed of midsized producers, with a large merchant and professional sector centered in Santiago. This region's political elite aspired to a free trade system, representative democracy, and political rights for the bulk of the population. The region's close ties with its traditional tobacco markets (Germany, St. Thomas, and Curaçao), moreover, explain its elite's aversion toward any maneuver to incorporate part or all of the country into the United States. In contrast, a hierarchical social structure and conservative political tendencies characterized the ranching and woodcutting West and South.

The first few years of the Second Republic was a period of great political instability. Nine different administrations governed the Dominican Republic between March 1865 and May 1868. Pimentel, the head of the provisional government, was unable to reach Santo Domingo because Cabral's and Eusebio Manzueta's troops blocked his path. Six months later, with opposition mounting, Cabral arranged Báez's return to power. In a conciliatory gesture, Báez appointed Pimentel and Cabral to his new cabinet. At this point the North became once again the focus of insurrection, this time led by the Blue party under Luperón. By August 1866 the Blue party had retaken the national government. It proceeded to establish a triumvirate, which was short-lived. Blue leaders yielded control to Cabral—now momentarily in the Blue party—because they believed he was the only one capable of keeping Báez out of power.[109]

True to his model, Santana, Cabral sought to consolidate his command by offering to sell Samaná and by seeking a U.S. protectorate. His weak grip on national power and unfavorable political circumstances in the United States, however, frustrated Cabral's annexationist overtures. His antinational agenda, furthermore, alienated Luperón and other nationalists in his party, while the Baecistas exploited his annexationist plots to rally the opposition against him.[110] This opposition included the Haitian government, then under Silvain Salnave, who turned Haiti into a haven for Baecista rebels and provided them with funds and weapons. By January 1868 the Baecistas were already in control, and Báez became president for the fourth time.[111]

Even though the Baecista opposition to Cabral had rested on nationalist, antiannexationist grounds, one of the first official acts of Báez's fourth administration was to approach the United States with offers to yield control over portions of Samaná bay and peninsula. Only six days after his inauguration, Báez spelled out his desire to come to an agreement whereby the United States would help him stay in power with "moral" and "material" support in exchange for sovereignty over Samaná. He set the price at two million dollars for a fifty-year lease: half the amount was to be paid in cash, the other half in weapons. In his offer to the United States, Báez described his country's situation as one of "absolute penury." He also had recourse to the traditional annexationist line, stating that the Haitians were behind Cabral and Luperón. Báez's secretary of state described the latter as a man of "backward ideas" who professed that "the African race must predominate in the island and that it should band together to exterminate other races."[112]

As Báez's survival appeared more doubtful, he became more desperate. By July 1868 he was talking of sale rather than lease, and by October he was advocating the establishment of a protectorate over the entire republic, not only Samaná. He even signaled that he was willing to annex the whole country to the United States. The U.S. envoy reported that Báez had assured him that "the Dominican Republic would at once apply for admission into the Union." Aware of opposition to Dominican annexation in the United States, Báez engaged in parallel negotiations for a British loan backed with state properties and lands, coal mines in Samaná, guano deposits in Alta Vela, and a mortgage of the republic's customs receipts. The agreement also included a hefty commission for the British agent, Edward Hartmont.[113]

During his six-year administration (1868–74), Báez became more repressive and authoritarian than he had been in his previous presidential terms. He banished dozens of political opponents and treated guerrillas with a heavy hand. He also resorted to wholesale electoral fraud, rigging the February 1870 plebiscite to create the impression that Dominicans overwhelmingly supported annexation to the United States. The result of this farce was 15,169 votes in favor, 11 votes against. Not satisfied with the U.S. Senate's rejection of the annexation treaty, Báez sought desperately needed funds through the lease of portions of Samaná to a group of U.S. speculators. Ratified in February 1873, the lease treaty remained in place only briefly until a successful insurrection put an end to both Báez's fourth administration and the Samaná lease. The Blue opposition to Báez and his pro-U.S. annexationism derived considerable support from foreign and national merchants and tobacco producers whose ties to the traditional tobacco markets were threatened by the prospect of annexation to the United States. The nationalist leader Luperón, himself a wealthy merchant from Puerto Plata, received monetary assistance from business associates in St. Thomas for the struggle against Báez and annexation.[114]

The period following Báez's fall proved even more unstable than the first decade of the Second Republic. Sixteen different administrations assumed political control between January 1874 and October 1879. Báez himself returned to power momentarily, from December 1876 to March 1878, in this bloody game of political musical chairs. During his brief fifth administration, Báez once again sought to annex his country to the United States, but to no avail. He finally left the island for good on March 2, 1878, with a 370,000-peso booty.[115]

Báez's annexationist schemes won him the antipathy not only of the nationalist Blue party but also of his former ally, the Dominican church. In an amazing shift, Báez, who during the 1850s figured as the anti-U.S. caudillo of the "black" and "clerical" parties, now attempted to sell his country to the United States.[116] In the process he was forced to assume anti-Haitian and anticlerical postures. This annexationist flip-flopping could be explained using the traditional interpretation that mid–nineteenth-century annexationists were opportunistic, self-serving politicians. Indeed they were. A sounder set of explanations, however, could be found by looking at broader changes in the international climate in the region. Attention to the Atlantic context, the balance of power, and international tensions helps explain why Santana, the "friend of the United States," suddenly became an anti–North American Hispanophile in 1859–61, and why Báez, the man who "hated" the United States, became an ardent advocate of his country's annexation to that country in 1865–66, 1868–74, and 1876–78.

Conclusion

On the surface, no changes in the political status of Cuba and Puerto Rico took place during the mid–nineteenth century. Both islands remained under Spain's aegis. Meanwhile, with the exception of the period of the Spanish annexation, the Dominican Republic retained its independent status and territorial integrity. Despite this illusion of stability, profound geopolitical changes and transformations in the balance of power occurred between 1840 and 1878. During this period the United States asserted its influence over the Hispanic Caribbean, to become the de facto authority dictating the paths of economic and political change in the region, shifting from a defensive position vis-à-vis Great Britain and other European powers to an offensive and expansionist stance both commercially and politically.

The United States did not assume de jure control over the Spanish colonies of the Caribbean for a number of reasons. First, internal tensions between two brands of expansionism in the United States during the antebellum period canceled each other out, thus preventing any real encroachment in the Hispanic Caribbean. Second, a tacit agreement existed whereby the United States as the region's de facto commercial leader accepted the continuation of Spanish domination over Cuba and Puerto Rico as long as Spain kept open the avenues of trade and maintained control of the slaves. U.S. influence continued to increase in the region. The Creoles certainly perceived it that way.

Policies toward slavery and the slave trade were crucial in this transition. During the 1840s and 1850s U.S. policy favored the continuation of slavery in the region as long as the slave population was kept under control. This posture neatly matched the aspirations of both the

Cuban planter class and the Spanish colonial bureaucracy and merchant class. Meanwhile, British abolitionist zeal backfired, because it alienated Great Britain from Creole and resident Spaniard support. Spain's standing also eroded: in the eyes of the Creole population, Spain appeared to have lost the ability to maintain social equilibrium—keeping the slaves under control. In 1854 both brands of U.S. expansionism—southern agrarian and northern commercial—surfaced in official attempts by the United States to purchase Cuba and territory for a coaling station in Samaná Bay.

As the United States gained the upper hand in the region, polarization sharpened. The European powers allied to counterbalance the growing U.S. hegemony. In 1853, the British and French governments, in accordance with Spain, proposed that the United States join them in a treaty to guarantee Cuba to Spain. The following year representatives of Spain, Great Britain, and France came together in the Dominican Republic in an attempt to bring down the pro-U.S. administration of Pedro Santana. At that juncture British officials expressed confidence in the fact that France would side with them in the event of a confrontation with the United States.

The crisis leading to the U.S. Civil War and the actual developments in the conflict had profound repercussions in the Hispanic Caribbean. As war became more likely, the United States retreated from expansionism, and Spain became more aggressive in the Dominican Republic and assured its control over Cuba and Puerto Rico. The secession of eleven southern states and the all-out war that followed debilitated the U.S. government, making it unable to enforce the Monroe Doctrine. The European powers thus moved into the sphere of influence of the United States, occupying both Mexico and the Dominican Republic. During this period the European coalition actually gained strength: the invasion of Mexico in 1862 was a joint venture of French, Spanish, and British troops.

With the Union victory in 1865 came the end of southern-based agrarian expansionism, which gave way to another brand of expansionism that was northern-based and abolitionist, seeking the establishment of new bases to protect trade routes and the region's markets. The abolitionist character of this new brand of expansionism completely transformed the rules of the game in the Spanish Caribbean. Thus far, slavery and even the continuation of the slave trade had been acceptable because they did not conflict with the Caribbean policy of the United States. During and after the war, however, the United States began to actively pressure for the abolition of slavery in Cuba and Puerto Rico. Creoles in Cuba and Spanish officials on both sides of the Atlantic realized that slavery would soon have to be abolished. This fact is still another indication of U.S. influence over events in the Spanish colonies of the Caribbean.

Internal divisions within the United States during the post–Civil War years continued to hamper the actual expansion of the United States into the Hispanic Caribbean. Ironically, the strong position of the United States and the certainty that the European naval powers no longer posed a threat in the region served as deterrents to physical expansion into the region. Moreover, U.S. officials continued to adhere to the policy that Spain could retain administrative control over Cuba and Puerto Rico. In fact, the Grant administration systematically worked against the Cuban revolutionary cause in favor of a continued Spanish presence. Despite the changes that had occurred in the United States, the Cuban Ten Years' War still provoked reactions similar to those produced by the Africanization scare of 1853–54. An "Africanized" Cuba was as unacceptable to the United States in the 1870s as it had been in the mid-1850s. In the aftermath of the Civil War, the Johnson and Grant administrations made serious attempts to acquire territorial concessions in the Dominican Republic. These efforts failed, however, not because of European pressures but because of internal opposition within the United States and nationalistic resistance within the Dominican Republic.

The Civil War in the United States also had profound repercussions in the Caribbean policies of the European naval powers. Great Britain moved further away from official abolitionism, and Spain markedly relaxed its colonial grip on Cuba and Puerto Rico. Moreover, developments in the United States during the Civil War made Spanish officials realize that the days of slavery in the hemisphere were numbered. The war also profoundly affected the policy of Spain toward the Dominican Republic, allowing it to annex its former colony until the end of the conflict, when Spanish troops withdrew from Santo Domingo.

Strong parallels emerged between the geopolitical and balance of power transformations and the patterns of trade between the Hispanic Caribbean and the northern Atlantic. The growth of U.S. hegemony over the islands went hand in hand with increased U.S. control of the region's commerce. During the 1850s the United States gained commercial superiority in the Spanish Caribbean, supplying 25 percent of the region's imports and receiving 40 percent of its exports. Besides controlling such large shares of the trade, the United States dictated the course of production in the region. This neocolonial system, in which the United States became the region's de facto commercial metropolis while Spain retained fiscal and administrative control, also helps explain why the United States failed to move into the region during the period covered by this study. Preserving Spanish colonialism was a means of preserving U.S. neocolonialism. The close links between political and commercial influence remained evident during the Civil War and its aftermath. Disruptions in the patterns of trade during the conflict meant temporary loss of U.S. commercial domination in the region. While the French and Spanish armies gained footholds in Mexico and the Dominican Republic, British, French, and Spanish vessels and goods moved in to fill the vacuum produced by the commercial retrenchment of the United States. After 1865, however, the United States reasserted its commercial and political influence over the region with greater vigor.

The contending policies of the various northern Atlantic powers had profound reverberations in the societies of the Hispanic Caribbean. The course of international rivalry and the transition in hegemony over the region to a great extent shaped political thought. British abolitionist pressures, for example, in 1840–42, 1848, and 1853–54 were instrumental in the politicization of the Cuban Creole elite, who began to pursue radical political alternatives such as annexationist separatism. One clear indicator of the influence of international pressures in the shaping of political patterns in the Hispanic Caribbean was that parallel polarization took place in Cuban and Dominican politics and in tensions between the United States and the European naval powers. This was evident in Cuba beginning in the early to mid-1840s and in the Dominican Republic after 1854. Moreover, polarization in Dominican and Cuban politics reached their peaks at precisely the moments of highest international tension over the region. In Puerto Rico, where international rivalries were not as marked, the Creole elite's politicization and polarization took place in a considerably lower key.

In this increasingly polarized, highly charged atmosphere of international rivalry, the Cuban elite responded by gravitating to one of two poles. Annexationists looked to the United States, embracing republicanism. Cuba's reformists reaffirmed their ties to Spain, seeking to strengthen their links with Europe on the basis of Catholic monarchism. Cuban annexationism entered a crisis beginning in the mid-1850s. The Cuban separatist-annexationist party became disillusioned with the U.S. government, resenting its insistence on attempting to solve the Cuba "problem" through the purchase route. Moreover, the political crisis during the latter years of the antebellum era and the period of the U.S. Civil War eliminated the alternative of annexation. Also, during this period of U.S. retrenchment, the conditions arose for the establishment of the *política de atracción,* which allowed the emergence of a Cuban reform movement seeking to solve the region's problems within the mechanisms of the Spanish empire. During the Cuban Ten Years' War, however, some Cuban patriots looked once again to the United States as the source of moral and material support in the struggle against Spanish colonialism. Thus, annexationism resurfaced once again, only to abate soon afterward in the face of the Grant administration's hostility.

Despite the profound differences separating Cuba and the Dominican Republic, similar patterns of political thought evolved in them. In the precariously established Caribbean republic, contending political factions emerged in the 1850s under the leadership of two caudillos: Pedro Santana and Buenaventura Báez. During the antebellum period the Santana party sought on numerous occasions to incorporate the republic into the United States. Meanwhile, the Báez party looked to Europe for the establishment of a protectorate over the Dominican Republic. Then in 1861 the so-called friend of the United States, Santana, successfully annexed his country, not to the United States, but to Spain. After the Dominicans regained their independence in 1865, Báez, "the anti-American," again paradoxically offered to sell his country, not to France or Spain, but to the United States.

One could try to understand these radical shifts by invoking the old explanation that Santana, Báez, and their Cuban counterparts were opportunistic, self-serving politicians. One could also see these shifts as reflections of equally dramatic changes in the international balance of power in the Hispanic Caribbean. Santana's shift in 1860 and 1861 took place in a context of deep political crisis in the United States that resulted in a reduction in U.S. influence over the region and the temporary demise of the pro-U.S. annexationist alternative. Shortly after the Civil War the United States once again assumed the position of indisputable hegemonic power in the region, this time without the antebellum constraints of sectional compromises. Amid these new geopolitical realities, Báez and the other annexationists of the Second Republic converted to pro–North Americanism. They could no longer look to the European powers for political support. These nations, except for Spain, which precariously held on to Cuba and Puerto Rico, had retreated from the Hispanic Caribbean, never to return.

Notes

Abbreviations Used

AGI	Archivo General de Indias, Seville
AGNRD	Archivo General de la Nación, Santo Domingo
AGPR	Archivo General de Puerto Rico, San Juan
AHN	Archivo Histórico Nacional, Madrid
AHP	Archivo Histórico de Ponce
ASHM	Archivo del Servicio Histórico Militar, Madrid
BPP	*British Parliamentary Papers*
CIH	Centro de Investigaciones Históricas, Universidad de Puerto Rico, Río Piedras
Duke	Special Collections Department, Perkins Library, Duke University, Durham, North Carolina
exp.	*expediente* (file)
HAHR	*Hispanic American Historical Review*
HLHU	Houghton Library, Harvard University, Cambridge, Massachusetts
LC	Library of Congress, Washington, D.C.
leg.	*legajo* (bundle)
MDA	Maryland Diocesan Archives, Baltimore
NA	National Archives, Washington, D.C.
PRFA	*Papers Relating to Foreign Affairs of the United States*
PRO	Public Record Office, Kew, England
RCSA	Records of the Confederate States of America
RG	Record Group
SHC	Southern Historical Collection, Chapel Hill, North Carolina
VHS	Virginia Historical Society, Richmond

Introduction

1. Throughout this book the term *hegemony* is defined simply as preponderant influence and domination. Hilbourne Watson recently presented a definition of *hegemony* that relates closely to the one applied here. Hegemony, Watson argues, occurs when a nation is able to impose on another a consensus that recognizes domination without recourse to military subordination or a physical metropolitan presence. This consensus allows the dominant power to define and dictate the economic and political alternatives of the subordinate nation. The recourse to military force, Watson suggests, is in fact a sign of the breakdown of consensus and loss of hegemony. Hilbourne Watson, "The United States and the Caribbean: Whose New World Order?" (Paper presented at the seventeenth annual conference of the Caribbean Studies Association, St. George's, Grenada, May 26, 1992).

2. For a good assessment of U.S.-British tensions over Cuba to 1830, see John J. Johnson, *A Hemisphere Apart: The Foundations of United States Policy Toward Latin America* (Baltimore: Johns Hopkins University Press, 1990). Johnson argues that during this period a stalemate emerged, and both nations sought to curb Cuba's independence and to stop its transfer to another northern Atlantic power.

3. An extensive body of literature treats the U.S. road to empire, but attention to the Caribbean has been almost exclusively limited to the maturation of expansionism in the 1890s, culminating in the Spanish-Cuban-American War. An early work by Walter Millis, strongly influenced by Frederick Jackson Turner's frontier thesis, argued that the lack of "unified psychological patterns" until around 1895 prevented the United States from embarking on empire building. Later works by Ernest E. May, Richard Hofstadter, Walter LaFeber, and William Appleman Williams sought more profound explanations for questions such as what forces led the United States into creating an empire and what factors explain the timing of its formation. In *Imperial Democracy*, May emphasized pivotal political transformations and shifts in public opinion in the late 1880s and early 1890s as well as the leadership role played by Boston's intelligentsia and New York's financial and industrial elite. He stressed the fact that in the 1890s the United States suddenly found itself in the position of empire builder. A different approach guided LaFeber's now classic *New Empire*. His study broadened the debate by incorporating economic motivations for imperialism—basically, that the industrial revolution in North America and the increased productivity that came with it made necessary the guarantees of access to new markets abroad. His study also went beyond attention to actual physical expansion as he traced the development of an empire that did not call for military and administrative domination but

rather for economic subordination. Still, his study viewed the decades leading to the 1890s as a period of "incubation." A similar approach, but one focusing on the expansionist demands of commercial agriculture, guided Williams's work. In *The Roots of the Modern American Empire* he explored the dramatic changes in agricultural productivity between 1875 and 1881, along with the partial closing of the European markets, to explain the expansionism that characterized commercial agriculturalists. He argued that these developments put the nation's agrarian sector in the paradoxical position of being "economic imperialists" while themselves enduring a "quasi-colonial" form of domination within the United States. His study linked economic transformations and political developments, as he argued that only shortly before the war with Spain did the metropolitan political leadership come to recognize the expansionist plight of the agrarian majority. A later work by Ernest N. Paolino, *The Foundations of the American Empire* (Ithaca, N.Y.: Cornell University Press, 1973), carefully traces the transition from agrarian expansionism to commercial imperialism during the critical period of the Civil War and its aftermath. He argued that 1898 was neither "inexplicable" nor "pathological" but rather the culmination of decades of imperialist preparation.

See A. E. Campbell, ed., *Expansion and Imperialism* (New York: Harper and Row, 1970); Ernest E. May, *Imperial Democracy* (New York: Harcourt, Brace and World, 1961); Walter LaFeber, *The New Empire: An Interpretation of American Expansion, 1860–1898* (Ithaca, N.Y.: Cornell University Press, 1963); William Appleman Williams, *The Roots of the Modern American Empire* (New York: Random House, 1969). See also Robert E. May, *The Southern Dream of a Caribbean Empire, 1854–1861* (Baton Rouge: Louisiana State University Press, 1973; Athens: University of Georgia Press, 1989). Robert May's book, written from a North American perspective and informed by sources pertaining to U.S. history, also deals with earlier manifestations of expansionism and with national restraints blocking such efforts.

4. These dates indicate significant events: 1762, British occupation of Havana; 1815, Cédula de Gracias reform package granted to Puerto Rico; 1837, first railroad in Cuba; 1844, Dominican independence from Haitian domination; 1861, Spanish annexation of the Dominican Republic; 1868, start of Cuba's Ten Years' War; and 1873, abolition of slavery in Puerto Rico.

5. In justifying the study of Cuba, Puerto Rico, and the Dominican Republic as a whole unit, albeit through monographs focusing on individual components, the editors of *Between Slavery and Free Labor* enumerate seven characteristics separating the Hispanic islands from the rest of the archipelago: larger size, early settlement pattern of colonization, late development of plantation systems, lighter-skinned population patterns, colonial links with a weaker metropolis, greater native economic initiative, and early establish-

ment of simultaneous colonialism and neocolonialism. See Manuel Moreno Fraginals, Frank Moya Pons, and Stanley L. Engerman, eds., *Between Slavery and Free Labor: The Spanish-Speaking Caribbean in the Nineteenth Century* (Baltimore: Johns Hopkins University Press, 1985). There is a vast and growing body of secondary literature on each of the three particular components of the Hispanic Caribbean. As will become evident to the reader, I am profoundly indebted to the corpus of recent monographic output on Cuba, Puerto Rico, and the Dominican Republic.

6. The Dominicans severed their already weak political ties with Spain in 1822. Shortly after independence, Haitian troops unified the island under Haitian rule, a domination that lasted twenty-two years. The First Dominican Republic came to an end in 1861, when Spain annexed Dominican territory. The Second Republic began in 1865.

7. Franklin W. Knight, *The Caribbean, the Genesis of a Fragmented Nationalism*, 1st and 2d eds. (New York: Oxford University Press, 1978 and 1990); Sidney W. Mintz, *Caribbean Transformations* (Chicago: Aldine Publishing Co., 1974); Gordon K. Lewis, *Main Currents in Caribbean Thought: The Historical Evolution of Caribbean Society in Its Ideological Aspects, 1492–1900* (Baltimore: Johns Hopkins University Press, 1983).

8. Recently some attempts have been made to compare the different components of the Hispanic Caribbean. These, however, tend to emphasize the "enormous differences" separating Cuba from Puerto Rico and the Dominican Republic. See, for example, Laird W. Bergad, "¿Dos alas del mismo pájaro?: Notas sobre la historia socioeconómica comparativa de Cuba y Puerto Rico," *Historia y Sociedad* 1 (1988): 143–54; Roberto Marte, *Cuba y la República Dominicana: Transición económica en el Caribe del siglo xix* (Santo Domingo: Universidad APEC, [1988?]). See also Andrés A. Ramos Mattei, *Betances en el ciclo revolucionario antillano: 1867–1875* (San Juan: Instituto de Cultura, 1987).

9. Turnbull's abolitionist activities soon gained him the antipathy of Spanish colonial administrators and of those sectors depending on slave labor. Turnbull was charged with organizing slave revolts in the early 1840s.

10. Among the works dealing with the earlier period are Arturo Santana, "The United States and Puerto Rico, 1797–1830," Ph.D. diss., University of Chicago, 1953; Arturo Morales Carrión, "Los orígenes de las relaciones entre los Estados Unidos y Puerto Rico, 1700–1815," *Historia* 2, no. 1 (1952): 1–50; Jaques A. Barbier and Allan J. Kuethe, eds., *The North American Role in the Spanish Imperial Economy, 1760–1819* (Manchester: Manchester University Press, 1984); John H. Coatsworth, "American Trade with European Colonies in the Caribbean and South America, 1790–1812," *William and Mary Quarterly* 24 (1967): 243–61; and Johnson, *Hemisphere Apart*. For the post-1868 period, see Dulce María Tirado Merced, "Las raíces sociales del liberalismo criollo: El Partido Liberal Reformista, 1870–1875," M.A. thesis, Universidad de Puerto Rico,

1981; Carmelo Rosario Natal, *Puerto Rico y la crisis de la Guerra Hispanoamericana* (Hato Rey, P.R.: Ramallo Printing, 1975); Louis A. Pérez, Jr., *Cuba Between Empires, 1878–1902* (Pittsburgh: University of Pittsburgh Press, 1983); Ramiro Guerra y Sánchez, *Guerra de los Diez Años, 1868–1878*, 2 vols. (Havana: Editorial de Ciencias Sociales, 1972); Philip S. Foner, *The Spanish-Cuban-American War and the Birth of American Imperialism*, 2 vols. (New York: Monthly Review Press, 1972); and Fernando Picó, *1898: La guerra después de la guerra* (Río Piedras: Ediciones Huracán, 1987). Among the works dealing with part or all of the period covered here are May, *Southern Dream;* Basil Rauch, *American Interest in Cuba: 1848–1855* (New York: Columbia University Press, 1948); Lester D. Langley, *The Cuban Policy of the United States: A Brief History* (New York: John Wiley and Sons, 1968); idem, *Struggle for the American Mediterranean* (Athens: University of Georgia Press, 1976); Herminio Portell Vilá, *Historia de Cuba en sus relaciones con los Estados Unidos y España*, 4 vols. (Havana: Montero, 1938–41); idem, *Narciso López y su época, 1848–1850*, 3 vols. (Havana: Cultural, S.A., 1930–58); and Robert Louis Paquette, *Sugar Is Made with Blood: The Conspiracy of La Escalera and the Conflict Between Empires over Slavery in Cuba* (Middletown, Conn.: Wesleyan University Press, 1988).

11. Manuel Moreno Fraginals, "Plantations in the Caribbean: Cuba, Puerto Rico, and the Dominican Republic in the Late Nineteenth Century," in Moreno Fraginals, Moya Pons, and Engerman, eds., *Between Slavery and Free Labor*, 15–16.

12. Theotonio dos Santos defined *dependency* as "a situation in which the economy of certain countries is conditioned by the development and expansion of another economy to which the former is subjected. The relation of interdependence between two or more economies, and between these and the world trade, assumes the form of dependence when some countries (the dominant ones) can expand and can be self-sustaining, while other countries (the dependent ones) can do this only as a reflection of that expansion, which can have either a positive or negative effect on their immediate development." See Theotonio dos Santos, "La crisis de la teoría del desarrollo y las relaciones de dependencia en América Latina," *Boletín del Centro de Estudios Socioeconómicos* 3 (Oct. 1968), 26.

Chapter 1: Clash of Empires

1. For a discussion of these differences, see Langley, *Cuban Policy*, 1–19.

2. Not only was Cuba geographically close to the United States, but it was also considered a "contiguous territory," following Thomas Jefferson's argument that it could be defended without a navy.

3. William L. Brent, one of the U.S. delegates to the Panama Conference in

1826, expressed the official concern that Cuban independence would translate into "a certain part of its population [namely blacks] attaining the ascendancy." Johnson, *Hemisphere Apart*, 146.

4. William Spence Robertson, *Hispanic-American Relations with the United States* (New York: Oxford University Press, 1923), 420.

5. Johnson, *Hemisphere Apart*, 78.

6. Samuel Flagg Bemis, *The Latin American Policy of the United States* (New York: Harcourt, Brace, and Co., 1943), 27; Manuel Quesada, *Address of Cuba to the United States* (New York: N.p., 1873), 32; Emilio Roig de Leuchsenring, *Cuba y los Estados Unidos, 1805–1898* (Havana: Sociedad Cubana de Estudios Históricos e Internacionales, 1949), 118. For a discussion of the role of the United States, see Langley, *Cuban Policy*, 14–17; and Johnson, *Hemisphere Apart*, 140–49.

7. David Murray, *Odious Commerce: Britain, Spain, and the Abolition of the Cuban Slave Trade* (Cambridge: Cambridge University Press, 1980), 169.

8. Henry Clay to Alexander Everett, April 13, 1826, quoted in José de Armas y Céspedes, *Position of the United States on the Cuban Question* (New York: N.p., 1872), 3; John Quincy Adams to Hugh Nelson, April 28, 1823, in Robert F. Smith, ed., *What Happened in Cuba? A Documentary History* (New York: Twayne Publishers, 1963), 29. In 1839 Secretary of State John Forsyth reminded the Havana consul of this policy and instructed him to exercise caution in maintaining it. Forsyth to Nicholas Trist, March 19, 1839, quoted in Kenneth W. Bunce, "American Interests in the Caribbean Islands, 1783–1850," Ph.D. diss., Ohio State University, 1939, p. 174.

9. Forsyth to Aaron Vail, July 15, 1840, quoted in Leland H. Jenks, *Our Cuban Colony: A Study in Sugar* (New York: Vanguard Press, 1928), 10; Leví Marrero, *Cuba: Economía y sociedad*, 14 vols. (Madrid: Editorial Playor, 1971–88), 9:89; instructions of James Buchanan to John Slidell, March 12, 1846, quoted in Dexter Perkins, *The Monroe Doctrine, 1826–1867* (Baltimore: Johns Hopkins University Press, 1933), 147.

10. Eric Williams, *Capitalism and Slavery*, 7th ed. (New York: Capricorn Books, 1966); Lord Palmerston quoted in C. Stanley Urban, "The Africanization of Cuba Scare, 1853–1855," *HAHR* 37, no. 1 (Feb. 1957): 32.

11. David Turnbull, *Travels in the West: Cuba with Notices of Porto Rico and the Slave Trade* (London, 1840; New York: Negro Universities Press, 1969), 40; Paquette, *Sugar*, 134.

12. These militant abolitionists replaced notoriously lax judges James Kennedy and Campbell J. Dalrymple, and Consul Charles Tolmé.

13. After increased pressures from the British government, Turnbull was finally recognized in March 1841. See Emilio Roig de Leuchsenring, "Cuba en 1840," *Revista Bimestre Cubana* 46, no. 2 (1940): 165. Parallel to the activities

of the British consular corps ran those of evangelical missionaries, who combined the Gospel with abolitionist teachings. Captain-General Miguel Tacón was quite active in the repression of such missionaries. In 1838, for example, Spanish authorities arrested James Thompson of the London Bible Society. See Miguel Tacón to the Spanish minister of state, Aug. 31, 1835, and March 5, 1836, in Miguel Tacón, *Correspondencia reservada del Capitán General don Miguel Tacón con el gobierno de Madrid, 1834–1836*, ed. Juan Pérez de la Riva (Havana: Biblioteca Nacional José Martí, 1963), 177–79, 223–25; and Marcos Antonio Ramos, *Panorama del protestantismo en Cuba* (San José, Costa Rica: Editorial Caribe, 1986), 57–69.

14. For a partial listing of slave conspiracies during this period, see [Richard Burleigh Kimball], *Cuba, and the Cubans: Comprising a History of the Island of Cuba, Its Present Social, Political, and Domestic Conditions . . .* (New York: S. Hueston, 1850), 81. For a discussion of the historiography of this topic, see Murray, *Odious Commerce*, 159–61; and Paquette, *Sugar*, 3–26.

15. Arturo Morales Carrión, *Auge y decadencia de la trata negrera en Puerto Rico (1820–1860)* (San Juan: Instituto de Cultura, 1978), 124; royal decree of July 28, 1841, in Archivo Nacional de Cuba, Asuntos Políticos, leg. 47, signatura 11, copy in CIH; Paquette, *Sugar*, 140–41; Laird W. Bergad, *Cuban Rural Society in the Nineteenth Century: The Social and Economic History of Monoculture in Matanzas* (Princeton, N.J.: Princeton University Press, 1990), 242. See also Joseph T. Crawford to Lord Palmerston, Oct. 23, 1851, PRO, FO 72, 793.

16. Madden also clashed with Captain-General Tacón. Trist and Tacón remained on very good terms. As a token of his friendship, Trist gave Tacón the first Colt revolver to be imported into Cuba. Richard Robert Madden, *The Island of Cuba: Its Resources, Progress, and Prospects* (London: Partridge and Oakey, 1853), 3; Tacón, *Correspondencia*, 19.

17. Jerónimo Bécker, *Historia de las relaciones exteriores de España durante el siglo xix*, 2 vols. (Madrid: Voluntad, 1924–26), 2:65; Westcott quoted in Rauch, *American Interest*, 70; Murray, *Odious Commerce*, 141–42.

18. For contemporary accounts of the extent of repression in 1844, see VHS, Diary of the Reverend William Norwood; and HLHU, José Agustín Escoto Papers (hereinafter cited as Escoto), box 10.

19. Miguel Aldama to Domingo del Monte, June 29, 1844, in Domingo Figarola-Caneda, ed., *Centón epistolario de Domingo del Monte*, 7 vols. (Havana: Imprenta El Siglo XX, 1923–57), 6:59; CIH, *El proceso abolicionista en Puerto Rico: Documentos para su estudio*, 2 vols. (San Juan: CIH–Instituto de Cultura, 1974–78), 1:297. Miguel Aldama to del Monte, April 9, 1844; José Luis Alfonso to del Monte, July 4, 1844; and Gaspar Betancourt Cisneros to del Monte, May 15, 1843, all in Figarola-Caneda, ed., *Centón epistolario* 6:21, 6:62–64, 5:99–100.

20. See "Bando de Prim contra la raza africana del 31 de mayo de 1848," in

Cayetano Coll y Toste, ed., *Boletín histórico de Puerto Rico*, 14 vols. (San Juan: Tipografía Cantero Fernández y Cía., 1914–27), 2:122–24. By 1860 the official census no longer distinguished between *pardos* (mulattoes) and *morenos* (blacks). Both categories were now grouped under the rubric of *gente de color* (people of color).

21. Paquette, *Sugar*, 170.

22. Estimate by Thomas C. Reynolds, cited in Morales Carrión, *Auge y decadencia*, 156. A higher estimate of 630 million is provided in "Del estado financiero de España," *La Verdad*, May 20, 1853, p. 132. Figures throughout this book are given in U.S. dollars unless otherwise noted.

23. Marvin Harris, *Patterns of Race in the Americas* (New York: B. Walker and Co., 1964), 76.

24. Arthur F. Corwin, *Spain and the Abolition of Slavery in Cuba, 1817–1886* (Austin: University of Texas Press, 1967), 84; Aldama to del Monte, May 8, 1845, in Figarola-Caneda, ed., *Centón epistolario* 6:196–98.

25. Responding to plans to stop the further importation of slaves into Cuba, O'Donnell told colonial authorities in Spain that such measures would "destroy assurances to the conservation of territorial integrity and colonial dependence." See O'Donnell's response, dated Feb. 15, 1845, quoted in Reyneiro G. Lebroc, *Cuba: Iglesia y sociedad (1830–1860)* (Madrid: N.p., 1976), 36 n. 167; Paquette, *Sugar*, 81; Philip S. Foner, *A History of Cuba and Its Relations with the United States*, 2 vols. (New York: International Publishers, 1962–63), 1:222.

26. Federico Roncali to the Spanish minister of state, July 9, 1848, quoted in Corwin, *Spain and the Abolition*, 93.

27. Frank Moya Pons, *Manual de historia dominicana*, 8th ed. (Santiago, Dominican Republic: Universidad Católica Madre y Maestra, 1984), 276; French consul at Santo Domingo to the French minister of foreign affairs, Jan. 20, 1848, and Jan. 24, 1849, in Emilio Rodríguez Demorizi, ed., *Correspondencia del consul de Francia en Santo Domingo, 1846–1850*, 2 vols. (Santo Domingo: Editora Montalvo, 1944–47), 2:34–38, 112–13; Schomburgk to Lord Palmerston, May 22 and July 14, 1849, both in PRO, FO 140, 1; text of Franco-Dominican treaty signed Oct. 22, 1848, in República Dominicana, *Colección de leyes, decretos y resoluciones*, 52 vols. to date (Santo Domingo: Publicaciones ONAP, 1982–), 2:172–83. The treaty did not include provisions for the payments of debts to France.

28. Captain-general of Puerto Rico to Antonio de Benavides, May 18 and Oct. 11, 1847, AHN, Ultramar, leg. 3524, exps. 43, 47. British subject Herman Hendrick attempted to force a loan on the emerging republic under quite usurious conditions, but the Dominican Congress rejected the offer. See congressional proclamation in Roberto Marte, *Estadísticas y documentos históricos sobre Santo Domingo (1805–1890)* (Santo Domingo: Museo Nacional de Historia y Geografía, 1984), 115–18.

29. Report of John Hogan to James Buchanan, Oct. 4, 1845, in Alfonso Lockward, ed., *Documentos para la historia de las relaciones dominico americanas (1837–1860)* (Santo Domingo: Editora Corripio, 1987), 54; Charles C. Tansill, *The United States and Santo Domingo, 1798–1873* (Baltimore: Johns Hopkins University Press, 1938), 134.

30. Also in 1848 Colonel Bristow, a British officer stationed in Madrid, was arrested by Spanish authorities; Lord Palmerston to the Spanish minister at London, May 30, 1848, AHN, Estado, leg. 8565.

31. Emeterio Santiago Santovenia y Echaide, *El presidente Polk y Cuba* (Havana: Academia de la Historia de Cuba, 1935), 112; Portell Vilá, *Narciso López* 2:27.

32. Foner, *History of Cuba* 2:21–23. Julius W. Pratt, C. Stanley Urban, Robert E. May, and others have demonstrated in their works that before the 1850s expansionism was a party issue, rather than a sectional one. See Julius W. Pratt, "The Ideology of American Expansion," in *Essays in Honor of William Dodd*, ed. Avery Craven (Chicago: University of Chicago Press, 1935), 346; C. Stanley Urban, "The Ideology of Southern Imperialism: New Orleans and the Caribbean, 1845–1860," *Louisiana Historical Quarterly* 34, no. 1 (1956): 48–73; May, *Southern Dream*, 19–21.

33. James Buchanan to Romulus Saunders, June 17, 1848, in Smith, ed., *What Happened in Cuba?*, 41.

34. Rauch, *American Interest*, 97.

35. John Clayton to Daniel Barringer, Aug. 2, 1849, in Smith, ed., *What Happened in Cuba?* 45; Paquette, *Sugar*, 195.

36. Foner, *History of Cuba* 2:73.

37. The Compromise of 1850 consisted of five provisions aimed at reducing sectional antagonism between the North and South in the United States. These were the admission of California as a free state, the organization of New Mexico as a territory without restrictions on slavery, the organization of Utah as a territory under similar provisions, a stringent fugitive slave law, and the abolition of the slave trade in the District of Columbia.

38. According to Robert E. May, one expansionist group aspired to gain fifty new senatorial seats and more than sixty new seats in the House. May, *Southern Dream*, 150.

39. As the main exporting port of the United States, New Orleans had long-established commercial ties with Cuba. During the 1830s and 1840s, however, New Orleans's relative importance as a trading partner and a source of capital diminished steadily, while that of Boston, New York, Philadelphia, and other northeastern ports grew. This was in part the result of the U.S. trade policy toward Spain and its colonies. Ramiro Guerra y Sánchez, *Manual de historia de Cuba* (Madrid: Editorial R., 1975), 489.

40. According to Charles W. Ramsdell, by 1850 cotton cultivation had ex-

tended as far west as geographic and climatic conditions allowed. Ramsdell, "The Natural Limits of Slavery Expansion," *Mississippi Valley Historical Review* 16 (1929): 151–71.

41. James Oaks, *The Ruling Race: A History of American Slaveholders* (New York: Alfred A. Knopf, 1982), 78, 80. A slave in the United States cost an average of $1,200, compared with only $500 in Cuba. See Rauch, *American Interest*, 200–202.

42. A number of southern planters are registered in "Register of Americans [in Cuba]," NA, Records of Foreign Service Posts of the Department of State, RG 84, Havana, vol. c.14.1; see also Urban, "Ideology," 66–68.

43. Rauch, *American Interest*, 208. Bryant and other northern abolitionist expansionists maintained that if Cuba was acquired by the United States, the slave trade would immediately end. See William Cullen Bryant, *Letters of William Cullen Bryant*, ed. William Cullen Bryant II and Thomas G. Voss, 4 vols. (New York: Fordham University Press, 1975–84), 3:48; and Robert B. Leard, "Bonds of Destiny: The United States and Cuba, 1848–1861," Ph.D. diss., University of California, Berkeley, 1953, pp. 150–53.

44. Proclamation of Zachary Taylor of Aug. 11, 1849, in James D. Richardson, ed., *A Compilation of the Messages and Papers of the Presidents, 1789–1897*, 10 vols. (Washington, D.C.: GPO, 1896–99), 5:7–8; John Clayton to J. Prescott Hall, Sept. 6, 1849, NA, General Records of the Department of State, RG 59, Records of Special Agents, Cuba, vol. 18; Clayton to Logan Hunton, June 9, 1850, quoted in Lester D. Langley, "The Whigs and the López Expeditions to Cuba, 1849–1851," *Revista de Historia de América* 71 (Jan.–June 1971): 14–15.

45. Proclamation of Millard Fillmore of April 25, 1851, in Richardson, ed., *Compilation* 5:111–12.

46. Ángel Calderón de la Barca to the Spanish minister of state, Aug. 14, 1849, AHN, Estado, leg. 5588, exp. 4; Calderón de la Barca to the Spanish minister of state, Aug. 22, 1852, ASHM, Ultramar, leg. 90; José de la Concha to the president of the Council of Ministers, March 31, 1851, quoted in Robert G. Caldwell, *The López Expeditions to Cuba, 1848–1851* (Princeton, N.J.: Princeton University Press, 1915), 41.

47. Mariano Torrente, *Bosquejo económico político de la isla de Cuba*, 2 vols. (Madrid: M. Pita-Barcina, 1852–53), 1:65; idem, "Memoria del 28 de septiembre de 1852," in España, Ministerio de Ultramar, *Cuba desde 1850 a 1873*, comp. Carlos de Sedano (Madrid: Imprenta Nacional, 1873), 168–74; idem, *Política ultramarina que abraza todos los puntos referentes a las relaciones de España con los Estados Unidos, con la Inglaterra y las Antillas, y señaladamente con la isla de Santo Domingo* (Madrid: Compañía General de Impresos y Libros del Reino, 1854), 81–82, 105; Thomas W. Wilson, *An Authentic Narrative Upon the Piratical Descents Made Upon Cuba* (Havana, 1851), 18; Demoticus Philalethes, *Yankee*

Travels Through the Island of Cuba; or, The Men and Government, the Laws and Customs of Cuba, as Seen by American Eyes (New York: D. A. Appleton, 1856), 73; de la Pezuela to Leopoldo A. de Cueto, July 10, 1854, AHN, Ultramar, leg. 4648, exp. 15, doc. 2; and de la Pezuela to José María Magallón, March 22, 1854, AHN, Ultramar, leg. 4645, exp. 33, doc. 8.

48. Cuban colonial records for this period housed in the Spanish Military Archives (ASHM) are dotted with reports by consuls about filibusterers and their activities. See, for example, captain-general of Cuba to the president of the Council of Ministers, April 30, 1852, and Spanish consul at New York to the minister of state, Aug. 20, 1852, and May 3, 1852, all in ASHM, Ultramar, leg. 90.

49. Portell Vilá, *Narciso López* 2:200.

50. Federico Roncali to the Spanish minister of government, Sept. 9, 1849, quoted in Portell Vilá, *Narciso López* 2:197; Roncali to the Spanish minister of state, Sept. 29, 1849, quoted in Foner, *History of Cuba* 2:19; Un hacendado [Cristóbal F. Madan], *Llamamiento de la isla de Cuba a la Nación Española* (New York: Hallet, 1854), 56.

51. Torrente, *Bosquejo* 1:25, 151–52; Un español americano, *Alerta a los cubanos* (New Orleans: La Patria, 1850), 10; president of the Spanish Council of Ministers to the minister of state, June 9, 1852, ASHM, Ultramar, leg. 90.

52. Torrente, *Política ultramarina*, 105–8; Rauch, *American Interest*, 138; Leard, "Bonds of Destiny," 109; Captain-General Cañedo to the president of the Spanish Council of Ministers, Nov. 8, 1852, AHN, Ultramar, leg. 4637, exp. 52, doc. 1. A Franco-British entente had, in fact, been brewing since the mid-1830s, as two blocs began to form in Europe, one authoritarian and conservative (Austria, Prussia, and Russia), the other liberal and parliamentarian (Britain and France). Anglo-Franco cooperation on foreign issues was not limited to Cuba. It was also evident with regard to the Dominican Republic, Hawaii, and Texas. Significantly, in 1840 Earl Spencer described France as "the nation in Europe most fitted to be our friend by situation, institutions, and civilization." Kenneth Bourne, *The Foreign Policy of Victorian England* (Oxford: Clarendon Press, 1970), 32, 87, 226–27, 249–50; idem, *The Balance of Power in North America* (Berkeley: University of California Press, 1967), 124.

53. United States, Department of State, *Correspondence on the Proposed Tripartite Convention Relative to Cuba* (Boston: Little, Brown and Co., 1853).

54. Secretary Everett to Lord John Russell and the Comte de Sartiges, Dec. 1, 1852, in U.S. Dept. of State, *Correspondence*, 42–44.

55. See Duff Green and Benjamin Green to the Dominican government, Aug. 26, 1850, in Marte, *Estadísticas*, 61.

56. Secretary Clayton to Benjamin Green, June 13, 1849 (confidential), NA, State, RG 59, Records of Special Missions, reel 152; Consul Robert B. Campbell

to Clayton, June 4, 1850, NA, State, RG 59, Diplomatic Despatches, Havana, vol. 23.

57. French consul at Santo Domingo to the French minister of foreign affairs, April 2, 1850, and French consul at Port-au-Prince to the French minister of foreign affairs, April 30, 1850, both in Rodríguez Demorizi, ed., *Correspondencia* 2:223–27, 234; Lord Palmerston to Robert Schomburgk, March 25, 1850, PRO, FO 140, 2; Schomburgk to Lord Palmerston, July 26, 1852, and the earl of Malmesburg to Schomburgk, May 24, 1852, both in PRO, FO 140, 3; Benjamin Green to Secretary Clayton, Sept. 27, 1849, in Lockward, ed., *Documentos*, 92; Jaime de Jesús Domínguez, *Economía y política: República Dominicana, 1844–1861* (Santo Domingo: Editora de la UASD, 1977), 110. See James A. Williamson, *A Short History of British Expansion*, 6th ed. (New York: St. Martin's, 1967), 18, 56; Edward Grierson, *The Death of the Imperial Dream* (Garden City, N.Y.: Doubleday and Co., 1972), 68; and Bourne, *Balance of Power*, 122. Also see instructions to Consul Schomburgk regarding Dominican requests for a British protectorate, June 8, 1849, PRO, FO 140, 1.

58. Sumner Welles, *Naboth's Vineyard: The Dominican Republic, 1844–1924*, 2 vols. (New York: Payson and Clarke, 1928), 1:102; French consul at Santo Domingo to Captain-General Valentín Cañedo, Sept. 7, 1852, AHN, Ultramar, leg. 3524, exp. 56, doc. 8.

59. José M. Pando to Valentín Cañedo, Aug. 7, 1852, AHN, Ultramar, leg. 3524, exp. 56bis, doc. 1; see also doc. 4 (copies in CIH).

60. Spanish minister of state to the president of the Spanish Council of Ministers, Nov. 24, 1852, AHN, Ultramar, leg. 3524, exp. 64, doc. 1.

61. Buenaventura Báez to French consul Pierre Levasseur, Feb. 15, 1845, and French consul to the French minister of foreign affairs, Feb. 19, 1849, both in Rodríguez Demorizi, ed., *Correspondencia* 2:76, 127; Welles, *Naboth's Vineyard* 1:110.

62. Jonathan Elliot to James Buchanan, April 13, 1849, in Lockward, ed., *Documentos*, 80–81; French consul at Santo Domingo to the French minister of foreign affairs, May 3 and April 12, 1849, in Rodríguez Demorizi, ed., *Correspondencia* 2:130, 142; Schomburgk to Commodore Bennet, April 9, 1849, PRO, FO 140, 1; letter to the captain-general of Puerto Rico, April 4, 1849, AHN, Ultramar, leg. 3524, exp. 52, doc. 3 (copy in CIH). On the mediation process, see PRO, FO 140, 2; and Lord Palmerston to Schomburgk, Aug. 18, 1851, PRO, FO 140, 3.

63. Pierce's inaugural message, March 4, 1853, in Richardson, ed., *Compilation* 5:197–203.

64. Portell Vilá, *Historia de Cuba* 2:13; Buchanan to William Marcy, March 8, 1853, quoted in Portell Vilá, *Historia de Cuba* 2:19.

65. Edward Everett to Lord John Russell, Sept. 17, 1853, Lord John Russell Papers, Special Collections Department, Perkins Library, Duke University.

66. Quitman was offered dictatorial powers, with control over civil and military matters, along with an eight hundred thousand–dollar bonus. May, *Southern Dream*, 47.

67. Rauch, *American Interest*, 273.

68. U.S. consuls, Marcy, and the filibuster movement attributed the measures of Juan de la Pezuela to British pressure. See Marcy to Charles W. Davis, March 15, 1854, NA, State, RG 59, Special Missions, reel 154.

69. Corwin, *Spain and the Abolition*, 112. In the May 30, 1853, session of the House of Lords, the English prime minister personally accused Valentín Cañedo of being implicated in the slave trade. See Lebroc, *Cuba*, 181; Joseph T. Crawford to Lord Palmerston, Jan. 20, 1853, and Crawford to the Foreign Office, Jan. 27, 1853, both in PRO, FO 84, 905; Crawford to Lord Palmerston, Jan. 20, 1853, and Crawford to Lord Clarendon, Oct. 11, 1853, both in PRO, FO 72, 858, 830.

70. De la Pezuela's short but eventful tenure extended from December 1853 to September 1854.

71. Morales Carrión, *Auge y decadencia*, 174. It is interesting to note that de la Pezuela is remembered among Puerto Ricans not as an abolitionist colonial administrator but as the despotic creator of vagrancy and serfdom laws that restricted the liberty and mobility of the island's displaced peonage. De la Pezuela received praise from British officials on both sides of the Atlantic: British minister at Madrid to Ángel Calderón de la Barca, May 17, 1854, and British minister at Madrid to J. Francisco Pacheco, Oct. 10, 1854, both in AHN, Estado, leg. 8047; Crawford to Lord Clarendon, June 28, 1854, PRO, FO 84, 936.

72. A British visitor had described the *emancipados'* fate: "[They are made] lamplighters, at five ounces apiece, or sent to the sugar estates to furnish sweets for the cup of life of [Queen Mother] Doña Cristina and El Marquis de las Delicias." John G. Taylor, *The United States and Cuba: Eight Years of Change and Travel* (London: Richard Bentley, 1851), 280–89. According to the British consul at Havana, some four thousand *emancipados* were fraudulently reenslaved. See Franklin W. Knight, *Slave Society in Cuba During the Nineteenth Century* (Madison: University of Wisconsin Press, 1970), 29.

73. The majority of the slaves had either been born in or been brought to Cuba after 1835. The life expectancy of plantation slaves in Cuba has been estimated at only seven years. The first Anglo-Spanish agreement to stop the slave trade dated to 1817, when Great Britain paid Spain four hundred thousand pounds in compensation. Treaties of 1817 and 1835 in Great Britain,

British and Foreign State Papers (1816–17, 1834–35) (London: James Ridgway and Sons, 1838, 1852), 1816–17:33–74, 1834–35:343–74.

74. See *La Gaceta de La Habana*, May 3 and 4, 1854. Other controversial decrees by de la Pezuela included provisions allowing blacks to be educated and to marry whites.

75. Guerra y Sánchez, *Manual*, 546; Torrente, *Política ultramarina*, 113–14; Rauch, *American Interest*, 299.

76. Murray, *Odious Commerce*, 253; Consul Joseph T. Crawford to Lord Clarendon, Sept. 27, 1854, in Great Britain, Parliament, House of Commons, *British Parliamentary Papers [Slave Trade]* (hereinafter cited as *BPP*), 95 vols. (Shannon, Ireland: Irish University Press, 1968–71), vol. 41, class B, p. 533.

77. For official British reactions, see Crawford to Lord Clarendon, Sept. 27, 1854, and July 26, 1854, *BPP*, vol. 41, class B, pp. 523, 533; George C. Backhouse to Lord Clarendon, July 31, 1854, *BPP*, vol. 40, class A, p. 23, and vol. 41, class A, p. 17.

78. Rauch, *American Interest*, 278. Torrente argued that because of the high demand for slave labor and the huge profits linked to the slave trade, slave trading could not be stopped by using force alone. See Mariano Torrente, *Memoria sobre la esclavitud en la isla de Cuba* (London: Wood, 1853), 46–50; idem, *Política ultramarina*, 169–71, 207–8, 218.

79. In Puerto Rico there were only 51,265 slaves out of a population of 443,139 in 1846, and 41,736 out of a population of 583,308 in 1860. Coll y Toste, ed., *Boletín histórico* 5:289.

80. Fernando de Norzagaray, "Diario del Gobernador Norzagaray," *Anales de Investigación Histórica* 6, nos. 1–2 (Jan.–Dec. 1979): 108.

81. Alexander Clayton to Marcy, Dec. 15, 1853, quoted in Portell Vilá, *Historia de Cuba* 2:77; William H. Robertson to Marcy, April 21 and May 10 and 14, 1854, NA, State, RG 59, Havana, vol. 27.

82. Marcy to Charles W. Davis, March 15, 1854, NA, State, RG 59, Special Missions, reel 154; report of Charles W. Davis to Marcy, May 22, 1854, NA, State, RG 59, Havana, vol. 27.

83. The Kansas-Nebraska Act was in essence a repeal of the Missouri Compromise. It established that the territories of Kansas and Nebraska could be organized without congressional intervention regarding the issue of slavery. U.S. Congress, House, 33d Cong., 1st sess., House Miscellaneous Docs., no. 79.

84. Robertson to Marcy, May 7, 1854, NA, State, RG 59, Havana, vol. 27.

85. One of the most vociferous of the expansionist publicists was John S. Thrasher. In his book *A Preliminary Essay on the Purchase of Cuba* (New York: Derby and Jackson, 1859), he denounced de la Pezuela's decrees as leading to a war of races.

86. Brown quoted in May, *Southern Dream*, 9; George Fitzhugh, "Destiny of the Slave States," *DeBow's Review* 17, no. 3 (Sept. 1854): 280–84; Soulé quoted in Carlos de Sedano, *Cuba, estudios políticos* (Madrid: Manuel G. Hernández, 1872), 91–93; May, *Southern Dream*, 57, 75 (quoting Quitman).

87. Fitzhugh quoted in Rauch, *American Interest*, 185–89; John S. Thrasher, "Cuba and the United States," *DeBow's Review* 17, no. 1 (July 1854): 43–49; Wickliffe quoted in May, *Southern Dream*, 14.

88. See Foner, *History of Cuba* 2:101.

89. *La Verdad* started out as a bilingual publication advocating expansionist and annexationist solutions for the Cuban "problem." One of the most vociferous of the New York–based expansionists was Jane M. Cazneau (pseud., Cora Montgomery), wife of expansionist diplomat William Cazneau. She wrote in an article for the March 20, 1853, issue that "Island America [the islands of the Caribbean], must soon be sealed to the service of the Union, by the annexation of its Queen, the Island of Cuba." "It must in any event," she continued, "be secured to the white race, by detaching it from European and colored rule." In a similar article, titled "European Intervention," Cazneau warned: "If Spain arms a single black in the quarrel, the citizens and government of the United States will hold her an outlaw among civilized nations, and our whole people will make the cause of the Cubans their own." Later articles by Cazneau continued to point to the peril of a black empire and its nefarious consequences for U.S. commercial interests. The topics of Great Britain as the instigator nation and the peril of Cuba's Africanization constantly surfaced: "The torch is lighted and there is but one power that can save Cuba from the knife of the African War." Cazneau concluded another article by saying that the United States could not permit Cuba to be turned "into an unproductive and lawless den of savages." See *La Verdad*, March 20 and 30 and April 10, 1853. See also Robert E. May, "'Plenipotentiary in Petticoats': Jane M. Cazneau and American Foreign Policy in the Mid-Nineteenth Century," in *Women and American Foreign Policy*, ed. Edward P. Crapol (New York: Greenwood Press, 1987), 19–44.

90. Running the Mobile–New York route with calls in Havana, this vessel ran into difficulties with Spanish port authorities on February 18, 1854. Accused of failing to report the ship's cargo accurately, Captain James D. Bulloch was imprisoned and fined six thousand dollars; the cargo was confiscated. Evidence indicates that this fraud was the norm rather than the exception. What made the *Black Warrior* affair exceptional was the severity of the Spanish response. Joseph T. Crawford to the British minister in Washington, D.C., March 1, 1854, PRO, FO 72, 852; Rauch, *American Interest*, 279; Foner, *History of Cuba* 2:97; Miguel Blanco Herrero, *Isla de Cuba, su situación actual y reformas que reclama* (Madrid: Agustín Jubera, 1876), 46–51, 75.

91. Marcy to Pierre Soulé, April 3, 1854, in Smith, ed., *What Happened in Cuba?*, 59–60.

92. See Portell Vilá, *Historia de Cuba* 2:63–64. At one point Buchanan devised a scheme whereby the United States would persuade the principal holders of Spanish bonds to pressure Spain into selling Cuba.

93. On June 24, 1854, a radical Liberal military uprising took place under the leadership of Leopoldo O'Donnell. Reaction, however, soon brought down the radical wing and led to the establishment of a moderate government under Baldomero Espartero. Soulé to Marcy, July 15, 1854, in Portell Vilá, *Historia de Cuba* 2:51.

94. Interim minister Horatio Perry to Marcy, Sept. 6, 1854, quoted in Smith, ed., *What Happened in Cuba?* 62–63; Foner, *History of Cuba* 2:113.

95. The document began with an outline for a renewed attempt to purchase Cuba. Rejecting the failed tactics of 1848 and early 1854, it called for "open, frank, and public" proceedings. It also included an enumeration of reasons why the sale of Cuba would benefit both the United States and Spain. Soulé, Buchanan, and Mason underscored reasons of national security among the benefits for the buyer: "Cuba has . . . become to us an unceasing danger, and permanent cause of anxiety and alarm." They also mentioned reasons of commercial and trade advantages. For the "selling" nation it was deemed an excellent opportunity to make a profit and to avoid losing Cuba and getting nothing in return. The last paragraphs of the Ostend Manifesto are its most striking, stating that the United States would prefer to acquire Cuba by peaceful purchase, but if Spain rejected such overtures then the United States would be "justified" in taking control of Cuba "and this upon the very principle that would justify an individual in tearing down the burning house of his neighbor if there were no other means of preventing the flames from destroying his own home." Smith, ed., *What Happened in Cuba?* 64–67.

96. Marcy to William Cazneau, Nov. 2, 1853, NA, State, RG 59, Special Missions, reel 154. For a discussion of the U.S. expansionist agenda in the Dominican Republic and the role played by William and Jane M. Cazneau, see May, "Plenipotentiary"; and Robert E. May, "Lobbyists for Commercial Empire: Jane M. Cazneau, William Cazneau, and U.S. Caribbean Policy, 1846–1878," *Pacific Historical Review* 48, no. 3 (1979): 383–412.

97. Secretary of State Daniel Webster to Robert M. Walsh, Jan. 18, 1851, NA, State, RG 59, Special Missions, reel 152.

98. Report of John Hogan to Buchanan, Oct. 4, 1845, NA, State, RG 59, Special Agents, vol. 13. According to contemporary estimates by Spanish observer Antonio López Villanueva, the population comprised four-eighths *pardos* (mulattoes), three-eighths *morenos* (blacks), and one-eighth *blancos* (whites). Domínguez, *Economía y política*, 13.

99. Lockward, ed., *Documentos*, li.

100. Secretary Clayton to Benjamin Green (confidential), June 13, 1849, NA, State, RG 59, Special Missions, reel 152; Green to Clayton, Aug. 27, 1849, NA, State, RG 59, Special Agents, Dominican Republic, vol. 15; Green to Clayton, Oct. 14, 1849, and June 15, 1850, in Lockward, ed., *Documentos*, 111, 147–48.

101. Cazneau to Quitman, April 25, 1856, appendix to John A. Quitman, *Speech of John A. Quitman, of Mississippi, on the Subject of the Neutrality Laws: April 29, 1856* (Washington, D.C.: Union Office, 1856), 20–21; Cazneau to Marcy, Jan. 23, 1854, in Lockward, ed., *Documentos*, 220–26; report of John Hogan to Buchanan, Oct. 4, 1845, and Benjamin Green to Clayton, Aug. 27, 1849, both in NA, State, RG 59, Special Agents, Dominican Republic, vols. 13 and 15; David D. Porter, "Diario de una misión secreta a Santo Domingo [1846]," and Green to Clayton, Oct. 14, 1849, both in Lockward, ed., *Documentos*, li, 111.

102. William Cullen Bryant, Charles Sumner, and other northerners opposed to the recognition of the Dominican Republic based their stance on pro-Haitian arguments linked to the desire to open the Haitian market and to promote the emigration of free blacks from the United States.

103. [William Cullen Bryant], "The St. Domingo Intrigue," New York *Evening Post*, May 25, 1854; Cazneau to the editor of the New York *Herald*, letter reprinted in the New York *Evening Post*, May 31, 1854; [William Cullen Bryant], editorial, New York *Evening Post*, May 31, 1854.

104. Quitman, *Speech*, 5, 10; Thrasher, *Preliminary Essay*, 50; United States, Congress, Senate, Senator George E. Pugh of Ohio speaking on the acquisition of Cuba, 35th Cong., 2d sess., *Congressional Globe*, Feb. 10, 1859, vol. 28, pt. 1, p. 940; David Campbell to William B. Campbell, Feb. 20, 1854, Duke, Campbell Family Papers.

105. Green to Clayton, Feb. 19, 1850, in Lockward, ed., *Documentos*, 125–30; deputies quoted in French consul at Santo Domingo to the French minister of foreign affairs, Feb. 10, 1849, in Rodríguez Demorizi, ed., *Correspondencia* 2:119.

106. Jonathan Elliot to Webster, Jan. 17, 1853, in Lockward, ed., *Documentos*, 206–7 (italics mine). Báez was the illegitimate son of a white merchant and a black slave. Miguel Ángel Monclús, *El caudillismo en la República Dominicana*, 4th ed. (Santo Domingo: Universidad CETEC, 1983), 21–22.

107. William Cazneau to Marcy, June 9, 1855; Elliot to Marcy, Sept. 10, 1856; and Cazneau to Cass, July 2, 1859, all in Lockward, ed., *Documentos*, 278–80, 290–92, 332. Eduardo San Just to the captain-general of Puerto Rico, Oct. 20, 1855, and San Just to the captain-general of Cuba, Feb. 7, 1855, both in AHN, Ultramar, leg. 3524, exps. 116, 101.

108. Portell Vilá, *Historia de Cuba* 2:95, 100; George C. Backhouse to Johnny

Backhouse, April 7, 1855, Duke, John Backhouse Papers. Spanish ministry of state to the Spanish agent in Santo Domingo, Jan. 22, 1855; O'Donnell to the Spanish minister of state, June 4, 1855; and Captain-General de la Pezuela to Leopoldo A. de Cueto, July 10, 1854, all in AHN, Ultramar, leg. 3524, exp. 96; leg. 4645, exp. 42; and leg. 4648, exp. 15.

109. Cazneau to Marcy, Jan. 23, 1854, and Marcy to Cazneau, June 17, 1854, both in Lockward, ed., *Documentos*, 220–26, 228.

110. Consul Segovia to Pedro Santana, Jan. 28, 1856, in Emilio Rodríguez Demorizi, ed., *Documentos para la historia de la República Dominicana*, 4 vols. (Santo Domingo: Editora Montalvo–Academia Dominicana de la Historia, 1944–81), 2:192–94; Cazneau to Marcy, Sept. 23 and Dec. 6, 1854, in Lockward, ed., *Documentos*, 242–43, 256–59; San Just to Captain-General de la Concha, Dec. 10, 1854, AHN, Ultramar, leg. 3524, exp. 93; Lord Aberdeen to Lord Clarendon, Nov. 5, 1854, and First Lord of the Admiralty to Lord Clarendon, Oct. 24, 1854, cited in Richard W. Van Alstyne, ed., "Anglo-American Relations, 1853–57," *American Historical Review* 42 (1937): 497–98.

111. Cazneau to Marcy, July 24, 1854, in Lockward, ed., *Documentos*, 230–32; May, "Plenipotentiary," 27; Robert Schomburgk to Lord Clarendon, Dec. 18, 1854, quoted in Tansill, *United States*, 197; Schomburgk to Lord Clarendon, March 22, 1855, PRO, FO 140, 4; J. Francisco Pacheco to Eduardo San Just, Sept. 11, 1854, AHN, Ultramar, leg. 3524, exp. 77, doc. 1; Juan de Abril to Fernando de Norzagaray, Nov. 6, 1854, AHN, Ultramar, leg. 3524, exp. 89; Cazneau's letter of Oct. 20, 1854, in *El Porvenir*, Oct. 22, 1854; Juan N. Tejera to Marcy, Dec. 13, 1854, and Marcy to Jonathan Elliot, Oct. 9, 1855, both in Lockward, ed., *Documentos*, 259–63, 282–83; San Just to de la Concha, Dec. 7, 1854, and Feb. 13, 1855, AHN, Ultramar, leg. 3524, exps. 93, 101.

112. Consul Pierre Levasseur to the French minister of foreign affairs, April 1848, in Rodríguez Demorizi, ed., *Correspondencia* 2:61; J. Francisco Pacheco to Manuel Dionisio Cruzat, Nov. 4, 1854, AHN, Ultramar, leg. 3524, exp. 86; instructions to San Just, quoted in Luis Álvarez López, "Historia de la anexión de Santo Domingo a España, 1861–1863," M.A. thesis, Universidad de Puerto Rico, 1977, pp. 56–57; Welles, *Naboth's Vineyard* 1:156; Cazneau to Marcy, Dec. 26, 1854, in Lockward, ed., *Documentos*, 274; Cazneau to Marcy, June 9, 1855, NA, State, RG 59, Special Agents, Dominican Republic, vol. 19; Cazneau to John Quitman, April 25, 1856, in Quitman, *Speech*, 20–21.

In December 1854 the British and French consuls wrote to Pedro Santana, spelling out the conditions under which they would mediate to appease Haiti. The first of six conditions was "not to alienate, lease, mortgage, or transfer or donate, either permanently or temporarily, any portion of the Dominican territory, particularly the Samaná Bay, to any government whatsoever." The other five points included prohibitions against the establishment of financial agreements with any foreign nation, the landing of foreign armies of adventurers, and the signing of any treaty that would not guarantee reciprocity of rights and privileges regardless of race. These restrictions obviously referred to the United States. P. Darasse and Robert Schomburgk to Pedro Santana, Dec. 14, 1854, in Lockward, ed., *Documentos*, 275–76.

113. Cazneau to Marcy, June 9, 1855, and Marcy to Cazneau, Dec. 18, 1854, both in Lockward, ed., *Documentos*, 280, 264.

114. See, for example, orders of J. Francisco Pacheco to San Just, Sept. 11, 1854, and president of the Spanish Council of Ministers to the overseas minister, March 16, 1854, both in AHN, Ultramar, leg. 3524, exps. 77, 72.

115. De Norzagaray to the Spanish minister of state, July 1, 1854, AHN, Ultramar, leg. 3524, exp. 75; de Norzagaray, "Diario," 109, 112; de Abril to de la Concha, Oct. 7, 1854, AHN, Ultramar, leg. 3524, exp. 81; Carlos F. Pérez, *Historia diplomática de Santo Domingo (1492–1861)* (Santo Domingo: Escuela de Servicios Internacionales, Universidad Nacional Pedro Henríquez Ureña, 1973), 286–88. Spanish minister of state to San Just, Sept. 11, 1854; San Just to de la Concha, Feb. 2, 1855; and San Just to the captain-general of Puerto Rico, Feb. 13, 1855, all in AHN, Ultramar, leg. 3524, exps. 77, 101, 99.

116. Spanish minister of state to Matías Ramón Mella, Feb. 18, 1854, in David G. Yungling, ed., *Highlights in the Debates in the Spanish Chamber of Deputies Relative to the Abandonment of Santo Domingo* (Washington, D.C.: Murray and Heister, 1941), 146; Matías Ramón Mella to Santana, March 1, 1854, in Rodríguez Demorizi, ed., *Documentos* 2:158–60; Spanish minister of state to the president of the Council of Ministers, March 16, 1854, AHN, Ultramar, leg. 3524, exp. 72, doc. 2; Torrente, *Política ultramarina*, 343; Welles, *Naboth's Vineyard* 1:155.

117. *Tratado de Reconocimiento, Paz, Amistad, Comercio, Navegación y Extradicción entre S.M. la Reina de España y la República Dominicana* (N.p., 1855); de la Concha to the Spanish minister of state, Oct. 25, 1854, AHN, Ultramar, leg. 3524, exp. 81. The treaty was ratified six months later.

118. Foner, *History of Cuba* 2:94; May, *Southern Dream*, 48; "Resignation of General Quitman," New York *Tribune*, April 30, 1855.

119. De la Concha was Spain's "fire-fighting" captain-general. He was dispatched to Cuba at the difficult junctures of 1850–52 and 1854–59 and again during the Ten Years' War, in 1874–75.

120. Torrente, *Política ultramarina*, 123–25. See *La Gaceta de la Habana*, May 24, 1855; José de la Concha, *Reseña de lo ejecutado en la Capitanía General de la isla de Cuba en los dos períodos en que se ha desempeñado el teniente general D. José de la Concha* (Havana: N.p., 1859), 15–17; Crawford to the earl of Malmesbury, April 20, 1852, PRO, FO 72, 793; Urban, "Africanization," 42.

121. Acting U.S. consul at Havana to Marcy, Jan. 22, 1856, NA, State, RG 59, Havana, vol. 33.

122. Murray, *Odious Commerce*, 219–20; Taylor, *United States*, 320–22;

Anthony Trollope, *The West Indies and the Spanish Main*, rpt. (London: Frank Cass, 1968), 143–48; Amelia Matilda Murray, *Letters from the United States, Cuba and Canada* (New York, 1856; New York: Negro Universities Press, 1969), 243–67.

123. Christopher J. Bartlett, "British Reaction to the Cuban Insurrection of 1868–1878," *HAHR* 37, no. 3 (Aug. 1957): 297; see also Charles C. Hauch, "Attitudes of Foreign Governments Towards the Spanish Reoccupation of the Dominican Republic," *HAHR* 27, no. 2 (May 1947): 249.

124. "La misión a España—Mr. Soulé—Cuba," *La Verdad*, April 20, 1853. In a revealing letter to Lord Clarendon, Lord Palmerston blamed the weakness of his country's Caribbean policy on distance, the indifference of the British public, and "strong commercial Interest in maintaining Peace with the United States." Van Alstyne, ed., "Anglo-American Relations," 500.

125. Lord Napier to Lord Clarendon, May 26, 1857, quoted in Gavin B. Henderson, ed., "Southern Designs on Cuba, 1854–1857, and Some European Opinions," *Journal of Southern History* 5 (Aug. 1939): 384; Murray, *Letters*, 258.

126. Kenneth Bourne, "The Clayton-Bulwer Treaty and the Decline of British Opposition to the Territorial Expansion of the United States, 1857–1860," *Journal of Modern History* 33 (1961): 287–91. For a discussion of British-American relations reaching "near levels of cooperation and understanding" during the 1850s, see Martin Crawford, *The Anglo-American Crisis of the Mid-Nineteenth Century* (Athens: University of Georgia Press, 1987), 5–10.

127. James Buchanan had a long history of expansionism dating back to at least 1848, when as secretary of state he actively promoted the first Cuba purchase initiative. During the Whig interlude he continued to fight for the acquisition of Cuba. Later, his role in the Ostend affair probably earned him his party's nomination and ultimately the presidency.

128. Portell Vilá, *Historia de Cuba* 2:119–25; May, *Southern Dream*, 188, 125, 134; Lincoln quoted in Richard N. Current, *The Lincoln Nobody Knows* (New York: Hill and Wang, 1984), 92. The compromise consisted of a bill that would have allowed for the westward extension of slavery in territories south of 36°30′.

129. John P. Hale, *The Acquisition of Cuba. Speech of Hon. John P. Hale, of New Hampshire* (Washington, D.C.: Buell and Blanchard, 1859), 13.

130. United States, Congress, Senate, Senator Zachariah Chandler of Michigan speaking on the acquisition of Cuba, 35th Cong., 2d sess., *Congressional Globe*, Feb. 17, 1859, vol. 28, pt. 2, p. 1080; United States, Congress, House, Congressman William W. Boyce of South Carolina speaking on the acquisition of Cuba, 33d Cong., 2d sess., *Congressional Globe*, Jan. 15, 1855, vol. 24, appendix, pp. 91–94; Chandler in *Congressional Globe*, vol. 28, pt. 2, p. 1080.

131. Hale, *Acquisition*, 15; Chandler in *Congressional Globe*, vol. 28, pt. 2,

p. 1081; John J. Perry, *The Filibuster Policy of the Sham Democracy* (Washington, D.C.: National Republican Committee, 1860), 4; United States, Congress, Senate, Senator Stephen R. Mallory of Florida speaking on the acquisition of Cuba, 35th Cong., 2d sess., *Congressional Globe*, Feb. 25, 1859, vol. 28, pt. 2, p. 1330.

132. May, *Southern Dream*, 184; Raymond Carr, *España, 1808–1975* (Barcelona: Ariel, 1985), 301.

133. Correspondence between the minister of the navy and the overseas minister also reveals an increased concern with the defense of trade routes and the Spanish possessions. In one letter the Spanish minister of the navy recommended the establishment of naval stations in Spain's former colonies of South and Central America. Minister of the navy to the overseas minister, April 1, 1856, AHN, Ultramar, leg. 4646, exp. 2.

134. Torrente, *Política ultramarina*, 326–27; Álvarez López, "Historia de la anexión," 60.

135. Consul Segovia traveled personally to St. Thomas to offer his support to Buenaventura Báez. Moya Pons, *Manual*, 319.

136. "La Matrícula Española II," *La República*, Aug. 26, 1856; Elliot to Marcy, March 22 and July 5, 1856, in Lockward, ed., *Documentos*, 284–85; Schomburgk to Lord Clarendon, June 20 and 26, 1856, PRO, FO 140, 4; Fernando Calderón Collantes to Francisco Serrano, quoted in Álvarez López, "Historia de la anexión," 80–81.

137. Emilio Rodríguez Demorizi, *Santana y los poetas de su tiempo* (Santo Domingo: Academia Dominicana de la Historia, 1969), 223; *La Gaceta de Santo Domingo*, June 7, 1859; Segovia to the captain-general of Puerto Rico, May 26, 1859, AHN, Ultramar, leg. 5082, exp. 19; Elliot to Cass, May 21, 1859, in Lockward, ed., *Documentos*, 326.

138. For correspondence on this crisis, see AGNRD, Fondo de Relaciones Exteriores, leg. 12, exps. 2, 3, 4; and PRO, FO 140, 4.

Chapter 2: Economic Transformations and the State

1. For a fine study of the impact of Bourbon reformism in Puerto Rico, see Altagracia Ortiz, *Eighteenth-Century Reforms in the Caribbean* (Rutherford, N.J.: Fairleigh Dickinson University Press, 1981).

2. Allan J. Kuethe, "Los Llorones Cubanos: The Sociomilitary Basis of Commercial Privilege in the American Trade Under Charles IV," in Barbier and Kuethe, eds., *North American Role*, 142.

3. As late as the mid-1830s Creoles controlled key positions in Cuba's colonial government, particularly in the municipal councils, Royal Audiencia,

Royal Hacienda, Intendancy, and tribunals. See Tacón, *Correspondencia*, 302–9; Francisco A. Scarano, "Inmigración y estructura de clases: Los hacendados de Ponce, 1815–1845," in *Inmigración y clases sociales en el Puerto Rico del siglo xix*, ed. Francisco A. Scarano (Río Piedras: Ediciones Huracán, 1981), 22; Knight, *Caribbean*, 2d ed., p. 232. See also Aída Caro Costas, ed., *Ramón Power y Giralt* (San Juan: Privately printed, 1969).

4. Knight, *Slave Society*, 88–89; Abiel Abbot, *Letters Written in the Interior of Cuba* (Boston: Bowles and Dearborn, 1829), 114.

5. Besides the causes mentioned in the text stands out the obvious geographic factor that both Cuba and Puerto Rico were islands, a condition that made the importation of revolution a more difficult task. Furthermore, the United States not only did not aid insurrection in Cuba but systematically obstructed any effort in that direction. Finally, the black population in both islands served as a neutralizing element that Creoles feared could get out of control in the event of a separatist insurrection.

6. For a discussion of these matters as they pertain to Cuba's failure to fight Spain during the general emancipation era (1810–25), see the sections on Cuba in Jorge Domínguez, *Insurrection or Loyalty: The Breakdown of the Spanish American Empire* (Cambridge, Mass.: Harvard University Press, 1980).

7. Jaime de Jesús Domínguez, *La anexión de la República Dominicana a España* (Santo Domingo: Editora de la UASD, 1979), 34; Manuel Moreno Fraginals, *El ingenio: El complejo económico social del azúcar*, 3 vols. (Havana: Editorial de Ciencias Sociales, 1978), 2:138.

8. English translation of decree in United States, Department of State, *Papers Relating to Foreign Affairs of the United States* (hereafter cited as *PRFA*), 1861–68 (Washington, D.C.: GPO, 1861–68) 1873:1000; Richard Henry Dana, Jr., *To Cuba and Back: A Vacation Voyage* (Boston: Ticknor and Fields: 1859; rpt., ed. C. Harvey Gardiner, Carbondale, Ill.: Southern Illinois University Press, 1966), 114–15.

9. Madden, *Island of Cuba*, 80. See also detailed explanations by Tacón regarding public works and repression, in Tacón, *Correspondencia*, esp. 111–16.

10. Turnbull, *Travels*, 57–58. See also Tacón, *Correspondencia;* and Nelly Vázquez Sotillo, "La represión política en Puerto Rico durante la administración de Miguel López de Baños (1837–1840)," M.A. thesis, Universidad de Puerto Rico, 1983.

11. Coll y Toste, ed., *Boletín histórico* 2:29; Saco quoted in Fernando Ortiz Fernández, *José Antonio Saco y sus ideas cubanas* (Havana: Universo, 1929), 50. See also "Protesta de los diputados electos por la isla de Cuba," supplement to *El Mundo*, Feb. 22, 1837, HLHU, Escoto, box 9.

12. See various letters of Tacón to the Madrid government in which he denounces the perils of sustaining institutions such as the Audiencia and

delegations to the Cortes. He attacks many of his adversaries personally and questions their loyalty to Spain as well as their morality. Tacón, *Correspondencia*, 120–25, 132–35, 148–51.

13. Torrente, *Bosquejo* 1:20–21. In a later work, which compared historical experiences of republicanism and despotism in Haiti, Torrente argued that the territory under Henry Cristophe's authoritarian monarchy prospered at an astonishing rate. In contrast, the south of Haiti under Alexander Petión deteriorated and became impoverished because of its republican institutions. See Torrente, *Memoria*, 34.

14. Duvon C. Corbitt, "The Junta de Fomento of Havana and the López Expeditions," *HAHR* 17, no. 3 (Aug. 1937): 344; Bécker, *Historia de las relaciones* 2:330; Duvon C. Corbitt, "A Petition for the Continuation of O'Donnell as Captain General of Cuba," *HAHR* 16, no. 4 (Nov. 1936): 541; "Manifesto," signed by Antonio Franchi de Alfaro, New York, Oct. 25, 1852, LC, Rare Book Room, Broadsides, portfolio 316.

15. De Norzagaray, "Diario"; Luis Estrada, *Las provincias ultramarinas y sus presupuestos* (Madrid: Imprenta La España, 1864), 40–43; [José Antonio Saco], *Algunas reformas en la isla de Cuba* (London: N.p., 1865), 34. Pesos fuertes were equivalent to U.S. dollars.

16. Estrada, *Provincias ultramarinas*, 43; [Saco], *Algunas reformas*, 34.

17. Portell Vilá, *Narciso López* 2:390; Torrente, *Bosquejo* 1:247; Diego González y Gutiérrez, *Historia documentada de los movimientos revolucionarios por la independencia de Cuba, de 1852 a 1867*, 2 vols. (Havana: Imprenta El Siglo XX, 1939), 2:223–24; de la Concha's decree of Feb. 12, 1855, establishing the *voluntarios*, PRO, FO 72, 878; José Elías Hernández, "Elementos con que creen poder contar el gobierno español para sostener su tiranía en Cuba," *La Verdad*, June 10, 1853. The number of troops in Puerto Rico in 1859 ascended to four thousand, according to an estimate by George Latimer; see Latimer to Mr. Tracks, March 19, 1859, Duke, George Latimer Papers. See also de la Concha, *Reseña*, 11–13. According to another contemporary observer, troop numbers reached twenty thousand regulars during the crisis of La Escalera. VHS, Norwood Diary.

18. Dana, *To Cuba and Back*, 117; Jane M. Cazneau cited in May, "Plenipotentiary," 23.

19. José de la Concha, "Memoria de Mirasol de 1850," in España, Ultramar, *Cuba*, 141; Portell Vilá, *Narciso López* 2:390; O'Donnell to the Spanish minister of state, Aug. 10, 1846, AHN, Ultramar, leg. 4645, quoted in Lebroc, *Cuba*, 22, n. 92; Fernando Picó, *Libertad y servidumbre en el Puerto Rico del siglo xix (los jornaleros utuadeños en vísperas del auge del café)*, 2d ed. (Río Piedras: Ediciones Huracán, 1982); Olga Jiménez de Wagenheim, *El Grito de Lares: Sus causas y sus hombres* (Río Piedras: Ediciones Huracán, 1984), 48.

20. [Gaspar Betancourt Cisneros], *Algunas observaciones a "La Crónica" de New York* (New York: La Verdad, 1848), 5; letter by Betancourt Cisneros, Oct. 19, 1852, quoted in González y Gutiérrez, *Historia documentada* 2:268; Torrente, *Bosquejo* 1:18–19.

21. Betancourt Cisneros to del Monte, April 2, 1843, in Figarola-Caneda, ed., *Centón epistolario* 5:92–93; John George F. Wurderman, *Notes on Cuba* (Boston: J. Munro and Co., 1844; New York: Arno Press, 1971), 1; James Mursell Phillippo, *The United States and Cuba* (London: Pewtress and Co., 1857), 414; letter of José García, Oct. 26, 1835, HLHU, Escoto, box 9; Consul Robert B. Campbell to Mrs. Burham and Co., Oct. 23, 1848, and Valentín Cañedo to Carlos Drake, Sept. 21, 1852, both in NA, State, RG 59, Havana, vols. 22, 25; Ángel Calderón de la Barca to the Spanish secretary of state, Oct. 21, 1852, and Cañedo to the president of the Spanish Council of Ministers, Sept. 4, 1852, both in AHN, Ultramar, leg. 4637, exp. 57; Valentín Carrillo, political secretary of Cuba, to the Spanish consul at Charleston, Oct. 24, 1852, Duke, Papers of Spain, Ministry of Foreign Affairs, Charleston Consulate (hereinafter cited as Spanish Ministry–Charleston), box 5; acting consul Morlan to the U.S. secretary of state, Aug. 25, 1852, and John S. Thrasher to the government and people of the United States, Nov. 21, 1851, both in NA, State, RG 59, Havana, vols. 25, 24; de Norzagaray, "Diario," 114 (italics mine); de Norzagaray to the president of the Spanish Council of Ministers, July 31, 1854, AHN, Ultramar, leg. 5072, exp. 13.

22. Edward Everett to Webster, quoted in Portell Vilá, *Historia de Cuba* 2:18–19; Alexander Jones, *Cuba in 1851* (New York: Stringer and Townsend, 1851), 17; Crawford to Lord Palmerston, June 5, 1851, PRO, FO 72, 793. Ambrosio José González, *Manifesto on Cuban Affairs Addressed to the People of the United States, September 1st, 1852* (New Orleans: Daily Delta Press, 1853), 3; Madden, *Island of Cuba*, 63; Lidio Cruz Monclova, *Historia de Puerto Rico (siglo xix)*, 3 vols. (Río Piedras: Editorial Universitaria, 1952–64), 1:483.

23. José de la Concha, *Memoria del Exmo. Sr. D. José de la Concha al actual Capitán General de la isla de Cuba sobre la hacienda pública de la misma* (Madrid: El Clamor Público, 1861), 20–21. Tax totals produced by critics of the Spanish government were higher than official figures because they included such costs as municipal taxes, tithes, post office fees, and costs of lawsuits. Other estimates are eighteen million (1849) in Editors of *La Verdad, A Series of Articles on the Cuban Question* (New York: La Verdad, 1849), 18; twenty-five million (1850) in A. W. Ely, "Cuba: Its Present Condition—The Revenues—Taxes—Agricultural Industry, Etc., of the Island," *DeBow's Review* 18, no. 1 (Feb. 1855): 163–67; and sixteen million (1859) in Dana, *To Cuba and Back*, 116.

24. Cristóbal F. Madan, quoted in Roland T. Ely, *Cuando reinaba su majestad el azúcar: Estudio histórico-sociológico de una tragedia latinoamericana* (Buenos Aires:

Editorial Sudamericana, 1963), 449–50; González, *Manifesto*, 3; V. de Roches, *Cuba Under Spanish Rule* (New York: Great American Engraving and Printing, [1869?]), 44. These calculations do not include money going directly to the queen mother ($222,000 in 1846 and $1,498,500 up to 1854). Ely, "Cuba: Its Present Condition," 166.

25. Betancourt Cisneros to del Monte, May 15, 1843; José Antonio Echeverría to del Monte, May 14, 1844; Félix Tanco to del Monte, April 3, 1845; and Manuel de Castro to del Monte, June 9, 1844, all in Figarola-Caneda, ed., *Centón epistolario* 5:100 and 6:33, 177, 42. Editors of *La Verdad*, *Cuestión negrera de la isla de Cuba* (New York: La Verdad, 1851), 2. See O'Donnell to the governor of Matanzas, March 2, 1844, and other related letters, in HLHU, Escoto, box 10.

26. Cristóbal F. Madan to Consul Allen Owen, June 6, 1851, NA, State, RG 59, Havana, vol. 24; González y Gutiérrez, *Historia documentada* 2:47. See also the file on repressive measures against those implicated in the Pintó conspiracy, in HLHU, Escoto, box 11; and files in AHN, Ultramar, leg. 4645, exps. 4 and 11. For a contemporary account by a British observer, see George C. Backhouse to Johnny Backhouse, April 7, 1855, Duke, John Backhouse Papers.

27. José García de Arboleya, *Manual de la isla de Cuba* (Havana: Imprenta del Tiempo, 1859), 217. For a revealing discussion of the new colonial pact, see José María Zamora, *Pronta contestación a "La memoria sobre el comercio de harinas" escrita por el señor don Manuel Gutiérrez* (Madrid: Imprenta del Amor de Dios, 1834), 6–7.

28. Moreno Fraginals, *Ingenio* 1:25.

29. Francisco López Segrera, *Cuba: Capitalismo dependiente y subdesarrollo (1510–1959)*, 2d ed. (Mexico City: Editorial Diógenes, 1979), 147; de Norzagaray, "Diario," 73–74; de la Concha to the Spanish minister of Development and Overseas, Oct. 26, 1856, AHN, Ultramar, leg. 726.

30. Cuban averages in J. M. de la Torre, "Cuba," in *The Spanish West Indies: Cuba and Porto Rico*, ed. Richard S. Fisher (New York: J. H. Colton, 1861), 127; Puerto Rican averages calculated using "Cuadros de movimiento comercial de Puerto Rico, 1850–1872," AHN, Ultramar, leg. 1152, exp. 14 (for 1850) and exp. 7 (for 1846–49).

31. Ratios estimated using numbers from J. T. O'Neil, "Porto Rico," in Fisher, ed., *Spanish West Indies*, 186; Charles De Ronceray to Lewis Cass, Nov. 10, 1860, NA, Foreign Service, RG 84, San Juan, vol. 7228; Félix Goizueta-Mimó, *Bitter Cuban Sugar: Monoculture and Economic Dependence from 1825 to 1899* (New York: Garland Publishing, 1987), 14, 25; and Moreno Fraginals, *Ingenio* 3:45. During the 1855–59 quinquennium, Cuba and Puerto Rico exported a value of $222,624,200 in sugar and only $110,275 in coffee.

32. O'Neil, "Porto Rico," 186; Moreno Fraginals, *Ingenio* 3:44–45. Cuba's

sugar exports nearly doubled from 3,216,925 quintals in 1841–45 to 5,784,811 quintals in 1856–59. See Ramiro Guerra y Sánchez, *Azúcar y población en las Antillas*, 3d ed. (Havana: Cultural, S.A., 1944), 71–72.

33. If beet sugar is considered, these percentage shares are lower: 21 and 4 percent respectively. See Ely, *Cuando reinaba*, 428.

34. Calculations based on numbers in O'Neil, "Porto Rico," 186; De Ronceray to Cass, Nov. 10, 1860, NA, Foreign Service, RG 84, San Juan, vol. 7228; and Goizueta-Mimó, *Bitter Cuban Sugar*, 25.

35. "Cuadros de movimiento," AHN, Ultramar, leg. 1152, exp. 14; Marrero, *Cuba* 12:201. U.S. control over the exports from certain Cuban ports was overwhelming. In 1852, for example, the United States absorbed 100 percent of exports from Mariel, 100 percent of exports from Guantánamo, and between 97 and 100 percent of the exports of Sagua, Cárdenas, and Remedios. See Franklin W. Knight, "Origins of Wealth and the Sugar Revolution in Cuba, 1750–1850," *HAHR* 57, no. 2 (May 1977): 248.

36. Consumption rates from Un emigrado cubano, *Información sobre reformas en Cuba y Puerto Rico*, 2d ed. (New York: Hallet and Green, 1877), 283. In *Sweetness and Power: The Place of Sugar in Modern History* (New York: Viking, 1985), Sidney W. Mintz traces the growth of sugar consumption as a process parallel to urbanization and industrialization. Sugar became the staple of the industrial worker's diet, a quick source of calories to meet the demands of the factory shop.

37. "Extracto de la balanza mercantil de España respectiva al año 1851," Duke, Spanish Ministry–Charleston, box 5. Total sugar imports amounted to 535,815 quintals from Cuba and 3,572 quintals from Puerto Rico.

38. Letter addressed to the queen of Spain by a group of Puerto Rican planters and merchants dated Sept. 23, 1863, AGPR, Fondo de Gobernadores Españoles, Municipios, Ponce, box 534.

39. Calculations based on numbers in "Cuadros de movimiento," AHN, Ultramar, leg. 1152, exp. 14; and Knight, "Origins of Wealth," 248. Great Britain dominated as receptor of Santiago's exports (the island's third exporting port), with 38 percent of the values exported. Regional percentages do not include Dominican exports. Great Britain received 14, 12, and 15 percent of Cuba's sugar exports during the 1846–50, 1851–55, and 1856–60 quinquennia. Marrero, *Cuba* 12:117, 122.

40. United States, Congress, House, *The World's Sugar Production and Consumption, 1800–1900*, 57th Cong., 1st sess., 1902, H. Doc. 15, pt. 7, serial set 4314, p. 2628.

41. Marrero, *Cuba* 12:117, 122; D. C. M. Platt, *Latin America and British Trade, 1806–1914* (New York: Barnes and Noble, 1973), 320.

42. Moreno Fraginals, *Ingenio* 3:70; Brigit Sonesson, "Puerto Rico's Com-

merce, 1835–1865: From Regional to Worldwide Market Relations," Ph.D. diss., New York University, 1985, p. 249; John Alfred Heitman, *The Modernization of the Louisiana Sugar Industry, 1830–1910* (Baton Rouge: Louisiana State University Press, 1987), 58; Moreno Fraginals, *Ingenio* 2:187; Goizueta-Mimó, *Bitter Cuban Sugar*, 25; United States, Department of Commerce, Bureau of the Census, *Historical Statistics of the United States, Colonial Times to 1957* (Washington, D.C.: GPO, 1960), 549.

43. The estimate is for 1854–58 using Moreno Fraginals's figure of $86.64 million. Applying a factor of .10 gives a rounded figure of $9 million from Puerto Rico, the total for both islands being roughly $96 million out of a total of $119 million imported. De la Sagra estimates for 1860 that both islands supplied 75 percent *not* of the United States's sugar imports but of that country's total sugar consumption.

44. U.S. Dept. of Commerce, Bureau of the Census, *Historical Statistics* (1960 ed.), 539; Robertson, *Hispanic-American Relations*, 420–21. Throughout this period Brazil was Latin America's second largest exporter to the United States.

45. U.S. tariffs had a similar impact on the Cuban cigar industry. High import duties forced Cuban *tabaqueros* to relocate to the United States, threatening to reduce Cuba to an exporter of tobacco leaves. See Louis A. Pérez, Jr., *Cuba: Between Reform and Revolution* (New York: Oxford University Press, 1988), 113–14; Ramón de la Sagra, *Cuba: 1860: Selección de artículos sobre agricultura cubana* (Havana: Comisión Nacional Cubana de la Unesco, 1963), 184.

46. Sonesson, "Puerto Rico's Commerce," 259; report in Charles De Ronceray to Lewis Cass, Jan. 14, 1860, in United States, Department of State, San Juan Consulate, *Despachos de los cónsules norteamericanos en Puerto Rico (1818–1868)*, ed. CIH (Río Piedras: Editorial Universitaria, 1982), 427; Moreno Fraginals, *Ingenio* 3:83–85.

47. Francisco Pérez de la Riva, *El café: Historia de su cultivo y explotación en Cuba* (Havana: Jesús Montero, 1944), 73; Sonesson, "Puerto Rico's Commerce," 259; O'Neil, "Porto Rico," 186. See also Laird W. Bergad, *Coffee and the Growth of Agrarian Capitalism in Nineteenth-Century Puerto Rico* (Princeton, N.J.: Princeton University Press, 1983), 226–27.

48. Pérez de la Riva, *Café*, 73.

49. Exports for 1850–60 amounted to $57,126,551; imports were $70,589,942. "Cuadros de movimiento," AHN, Ultramar, leg. 1152, exp. 14.

50. Numbers for 1846–51 from de la Torre, "Cuba," 127; numbers for 1852 from Knight, "Origins of Wealth," 247–48.

51. Calculations based on the rate of growth of sugar exports derived from Moreno Fraginals, *Ingenio* 3:45 (7,273,086 quintals in 1852 and 10,345,372 quintals in 1859), and import figures from [Saco], *Algunas reformas*, 8 ($29,780,242 in 1852 and $43,465,679 in 1859).

52. [Saco], *Algunas reformas*, 8. In his recent book on Cuban rural society, Bergad argues that the establishment of a railroad network in Cuba as early as the late 1830s facilitated the importation and transportation of bulky foodstuffs that heretofore had to be produced locally. See Bergad, *Cuban Rural Society*, 235.

53. "Cuadros de movimiento," AHN, Ultramar, leg. 1152, exp. 14. Importation capacity for Cuba estimated on the basis of 1859 import figures in [Saco], *Algunas reformas*, and a population of 1,396,530 for 1861; for Puerto Rico, 1854 import figures in "Cuadros de movimiento," AHN, Ultramar, leg. 1152, exp. 14, and a population of 523,236 for that year arrived at by interpolation of census figures; for the Dominican Republic, the conservative 1852 population estimate of 130,000 by Torrente, quoted in Domínguez, *Economía y política*, 13, and import figures in Torrente, *Política ultramarina*, 282–84.

54. Coll y Toste, ed., *Boletín histórico* 5:289. In the staple-producing region of Mayagüez, Puerto Rico, for example, while sugarcane acreage increased from 1,344 to 2,577 (1837–48), acreage devoted to rice and corn fell from 862 to 524. Meanwhile, acreage for plantain, a staple in the slave diet not produced in the United States, also increased, from 1,361 to 2,350. See Bergad, *Coffee*, 36.

55. See figures in Marrero, *Cuba* 12:201; and "Cuadros de movimento," AHN, Ultramar, leg. 1152, exp. 14.

56. U.S. control over Cuba's exports was particularly noticeable in the ports of Cárdenas, Sagua, Remedios, and Guantánamo, where more than 75 percent of exports headed to the United States. See Knight, "Origins of Wealth," 247–48.

57. Numbers for Cuba in 1859 are as follows: $12.2 million imported from the United States and $24 million exported to the United States; $12.3 million imported from Spain and $7.4 million exported to Spain. Numbers for Puerto Rico in 1859 are as follows: $1,903,779 imported from the United States and $1,897,082 exported to the United States; $1,820,609 imported from Spain and $217,747 exported to Spain. Marrero, *Cuba* 12:96; "Cuadros de movimiento," AHN, Ultramar, leg. 1152, exp. 14.

58. Marrero, *Cuba* 12:96; "Cuadros de movimiento," AHN, Ultramar, leg. 1152, exp. 14. These figures are based on official trade. If smuggling figures could be reached and included, U.S. domination of the Spanish Caribbean's trade would have been greater, both in exports and imports.

59. Numbers for Puerto Rico in "Cuadros de movimiento," AHN, Ultramar, leg. 1152, exp. 14. Numbers for Cuba calculated from data in [Saco], *Algunas reformas*, 8; de la Torre, "Cuba," 126–27; United States, Congress, Senate, *Report of the Secretary of the Treasury in Answer to a Resolution of the Senate, Calling for Statistics of Trade with Cuba for the Last Five Years (March 2, 1859)*, 35th

Cong., 2d sess., 1859, S. Exec. Doc. 45, serial set 984; Marrero, *Cuba* 12:96; and Knight, "Origins of Wealth," 247–48. In fact, the U.S. trade imbalance with Cuba and Puerto Rico was responsible for the United States's overall negative trade balance during this period. This trade imbalance with Cuba and Puerto Rico (−$148,566,120) was greater than that with all trading partners combined, including Cuba and Puerto Rico (−$115,893,000). Put another way, had the United States established balanced trade with Cuba and Puerto Rico, it would have enjoyed an overall positive trade balance of $32,673,120. Estimate based on $246,504,530 exported from Cuba and Puerto Rico to the United States and $97,008,852 imported into Cuba and Puerto Rico from the United States (1850–59). The overall imbalance figure is given in Douglass C. North, "The United States Balance of Payments, 1790–1860," in *Trends in the American Economy in the Nineteenth Century* (Princeton, N.J.: National Bureau of Economic Research, 1960), 605.

60. Cuban figures calculated from numbers in de la Torre, "Cuba," 126; Puerto Rico's numbers from "Cuadros de movimiento," AHN, Ultramar, leg. 1152, exp. 14.

61. George Latimer to the U.S. secretary of the treasury, June 19, 1852, in U.S. Dept. of State, San Juan Consulate, *Despachos*, 321; dispatch of the French consul in San Juan, Jan. 4, 1854, quoted in Morales Carrión, *Auge y decadencia*, 206; de la Torre, "Cuba," 126.

62. "Cuadros de movimiento," AHN, Ultramar, leg. 1152, exp. 14; De Ronceray to Cass, Jan. 16, 1860, NA, Foreign Service, RG 84, San Juan, vol. 7228.

63. Emigrado cubano, *Información*, 277; Gustave Hespel D'Harponville, *La Reine des Antilles* (Paris: Gide et Baudry, 1850), 352.

64. Thrasher, "Cuba," 44–45; Jones, *Cuba in 1851*, 17; O'Neil, "Porto Rico," 187. Not only was flour expensive, but sometimes Spain could not supply the islands' demand and special concessions had to be made. See request of the captain-general of Puerto Rico to the Spanish overseas minister, Feb. 29, 1856, AHN, Ultramar, leg. 1128, exp. 11; and Robert B. Campbell to Buchanan, May 4, 1845, NA, State, RG 59, Havana, vol. 21.

65. Thrasher, "Cuba," 44–45; "Harinas en Cuba," *La Verdad*, May 30, 1853, pp. 137–38; Jones, *Cuba in 1851*, 16; Madden, *Island of Cuba*, 61–62.

66. Editors of *La Verdad, Series of Articles*, 11–13; Thrasher, "Cuba," 44–45; Mallory in *Congressional Globe*, vol. 28, pt. 2, p. 1327; U.S. Senate, *Report of the Secretary of the Treasury*.

67. In 1834 duties on rice were raised to 25 percent ad valorem. See United States, Congress, House, *Duties at Porto Rico*, 23d Cong., 2d sess., 1834–35, H. Doc. 173.

68. Stephen R. Mallory, *Report of Mr. Mallory of Florida, on the Relations of the United States with Cuba* (Washington, D.C.: Towers, [1851]), 18; Félix Erenchun,

Anales de la isla de Cuba (Havana: Imprenta La Habanera, 1856), 733. Rice calculations for Cuba are based on the import price of $5.88 per quintal (1858) and an estimated population of 1,338,194.

69. O'Neil, "Porto Rico," 158–59. Given the fact that each *caballería* of land (thirty-three and a third acres) produced two and a half times as much income if planted in sugar rather than rice, it made perfect sense to devote the totality of the cultivated surface to sugar and to import rice to feed the work force. Hespel D'Harponville, *Reine*, 303.

70. The comparison that follows is based on itemized import data for Cuba (1847, 1853) and Puerto Rico (1851) and estimated populations of 1,124,296 and 1,240,968 for Cuba (1847, 1853) and 473,960 for Puerto Rico (1851), arrived at by interpolation of census figures.

71. For a good discussion of the slave diet, see Kenneth F. Kiple, *The Caribbean Slave: A Biological History* (Cambridge: Cambridge University Press, 1981), 66–78.

72. Figures for Puerto Rico (1854) from the official "Balanza mercantil de la isla de Puerto Rico" (microfilm in CIH) include 1,217,256 reales de vellón of "carnes saladas y embutidos" and 1,656,561 reales de vellón of "pesca." Cuban numbers are from U.S. Senate, *Report of the Secretary of the Treasury*. They include $113,567 worth of "fish," $190,007 of "beef and tallow," and $1,375,281 of "pork, lard, hams, and bacon" (1854). Another factor to consider is the extent of urbanization, which in the region paralleled the growth of the export sector. One barrel is equivalent to 181 to 200 pounds.

73. "Balanza mercantil de la isla de Puerto Rico," 1854 (microfilm in CIH); U.S. Senate, *Report of the Secretary of the Treasury;* O'Neil, "Porto Rico," 158–59.

74. Moreno Fraginals, *Ingenio* 1:163; Leard, "Bonds of Destiny," 17; José de Armas y Céspedes, *Manifiesto de un cubano al Gobierno de España* (Paris: Librería Española, 1876), 5.

75. Leard, "Bonds of Destiny," 17; O'Neil, "Porto Rico," 158–59; U.S. Senate, *Report of the Secretary of the Treasury;* "Balanza mercantil de la isla de Puerto Rico," 1854 (microfilm in CIH). Numbers refer to imports from the United States. Studies on the mechanization of Puerto Rico's sugar industry by Andrés A. Ramos Mattei reveal that Puerto Rican planters had a predilection for British- and French-made machinery, which they acquired through intermediary firms in St. Thomas. Andrés A. Ramos Mattei, "The Influence of Mechanization on the Puerto Rican System of Sugar Production, 1873–1898," Ph.D. diss., University of London, 1977; idem, *La hacienda azucarera: Su crecimiento y crisis en Puerto Rico (siglo xix)* (San Juan: CEREP, 1981).

76. U.S. Senate, *Report of the Secretary of the Treasury;* "Balanza mercantil de la isla de Puerto Rico," 1854 (microfilm in CIH). Numbers refer to imports from the United States.

77. "Cuadros de movimiento," AHN, Ultramar, leg. 1152, exp. 14; Marrero, *Cuba* 12:119.

78. De la Torre, "Cuba," 80; Andrew Blythe to Lewis Cass, July 20, 1857, NA, State, RG 59, Havana, vol. 36; Marte, *Cuba y la República Dominicana*, 49.

79. Caldwell, *López Expeditions*, 15; Rauch, *American Interest*, 192; Marrero, *Cuba* 12:119; Charles Helm to Cass, May 5, 1860, quoted in Portell Vilá, *Historia de Cuba* 2:130; report included with De Ronceray to Cass, July 29, 1859, in U.S. Dept. of State, San Juan Consulate, *Despachos*, 390; De Ronceray to Cass, Jan. 16, 1860, NA, Foreign Service, RG 84, San Juan, vol. 7228.

80. For comparable data on maritime and nonmaritime revenue, see de la Concha, *Memoria*, 20–21; de la Torre, "Cuba," 127; and Sonesson, "Puerto Rico's Commerce," 125.

81. "Cuadros de movimiento," AHN, Ultramar, leg. 1152, exp. 14.

82. Calculations based on data for Cuba's general trade, 1846–1850. De la Torre, "Cuba," 127; and "Cuadros de movimiento," AHN, Ultramar, leg. 1152, exp. 14.

83. De la Concha, *Memoria*, 20–21; de la Torre, "Cuba," 127.

84. Maritime taxes were subdivided into various categories: import and export tariffs, tonnage duties of $1.50 plus 1 percent per ton, 4-percent storage fees, registration, charitable tax, flag registration, weighing fees, translation fees, currency exchange fees, 2-percent "extraordinary" duty on imports, fines (when applicable), health fees, fees for the Royal Consulate, pontoon and lighthouse fees, and so on. See Miguel Estorch, *Apuntes para la historia sobre la administración del Marqués de la Pezuela en la isla de Cuba* (Madrid: M. Galiano, 1856), 130; and Ely, *Cuando reinaba*, 261.

85. Campbell to Secretary Clayton, June 13, 1850, quoted in Foner, *History of Cuba* 2:29. Tax data from Turnbull, *Travels*, 103; *Aranceles generales para el cobro de derechos de introducción y extracción en todas las aduanas de los puertos habilitados de la siempre fiel isla de Cuba desde 1ro de febrero de 1853* (Havana: Imprenta del Gobierno, 1860), 94; Rauch, *American Interest*, 182.

86. Julio Le Riverend, *Historia económica de Cuba* (Barcelona: Ariel, 1972), 169; Mallory, *Report*, 6–18, 9, 19–20; Moreno Fraginals, *Ingenio* 2:147.

87. U.S. House, *Duties;* Madden, *Island of Cuba*, 56; Rauch, *American Interest*, 46; Torrente, *Bosquejo* 1:355–57, 2:212–21.

88. John A. Leon, *On Sugar Cultivation in Louisiana and Cuba*, 2 vols. (London: Ollivier, 1848), 1:27; Ely, *Cuando reinaba*, 516; Madden, *Island of Cuba*, 83; Bryant, *Letters* 3:35; [Carlton H. Rogers], *Incidents of Travel in the Southern States and Cuba* (New York: R. Craighead, 1862), 110; Lewis Leonidas Allen, *The Island of Cuba; or, Queen of the Antilles* (Cleveland: Harris, Fairbanks and Co., 1852), 19; Marrero, *Cuba* 10:272; Moreno Fraginals, *Ingenio* 1:212.

89. Joaquín Freire, *Presencia de Puerto Rico en la historia de Cuba* (San Juan:

Instituto de Cultura, 1966), 102; Robertson to Marcy, Jan. 10, 1856, NA, State, RG 59, Havana, vol. 32.

90. Francisco A. Scarano, *Sugar and Slavery in Puerto Rico: The Plantation Economy of Ponce, 1800–1850* (Madison: University of Wisconsin Press, 1984), 107–8; Caldwell, *López Expeditions*, 11; Edward Kenney to William R. Whittingham, April 1, 1876, MDA, file V; Paquette, *Sugar*, 187; Robert W. Gibbes, *Cuba for Invalids* (New York: W. A. Townsend and Co., 1860), 109. For similar assessments, see Samuel Hazard, *Cuba with Pen and Pencil* (Hartford, Conn.: Hartford, 1871), 318; Maturin M. Ballou, *Due South; or, Cuba, Past and Present* (Cambridge, Mass.: 1891; New York: Negro Universities Press, 1969), 47.

91. In a letter dated September 28, 1840, Cuban planter Francisco Diago communicated to sugar broker Henry Coit that some of his friends needed machinists and asked if Coit knew any that might be willing to come to Cuba. Ely, *Cuando reinaba*, 466–67, contains information on salaries. Other sources of information on machinists in Cuba are Allen, *Island of Cuba*, 19; Caldwell, *López Expeditions*, 11; Wurderman, *Notes*, 152; William J. Karras, "Yankee Carpenter in Cuba, 1848," *Americas* 30, nos. 6–7 (1978): 17–23; Philalethes, *Yankee Travels*, 157. For occupational information about U.S. citizens residing in Cuba in the early 1870s, see "Register of Americans [in Cuba]," NA, Foreign Service, RG 84, Havana, vol. c.14.1.

92. I found six specific references to engineers and skilled craftsmen from the United States in Cuba, with information about their place of origin (1840–60): two were from Lowell, Massachusetts; one from New Bedford, Massachusetts; one from Cambridgeport, Massachusetts; one from Concord, New Hampshire; and one from New York. According to a report in the Boston *Journal* of October 19, 1852, by that time of the year thirty-nine or forty machinists had left for Cuba from South Boston alone. News article cited in Foner, *History of Cuba* 2:129–30.

93. George W. Williams, *Sketches of Travel in the Old and New World* (Charleston: Walker, Evans and Cogswell, 1871), 21; Taylor, *United States*, 297. For information on the *fiador* system, see de Norzagaray, "Diario," 130. See also bond documents of a Maine machinist in AHP, leg. 53, box 51, exp. 14.

94. B. J. Smith to Vice-Consul Dimas Ponce, Feb. 24, 1842, and Spanish minister at Washington, D.C., to the Spanish consul at Savannah, March 8, 1859, both in Duke, Spanish Ministry–Savannah; Rauch, *American Interest*, 42.

95. José de la Concha, "Informe sobre instrucción, 15 de marzo de 1851," in España, Ultramar, *Cuba*, 41; *La Gaceta de La Habana*, Sept. 28, 1855. De la Concha also passed new, more restrictive decrees, seeking to limit the mobility of foreign visitors. See enclosure with George C. Backhouse to Lord Clarendon, June 20, 1855, *BPP*, vol. 42, class A, p. 67.

96. One of the profit mechanisms applied by U.S. sugar brokers during this

period was purchase on consignment, with charges for shipping expenses (set by the shipper) plus a 5-percent commission. Through these means, Moses Taylor, a New York sugar broker, raised a thirty-five-million-dollar fortune without ever having risked a single cent in the agricultural and industrial phases of sugar production. According to data presented by Bergad, in an 1861 transaction in which he bought sugar at 3.00 cents per pound and sold it at 7.31 cents per pound, Taylor netted a 66-percent profit. See Ely, *Cuando reinaba*, 175, 187; and Bergad, *Cuban Rural Society*, 177.

97. Sonesson, "Puerto Rico's Commerce," 334.

98. Ibid., 336; Alfred S. Eichner, *The Emergence of Oligopoly: Sugar Refining as a Case Study* (Baltimore: Johns Hopkins University Press, 1969), 39. See also Paul L. Vogt, *The Sugar Refining Industry in the United States, Its Development and Present Condition* (Philadelphia: University of Pennsylvania Press, 1908).

99. Marrero, *Cuba* 10:216; Aldama quoted in Carlos Rebello, *The Pith of the Sugar Question* (New York: MacGowan and Slipper, 1879), 32; Goizueta-Mimó, *Bitter Cuban Sugar*, 89.

100. Marte, *Cuba y la República Dominicana*, 19, 285; Roberto Cassá, *Historia social y económica de la República Dominicana*, 2 vols., 10th ed. (Santo Domingo: Alfa y Omega, 1991), 2:24–25. While in 1860 the Dominican Republic exported 80,000 quintals of tobacco, Cuba in 1861 produced 540,000 quintals. Marte, *Cuba y la República Dominicana*, 28–30, 287.

101. Moya Pons, *Manual*, 404–5.

102. For a fine discussion of land legislation and patterns of land distribution, see Frank Moya Pons, "The Land Question in Haiti and Santo Domingo: The Sociopolitical Context of Transition from Slavery to Free Labor, 1801–1843," in Moreno Fraginals, Moya Pons, and Engerman, eds., *Between Slavery and Free Labor*, 181–214.

103. H. Hoetink, *The Dominican People, 1850–1900*, trans. Stephen K. Ault (Baltimore: Johns Hopkins University Press, 1982), 4. Population and territorial information for the Dominican Republic comes from Mariano Álvarez, "Informe del Cónsul Mariano Álvarez del 20 de abril de 1860," in *Antecedentes de la anexión a España*, ed. Emilio Rodríguez Demorizi (Santo Domingo: Academia Dominicana de la Historia, 1955), 87–100.

104. Moya Pons, "Land Question," 186; Marte, *Cuba y la República Dominicana*, 232–37.

105. Cuban averages in de la Torre, "Cuba," 127; Puerto Rican averages calculated using "Cuadros de movimiento," AHN, Ultramar, leg. 1152, exps. 14 and 7; Dominican figures from Torrente, *Política ultramarina*, 282–85. Rate used for conversions: £1.00 equals $5.35.

106. Cassá, *Historia social* 2:27; "Informe de Antonio Peláez Campomanes del 8 de noviembre de 1860," in Rodríguez Demorizi, ed., *Antecedentes*, 106–

7. In 1855 France and Great Britain received 63 percent of Santo Domingo's mahogany exports; in 1856 the proportion went up to 72 percent. Marte, *Cuba y la República Dominicana*, 350.

107. Marte, *Cuba y la República Dominicana*, 350; Domínguez, *Anexión*, 9–10. Other export data in Marte, *Estadísticas*, 84–94, 194.

108. Marte, *Cuba y la República Dominicana*, 222; *La Gaceta de La Habana*, April 28, 1858, quoted in Rodríguez Demorizi, ed., *Documentos* 2:245; "Informe del Consul Álvarez," in Rodríguez Demorizi, ed., *Antecedentes*, 88.

109. [Saco], *Algunas reformas*, 8; "Cuadros de movimiento," AHN, Ultramar, leg. 1152, exp. 14; Torrente, *Política ultramarina*, 282–85. See Cassá, *Historia social* 2:27.

110. Torrente, *Política ultramarina*, 281; Domínguez, *Economía y política*, 82.

111. Calculations based on figures from Torrente, *Política ultramarina*, 282–85. Between October 1858 and September 1859 the United States exported only $94,846 worth of goods to Dominican ports. The Dominican market for northern Atlantic technology and implements was practically nonexistent. The first plow was introduced in Santiago in 1898, and even at that late date, according to H. Hoetink, it was slow to be accepted. According to a contemporary visitor, not a single steam engine was in operation there in 1872. Domínguez, *Anexión*, 9–10; Hoetink, *Dominican People*, 5; Samuel Hazard, *Santo Domingo, Past and Present, with a Glance at Hayti* (London: Sampson, Low, Marston and Searle, 1873), 307.

112. Averages are for 1849 and 1850, for the ports of Santo Domingo and Puerto Plata, departures and arrivals. Torrente, *Política ultramarina*, 282–85; and "Cuadros de movimiento," AHN, Ultramar, leg. 1152, exp. 14.

113. Torrente, *Política ultramarina*, 282–85; Jonathan Elliot to William S. Hodge, Sept. 1, 1851, in Lockward, ed., *Documentos*, 195–96.

114. "Informe de Peláez Campomanes," in Rodríguez Demorizi, ed., *Antecedentes*, 108; Captain-general of Puerto Rico, citing reports of the Spanish agent in Santo Domingo, to the overseas minister, Nov. 15, 1855, AHN, Ultramar, leg. 3524, exp. 116, doc. 1; Moya Pons, *Manual*, 290–91; *Diario de la Marina*, July 23, 1861, reproduced in Rodríguez Demorizi, ed., *Antecedentes*, 143.

115. Official report dated June 30, 1845, in Lockward, ed., *Documentos*, 38–44. I used 2.3 pesos per dollar for 1845 and 50.3 pesos per dollar for 1853.

116. Editors of *La Verdad*, *Series of Articles*, 18; Hazard, *Santo Domingo*, 259; Domínguez, *Economía y política*, 80; official report dated June 30, 1845, in Lockward, ed., *Documentos*, 38–44; Cassá, *Historia social* 2:48.

117. Rates derived from the following information: 11 pesos per dollar in March 1847, 44 pesos per gold ounce in 1844, 210 pesos per gold ounce in December 1847, 700 pesos per gold ounce in July 1851, 960 pesos per gold ounce in October 1854, and 1,100 pesos per gold ounce in November 1855. Lockward, ed., *Documentos*, 38–44; Domínguez, *Economía y política*, 25.

118. Cassá, *Historia social* 2:34; Domínguez, *Economía y política*, 29–30. See congressional proclamation in Marte, *Estadísticas*, 115–18.

119. Domínguez, *Economía y política*, 73–76.

120. Bunce, "American Interests," 231; Duff Green and Benjamin Green to the Dominican government, Aug. 26, 1850, in Marte, *Estadísticas*, 61; Allan Nevins, *Hamilton Fish: The Inner History of the Grant Administration* (New York: Dodd, Mead and Co., 1936), 253–54.

121. The company's prospectus and several related letters are among the Duff Green Papers, SHC.

122. Cazneau to Marcy, Jan. 23, 1854, in Lockward, ed., *Documentos*, 221; William Jaeger to William Seward, Dec. 27, 1863, NA, State, RG 59, Diplomatic Despatches, Santo Domingo, vol. 4; AGNRD, Relaciones Exteriores, leg. 21, exp. 6; Tansill, *United States*, 290–92.

Chapter 3: Dual Colonialism in Cuba and Puerto Rico

1. Mintz, *Sweetness and Power*, 148.

2. Moreno Fraginals, *Ingenio* 3:36. The percentage of beet sugar among British sugar imports increased consistently during the second half of the nineteenth century, from 14 percent in 1853 to 23 percent in 1863, and further to 38 percent in 1873. Eric Williams, *From Columbus to Castro: The History of the Caribbean, 1492–1969* (New York: Vintage Books, 1984), 383.

3. According to Mintz, sugar prices fell by 30 percent between 1840 and 1850, and by a further 25 percent between 1851 and 1870. Mintz, *Sweetness and Power*, 144. Bergad's figures show that sugar prices in Matanzas remained fairly stable during 1840–56 and then shot up in 1857–58. Bergad, *Cuban Rural Society*, 162.

4. García de Arboleya, *Manual*, 238, quoted in Knight, *Slave Society*, 45; Marrero, *Cuba* 10:101.

5. Susan Schroeder, *Cuba: A Handbook of Historical Statistics* (Boston: G. K. Hall, 1982), 239. A series of ravishing hurricanes hit the Cuban coffee regions in the mid-1840s, causing enormous destruction.

6. See Thomas W. Wilson, *Island of Cuba in 1850; Being a description of the Island, Its Resources, Productions, Commerce & Co.* (New Orleans: La Patria, 1850), 7; Corwin, *Spain and the Abolition*, 295; Knight, *Slave Society*, 39; and Marrero, *Cuba* 10:176.

7. Knight, *Slave Society*, 40–41; Dana, *To Cuba and Back*, 129; de la Sagra, *Cuba*.

8. See Wilson, *Island of Cuba*, 7; Marrero, *Cuba* 10:176; Knight, *Slave Society*, 39; and David A. Denslow, Jr., "Sugar Production in Northeastern Brazil and Cuba, 1858–1908," Ph.D. diss., Yale University, 1974, p. 77.

9. Marrero, *Cuba* 10:250; Ely, *Cuando reinaba*, 539; testimony of José Julián Acosta to the Junta de Información, Feb. 6, 1867, in España, Ultramar, *Cuba*, 72.

10. Marrero, *Cuba* 10:194–95; Marte, *Cuba y la República Dominicana*, 296 n. 68.

11. Moreno Fraginals, *Ingenio* 1:272; Knight, *Slave Society*, 38; Bergad, *Cuban Rural Society*, 109–14; García de Arboleya, *Manual*, 200–201. For an assessment on the origins, development, and impact of Cuban railroads, see Gert J. Oostindie, "Cuban Railroads, 1803–1868: Origins and Effects of Progressive Entrepreneurialism," *Caribbean Studies* 20, nos. 3–4 (1988): 24–45; and idem, "La burguesía cubana y sus caminos de hierro, 1830–1868," *Boletín de Estudios Latinoamericanos y del Caribe* 37 (Dec. 1984): 99–115.

12. Ely, *Cuando reinaba*, 446–47; Knight, *Slave Society*, 69.

13. García de Arboleya, *Manual*, 137–38; Knight, *Slave Society*, 39; Wilson, *Island of Cuba*, 7; Corwin, *Spain and the Abolition*, 295; Marrero, *Cuba* 10:176; Moreno Fraginals, *Ingenio* 1:222.

14. Hacendado [Madan], *Llamamiento*, 32.

15. See Joseph T. Crawford to Lord Clarendon, Aug. 7 and 16, 1855, *BPP*, vol. 42, class B, pp. 397–401; and Bergad, *Cuban Rural Society*, 250–51.

16. Ely, *Cuando reinaba*, 616; "Report of Coolie Importations to Cuba, June 14, 1858," NA, State, RG 59, Havana, vol. 39; *La Gaceta de La Habana*, Jan. 30, 1856.

17. Raúl Cepero Bonilla, *Azúcar y abolición* (1948; Barcelona: Editorial Crítica, 1976); Moreno Fraginals, *Ingenio* 1:27, 49; Fe Iglesias García, "The Development of Capitalism in Cuban Sugar Production, 1860–1900," in Moreno Fraginals, Moya Pons, and Engerman, eds., *Between Slavery and Free Labor*, 59; Herbert S. Klein, "Consideraciones sobre la viavilidad de la esclavitud y las causas de la abolición en la Cuba del siglo xix," *La Torre* 21 (July–Dec. 1973): 307–15; Rebecca J. Scott, *Slave Emancipation in Cuba: The Transition to Free Labor, 1860–1899* (Princeton, N.J.: Princeton University Press, 1985), 89; Laird W. Bergad, "The Economic Viability of Sugar Production Based on Slave Labor in Cuba, 1859–1878," *Latin American Research Review* 24, no. 1 (1989): 95–113; Bergad, *Cuban Rural Society*, chap. 11. For my assessment of forces leading to emancipation, see chapter 6.

18. See David Eltis, "The Nineteenth-Century Transatlantic Slave Trade: An Annual Time Series of Imports into the Americas Broken Down by Region," *HAHR* 67, no. 1 (Feb. 1987): 109–38.

19. Murray, *Odious Commerce*, 244, 259; Crawford to Lord Clarendon, Oct. 6, 1855, PRO, FO 84, 965.

20. Schroeder, *Cuba*, 107; Knight, *Slave Society*, 181; Dana, *To Cuba and Back*, 45. According to an 1850 report by the British judge of the Havana Mixed Commission, three or four cargoes of Brazilian slaves arrived yearly at the island. *BPP*, vol. 7, pp. 173–77.

21. Morales Carrión, *Auge y decadencia*, 200, 203. Morales Carrión recounts dramatic instances of slaves' jumping off ships to avoid being sent to Cuba. Several documents on the slave trade between Puerto Rico and Cuba are housed in AHN, Ultramar, leg. 5070, exp. 39, and leg. 5072, exps. 37–38.

22. Luis Manuel Díaz Soler, *Historia de la esclavitud negra en Puerto Rico* (Río Piedras: Editorial Universitaria, 1967), 407–8.

23. Editors of *La Verdad*, *Cuestión negrera*, 4; Ely, *Cuando reinaba*, 585; Crawford to Lord Clarendon, Aug. 29, 1853, PRO, FO 84, 906; Mallory, in *Congressional Globe*, vol. 28, pt. 2, p. 1328; Gibbes, *Cuba*, 39.

24. Murray, *Odious Commerce*, 266; Robert W. Shufeldt, "Secret History of the Slave Trade to Cuba," ed. Frederick C. Drake, *Journal of Negro History* 55, no. 3 (July 1970): 218–35; Hiram Fuller of the New York *Mirror*, quoted in Marrero, *Cuba* 10:269; Corwin, *Spain and the Abolition*, 118. Similar estimates were produced by the British consul at Havana, who calculated that a 450-slave expedition could net a $389,850 profit and that twice as much was spent in bribes as in purchasing the slaves. Joseph T. Crawford to Lord Russell, Feb. 5, 1861, PRO, FO 541, vol. 5.

25. Knight, "Origins of Wealth," 249, 231–53; Paquette, *Sugar*, 45. For a discussion of native wealth expanding to Matanzas, see Bergad, *Cuban Rural Society*, 14–15, 22–23.

26. Moreno Fraginals, *Ingenio* 1:63.

27. Justo Zaragoza, *Isla de Cuba, suspención de conventos y contribución extraordinaria de guerra* (Madrid: N.p., 1837), 24; Ely, *Cuando reinaba*, 324–25; Bergad, *Cuban Rural Society*, 174.

28. Arango y Parreño quoted in Marrero, *Cuba* 10:210; de Roches, *Cuba*, 15–17; *La Gaceta de Puerto Rico*, vol. 17, no. 137, quoted in Cruz Monclova, *Historia de Puerto Rico* 1:292. Between 1850 and 1853 planter Fernando Diago paid a total of $333,815 in interest on his debts to *refaccionistas*, while his colleague Joaquín de Ayestarán paid $284,691. Pérez, *Cuba: Between Reform and Revolution*, 94.

29. Pérez, *Cuba: Between Reform and Revolution*, 113; López Segrera, *Cuba*, 114; Moreno Fraginals, "Plantations," 16.

30. A variety of popular sayings described the extent of official corruption in Cuba: "To leave one's shame in Cádiz," "Nobody comes to Cuba for the fresh air," "To kill leaves" (to destroy incriminating government documents). Mariano Cancio Villa-Amil, *Situación económica de la Isla de Cuba* (Madrid: M. Ginesta, 1875), 44.

31. Philalethes, *Yankee Travels*, 64–65; Dana, *To Cuba and Back*, 111–12; Thrasher, *Preliminary Essay*, 77; James Rawson, *Cuba* (New York: Lane and Tippet, 1847), 12.

32. For a discussion of how these mechanisms operated, see Ely, *Cuando reinaba*, 306–7; and Roland T. Ely, "The Old Cuba Trade: Highlights and Case

Studies of Cuban American Interdependence During the Nineteenth Century," *Business History Review* 38, no. 4 (1964): 470–72.

33. Ely, *Cuando reinaba*, 330–31; Paquette, *Sugar*, 46–47; Crawford to Lord Clarendon, May 28, 1853, PRO, FO 84, 905; Corwin, *Spain and the Abolition*, 136–37; Marrero, *Cuba* 10:269–71. Bergad contends that Zulueta's humble origins were fictional, but he fails to present supporting evidence for this contention. Bergad, *Cuban Rural Society*, 51–52.

34. Other examples are Antonio Tellería, Ramón Herrera, and Rafael Toca. See Marte, *Cuba y la República Dominicana*, 178–79.

35. By 1895 only 17 percent of the island's planter class could trace its origins to the "old plantation families." Moreno Fraginals, "Plantations," 5.

36. Data from "Balanzas mercantiles de la isla de Puerto Rico" (microfilm in CIH). The average yearly change rate is calculated by finding all the yearly fluctuations between 1850 and 1859 and then determining the average.

37. Scarano, "Inmigración," in Scarano, ed., *Inmigración*, 23.

38. Cuban *ingenios* produced a mean of 391 tons (1860), while the Puerto Rican average remained at around 87 tons (1845). Scarano, *Sugar*, 66–67.

39. Andrés A. Ramos Mattei, "La importación de trabajadores contratados para la industria azucarera puertorriqueña: 1860–1880," in Scarano, ed., *Inmigración*, 126; Bergad, *Coffee*, 68; Ramos Mattei, *Hacienda*, 22–23. Indicative of the stagnation of the sugar industry is the fact that in 1899 still one-half of the sugar mills were driven by oxen. The railroad also arrived in Puerto Rico some forty years after it had been established in Cuba. Laird W. Bergad, "Agrarian History of Puerto Rico, 1870–1930," *Latin American Research Review* 13, no. 3 (1978): 65–66.

40. Scarano, *Sugar*, 5; consul quoted in Morales Carrión, *Auge y decadencia*, 134–35; Bergad, *Coffee*.

41. H. Augustus Cowper to Lord Clarendon, Feb. 11, 1866, in CIH, *Proceso abolicionista* 1:53. See Picó, *Libertad y servidumbre*.

42. Data on slave population and imports come from Philip D. Curtin, *The Atlantic Slave Trade: A Census* (Madison: University of Wisconsin Press, 1969), 31–44, 88.

43. José A. Curet, "De la esclavitud a la abolición: Transiciones económicas en las haciendas azucareras de Ponce, 1845–1873," in *Azúcar y esclavitud*, ed. Andrés A. Ramos Mattei (San Juan: Privately published, 1982), 84–85; Charles De Ronceray to Lewis Cass, Aug. 22, 1860, NA, Foreign Service, RG 84, San Juan, vol. 7228.

44. Morales Carrión, *Auge y decadencia*, 11–14; Rafael María de Labra y Cadrana, *La cuestión de ultramar* (Madrid: Nogueras, 1871), 25. See also Jay Kinsbruner, "Caste and Capitalism in the Caribbean: Residential Patterns and House Ownership Among the Free People of Color of San Juan, Puerto Rico, 1823–46," *HAHR* 70, no. 3 (Aug. 1990): 445.

45. Census figures reproduced in Cuba, Instituto de Investigaciones Estadísticas, *Los censos de población y viviendas en Cuba*, vol. 1, pt. 2 (Havana: Instituto de Investigaciones Estadísticas, 1988), 89–91.

Chapter 4: Political Patterns

1. Quoted in Hacendado [Madan], *Llamamiento*, vii–xx.

2. The conservatism basically responded to the desire to keep the social structure intact, with slaves subdued at the bottom and the elite enjoying social privileges. Loyalty to Spain was the logical consequence of this brand of conservatism, because, generally speaking, the crown appeared to be the best guarantor of such goals. Liberal postures such as espousing representative democracy, religious toleration, and free trade were not perceived as dangerous to the social status quo and therefore were welcomed by Cuba's conservative elite.

3. Knight, *Caribbean*, 1st ed., p. 133; Elsa V. Goveia, *Slave Society in the British Leeward Islands at the End of the Eighteenth Century* (New Haven, Conn.: Yale University Press, 1965), 102.

4. Note the use of the inclusive term *propertied elite*, which groups together planters and merchants. This term points also to the commonality of interests existing between these sectors when racial war was perceived as a threat.

5. Corbitt, "Petition," 538–40; idem, "Junta de Fomento," 339, 341–42.

6. Herminio Portell Vilá wrote a three-volume history of Narciso López between 1930 and 1958. In these volumes he asserted that López was not an annexationist but actually a separatist who cunningly used annexationist rhetoric to obtain support for the Cuban cause among U.S. expansionists and Cuban planters. Portell Vilá, however, produced little evidence to substantiate his thesis. His interpretation has come under severe attack from other students of the period, such as Sergio Aguirre, Philip S. Foner, and C. Stanley Urban. For a historiographic discussion on the role of Narciso López, see Sergio Aguirre, ed., *Eco de caminos* (Havana: Editorial de Ciencias Sociales, 1974), 117–61.

7. Despite two failures in 1849 and 1850, López organized a third and final expedition. This time López's troops left hastily, before the scheduled departure date in the summer of 1851, in an attempt to join an ongoing insurrection in Camagüey. The rebels were smashed, however, and their leaders were shot before López's troops reached the shores of Bahía Honda, at the western tip of the island. The outcome for the invading forces was also tragic. Once again they found no support among the populace and had to face well-armed and well-trained regular troops. The population gave its support to the Spanish troops. Carts of plantains were donated to feed the Spanish troops, and

cries of "Viva España," and "Viva Isabel" could be heard amid the gunfire. López and one of his divisions retreated to the hinterland. One eyewitness recounted: "He marches in shirt sleeves, over which crosses a rain-soaked discolored red flag; his beard is long and white. . . . Another ten or twelve are riding with him. They appeared shocked and were wordless." In a few days roughly five hundred filibuster troops had been either killed in action or captured. Several members of the expedition charged that they had been tricked into participating, led to believe that they were actually going to California. For his part, William Crittenden, the expedition's second-ranking officer, blamed López before being executed by the Spanish authorities. "I was deceived by López," he said. "He as well as the public press, assured me that the island was in a state of prosperous revolution." López, in turn, passed the blame to his local contacts: "I have been deceived," he asserted, adding that he had been led to believe that he could count on the army and the people. Roughly half of the invading force was captured alive. Firing squads executed fifty on August 15, including Colonel Crittenden, nephew of the U.S. attorney general. Two weeks later López himself was garroted. About 175 of the survivors were sent to work camps in Spain and were eventually pardoned. *Colección de los partes y otros documentos publicados en la Gaceta Oficial de La Habana referentes a la invasión de la gavilla de piratas capitaneada por el traidor Narciso López* (Havana: Imprenta del Gobierno, 1851); Crawford to Lord Palmerston, PRO, FO 72, 793; Smith, ed., *What Happened in Cuba?* 48–49; Leard, "Bonds of Destiny," 49; May, *Southern Dream*, 29.

8. Cepero Bonilla, *Azúcar*, 58. For information on the composition of the filibuster expeditions, see *Colección de los partes*, 8, 12–13, 25–27; Guerra y Sánchez, *Manual*, 490; Jones, *Cuba in 1851*, 57; John S. Thrasher to Daniel Barringer, Oct. 1, 1851, SHC, Moreau Barringer Papers.

9. Rauch, *American Interest*, 108.

10. Ibid., 76; Portell Vilá, *Narciso López* 1:266.

11. López to José Antonio Echeverría, Jan. 10, 1850, quoted in Portell Vilá, *Narciso López* 2:99; also see 2:459, 107–8.

12. Madan quoted in Portell Vilá, *Narciso López* 2:123.

13. Significantly, a student of nineteenth-century Cuban political thought describes the period in which annexationist tendencies dominated (1840–55) as one in which scholars encounter shaky ground. Aguirre, ed., *Eco*, 87.

14. El Grito de Lares was an unsuccessful revolt staged by Puerto Rican separatists in September 1868.

15. Lewis, *Main Currents*, 156; Aguirre, ed., *Eco*, 88; Ramos Mattei, *Betances*, 5, 11.

16. See José Ignacio Rodríguez, *Estudio histórico sobre el origen, desenvolvimiento y manifestaciones de la idea de la anexión de la isla de Cuba a los Estados*

Unidos (Havana: La Propaganda Política, 1900); Roig de Leuchsenring, *Cuba*, 120–21; and works by Portell Vilá cited earlier.

17. Fernando Portuondo, quoted in Aguirre, ed., *Eco*, 131.

18. In this and subsequent chapters the annexationist label is also applied to those who were willing to grant partial territorial concessions to foreign powers in exchange for political and financial support. The definition of *annexationism* used throughout this book leaves out the U.S. part of the annexationist equation. It was certainly true that annexationism included both a Caribbean push and a U.S. pull. For analytical purposes, however, in this book only the Caribbean push receives the label of annexationism. Other terms, such as *expansionism*, are applied to the U.S. pull.

19. Lewis, *Main Currents*, 240; Rauch, *American Interest*, 68; David Bushnell and Neil Macaulay, *The Emergence of Latin America in the Nineteenth Century* (New York: Oxford University Press, 1988), 79. I have come across other references to annexationist aspirations in Honduras, El Salvador, and Nicaragua (early 1850s), and from planters in St. Thomas (1858) and Brazil (1878). One planter in Pernambuco seriously suggested that the Nordeste secede from Brazil and seek annexation to the United States.

20. Some recent works have looked at the political behavior of the region's Creole elites against the backdrop of imperial rivalries. See, for example, Paquette, *Sugar*, 191–96; and William J. Nelson, "The Haitian Political Situation and Its Effect on the Dominican Republic: 1849–1877," *Americas* 45, no. 2 (Oct. 1988): 232.

21. The writings of annexationists Betancourt Cisneros and López reveal a degree of latent anti–North Americanism, a feeling that would surface with greater strength after 1855. See Betancourt Cisneros to del Monte, July 18, 1841, and Sept. 5, 1843, in Figarola-Caneda, ed., *Centón epistolario* 5:33, 130; Betancourt Cisneros to Saco, April 3, 1849, in José Antonio Saco, *Contra la anexión*, ed. Fernando Ortiz Fernández (Havana: Instituto Cubano del Libro, 1974), 211; and López, quoted in Portell Vilá, *Narciso López* 2:96.

22. Foner, *History of Cuba* 1:204.

23. Decree quoted in Knight, *Slave Society*, 127; see also Foner, *History of Cuba* 1:206. According to Bergad, following the repressive onslaught of La Escalera, "no slave rebellions are recorded in the Matanzas historical record, notices of palenques disappear, and the number of cimarrones drastically decline." Bergad, *Cuban Rural Society*, 241.

24. Domingo del Monte to the Spanish minister of state, quoted in Guerra y Sánchez, *Manual*, 462.

25. José de la Concha, "Informe de Concha al Sr. Ministro de Gobernación, 21 de diciembre, 1850," in España, Ultramar, *Cuba*, 16; Guerra y Sánchez, *Manual*, 477; Roig de Leuchsenring, *Cuba*, 52–53; Adrián del Valle, "Esclavitud

y anexionismo en Cuba," *Revista Bimestre Cubana* 55, no. 1 (1945): 35.

26. Betancourt Cisneros to Saco, Feb. 20, 1848, quoted in del Valle, "Esclavitud," 29–41; Betancourt Cisneros to Saco, April 3, 1849, quoted in Saco, *Contra la anexión*, 210; [Gaspar Betancourt Cisneros], *Thoughts upon the Incorporation of Cuba into the American Confederation in Contra-position to Those Published by Don José Saco* (New York: La Verdad, 1849), 1, 15; Editors of *La Verdad, Cuestión negrera*, 8.

27. The junta was now led by Betancourt Cisneros, José Elías Hernández, Pedro Valiente, and Domingo Goicuría.

28. Charles De Ronceray to Lewis Cass, Jan. 6, 1860, NA, Foreign Service, RG 84, San Juan, vol. 7228; [Betancourt Cisneros], *Thoughts*, 21; Rafael María de Labra y Cadrana, *La brutalidad de los negros*, rpt. (Havana: Universidad de La Habana, 1961), 31. See also Alexander Jourdan to William Seward, March 30, 1868, NA, Foreign Service, RG 84, San Juan, vol. 7228; Jiménez de Wagenheim, *Grito de Lares*, 80.

29. Paquette, *Sugar*, 88.

30. Thrasher, *Preliminary Essay*, 78; Ely, *Cuando reinaba*, 683–86; Special Committee of the Cuban League of the United States, *The Present Condition of Affairs in Cuba* (New York: Douglas Taylor, 1877), 13; Betancourt Cisneros to Saco, Aug. 14, 1849, in Saco, *Contra la anexión*, 219.

31. Cruz Monclova, *Historia de Puerto Rico* 1:320; de la Concha, "Informe sobre instrucción," and Valentín Cañedo, "Memoria de Cañedo del 24 de agosto de 1852," both in España, Ultramar, *Cuba*, 47, 166; Torrente, *Bosquejo* 1:228–29; "Educación-Instrucción, II," *La Voz de Cuba*, July 28, 1870.

32. Foner, *History of Cuba* 2:11; González, *Manifesto*, 4; [Kimball], *Cuba*, 185; De Ronceray to Cass, Jan. 6, 1860, NA, Foreign Service, RG 84, San Juan, vol. 7228; and George Latimer to James Buchanan, Dec. 9, 1846, in U.S. Dept. of State, San Juan Consulate, *Despachos*, 190–91. The state granted a number of scholarships for needy students to pursue advanced studies in the natural sciences in Spain. José Julián Acosta and Román Baldorioty de Castro were two notable recipients of such scholarships.

33. De la Concha, "Informe sobre instrucción," in España, Ultramar, *Cuba*, 36–40; Torrente, *Bosquejo* 1:232.

34. Betancourt Cisneros to Saco, Oct. 19, 1848, quoted in del Valle, "Esclavitud," 37; [Betancourt Cisneros], *Algunas observaciones*, 1; idem, *Thoughts*, 24; Hacendado [Madan], *Llamamiento*, 188; Betancourt Cisneros to Saco, Oct. 19, 1848, in Saco, *Contra la anexión*, 206; Uno de sus amigos [Cristóbal F. Madan], *Contestación a un folleto titulado: "Ideas sobre la incorporación de Cuba en los Estados Unidos," por Don José Antonio Saco* (New York: La Verdad, 1849), 4.

35. Betancourt Cisneros to del Monte, March 30, June 20, and July 30, 1841, in Figarola-Caneda, ed., *Centón epistolario* 5:14–15, 31–33, 34–36; Betancourt

Cisneros quoted in Foner, *History of Cuba* 2:14; Hacendado [Madan], *Llamamiento*, 36, 92.

36. Editors of *La Verdad*, *Cuestión negrera*, 9; Hacendado [Madan], *Llamamiento*, 178.

37. "España," *La Verdad*, May 20, 1853; [Betancourt Cisneros], *Thoughts*, 20; idem, *Algunas observaciones*, 5; Hacendado [Madan], *Llamamiento*, 223.

38. Quoted in Cepero Bonilla, *Azúcar*, 58.

39. Uno de sus amigos [Madan], *Contestación*, 4, 14; quoted translated version in Rauch, *American Interest*, 111.

40. Francisco J. Ponte Domínguez, *La masonería en la independencia de Cuba, 1809–1869* (Havana: Masonic World, 1944), 13–15; [Betancourt Cisneros], *Thoughts*, 28; Gaspar Betancourt Cisneros and John S. Thrasher, *Addresses Delivered at the Celebration of the Third Anniversary in Honor of the Martyrs of Cuban Freedom* (New Orleans: Sherman, Wharton and Co., 1854), 6–7; Un cubano [Porfirio Valiente], *La anexión de Cuba y los peninsulares en ella*, 2d ed. (New York: Imprenta de J. Mesa, 1853), 11; Spanish minister at Washington to the minister of state, Aug. 30, 1852, ASHM, Ultramar, leg. 90.

41. Cubano [Valiente], *Anexión*, 19–20; Betancourt Cisneros to Saco, Aug. 30, 1848, in Saco, *Contra la anexión*, 203.

42. This portrayal of Cuban annexationists as cultural nationalists challenges Gerald Eugene Poyo's contention that "annexationism increasingly lost ground after the 1850s as a growing *cubanidad*, or sense of being distinctly Cuban, gave birth to a nationalist movement dedicated to establishing an independent republic." Gerald Eugene Poyo, *With All, and for the Good of All: The Emergence of Popular Nationalism in the Cuban Communities of the United States, 1848–1898* (Durham, N.C.: Duke University Press, 1989), xv.

43. [Betancourt Cisneros], *Thoughts*, 18; Uno de sus amigos [Madan], *Contestación*, 5; Cubano [Valiente], *Anexión*, 12.

44. See, for example, Andrew Blythe to Marcy, Feb. 24, 1857, NA, State, RG 59, Havana, vol. 36.

45. *El Filibustero*, Feb. 15, 1854, quoted in Gerald Eugene Poyo, "Cuban Emigré Communities in the United States and the Independence of Their Homeland, 1852–1895," Ph.D. diss., University of Florida, 1983, pp. 28–30; "M. Pierre Soulé y el Diario de la Marina," *La Verdad*, May 20, 1853, p. 126.

46. Porfirio Valiente, "Will Spain Cede Cuba to the United States?" *La Verdad*, Feb. 10, 1853, p. 12; editorial, *La Verdad*, May 30, 1853, pp. 145–46.

47. Betancourt Cisneros and Thrasher, *Addresses*, quoted in Foner, *History of Cuba* 2:108; Junta Cubana de Nueva York, *Exposición de la Junta Cubana al Pueblo de Cuba* (New York: Hallet, 1855), 7, 10.

48. Grace Backhouse to her mother-in-law, Oct. 5, 1854, Duke, John Backhouse Papers. Some of the annexationist leaders of the late 1840s and early

1850s were co-opted with amnesties and/or appointments within the Spanish state apparatus. Cristóbal F. Madan and Juan Manuel Macías, for example, received safe conducts to return to the island, Pedro de Agüero was pardoned and appointed to the Board of Public Education, and José Luis Alfonso was entrusted with the task of traveling to Europe to promote a European treaty to guarantee Cuba to Spain.

49. For some information on Puerto Ricans studying in Europe, see Ástrid Cubano Iguina, *El hilo en el laberinto: Claves de la lucha política en Puerto Rico (siglo xix)* (Río Piedras: Ediciones Huracán, 1990), 56, 66.

50. Quoted in Carmelo Rosario Natal, "Betances y los anexionistas, 1850–1870: Apuntes sobre un problema," *Revista de Historia* 1, no. 2 (1985): 114.

51. The negative term *antiannexationist* is used here without reservation because the movement was essentially a reaction to the annexationist party and because at times its members referred to themselves as antiannexationists.

52. Del Monte to Leopoldo O'Donnell, April 30, 1845, in Figarola-Caneda, ed., *Centón epistolario* 6:190–93; [Domingo del Monte], "Memorial on the Present State of Cuba, Addressed to the Spanish Government by a Native of the Island," *United States Magazine and Democratic Review* 15, no. 77 (Nov. 1844): 478, 483.

53. During the late 1830s Saco momentarily embraced the annexationist, pro-U.S. route. After a brief stay in the United States, however, he developed a strong anti–North American sentiment. Ortiz Fernández, *José Antonio Saco*, 63; Antonio González Ponce de Llorante, *¿Qué es la anexión?: Consideraciones sobre la pretendida unión de la isla de Cuba a la república de los Estados Unidos de América*, 2d ed. (Havana: A. M. Dávila, 1852), 27–28.

54. Saco quoted in Lewis, *Main Currents*, 152; Saco to Betancourt Cisneros, March 10, 1848, quoted in Caldwell, *López Expeditions*, 25; José Antonio Saco, "Ideas sobre la incorporación de Cuba en los Estados Unidos [1848]," in Saco, *Contra la anexión*, 100.

55. Del Monte to O'Donnell, April 30, 1845, in Figarola-Caneda, ed., *Centón epistolario* 6:190–93; del Monte to Saco, July 18, 1850, in Saco, *Contra la anexión*, 223.

56. [Del Monte], "Memorial," 483; José Antonio Saco, "La situación política de Cuba y su remedio [1852]," in Saco, *Contra la anexión*, 266.

57. Saco to José Luis Alfonso, Jan. 30, 1853, in Saco, *Contra la anexión*, 242. Saco was highly critical of the U.S. rejection of this treaty, which he said reflected an "egotistical" and self-serving policy. Quoted in Lebroc, *Cuba*, 120.

58. Saco, *Contra la anexión*, 174.

59. Saco to Betancourt Cisneros, March 19, 1848, in Saco, *Contra la anexión*, 198.

60. Saco, *Contra la anexión*, 56, 90–91. It is important to note that during

the second half of the 1830s Saco had momentarily embraced the idea of annexation to the United States.

61. Saco, "Ideas," in Saco, *Contra la anexión,* 104; González Ponce de Llorante, *¿Qué es la anexión?* 6, 12.

62. González Ponce de Llorante, *¿Qué es la anexión?* 38–39.

63. I disagree with Poyo's contention that Cuban annexationists were "liberals" whose "principal motivation was annexation per se (to be achieved through armed action) and not the preservation or extension of slavery." Poyo, *With All,* 13.

64. López quoted in Lewis, *Main Currents,* 156; *La Verdad,* April 27, 1848, quoted in Rauch, *American Interest,* 63; Hernández, "Elementos," *La Verdad,* April 20, 1853, p. 88; Hacendado [Madan], *Llamamiento,* 177; *El Filibustero,* Feb. 15, 1854, quoted in Cepero Bonilla, *Azúcar,* 54; article by Ramón de Palma, in *La Verdad,* June 12, 1851, quoted in Cepero Bonilla, *Azúcar,* 56–57.

65. Betancourt Cisneros to Saco, Oct. 19, 1848, in Saco, *Contra la anexión,* 205; Uno de sus amigos [Madan], *Contestación,* 3; Betancourt Cisneros quoted in Portell Vilá, *Narciso López* 1:209; Editors of *La Verdad, Cuestión negrera,* 10.

66. Saco, *Contra la anexión,* 119–20.

67. Betancourt Cisneros to del Monte, April 25, 1841, and Miguel Aldama to del Monte, April 9, 1844, both in Figarola-Caneda, ed., *Centón epistolario* 5:21, 6:20; Editors of *La Verdad, Cuestión negrera,* 8, 10; Foner, *History of Cuba* 2:82; Hacendado [Madan], *Llamamiento,* 97–98.

68. Saco, *Contra la anexión,* 60, 72.

69. [Betancourt Cisneros], *Thoughts,* 9, 22.

70. Paquette, *Sugar,* 95; Miguel Aldama to del Monte, Nov. 9, 1844, in Figarola-Caneda, ed., *Centón epistolario* 6:119–21; Leon, *Sugar Cultivation* 2:5–10; Francisco Calcagno, *Diccionario biográfico cubano* (New York: Imprenta Ponce de León, 1878), 18; Saco, *Contra la anexión,* 70–71.

71. De Roches, *Cuba,* 42; Torrente, *Política ultramarina,* 213.

72. Throughout this book, *Dominican annexationism* is broadly defined to include not only the desire to annex the entire country to another nation but also the various attempts to grant territorial concessions in Samaná or elsewhere in return for a foreign protectorate. The rationale behind the use of this definition rests on the fact that most Dominican annexationists were not willing to draw a line at the protectorate level but instead were quite flexible, willing to offer anything between a partial protectorate and full annexation.

73. Dominican historian Frank Moya Pons has identified at least four of these movements: one in Santo Domingo with pro-Spanish inclinations led by Catholic priests Gaspar Hernández and Pedro Pamiés; another under the leadership of Pedro Antonio Pimentel, an Anglophile; a third, the Trinitarios, led by Juan Pablo Duarte, seeking total independence; and finally, a

pro-French faction led by Buenaventura Báez and Manuel Joaquín Delmonte. Moya Pons, *Manual*, 270.

74. Declaration of Independence of the Dominican Republic, Jan. 16, 1844, in República Dominicana, *Colección de leyes* 1:7–15. For an interesting document on the Trinitarios, see José María Serra, "Apuntes para la historia de los Trinitarios, fundadores de la República Dominicana," *Boletín del Archivo General de la Nación* 32–33 (Jan.–April 1944): 49–69.

75. Moya Pons, *Manual*, 289–90, 291–95; Rodríguez Demorizi, ed., *Documentos* 1:35–40.

76. Dominican envoys to the French minister of foreign affairs, March 30, 1848, in Rodríguez Demorizi, ed., *Correspondencia* 2:43–45.

77. French consul at Santo Domingo to the French minister of foreign affairs, Jan. 20, 1848, and Dominican envoys to the French minister of foreign affairs, July 23 and March 30, 1848, all in Rodríguez Demorizi, ed., *Correspondencia* 2:34–38, 94, 43–45; Dominican minister of foreign relations to the French consul at Santo Domingo, Oct. 18, 1849, cited in Vetilio Alfau Durán, ed., *Controversia histórica: Polémica de Santana* (Santo Domingo: Editora Montalvo, 1968), 118.

78. For contemporary criticisms of cultural mimicry, see "Manía de la época," *El Dominicano*, June 29, 1855; and "Ecleptomanía social," *La Española Libre*, Oct. 28, 1856.

79. Poem by Father Vázquez, in Rodríguez Demorizi, *Santana*, 11.

80. Moya Pons, *Manual*, 304–5; Dominican Council of Ministers to the captain-general of Puerto Rico, April 4, 1849, AHN, Ultramar, leg. 3524, exp. 52, doc. 2 (copy in CIH); Báez to the French consul at Santo Domingo, April 19, 1849, in Rodríguez Demorizi, ed., *Correspondencia* 2:140; Valentina Peguero and Danilo de los Santos, *Visión general de la historia dominicana*, 10th ed. (Santiago, Dominican Republic: Universidad Católica Madre y Maestra, 1986), 191–93; Schomburgk to Lord Palmerston, May 22 and June 8, 1849, both in PRO, FO 140, 1; French consul at Santo Domingo to the French minister of foreign affairs, June 1 and Oct. 18, 1849, in Rodríguez Demorizi, ed., *Correspondencia* 2:153, 187; Alfau Durán, ed., *Controversia histórica*, 94; Jonathan Elliot to the U.S. secretary of state, May 2, 1849, in Lockward, ed., *Documentos*, 82–83; Perkins, *Monroe Doctrine*, 259; Lockward, ed., *Documentos*, xxiv, 106–7.

81. Monclús, *Caudillismo*, 9–10; Rodríguez Demorizi, *Santana*, 74. According to the British consul, Santana had an eight hundred–troop army with which he confronted and beat the entire Haitian army consisting of five to six thousand soldiers. Schomburgk to Commodore Bennet, May 5, 1849, PRO, FO 140, 1.

82. Rodríguez Demorizi, *Santana*, 70.

83. Nelson, "Haitian Political Situation," 232; Peguero and de los Santos, *Visión general*, 196.

84. For documentation on the rivalry between Santana and Báez, see Santana's proclamation of July 3, 1853, and Báez's proclamation of August 1, 1853, in Rodríguez Demorizi, ed., *Documentos* 1:272–82, 291–322.

85. Cassá, *Historia social* 2:58; British consul at Santo Domingo to the Dominican minister of foreign relations, Nov. 23, 1849, in Rodríguez Demorizi, ed., *Correspondencia* 2:196. See also Báez's inaugural speech (1849), quoted in Cassá, *Historia social* 2:52.

86. Rodríguez Demorizi, ed. *Documentos* 1:276–79. An indicator of the deterioration of the relations between Santana and the church is that while he had left two hundred pesos in his 1852 will to the church, he eliminated this entry from his 1862 will. See Emilio Rodríguez Demorizi, ed., *Papeles de Santana* (Rome: Tipografía G. Menaglia, 1952), 107–18; Rodríguez Demorizi, *Santana*, 101.

87. Peguero and de los Santos, *Visión general*, 197–98.

88. Expulsion decrees against Baecistas in República Dominicana, *Colección de leyes* 2:524–27; Elliot to Cass, Nov. 27, 1853, quoted in Tansill, *United States*, 175.

89. Rodríguez Demorizi, *Santana*, 155.

90. Domínguez, *Anexión*, 45; idem, *Economía y política*, 135; Rodríguez Demorizi, *Santana*, 159.

91. Schomburgk to Lord Clarendon, Feb. 6, 1856, PRO, FO 140, 4; Jacob Pereira (interim U.S. commercial agent) to Marcy, Aug. 7, 1856, in Lockward, ed., *Documentos*, 286–87; *La Gaceta de Santo Domingo*, Jan. 30, 1855; Spanish commercial agent to the captain-general of Cuba, May 28, 1855, AHN, Ultramar, leg. 3524, exp. 109 (see also exp. 110).

92. Moya Pons, *Manual*, 324–26.

93. Proclamation of Báez, Oct. 9, 1856, in Rodríguez Demorizi, ed., *Documentos* 1:353. Another characteristic of Báez's administration was its marked pro-Catholicism. Upon assuming the presidency, Báez promised "to restore to the Catholic Church all those things of which it was despoiled with sacrilegious impudence, in the time of our predecessor [Santana]." William L. Wipfler, "The Churches of the Dominican Republic in the Light of History," M.Div. thesis, Union Theological Seminary, 1964, p. 44. Jacob Pereira to Marcy, Oct. 30 and Nov. 22, 1856, in Lockward, ed., *Documentos*, 292–301.

94. Báez to the captain-general of Puerto Rico, July 12, 1857, quoted in Pérez, *Historia diplomática*, 335; captain-general of Puerto Rico to the Spanish minister of state, July 18, 1857, AHN, Ultramar, leg. 3524, exp. 133; Félix María del Monte to Cass, May 7, 1857, in Lockward, ed., *Documentos*, 306–8; del Monte to Cass, May 6, 1857, NA, State, RG 59, Notes from Foreign Missions, Dominican Republic, vol. 1. For peace terms, see República Dominicana, *Colección de leyes* 3:521–22; captain-general of Puerto Rico to the Spanish minister of state, Sept. 9, 1857, AHN, Ultramar, leg. 3524, exp. 138.

95. Copy of agreement in AHN, Ultramar, leg. 3525, exp. 4, doc. 2 (copy in CIH); see also *La Crónica de Ambos Mundos,* June 5, 1863, in Emilio Rodríguez Demorizi, ed., *Papeles de Buenaventura Báez* (Santo Domingo: Editora Montalvo, 1955), 169–73. Elliot to Cass, March 21, 1859, quoted in Tansill, *United States,* 207–8.

Chapter 5: The Rearrangement of Political and Commercial Ties

1. A clear indicator of the sectional transfer of power during the war was the fact that between 1861 and 1862 the U.S. consular corps in the Spanish colonies of the Caribbean went from being staffed by southerners to being staffed by northerners. In 1862 Robert W. Shufeldt suggested that "the appointment of U.S. Consuls & their subordinates to the island of Cuba ought to be of men whose proclivities are rather against than for slavery. Hitherto this has not been the case." Indeed, before the Civil War most members of the U.S. consular corps in the Spanish colonies of the Caribbean were southerners linked to the plantation economy of the South. This was so partially because Spanish officials in Cuba and Spain consistently obstructed the appointment of abolitionist foreign consuls. During the 1840s and 1850s William Sharkey, Thomas Dunu, and Andrew Blythe of Mississippi, Robert B. Campbell of South Carolina, and Charles Helm, originally of Kentucky with residence in Georgia, served as consuls in Havana. When the war broke out, Charles Helm and his counterpart in Puerto Rico, the Baltimorean Charles De Ronceray, were replaced by a northern staff: Robert W. Shufeldt, from Connecticut, became U.S. consul at Havana, and James Derby and John J. Hyde, from New York and Connecticut, respectively, were appointed consuls at San Juan. The new vice-consuls in Nuevitas, Cárdenas, Sagua, and Cienfuegos were either from New England or New York. Shufeldt, "Secret History," 230.

2. Frederic Bancroft, *The Life of William Seward,* 2 vols. (New York: Harper and Brothers, 1900), 2:132–33. Lester D. Langley described U.S. official reaction to European encroachments in Mexico as one reflecting "uneasy detachment." Langley, *Struggle,* 115.

3. See Shufeldt, "Secret History," 218–35.

4. Hauch, "Attitudes," 256; William Seward to Horatio Perry, Sept. 3, 1863, in U.S. Dept. of State, *PRFA* 1863:907.

5. Gabriel García Tassara to Seward, Oct. 7, 1863; García Tassara to Fernando Calderón Collantes, Dec. 31, 1863; and Captain Smith to the Spanish minister at Paris, Oct. 7, 1863, all in AHN, Ultramar, leg. 3525, exps. 104, 112, 103.

6. Horatio Perry to Seward, June 13, 1861, and March 8 and Sept. 21, 1862, in U.S. Dept. of State, *PRFA* 1861:261, and 1862:482–83, 515.

7. Bernard Kock was the promoter of the Ile à Vache project. Falsely posing as the island's governor, Kock managed to get financial support from the U.S. government and a group of New York capitalists for the relocation of five hundred former slaves from Virginia. The project turned out to be a fiasco. Many participants died as a result of an epidemic. The freed slaves were not paid for their labor, and by 1864 all of the survivors had returned to the United States. See Frederic Bancroft, "The Colonization of American Negroes, 1801–1865," in *Frederic Bancroft: Historian*, ed. Jacob E. Cooke (Norman: University of Oklahoma Press, 1957).

8. Jonathan Elliot to Seward, Oct. 3, 1862 (private), NA, State, RG 59, Santo Domingo, vol. 4; Robert W. Shufeldt to Seward, July 4, 1862, NA, State, RG 59, Havana, vol. 45. See Bancroft, "Colonization," 228–58.

9. See Frank Lawrence Owsley, *King Cotton Diplomacy: Foreign Relations of the Confederate States of America*, 2d rev. ed. (Chicago: University of Chicago Press, 1959).

10. Emory Thomas, *The Confederate Nation, 1861–1865* (New York: Harper Torchbook, 1979), 175; Francisco Muñoz Moncada to the Spanish minister of state, Aug. 12, 1861, Duke, Spanish Ministry–Charleston.

11. Thomas, *Confederate Nation*, 172; Owsley, *King Cotton*, 542–58.

12. R. M. T. Hunter to Pierre A. Rost, Aug. 24, 1861, quoted in Portell Vilá, *Historia de Cuba* 2:160; Charles Helm to Francisco Serrano (confidential), Feb. 22, 1863, LC, Manuscripts Department, vol. 7. Slavery had been abolished in the Dominican Republic four decades earlier and was not reestablished during Spanish annexation.

13. Robert Toombs to Helm, July 22, 1861, quoted in May, *Southern Dream*, 249; and in Portell Vilá, *Historia de Cuba* 2:144. In a similar communication Secretary of State Hunter instructed Rost: "If a party was found in these States during their connection with the former Union who desired the acquisition of Cuba it was for the purpose of establishing something like a balance of power . . . now they can fear nothing." Hunter to Rost, Aug. 24, 1861, quoted in Portell Vilá, *Historia de Cuba* 2:160.

14. The Spanish consul at Charleston reported that the annexation had been "applauded by the local press" and that North American intervention on that matter was "entirely unpopular" there. Francisco Muñoz Moncada to García Tassara, April 12, 1861, Duke, Spanish Ministry–Charleston.

15. Bourne, *Foreign Policy*, 90.

16. García Tassara to Muñoz Moncada, Dec. 31, 1860, Jan. 6 and 12, 1861, Duke, Spanish Ministry–Charleston.

17. García Tassara to Muñoz Moncada, March 12, 1861. See also comments

of the Spanish secretary of state regarding the blockade, dated June 25, 1861, Duke, Spanish Ministry–Charleston.

18. Bécker, *Historia de las relaciones* 2:589; royal decree of June 19, 1861, in U.S. Dept. of State, San Juan Consulate, *Despachos*, 542–43; García Tassara to Muñoz Moncada, Aug. 31, 1861, Duke, Spanish Ministry–Charleston.

19. Thomas Savage to Lewis Cass, Aug. 27, 1860, NA, State, RG 59, Havana, vol. 40; Perkins, *Monroe Doctrine*, 284; Portell Vilá, *Historia de Cuba* 2:153; O'Donnell quoted in Perkins, *Monroe Doctrine*, 284–85.

20. Santana declared his country's annexation to Spain on March 18, 1861. The Spanish government waited a few weeks before officially accepting this fait accompli. For an assessment of international reactions to this step, see Hauch, "Attitudes."

21. Bourne, *Balance of Power*, 255.

22. Savage to Seward, Oct. 4, 1861, NA, State, RG 59, Havana, vol. 42; Shufeldt to Seward, Nov. 27, 1861, NA, State, RG 59, Havana, vol. 41, Helm to the Confederate secretary of state, Jan. 23, 1864, LC, Manuscripts Department, RCSA, vol. 7; John J. Hyde to Seward, Aug. 12, 1864, U.S. Dept. of State, San Juan Consulate, *Despachos*, 642–43.

23. Shufeldt to Serrano, Dec. 12, 1861, AHN, Ultramar, leg. 4682, exp. 186; William Jaeger to Seward, Sept. 28, 1863, NA, State, RG 59, Santo Domingo, vol. 4.

24. Message of Andrew Johnson of Dec. 9, 1868, in Richardson, ed., *Compilation* 4:688–89. For an assessment of the postures of the Johnson administration and the general public regarding the issue of expansion, see Theodore Clarke Smith, "Expansion After the Civil War, 1865–71," *Political Science Quarterly* 16, no. 3 (1901): 412–36.

25. Report of Jan. 5, 1867, AHN, Ultramar, leg. 5094, exp. 46; Tansill, *United States*, 241–45; William Seward to Frederick Seward, Dec. 17, 1866, NA, State, RG 59, Special Missions, reel 153; article in the New York *Tribune*, June 15, 1870, quoted in Smith, "Expansion," 434. See also Harold T. Pinkett, "Efforts to Annex Santo Domingo to the United States, 1866–1871," *Journal of Negro History* 26, no. 1 (Jan. 1941): 15.

26. Tansill, *United States*, 363–71; George N. Robeson to Commander E. K. Owen, July 10, 1869, quoted in Welles, *Naboth's Vineyard* 1:370–71; and Admiral Poor to Robeson, March 12, 1870, in Emilio Rodríguez Demorizi, ed., *Proyecto para la incorporación de Santo Domingo a Norte América* (Santo Domingo: Editora Montalvo, 1945), 362; Pinkett, "Efforts," 30; Rodríguez Demorizi, ed., *Proyecto*, 405; Robeson to Poor, Jan. 29, 1870, and Poor to Nissage Saget, Feb. 10, 1870, in Rodríguez Demorizi, ed., *Proyecto*, 356–57; United States, Commission of Inquiry to Santo Domingo, *Report of the Commission of Inquiry* (Washington, D.C.: GPO, 1871), 6–7.

27. Seward to Benjamin Hunter, June 2, 1869, NA, State, RG 59, Special

Missions, reel 152; Samuel G. Howe, *Letters on the Proposed Annexation of Santo Domingo* (Boston: Wright and Potter, 1871), 17; U.S., Commission of Inquiry, *Report of the Commission*, 13; Cazneau to Seward, Oct. 9, 1866, NA, State, RG 59, Santo Domingo, vol. 5; Congressman Wood quoted in Rodríguez Demorizi, ed., *Proyecto*, 88–89 (my translation).

28. For information on the company's bond holders and a copy of the agreement, see Gregorio Luperón, *Notas autobiográficas y apuntes históricos sobre la República Dominicana*, 3 vols., 2d ed. (Santiago, Dominican Republic: Editorial El Diario, 1939), 2:172–75, 203–5; Emilio Rodríguez Demorizi, ed., *Samaná, pasado y porvenir* (Santo Domingo: Editora Montalvo, 1945), 35; and Rodríguez Demorizi, ed., *Proyecto*, 298–301. For a recent assessment of the Grant administration's pursuit of territories in the Dominican Republic, see William J. Nelson, *Almost a Territory: America's Attempt to Annex the Dominican Republic* (Newark, Del.: University of Delaware Press, 1990).

29. See, for example, Albert K. Weinberg, *Manifest Destiny: A Study of Nationalistic Expansion in American History* (Baltimore: Johns Hopkins University Press, 1935), 231.

30. The Union victory was not the primary motivation for Spain's withdrawal. The growing strength of the insurrectionary forces and the high casualty rate among Spanish troops would have produced the same result. Nonetheless, had things been different in the United States, Spain would probably have decided to reinforce its position in Santo Domingo.

31. For a pioneering, now classic study of the formation of the "new empire," see LaFeber, *New Empire*. Also see Paolino, *Foundations*.

32. Seward to Charles Hale, May 23, 1866, U.S. Dept. of State, *PRFA* 1866: 574. For another example of new attitudes toward slavery, see Williams, *From Columbus*, 388–89.

33. In an article entitled "Cuba or San Domingo?" the editors of the New York *Times* spelled out why it was preferable to annex the Dominican Republic rather than Cuba, using racial and economic justifications. New York *Times*, March 25, 1870.

34. See AHN, Ultramar, leg. 5094, exp. 46.

35. He continued, stating that "there are in the United States hundreds of officers belonging to the dissolved Northern army, who having become accustomed to military life and activity are always willing to participate in any adventure; next to these officers there are thousands of individuals who were soldiers and who either lost their work habits or means of support. All of these elements are to be feared." Francisco Lersundi to the Spanish overseas minister, Aug. 30, 1867, AHN, Ultramar, leg. 4713, exp. 220. Also see García Tassara to the captain-general of Cuba, April 28, 1865, AHN, Ultramar, leg. 4645, exp. 50, doc. 1.

36. "La neutralidad americana," *La Revolución*, June 9, 1869; [Francisco

Vicente Aguilera], *Notes About Cuba* (New York: N.p., 1872), 17, 28; Nevins, *Hamilton Fish*, 358; Daniel Sickles to Fish, telegram received Sept. 16, 1869, U.S. Congress, Senate, 41st Cong., 2d sess., S. Exec. Doc. 113, p. 4; Fernando Calderón Collantes to Fish, Feb. 3, 1876, NA, State, RG 59, Other Records, Confidential Correspondence Related to the Cuban War (hereinafter cited as Cuban War), entry 813; Roig de Leuchsenring, *Cuba*, 93, 100; Fish to Caleb Cushing, March 1, 1876, NA, State, RG 59, Other Records, Cuban War, entry 813; Nevins, *Hamilton Fish*, 125; Foner, *History of Cuba* 2:201, 213–16; Spanish minister at Washington to the Spanish minister of state, April 16, 1872, ASHM, Ultramar, leg. 90.

37. Spanish minister to Washington to the Spanish minister of state, May 26, 1869, AHN, Ultramar, leg. 4723, exp. 99. Foner, *History of Cuba* 2:244–46; Hudson Strode, *The Pageant of Cuba* (New York: Random House, 1934), 106–7; CIH, *Proceso abolicionista* 1:402; de Labra y Cadrana, *Cuestión de ultramar*, 44; James J. O'Kelly, *Mambí-Land; or, Adventures of a Herald Correspondent in Cuba* (Philadelphia: J. B. Lippincott and Co., 1874), 221; Cushing to Fish, Jan. 21, Feb. 21, and April 19, 1876, NA, State, RG 59, Other Records, Cuban War, entry 813; Francis L. Norton, *Cuba* (New York: N.p., 1873), 5–8.

38. In March 1876 the Grant administration spelled out its demands to Spain: "Peace, order and good government in Cuba. . . . Gradual but effectual emancipation of the slaves. . . . Improvement of commercial facilities and the removal of obstructions now existing in the way of trade and commerce." Fish to Fernando Calderón Collantes, March 1, 1876, NA, State, RG 59, Other Records, Cuban War, entry 813.

39. Muñoz Moncada to García Tassara, May 13, 20, and 24, 1861; Muñoz Moncada to the minister of state, June 11, 1861; Muñoz Moncada to García Tassara, June 11, 1861; and Muñoz Moncada to Francisco Serrano, Sept. 10, 1861, all in Duke, Spanish Ministry–Charleston. For a recent study on blockade-running activities, see Stephen R. Wise, *Lifeline of the Confederacy: Blockade Running During the Civil War* (Columbia: University of South Carolina Press, 1988).

40. García Tassara to the Spanish vice-consul at Savannah, March 16, 1861, Duke, Spanish Ministry–Savannah; Spanish minister of state to Muñoz Moncada, June 25, 1861, Duke, Spanish Ministry–Charleston; royal decree of June 19, 1861, in U.S. Dept. of State, San Juan Consulate, *Despachos*, 542–43; Francisco Serrano to Muñoz Moncada, Sept. 10, 1861, Duke, Spanish Ministry–Charleston. The principle stated that a blockade, to be binding, had to be effective.

41. Owsley, *King Cotton*, 230–31; blockade-running information published by Helm in the Havana *Mercantile Weekly*, Jan. 6, 1862; Shufeldt to Seward, Nov. 1861, quoted in Owsley, *King Cotton*, 236.

42. Owsley, *King Cotton*, 232; Havana *Mercantile Weekly*, Jan. 6, 1862; Muñoz

Moncada to the minister of state, Sept. 29 and Dec. 8 and 18, 1861, and "List of Vessels Cleared at the Port of Charleston," all in Duke, Spanish Ministry–Charleston.

43. "List of Vessels Cleared at the Port of Charleston," Duke, Spanish Ministry–Charleston; Owsley, *King Cotton*, 238.

44. Owsley, *King Cotton*, 253–54; enclosure with Hyde to Seward, Dec. 22, 1864, and Hyde to Seward, Sept. 7, 1863, both in U.S. Dept. of State, San Juan Consulate, *Despachos*, 665, 595–600. In July 1861 Consul De Ronceray left his post while the Confederate vessel *Jeff Davis* visited the port of San Juan. The Department of State received information that he "left [the] consulate without permission, and that in the meanwhile the duties of the office [were] discharged by a boy . . . a clerk in the British consulate." De Ronceray was discharged soon after the incident. See related correspondence in U.S. Dept. of State, San Juan Consulate, *Despachos*, 545–47.

45. Owsley, *King Cotton*, 230–31, 261; Hyde to Seward, June 30, 1864, and Hyde's register of blockade running, 1864, both in U.S. Dept. of State, San Juan Consulate, *Despachos*, 633–35, 665.

46. Havana *Mercantile Weekly*, Jan. 6, 1862; "List of Vessels Cleared at the Port of Charleston," Duke, Spanish Ministry–Charleston.

47. Muñoz Moncada to the minister of state, Sept. 29, 1861, and March 7, 1862, Duke, Spanish Ministry–Charleston; Hyde to Seward, Jan. 20 and Sept. 7, 1863, in U.S. Dept. of State, San Juan Consulate, *Despachos*, 574–75, 595–600; Savage to Seward, April 26, 1863, NA, State, RG 59, Havana, vol. 46; William Watson, *Adventures of a Blockade Runner* (London: T. Fisher Unwin, 1892), 199.

48. Savage to Seward, Sept. 10, 1863, NA, State, RG 59, Havana, vol. 46; Hamilton Cochran, *Blockade Runners of the Confederacy* (Indianapolis: Bobbs-Merrill Co., 1958), 224; Watson, *Adventures*, 145; Hyde to Seward, Aug. 22, 1864, and George Latimer to Seward, July 19, 1864, both in U.S. Dept. of State, San Juan Consulate, *Despachos*, 635–37, 647. The merchant involved was George Latimer, a native of Pennsylvania and a former U.S. consul at San Juan. In a letter addressed to Seward, Latimer denied the charges and stated that the blockade-runners took the coal without his knowledge.

49. Marcus W. Price, "Blockade Running as a Business in South Carolina During the War Between the States, 1861–1865," *American Neptune* 9 (1949): 41–42.

50. Shufeldt to Seward, Nov. 28, 1861, NA, State, RG 59, Havana, vol. 41; Helm to the Confederate secretary of state, May 6, 1862, and March 6, 1863, LC, Manuscripts Department, RCSA, vol. 7; "Report of Jan. 14, 1864," NA, Foreign Service, RG 84, Havana, vol. c.81.

51. J. Wilkinson, *The Narrative of a Blockade-Runner* (New York: Sheldon and

Co., 1877), 124; Watson, *Adventures*, 139; Thomas E. Taylor, *Running the Blockade: A Personal Narrative of Adventures, Risks, and Escapes During the American Civil War*, 4th ed. (London: John Murray, 1912), 146.

52. Watson, *Adventures*, 238.

53. Records do not show evidence of direct trade between Puerto Rico and Confederate ports. One exception to this was a Spanish resident of Charleston, one Mr. Malga, who shipped Puerto Rican coffee to the South. See Hyde to Seward, Feb. 28, June 27, and Sept. 7, 1863, and May 6 and Aug. 15, 1864, in U.S. Dept. of State, San Juan Consulate, *Despachos*, 581–83, 593–95, 595–600, 608–10, 645–46.

54. García Tassara to Muñoz Moncada, June 24, 1861; Muñoz Moncada to Judge A. G. Magrath, June 26, 1861; and court clerk to Muñoz Moncada, July 11, 1861, all in Duke, Spanish Ministry–Charleston.

55. Portell Vilá, *Historia de Cuba* 2:143; Ely, *Cuando reinaba*, 285. García Tassara to Muñoz Moncada, Aug. 3, 1861; Muñoz Moncada to García Tassara, Aug. 15, 1861; Muñoz Moncada to Salvador Zulueta, Aug. 5, 1861; Muñoz Moncada to García Tassara, Aug. 23, 1861; and Muñoz Moncada to the mayor of Savannah, April 22, 1862, all in Duke, Spanish Ministry–Charleston.

56. Seward to Gustavus Kroener, Jan. 30, 1863, in U.S. Dept. of State, *PRFA* 1863:967; Portell Vilá, *Historia de Cuba* 2:148; Ely, *Cuando reinaba*, 288.

57. Rafael Echagüe to the overseas minister, May 16, 1861, AHN, Ultramar, leg. 1128, exp. 29, doc. 2; De Ronceray to Seward, May 27, 1861, and Hyde to Seward, Feb. 4, 1863, 580, both in U.S. Dept. of State, San Juan Consulate, *Despachos*, 535–36, (also see 545–57); William Jaeger to Seward, Feb. 6, 1863, NA, State, RG 59, Santo Domingo, vol. 4.

58. Portell Vilá, *Historia de Cuba* 2:135.

59. De Ronceray to Cass, Jan. 1, 1861, and De Ronceray to J. S. Black, Jan. 31, 1861, both in NA, Foreign Service, RG 84, San Juan, vol. 7228; Muñoz Moncada to García Tassara, March 7, 1861, Duke, Spanish Ministry–Charleston.

60. Juan Prats and Francisco Marich to Rafael Echagüe, June 7, 1861; Eduardo Lino, Pedro Virella Duque, and Luis Sánchez to Echagüe, June 28, 1861; and R. Plaud, D. Bergazo, and E. T. Herpin to Echagüe, July 15, 1861, all in AHN, Ultramar, leg. 115, exp. 48.

61. Echagüe to the Spanish overseas minister, July 27, 1861, AHN, Ultramar, leg. 1115, exp. 48; Carlos Cabrera and others to the queen of Spain, Sept. 23, 1863, AGPR, Gobernadores Españoles, Municipios, Ponce, box 534.

62. [Saco], *Algunas reformas*, 12.

63. "Cuadros de movimiento," AHN, Ultramar, leg. 1152, exp. 14; Knight, *Slave Society*, 44; Moreno Fraginals, *Ingenio* 3:44–45, 84–85.

64. "Cuadros de movimiento," AHN, Ultramar, leg. 1152, exp. 14; Moreno Fraginals, *Ingenio* 3:44–45, 84–85.

65. Pre–Civil War sugar figures for Puerto Rico are for 1855–59, and wartime figures are for 1860–64; from Sonesson, "Puerto Rico's Commerce," 249. Pre–Civil War sugar figures for Cuba are for 1856–60, and wartime figures are for 1861–65; from Marrero, *Cuba* 12:121; and Moreno Fraginals, *Ingenio* 3:70–71. References to pre–Civil War combined sugar exports (Cuba and Puerto Rico) are based on the combination of 1855–59 for Puerto Rico and 1856–60 for Cuba; Civil War combined figures are based on 1860–64 for Puerto Rico and 1861–65 for Cuba.

66. The negligible increase in Cuban sugar exports to the United States and the decrease in sugar exports from Puerto Rico to the United States are stunning facts in light of the destruction of the sugar industry in the South during the Civil War. In 1861 the South had a bumper sugar crop of 459,410 hogsheads. Because of the closing of the North's market for southern sugar that year, most of the harvest was used to feed hogs. During the war 1,025 of Louisiana's 1,200 sugar estates were destroyed, and production fell to 87,000 hogsheads in 1862 and to 10,000 in 1864. Prewar levels would not be reached again until the second half of the 1880s. See Paul W. Gates, *Agriculture and the Civil War* (New York: Alfred A. Knopf, 1965), 103, 145; Joseph Carlyle Sitterson, *Sugar Country: The Cane Sugar Industry in the South, 1753–1950* (Lexington: University Press of Kentucky, 1953), 226, 233; and Marrero, *Cuba* 10:50.

67. Sonesson, "Puerto Rico's Commerce," 249; Moreno Fraginals, *Ingenio* 3:70–71; "Balanzas mercantiles de la isla de Puerto Rico," 1858–67 (microfilm in CIH). Refer to note 65 for an explanation of the data. By late 1862 the U.S. tariff on imported sugar had been raised to double its prewar level as a means to help finance the war. Eichner, *Emergence of Oligopoly*, 42.

68. Sonesson, "Puerto Rico's Commerce," 249; Moreno Fraginals, *Ingenio* 3:70–71; "Balanzas mercantiles de la isla de Puerto Rico" 1858–67 (microfilm in CIH).

69. Pérez de la Riva, *Café*, 74–79; Marrero, *Cuba* 10:101; Bergad, *Coffee*, 226–27; "Balanzas mercantiles de la isla de Puerto Rico" (microfilm in CIH); Bergad, "Agrarian History," 68.

70. United States, Department of Commerce, Bureau of the Census, *Historical Statistics of the United States*, 2 vols. (Washington, D.C.: GPO, 1975), 1:518, 208.

71. File on cotton cultivation dated Oct. 6, 1858, AHN, Ultramar, leg. 753; *La Gaceta de Puerto Rico*, April 8, 1862; Cruz Monclova, *Historia de Puerto Rico* 1:386.

72. "Expediente relativo al cultivo de algodón," AHP, box 111B, leg. 117, exp. 38; dispatch of the British consul at San Juan, June 12, 1863, quoted in Sonesson, "Puerto Rico's Commerce," 267. Plaja, Cortada, and Fornier to the superintendent of hacienda, March 4, 1864; superintendent of hacienda to the

Spanish overseas minister, Oct. 19, 1864; and overseas minister to the superintendent of hacienda, Dec. 12, 1864, all in AHN, Ultramar, leg. 1086, exp. 15, docs. 3, 1, 4. AHP, box 111B, leg. 117, exp. 908; Félix María de Messina to the overseas minister, Nov. 3, 1864, AHN, Ultramar, leg. 1086, exp. 16; AHP, box 111B, leg. 117, exp. 897; AGNRD, Fondo de la Anexión a España y Guerra de Restauración, leg. 11, exp. 40.

73. "Balanzas mercantiles de la isla de Puerto Rico" (microfilm in CIH); dispatch of the British consul at San Juan, June 12, 1863, quoted in Sonesson, "Puerto Rico's Commerce," 267; superintendent of Cuba to the Spanish overseas minister, May 22, 1863, AHN, Ultramar, leg. 753; Marrero, *Cuba* 10:101.

74. Alexander Jourdan to Seward, Nov. 28, 1865, NA, Foreign Service, RG 84, San Juan, vol. 7228; "Balanzas mercantiles de la isla de Puerto Rico" (microfilm in CIH); AHP, box 111B, leg. 117, exp. 897; *El Progreso*, Sept. 25, 1870, quoted in Tirado Merced, "Raíces sociales," 52.

75. Ely, *Cuando reinaba*, 283; Thomas, *Confederate Nation*, 183. Because of the destruction of vessels, changes in registration, and reduced trade, shipping in North America under the U.S. flag dropped from 3,298,000 tons in 1856–60 to 2,232,000 tons in 1861–65. During the Civil War, but particularly in 1864 and 1865, the United States ceased to control the majority of shipping in its ports. The national-to-foreign ratio went from 1:0.44 in 1856–60 to 1:0.65 in 1861–63, and further down to 1:1.47 in 1864–65. U.S. Dept. of Commerce, Bureau of the Census, *Historical Statistics* (1960 ed.), 450–51.

76. "Balanzas mercantiles de la isla de Puerto Rico" (microfilm in CIH). Information on tonnage refers to departures, while number of ships is the average of arrivals and departures. Shares refer to departing tons.

77. James Gallagher to Seward, March 7, 1863, NA, State, RG 59, San Juan, vol. 27; "Balanzas mercantiles de la isla de Puerto Rico" (microfilm in CIH); Jourdan to Seward, Nov. 28, 1865, NA, Foreign Service, RG 84, San Juan, vol. 7228.

78. "Balanzas mercantiles de la isla de Puerto Rico" (microfilm in CIH). Number of vessels refers to average of arrivals and departures, while tonnage refers to tons cleared.

79. J. C. Burnham to Moses Taylor, Aug. 14, 1861, quoted in Ely, *Cuando reinaba*, 286; Portell Vilá, *Historia de Cuba* 2:196; Havana *Mercantile Weekly*, [early 1863], in NA, State, RG 59, Havana, vol. 45.

80. Moreno Fraginals, *Ingenio* 2:195–99; Knight, *Slave Society*, 44. In 1868 Puerto Rico imported goods valued at 8,754,689 pesos, 2,803,160 pesos' worth of which came from the United States, and exported goods worth 5,730,239 pesos, of which 3,358,830 pesos' worth went to the United States. *El Progreso*, Sept. 25, 1870, quoted in Tirado Merced, "Raíces sociales," 51.

81. Jaime de Jesús Domínguez, *Notas económicas y políticas dominicanas sobre el período julio 1865–julio 1886*, 2 vols. (Santo Domingo: Editora de la UASD,

1983–84), 1:173, 177, 182–84. Five years later, in 1882, 51 percent of Dominican exports from the port of Santo Domingo headed for the United States.

82. In contrast, U.S. investors embarked on direct service and extractive ventures in the Dominican Republic, where the various administrations promoted U.S. investments. Shortly after the withdrawal of Spanish troops, the Dominican government granted concessions to a Davis Hatch from Connecticut to conduct a study for the construction of a railroad network and to exploit a salt mine. The following year Joseph W. Fabens, a personal friend of Buenaventura Báez's, received permission to establish a transportation company consisting of a fleet of camels. Fabens himself brought eighteen of the animals from the Sahara. Although certainly this was the most bizarre of Fabens's enterprises, his most lucrative one was the geological survey company established in July 1868. According to the contract signed between Fabens and the Dominican government, the company would receive "the one-fifth part of the lands that may have undergone the geological examination . . . with the right to select and set it apart." By February 1871 Fabens and his associates held claims to at least 10 percent of the Dominican territory in exchange for a dubious geological survey that had cost only thirty-five thousand dollars. Rodríguez Demorizi, ed., *Papeles de Buenaventura Báez*, 230; Pinkett, "Efforts," 17; Nevins, *Hamilton Fish*, 254–55; U.S. Commission of Inquiry, *Report of the Commission*, 185–87.

Chapter 6: Political Change

1. De Sedano, *Cuba*, 3.

2. Charles De Ronceray to Lewis Cass, Jan. 1, 1861, NA, Foreign Service, RG 84, San Juan, vol. 7228; Charles Helm to Pierre A. Rost, Nov. 6, 1861, quoted in Ely, *Cuando reinaba*, 287; Helm to Rost, Nov. 8, 1861, and Helm to the Confederate secretary of state, Dec. 18, 1862, both in LC, Manuscripts Department, RCSA, vol. 7.

3. These sentiments continued beyond the war. In the aftermath of the Civil War the Spanish minister at Washington announced that the victorious North was seeking to "subdue the white population under the former slaves, imbuing the blacks with a spirit of antisocial propaganda." He concluded that this posed great risks not only for the United States but also for the Antilles. Portell Vilá, *Historia de Cuba* 2:148; Ely, *Cuando reinaba*, 288; Gabriel García Tassara to Domingo Dulce, Feb. 7, 1866, AHN, Ultramar, leg. 4714, exp. 7.

4. Cochran, *Blockade Runners*, 25; Portell Vilá, *Historia de Cuba* 2:148; Ely, *Cuando reinaba*, 288–89; Helm to Rost, Nov. 8, 1861, LC, Manuscripts Department, RCSA, vol. 7.

5. Jasper Smith to Seward, Aug. 11, 1862, in U.S. Dept. of State, San Juan

Consulate, *Despachos*, 571–72; John J. Hyde to Seward, Jan. 31, 1863, NA, Foreign Service, RG 84, San Juan, vol. 7228; Hyde to Seward, March 5, 1863, in U.S. Dept. of State, San Juan Consulate, *Despachos*, 588–89.

6. Robert W. Shufeldt to Seward, Oct. 12, 1862, NA, State, RG 59, Havana, vol. 45; *El Siglo*, Nov. 4, 1863, quoted in Raúl Cepero Bonilla, *Obras históricas* (Havana: Instituto de Historia, 1963), 287; Cepero Bonilla, *Azúcar*, 92, 153; *El Siglo*, April 10, 1865.

7. [Oliver Wilson Davis], *Sketch of Frederic Fernández Cavada, a Native of Cuba* (Philadelphia: Privately printed, 1871), 24–25; Shufeldt to Seward, Oct. 12, 1862, and Thomas Savage to Seward, Oct. 3, 1863, both in NA, State, RG 59, Havana, vols. 45, 46.

8. Cepero Bonilla, *Obras*, 251; de Sedano, *Cuba*, 267.

9. Guerra y Sánchez, *Manual*, 547–49, 604; [Francisco de Frías y Jacott], *Recuerdo de la despedida del Excmo. Sr. Teniente General don Domingo Dulce* (Havana: Mencey, 1866), 11–12, 27; Knight, *Slave Society*, 56.

10. Cruz Monclova, *Historia de Puerto Rico* 1:363.

11. Ibid. 480–81. De Messina only permitted articles dealing with science, technical matters, or literature. Publishers had to post one-thousand-peso bonds, and their articles had to be preapproved by state censors. See corregidor of Ponce to the captain-general of Puerto Rico, June 1, 1861, AHP, leg. 84, exp. 2.

12. Among those banished were Ramón Emeterio Betances, Segundo Ruiz Belvis, Pedro Gerónimo Goyco, Julián Blanco Sosa, Carlos Elio Lacroix, Vicente María Quiñones, Calixto Romero, Luis de Leiras, José de Celis Aguilera, Vicente Rufino Goenga, and Félix del Monte.

13. For the social composition of Puerto Rico's reform movement, see Tirado Merced, "Raíces sociales."

14. *El Siglo*, March 9, 1863, March 10, 1866, and Aug. 17, 1865, quoted in Cepero Bonilla, *Obras*, 262.

15. Some of the leading reformists were José Morales Lemus, the count of Pozos Dulces, José Manuel Mestre, José Antonio Echeverría, Miguel Aldama, José Ricardo O'Farrill, José Luis Alfonso, José Silverio Jorrín, Nicolás Azcárate, and José Valdés Faulí.

16. Cepero Bonilla, *Obras*, 253–54. See Serrano to the count of Cañogo, July 12, 1865, HLHU, Escoto, box 9.

17. *El Siglo*, March 24, 1865, quoted in Cepero Bonilla, *Obras*, 27; also see *El Siglo*, March 23, 1865.

18. [Cristóbal F. Madan], *El trabajo libre y el liber-cambio en Cuba* (Paris: Bonaventure, 1864), 6.

19. Hacendado [Madan], *Llamamiento*, 178; [Madan], *Trabajo*, 1, 32.

20. Serrano quoted in España, Ultramar, *Cuba*, 256.

21. Moreno Fraginals, *Ingenio* 1:287; Murray, *Odious Commerce*, 244.

22. [Madan], *Trabajo*, 3; Schroeder, *Cuba*, 107; slave trade report of Vice-Consul Leopoldo Krug, Feb. 6, 1866, in CIH, *Proceso abolicionista* 1:48–51.

23. Around 125,000 Chinese coolies were imported between 1853 and 1874. A few hundred Yucatecan Indians were also brought to Cuba. For its part, the white male population more than doubled between 1846 and 1861. Knight, *Slave Society*, 116–19; Pérez, *Cuba: Between Reform and Revolution*, 116.

24. Coll y Toste, ed., *Boletín histórico* 5:289; Schroeder, *Cuba*, 106. The *coartación* was a legal mechanism whereby prices were fixed for slaves to purchase their own liberty.

25. Coll y Toste, ed., *Boletín histórico* 5:289; Knight, *Slave Society*, 86; letter addressed to the queen of Spain by a group of Cuban reformists, July 28, 1865, LC, Manuscripts Department, José Ignacio Rodríguez Collection (hereinafter cited as Rodríguez), Papers of José Manuel Mestre (hereinafter cited as Mestre), box 143.

26. Corwin, *Spain and the Abolition*, 162–63; Spanish minister of state to the Spanish vice-consul at Savannah, Aug. 26, 1863, Duke, Spanish Ministry–Savannah.

27. Knight, *Slave Society*, 123, 173–74; Scott, *Slave Emancipation*, 67, 70–83; Segismundo Moret to the captain-general of Cuba, quoted in Foner, *History of Cuba* 2:220; Fish to Daniel Sickles, June 20, 1870, U.S. Congress, Senate, 41st Cong., 2d sess., S. Exec. Doc. 113, pp. 12–14; Ramón Emeterio Betances, "La abolición de la esclavitud en Puerto Rico," in *Las Antillas para los antillanos*, by Ramón Emeterio Betances, ed. and trans. Carlos M. Rama (San Juan: Instituto de Cultura, 1975), 77.

28. *El Siglo*, Aug. 23, 1864, quoted in Cepero Bonilla, *Obras*, 285.

29. *El Siglo*, Oct. 11, 1865; [Madan], *Trabajo*, 11; *El Siglo*, March 9, 1863, quoted in Cepero Bonilla, *Obras*, 281; Echeverría to Saco, June 6, 1865, quoted in Cepero Bonilla, *Azúcar*, 89. Not all in Cuba were reluctant or timid abolitionists like the reformists; a separatist, radical minority had gained strength during and after the Civil War. In the mid-1850s a visitor reported that Cuban abolitionists were so scarce "that they can hardly be considered as forming a party." Among this minority, however, were those who, after failed filibuster attempts in the late 1840s and early 1850s, added abolitionism to the separatist agenda. Some Cuban exiles in Paris in the early 1850s, for example, blamed Narciso López's failure on his proslavery stance. Later in 1854 abolitionist-separatists Carlos Collins, Lorenzo Allo, Juán C. Zenea, and Agüero Estrada began to publish *El Mulato*, a newspaper underscoring the incompatibility of slavery and national political liberty. A few years later the count of Pozos Dulces began to speak out against slavery, recommending that taxes collected in Cuba be used to compensate slave owners after emancipation. Writing

under a false name, Pozos Dulces affirmed that "black slavery corrupts and demoralizes the white man." He also denounced the institution of slavery as a tool used by Spain to subordinate the Cubans. During the years of *política de atracción*, however, a mellowed Pozos Dulces considerably toned down his abolitionism. Philalethes, *Yankee Travels*, 389; French minister of police to the Spanish minister at Paris, 1852, ASHM, Ultramar, leg. 90; Poyo, "Cuban Emigré Communities," 35–36; Marrero, *Cuba* 10:49; Un cubano [Francisco de Frías y Jacott], *Isla de Cuba* (Paris: D'Aubusson y Kugelman, 1859), 12.

30. Poyo, *With All*, 16; Gabriel García Tassara to Dulce, Sept. 26, 1865, AHN, Ultramar, leg. 4669, exp. 132; leaflet signed "La Voz del Pueblo," May 1, 1866, LC, Manuscripts Department, Domingo Del Monte Collection, box 3; Julián M. Casamena, pseud. [Juan Manuel Macías], *Publicación de la Sociedad Democrática de los Amigos de América* 4 (July 1865): 5–7; Alexander Jourdan to Seward, Dec. 31, 1866, in U.S. Dept. of State, San Juan Consulate, *Despachos*, 760.

31. *El Siglo*, April 11, 1865; *El Siglo*, July 1, 1863, and Feb. 6, 1864, quoted in Cepero Bonilla, *Obras*, 291, 295; *El Siglo*, Jan. 3, 1867. A similar editorial in December 1866 recommended the erection of *centrales*, so that the white population could devote its energies and resources exclusively to cultivation. In an agricultural manual, José María Dau echoed the same views when he recommended the establishment of small *ingenios* that would go only as far as the earliest phases of sugar production. The Diago brothers are credited with establishing the first actual project based on a new division of labor: in 1862 their Tinguaro and Santa Elena estates began to receive cane from twelve growers (*colonos*). The number of *ingenios* decreased considerably between 1860 and 1878, from 2,000 to 1,190. The relationship between the *centrales* and the cane growers can be seen in the operation of the *central* La Gran Azucarera and its cane suppliers. Two and a half *caballerías* of land, of which one and a half *caballerías* were planted in cane, were rented out to *colonos* at a price of one hundred pesos per *caballería* per year (if cultivated in cane) and fifty pesos (if not cultivated). The *central* was obliged to rent out, at market rates, three carts and six pairs of oxen and other farming implements. If an ox died, the renter was responsible for half the cost of replacing it. For their part, *colonos* were obligated to take care of the land and provide the necessary labor in order to supply the cane to the *central* at an agreed time of the year. The cane was to be sold at sixteen reales per 2,500 pounds and had to be clean and of good quality. By virtue of these arrangements the *central* controlled the *colonos* in a variety of ways: the animals and the implements could not be used outside the *colonia*, the cane could not be sold to other parties, strange persons could not enter into the rented plots, the cane had to be delivered when the *central* wanted it, and the *central* operator reserved the right to enter into the

colonias "to put things in order." See "Contrato de arrendamiento.—División del trabajo (La Gran Azucarera)," LC, Manuscripts Department, Del Monte Collection, box 3; Marrero, *Cuba* 10:255–56.

32. *El Siglo*, March 29, 1865. Ramón Just stated: "Then, Cuba would have true toilers of the soil, such as there are in Europe; and this class, the most moderate, the most sober, and the one with the best habits everywhere, would become a new guarantee of order and peace, a most solid prop for the Spanish government." Ramón Just, *Las aspiraciones de Cuba* (Paris: Mourgues, 1859), 38.

33. *El Siglo*, Feb. 18, 1864, quoted in Cepero Bonilla, *Obras*, 292; *El Siglo*, Feb. 23, 1864. "The tropics, by providential ordainment, are designated the laboratory of the raw materials required by civilization. Why, then, should we insist on wasting our efforts on industrial and manufacturing operations, convenient only in more temperate latitudes, where the winter snow and the changing of the seasons force energies and rest indoors?" Count of Pozos Dulces, quoted in Moreno Fraginals, *Ingenio* 2:200–202. One clear indicator of the division of labor in the Cuban sugar industry was the disproportionate growth in molasses exports. Whereas in 1865–68 a yearly average of 2,525 tons of molasses was exported, in 1873–74 an average of 48,606 tons of molasses left the island annually.

34. De Sedano, *Cuba*, 295–96; Cruz Monclova, *Historia de Puerto Rico* 1:374–76. For an assessment of the political tendencies of the Puerto Rican delegates, see Captain-General Marchesi's report of Jan. 30, 1866, in Cruz Monclova, *Historia de Puerto Rico* 1:380–81.

35. Emigrado cubano, *Información;* Corwin, *Spain and the Abolition*, 186; José Morales Lemus to Aldama, Nov. 28, 1866, LC, Manuscripts Department, Del Monte Collection, box 3.

36. See Segundo Ruiz Belvis, José Julián Acosta, and Francisco Mariano Quiñones, *Proyecto para la abolición de la esclavitud* (Río Piedras: Editorial Edil, 1978). Puerto Rican abolitionism was consistently more radical than the Cuban brand. The emancipation of slaves was the first article in the Puerto Rican separatist agenda during the post-1867 period. Assimilationists like Rafael María de Labra y Cadrana, a delegate for Puerto Rico in the early 1870s, insisted that abolition should not be carried out gradually and that the master class was not entitled to compensation.

37. Conference no. 26 of the Junta de Información, Feb. 25, 1867, in CIH, *Proceso abolicionista* 2:10–19; Ruiz Belvis, Acosta, and Quiñones, *Proyecto*, 69, 80.

38. Morales Lemus to Aldama, Nov. 13, 1866, LC, Manuscripts Department, Rodríguez, Mestre, box 143; Echeverría quoted in Corwin, *Spain and the Abolition*, 193; Enrique José Piñeyro y Barry, *Morales Lemus y la revolución de Cuba* (New York: Zarzamendi, 1871; New York: Unión de Cubanos en el

Exilio, 1970), 46; letter by opponents to reform to the queen of Spain, June 28, 1865, in España, Ultramar, *Cuba*, 276.

39. Foner, *History of Cuba* 2:156; Conference no. 26 of the Junta de Información, Feb. 26, 1867, in CIH, *Proceso abolicionista* 2:11; Zeno's deposition of Nov. 20, 1866, and Manuel de Armas's deposition of Dec. 2, 1866, both in Emigrado cubano, *Información*, 50, 57.

40. España, Ultramar, *Cuba*, 33; statement by Morales Lemus and others, Nov. 26, 1866, LC, Manuscripts Department, Del Monte Collection, box 4. The antimissionary vote by the Cubans should also be seen as an attempt to curb the presence of the church on private estates.

41. Statement by Cuban delegates, 1867, LC, Manuscripts Department, Del Monte Collection, box 4; Ruiz Belvis, Acosta, and Quiñones, *Proyecto*, 53.

42. Piñeyro y Barry, *Morales Lemus*, 51; statement by fifteen Cuban delegates and Zeno, Nov. 29, 1866, LC, Manuscripts Department, Del Monte Collection, box 4.

43. Poyo, "Cuban Emigré Communities," 79–80.

44. Ramos Mattei, *Betances*, 16–17; Foner, *History of Cuba* 2:162. In 1865 Saco estimated that up to September 1864 the annexation of the Dominican Republic had cost fourteen million pesos and that this would increase to eighteen to twenty million pesos. In 1875 Cuba's treasury still owed six million pesos of the Dominican and Mexican expenses. Other estimates of the costs of Spanish expansionism in the 1860s are 19,623,219 pesos for the Dominican Republic and 3,355,341 pesos for Mexico, and 22 million pesos for the Dominican Republic and 10 million pesos for Mexico. See [Saco], *Algunas reformas*, 30; Miguel Blanco Herrero, *Los billetes de banco y la deuda de Cuba: Su arreglo y amortización* (Havana: José Valdepares, 1875), 16; Marrero, *Cuba* 10:52; Junta Cubana de Nueva York, *Facts About Cuba Published Under the Authority of the N.Y. Cuban Junta* (New York: Sun Job, 1870), 5–6.

45. Cancio Villa-Amil, *Situación económica*, 85.

46. Junta Cubana, *Facts*, 5–6; de la Concha, *Memoria*, 20. Tax figures have been rounded up to the nearest hundred thousand pesos.

47. Rafael María de Labra y Cadrana, *La abolición de la esclavitud en las Antillas Españolas* (Madrid: Morete, 1869), 43; Benjamín Vicuña MacKenna, "La independencia de Cuba y Puerto Rico," *Revista Cubana* 3 (1935): 318; [Saco], *Algunas reformas*, 32–33. The tax burden would increase further during the war to around 34.50 pesos. See "Gravámenes fiscales en Cuba," *El Triunfo*, May 22, 1879.

48. Estrada, *Provincias ultramarinas*, 40; Junta Cubana, *Facts*, 5–6; de Roches, *Cuba*, 4–5.

49. Estrada, *Provincias ultramarinas*, 42; [Saco], *Algunas reformas*, 45.

50. Marrero, *Cuba* 10:53–54; Knight, *Slave Society*, 158–59; Dulce to the Spanish overseas minister, Aug. 30, 1867, AHN, Ultramar, leg. 4713, exp. 223.

51. See revolutionary proclamations of July 16 and Sept. 1, 1867, in CIH, *Proceso abolicionista* 2:188; and Bolívar Pagán, *Procerato puertorriqueño del siglo xix* (San Juan: Librería Campos, 1961), 120.

52. For estimates, see Strode, *Pageant of Cuba*, 109; Langley, *Cuban Policy*, 80; and Foner, *History of Cuba* 2:274. In monetary terms, the war cost three hundred million dollars.

53. Betances, *Las Antillas*, vi.

54. Betances to Justo Barros, Dec. 16, 1868, and Sept. 20, 1869; Betances to José F. Basora, Jan. 14, 1868; Betances to Antonio Ruiz, April 21, 1868; and Betances to Juan Chavarri, April 21, 1868, all in Luis Bonafoux, ed., *Betances*, 3d ed. (San Juan: Instituto de Cultura, 1987), xl–xli, 77, 79, 88–89, 90–91.

55. Betances to Eugenio María de Hostos, April 10, 1871, in Betances, *Las Antillas*, 251; Hostos, July 11, 1874, quoted in Cubano Iguina, *Hilo en el laberinto*, 77; de Labra y Cadrana, *Cuestión de ultramar*, 19; de Labra y Cadrana, cited in Cruz Monclova, *Historia de Puerto Rico* 2:1, 9–10.

56. The *Virginius* case involved the capture of a ship with a U.S. flag used by Cuban expeditionary forces. Local colonial authorities in western Cuba executed some of the prisoners, among them several U.S. citizens. See files in AGPR, Gobernadores Españoles, box 188.

57. The correspondence of Cuban annexationists during this period shows that annexationism was not a profound sentiment but rather a political strategy dictated by the present geopolitical circumstances. See, for example, José Morales Lemus to José Manuel Mestre, Dec. 18, 1869, LC, Manuscripts Department, Rodríguez, Mestre, box 134; and Céspedes to Mestre, cited in Poyo, "Cuban Emigré Communities," 118–19.

58. Cepero Bonilla, *Azúcar*, 193; Roig de Leuchsenring, *Cuba*, 132.

59. Portell Vilá, *Historia de Cuba* 2:237–38; Cepero Bonilla, *Azúcar*, 113. In 1868, 21 percent of the people in Camagüey were slaves. In 1864 this district produced only 3 percent of the island's sugar output. See Ely, *Cuando reinaba*, 542; Guerra y Sánchez, *Guerra* 1:4. Also see Foner, *History of Cuba* 2:193.

60. See Un habanero, *Probable y definitivo porvenir de la isla de Cuba* (Key West, Fla., 1870), 3.

61. Poyo, *With All*, 27–28. Annexationist conspiratorial groups also sprang up in Puerto Rico between 1867 and 1869. According to U.S. consul Alexander Jourdan, these were more numerous than the proindependence groups. They were particularly strong in Mayagüez. See Rosario Natal, "Betances," 119–22; Ramos Mattei, *Betances*, 25.

62. O'Kelly, *Mambí-Land*, 28; Guerra y Sánchez, *Guerra* 1:139, 346–47. For

all practical purposes, the *voluntarios* had taken control of Cuba. These troops terrorized the population and succeeded in expelling Captain-General Dulce along with other liberal officials. A similar situation emerged in Puerto Rico, where pro-Spanish conservatives staged various acts of violence and came close to placing reform-oriented Captain-General Rafael Primo de Rivera on a ship heading for Spain. Guerra y Sánchez, *Guerra* 1:228–30; Foner, *History of Cuba* 2:176–81; de Sedano, *Cuba*, 398; [Aguilera], *Notes about Cuba*, 46; Consul Edward Conroy to the U.S. secretary of state, Feb. 18, 1873, NA, State, RG 84, San Juan, vol. 7230; *El Abolicionista*, April 15 and June 23, 1873, reproduced in CIH, *Proceso abolicionista* 2:295–98; Rafael Primo de Rivera to the Spanish overseas minister, July 26, 1873, AHN, Ultramar, leg. 5113, exp. 23, doc. 2.

63. Guerra y Sánchez, *Guerra*, 390; Poyo, "Cuban Emigré Communities," 119, 144–45.

64. Cepero Bonilla, *Azúcar*, 112–16; Knight, *Slave Society*, 162; Lewis, *Main Currents*, 194, 292; proclamation of Dec. 27, 1868, and abolitionist document dated Feb. 26, 1869, both in AHN, leg. 4882, vol. 4, exp. 10; Poyo, "Cuban Emigré Communities," 75.

65. Poyo, *With All*, 25.

66. Among these early portrayals are the poems of Félix Mota and Nicolás Ureña and the writings of Manuel María Gautier and Francisco Sánchez. See Rodríguez Demorizi, *Santana*, 106–7, 162, 183, 18, 25; and Alfau Durán, ed., *Controversia histórica*, 129.

67. For a journalistic debate on Santana and his achievements in which García participated, see Alfau Durán, ed., *Controversia histórica*. See also José Gabriel García, "Apuntes sobre la vida política de Báez [1871]," in Rodríguez Demorizi, ed., *Papeles de Buenaventura Báez*, 313–26.

68. See, for example, Monclús, *Caudillismo*, 33–39; and Cassá, *Historia social* 2:44, 55.

69. José Luis González, *Nueva visita al cuarto piso* (Madrid: Exlesa, 1986), 83; Nelson, "Haitian Political Situation," 231.

70. Rafael Senior, *Santana: Libertador, gobernante, anexionista* (Santo Domingo: La Información, 1938), 130, 33.

71. Rufino Martínez, *Hombres dominicanos* (Santiago, Dominican Republic: El Diario, 1943; Santo Domingo: Sociedad Dominicana de Bibliófilos, 1985), 315; Rodríguez Demorizi, *Santana*, 7, 8, 54, 274.

72. Detlev Julio K. Peukert, "Anhelo de dependencia: Las ofertas de anexión de la República Dominicana a los Estados Unidos en el siglo xix," *Jahrbuch für Geschichte von Staat, Wirtschaft und Gesellschaft Lateinamerikas* 23 (1986): 305–30; Nelson, "Haitian Political Situation"; Domínguez, *Anexión*, 68; Frank Moya Pons, "La economía dominicana y el Partido Azul," *Eme Eme* 5, no. 28 (Jan.–Feb. 1977): 6–7; Cassá, *Historia social* 2:109, 44.

73. "Informe de Peláez Campomanes" and "Informe del Cónsul Álvarez," both in Rodríguez Demorizi, ed., *Antecedentes*, 113–15, 100; Álvarez quoted in Álvarez López, "Historia de la anexión," 79; José Varela Project, 1863, in Rodríguez Demorizi, ed., *Samaná*, 189; Emilio Rodríguez Demorizi, "Antecedentes de la anexión," *Clio* 123 (Jan.–Aug. 1968): 38.

74. "Informe del Cónsul Álvarez," in Rodríguez Demorizi, ed., *Antecedentes*, 89–97; *El Diario de la Marina*, July 23, 1861; report of the Spanish vice-consul Emiliano Terrero, Nov. 1860, quoted in Esteban de la Puente García, "1861–1865: Anexión y abandono de Santo Domingo," *Revista de Indias* 22, nos. 89–90 (1962): 415.

75. Miguel Lavastida to Santana, May 1, 1860, in Rodríguez Demorizi, ed., *Documentos* 2:386–88; Alfau Durán, ed., *Controversia histórica*, 77.

76. Moya Pons, *Manual*, 338. See Santana's proclamations of March 18, 1861, and January 31, 1859, in Rodríguez Demorizi, ed., *Documentos* 1:504–6, 468–69. See his decree of January 19, 1861, in República Dominicana, *Colección de leyes* 4:140.

77. Santana to the queen of Spain, April 27, 1860, in José de la Gándara y Navarro, *La anexión y guerra de Santo Domingo*, 2 vols. (Madrid: El Correo Militar, 1884), 1:395–96; Álvarez López, "Historia de la anexión," 76–77.

78. Domínguez, *Anexión*, 50.

79. Ibid., 59–61; Moya Pons, *Manual*, 340; Cazneau to Cass, Oct. 13, 1860, in Lockward, ed., *Documentos*, 358–60; Peláez Campomanes cited in de la Gándara y Navarro, *Anexión* 1:404.

80. Santana's proclamations of Feb. 15, 1853, and July 16, 1861, in Rodríguez Demorizi, ed., *Documentos* 1:267, 2:393–94; president of the Spanish Council of Ministers to the overseas minister, May 20, 1861, AHN, Ultramar, leg. 5485, exp. 3; Domínguez, *Anexión*, 208; Rodríguez Demorizi, ed., *Documentos* 2:392–428; Rodríguez Demorizi, ed., *Papeles de Santana*, 153–62.

81. Santana quoted in Rafael Vival, prologue to Pedro María Archambault, *Historia de la Restauración* (Paris: Librerie Technique et Economique, 1938; Santo Domingo: Biblioteca Taller 20, 1973), xiii; de la Gándara y Navarro, *Anexión* 1:241–45; report of Commander Manuel Buceta, Sept. 25, 1864, and [A. A. Guridi], *Santo Domingo y España* (New York: 1864), both in Rodríguez Demorizi, ed., *Antecedentes*, 331, 355; Luperón, *Notas* 1:81.

82. De la Gándara y Navarro, *Anexión* 1:224; report of General J. Luis Golfín, 1861, in Rodríguez Demorizi, ed., *Samaná*, 162; report of Captain-General Serrano, Sept. 5, 1861, in Rodríguez Demorizi, ed., *Antecedentes*, 250. Also see AGNRD, Anexión a España, leg. 7, exp. 2.

83. Luperón, *Notas* 1:82; George A. Lockward, *El protestantismo en Dominicana*, 2d ed. (Santo Domingo: Universidad CETEC, 1982), 129–30; de la Gándara y Navarro, *Anexión* 1:223–29, 459; [Guridi], *Santo Domingo*, in Rodrí-

guez Demorizi, ed., *Antecedentes,* 356; *La Gaceta de Santo Domingo,* Feb. 26, 1863; overseas minister to the Spanish governor of Santo Domingo, Dec. 21, 1862, and orders for the general intendant of the army, Feb. 10, 1863, both in AGNRD, Anexión a España, leg. 7, exp. 4 (also see leg. 5).

84. This posture paralleled the annexationist inclinations of the Mexican clergy with regard to European intervention in 1862 and also those of the Ecuadorian clergy, which in the early 1860s sought a similar protectorate under France. De la Gándara y Navarro, *Anexión* 1:223; Pedro Santana, "Relación nominal de los eclesiásticos que cooperan con la anexión de Santo Domingo," in Rodríguez Demorizi, ed., *Antecedentes,* 308–9; Father Arturo Meriño to Father Carlos Nouel, Sept. 27, 1902, in Rodríguez Demorizi, ed., *Papeles de Santana,* 262; Domínguez, *Anexión,* 113, 122; Nathan L. Ferris, "The Relations of the United States with South America During the American Civil War," *HAHR* 21, no. 1 (Feb. 1941): 65–66.

85. De la Gándara y Navarro, *Anexión* 1:228–29.

86. Report of the Spanish vice-consul, quoted in de la Puente García, "1861–1865," 415; Serrano to the Spanish overseas minister, July 26, 1861, AHN, Ultramar, leg. 5085, exp. 12. See also AGNRD, Anexión a España, leg. 3, exp. 28.

87. Domínguez, *Anexión,* 222.

88. Varela project of 1863, in Rodríguez Demorizi, ed., *Samaná,* 193–94; Jonathan Elliott to Seward, Oct. 5, 1861, NA, State, RG 59, Santo Domingo, vol. 4; Domínguez, *Anexión,* 231; Marte, *Cuba y la República Dominicana,* 320.

89. Joseph Warren Fabens, *Life in Santo Domingo, by a Settler,* 3d ed. (New York: Carleton and Co., 1873), 304. This is a reedited version of an edition published during the period of annexation.

90. May, "Plenipotentiary," 34; Tansill, *United States,* 219.

91. AGNRD, Anexión a España, leg. 33, exp. 28; Nevins, *Hamilton Fish,* 253; Fabens, *Life;* William Jaeger to Seward, Dec. 27, 1863, NA, State, RG 59, Santo Domingo, vol. 4. Also see claims files in AGNRD, Relaciones Exteriores, leg. 21, exp. 6.

92. Moya Pons, *Manual,* 343.

93. Officer quoted in Domínguez, *Anexión,* 128; Elliot to Seward, March 22, 1861, NA, State, RG 59, Santo Domingo, vol. 4. To stop the rumors of reenslavement, Santana issued a decree prescribing the death sentence to anyone caught suggesting that annexation would mean the return of slavery. Decree of June 18, 1861, in República Dominicana, *Colección de leyes* 4:155–56.

94. Proclamation of Jan. 20, 1861, quoted in Archambault, *Historia de la Restauración,* 13; Santana to the Spanish overseas minister, Oct. 11, 1863, quoted in Luperón, *Notas* 1:177; *La Crónica de Ambos Mundos,* April 26, 1861, quoted in Rodríguez Demorizi, ed., *Antecedentes,* 166.

95. Geffrard assumed political leadership following a coup against Faustin Soulouque in 1859.

96. Moya Pons, *Manual*, 350.

97. Proclamation of Geffrard, March 18, 1861, quoted in de la Gándara y Navarro, *Anexión* 1:418; *La Crónica de Ambos Mundos*, July 2, 1861; Domínguez, *Anexión*, 151, 264; de la Puente García, "1861–1865," 463.

98. Marte, *Cuba y la República Dominicana*, 317, 326–27.

99. See, for example, governor of Santo Domingo to the Spanish overseas minister, Sept. 3, 1863; García Tassara to the minister of state, Nov. 9, 1863; and related correspondence, all in AHN, Ultramar, leg. 3525, exps. 28, 109, and leg. 5088, exp. 27.

100. Spanish vice-consul at Boston to the minister of state, Jan. 3, 1865, AHN, Ultramar, leg. 4697, exp. 202.

101. For an English translation of the debate, see Yungling, ed., *Highlights*.

102. Speech of Senator Alzugaray, March 28, 1865, in Yungling, ed., *Highlights*, 59; Dulce quoted in Domínguez, *Anexión*, 69. See de la Gándara y Navarro, *Anexión* 2:632; speech of Senator Saavedra Meneses, March 27, 1865, in Yungling, ed., *Highlights*, 39; Luperón, *Notas* 2:8.

103. De la Gándara y Navarro, *Anexión* 2:632; Torrente, *Política ultramarina*, 289; "Informe de Peláez Campomanes," in Rodríguez Demorizi, ed., *Antecedentes*, 106; speech of Senator Saavedra Meneses, March 27, 1865, in Yungling, ed., *Highlights*, 39, 55.

104. Speech of Manuel Seijas Lozano, March 30, 1865, in Yungling, ed., *Highlights*, 108.

105. Speech of Ulloa, March 24, 1865, and speech of Senator Seijas Lozano, March 30, 1865, both in Yungling, ed. *Highlights*, 9, 115; García Tassara to the Spanish overseas minister, Nov. 9, 1863, AHN, Ultramar, leg. 3525, exp. 119; de la Puente García, "1861–1865," 418.

106. Speech of Senator Ulloa, March 24, 1865, in Yungling, ed., *Highlights*, 9.

107. Even before Spain had left Dominican territory, agents of the provisional Dominican government approached U.S. agents with offers to rent portions of the Samaná bay and peninsula. DeBenneville Randolph Keim, *Pen Pictures and Leaves of Travel, Romance and History, from the Portfolio of a Correspondent in the American Tropics* (Philadelphia: Claxton, Remsen and Haffelfinger, 1870), 122.

108. Cassá, *Historia social* 2:44; Marte, *Cuba y la República Dominicana*, 405; Domínguez, *Notas* 2:494–95, 414; Hoetink, *Dominican People*, 114–19; Moya Pons, *Manual*, 404.

109. Moya Pons, *Manual*, 365, 367–68; Tansill, *United States*, 228; Luperón, *Notas* 1:371; Domínguez, *Notas* 2:431; Rodríguez Demorizi, ed., *Papeles de Buenaventura Báez*, 195–99.

110. Anti-Cabral leaflet, Dec. 24, 1867, NA, State, RG 59, Foreign Missions, Dominican Republic, vol. 1; Luperón to Cabral, April 20, 1868, in Monclús, *Caudillismo*, 68–70. Luperón's anti-U.S. nationalism was fueled by his experience as a man of color who resided in New York City at the time of the Civil War riots.

111. Luperón, *Notas* 2:21, 41; Moya Pons, *Manual*, 372.

112. Keim, *Pen Pictures*, 71–72; Báez to Fabens, April 2, 1868, in Tansill, *United States*, 260; Báez to Andrew Johnson, Jan. 8, 1869, NA, House of Representatives, RG 233, file 40-A-F9.13; Báez to Grant, Aug. 18, 1873, NA, State, RG 59, Diplomatic Despatches, Samaná, vol. 1; Domínguez, *Notas* 2:508; Manuel María Gautier to Fish, July 9, 1869, NA, State, RG 59, Foreign Missions, Dominican Republic, vol. 1.

113. J. Somers Smith to Seward, Oct. 24, 1868, quoted in Welles, *Naboth's Vineyard* 1:350; Moya Pons, *Manual*, 373.

114. Nevins, *Hamilton Fish*, 315; Mayor Raymond H. Perry to Fish, 7 June 1870, quoted in Welles, *Naboth's Vineyard* 1:386; Rodríguez Demorizi, ed., *Proyecto*, 298–301; Moya Pons, *Manual*, 379; Rodríguez Demorizi, ed., *Samaná*, 35; Captain Bunce to Poor, March 24, 1870, in Rodríguez Demorizi, ed., *Proyecto* 366–69; U.S. Commission of Inquiry, *Report of the Commission*, 11–12, 246.

115. Moya Pons, *Manual*, 373.

116. B. Báez to Damián Báez, Jan. 21, 1876, in Rodríguez Demorizi, ed., *Papeles de Buenaventura Báez*, 466–67; Luperón to the captain-general of Puerto Rico, Aug. 5, 1868, AHN, Ultramar, leg. 5096, exp. 46.

Bibliography

Primary Sources

Archival Materials

Archivo del Servicio Histórico Militar, Madrid.
Sección Ultramar, Cuba, legs. 90–91, 93, 98–99
Archivo General de Indias, Seville.
Sección X, Ultramar, legs. 881A, 881B
Sección XI, Cuba, legs. 1004B, 2265, 2268
Archivo General de la Nación, Santo Domingo.
Colección Herrera
Colección Lugo
Documentos de Asuntos Políticos de Santo Domingo procedentes del Archivo Nacional de Cuba, vols. 11–29
Fondo de la Anexión a España y Guerra de Restauración, legs. 1–37
Fondo de Relaciones Exteriores, legs. 1–34
Libros Copiadores de Oficios de Relaciones Exteriores, vols. 1–4
Archivo General de Puerto Rico, San Juan.
Fondo de Diputación Provincial, boxes 357, 469
Fondo de Gobernadores Españoles, boxes 3, 21, 27, 34, 88–114, 116, 134, 136, 142, 150, 188, 287, 288, 290, 530, 534, 535
Archivo Histórico de Ponce.
Legs. 5, 6, 7, 13, 20, 22, 30, 31, 32, 35, 43, 44, 53, 65, 68, 69, 77, 84, 88, 117
Archivo Histórico Nacional, Madrid.
Sección Estado, legs. 5583, 5585, 5587–89, 8045–48, 8565, 8588
Sección Ultramar, Cuba, legs. 725–26, 741, 750, 753, 4637, 4639, 4641–42, 4645–46, 4648–49, 4651, 4655–58, 4660, 4665, 4668–71, 4673–74, 4676–77, 4681–82, 4685–87, 4690–92, 4694, 4696–97, 4699, 4701, 4704, 4708, 4710,

4713–16, 4721–26, 4729–31, 4735–36, 4738–41, 4743, 4745–46, 4749–51, 4759–60, 4784, 4882

Sección Ultramar, Puerto Rico, legs. 1086, 1088, 1100, 1115, 1128, 1152–53, 2058, 2061, 5070, 5072, 5076, 5079, 5082, 5084–86, 5088–89, 5091, 5092, 5094–96, 5098, 5101, 5103, 5113

Sección Ultramar, Santo Domingo, legs. 3524–26, 3531, 5485

Centro de Investigaciones Históricas, Universidad de Puerto Rico, Río Piedras.

Balanzas mercantiles de la isla de Puerto Rico

Correspondencia de los capitanes generales de Puerto Rico con los de Santo Domingo y Cuba, 1843–1864

Houghton Library, Harvard University, Cambridge, Massachusetts.

José Agustín Escoto Papers

Library of Congress, Washington, D.C.

Manuscripts Department

Domingo Del Monte Collection

José Ignacio Rodríguez Collection

Nicholas Trist Collection

Papers of Robert W. Shufeldt

Puerto Rican Memorials Collection

Puerto Rico Collection

Records of the Confederate States of America

Rare Book Room

Broadsides, portfolio 316

Maryland Diocesan Archives, Baltimore.

Cuba Mission Files

National Archives, Washington, D.C.

RG 46, U.S. Senate, files 30A–F2, 34B–B15, 40B–B9

RG 59, General Records of the Department of State, Diplomatic Despatches, Havana, vols. 13–80, San Juan, vols. 3–14, Guayama, vol. 23, Ponce, vols. 25–28, Mayagüez, vol. 30, Santo Domingo, vols. 1–9, and Samaná, vol. 1; Diplomatic Instructions, Haiti, vols. 1–2, Dominican Republic, vol. 1; Notes from Foreign Missions, Cuba, vol. 1, Dominican Republic, vols. 1–2; Records of Special Agents, Cuba, vols. 18, 24, Dominican Republic, vols. 13, 15, 18, 19, 22, 24; Records of Special Missions, reels 152–54; Reports of the Diplomatic Bureau, vol. 1; Other Records, entries 813, 829

RG 84, Records of Foreign Service Posts of the Department of State, Havana, vols. c.81, c.82, c.14.1, c.18.1, San Juan, vols. 7115–21, 7172, 7204, 7212, 7214, 7228–31, 7236, Ponce, all vols.

RG 233, U.S. House of Representatives, files 40A–F9.8, 40A–F9.13, 41A–F10.6
Perkins Library, Special Collections Department, Duke University, Durham, North Carolina.
Appleton Oaksmith Papers
Campbell Family Papers
Charles Sumner Papers
George Latimer Papers
John Backhouse Papers
Lord John Russell Papers
Papers of Spain, Ministry of Foreign Affairs, Charleston Consulate
Papers of Spain, Ministry of Foreign Affairs, Savannah Consulate
Public Record Office, Kew, England.
FO 72, General Correspondence before 1906, Spain, nos. 771, 793, 811, 830, 852, 858, 878, 885–87, 902
FO 83, General Correspondence, Great Britain and General, nos. 154, 159, 247, 421, 462, 520, 1221
FO 84, General Correspondence before 1906, Slave Trade, nos. 870, 898–900, 905–6, 929–30, 935–37, 959, 965, 984, 988
FO 140, Embassy and Consular Archives, Dominican Republic, Correspondence, nos. 1–5, 8
FO 313, Archives of Havana Slave Trade Commission, nos. 24–29, 37–38, 53
FO 541, Confidential Print, Slave Trade, 1858–92, vols. 1–9
FO 683, Embassy and Consular Archives, Dominican Republic, nos. 1–3
Southern Historical Collection, Chapel Hill, North Carolina.
Duff Green Papers
John Quitman Papers
Moreau Barringer Papers
Virginia Historical Society, Richmond.
Diary of the Reverend William Norwood

Contemporary Sources

Abbot, Abiel. *Letters Written in the Interior of Cuba.* Boston: Bowles and Dearborn, 1829.

[Aguilera, Francisco Vicente]. *Notes About Cuba.* New York: N.p., 1872.

Allen, Lewis Leonidas. *The Island of Cuba; or, Queen of the Antilles.* Cleveland: Harris, Fairbanks and Co., 1852.

Aranceles generales para el cobro de derechos de introducción y extracción en todas las aduanas de los puertos habilitados de la siempre fiel isla de Cuba desde 1ro de febrero de 1853. Havana: Imprenta del Gobierno, 1860.

Ballou, Maturin M. *Due South; or, Cuba, Past and Present*. Cambridge, Mass., 1891; New York: Negro Universities Press, 1969.

[Betancourt Cisneros, Gaspar]. *Algunas observaciones a "La Crónica" de New York*. New York: La Verdad, 1848.

———. *Thoughts upon the Incorporation of Cuba into the American Confederation in Contra-position to Those Published by Don José Saco*. New York: La Verdad, 1849.

Betancourt Cisneros, Gaspar, and John S. Thrasher. *Addresses Delivered at the Celebration of the Third Anniversary in Honor of the Martyrs of Cuban Freedom*. New Orleans: Sherman, Wharton and Co., 1854.

Blanco Herrero, Miguel. *Los billetes de banco y la deuda de Cuba: Su arreglo y amortización*. Havana: José Valdepares, 1875.

———. *Isla de Cuba, su situación actual y reformas que reclama*. Madrid: Agustín Jubera, 1876.

Bryant, William Cullen. *Letters of William Cullen Bryant*. Edited by William Cullen Bryant II and Thomas G. Voss. 4 vols. New York: Fordham University Press, 1975–84.

Calcagno, Francisco. *Diccionario biográfico cubano*. New York: Imprenta Ponce de León, 1878.

Cancio Villa-Amil, Mariano. *Situación económica de la Isla de Cuba*. Madrid: M. Ginesta, 1875.

Casamena, Julián M., pseud. [Juan Manuel Macías]. *Publicación de la Sociedad Democrática de los Amigos de América* 4 (July 1865).

Colección de los partes y otros documentos publicados en la Gaceta Oficial de La Habana referentes a la invasión de la gavilla de piratas capitaneada por el traidor Narciso López. Havana: Imprenta del Gobierno, 1851.

Cubano, un [Francisco de Frías y Jacott]. *Isla de Cuba*. Paris: D'Aubusson y Kugelman, 1859.

Cubano, un [Porfirio Valiente]. *La anexión de Cuba y los peninsulares en ella*. 2d ed. New York: Imprenta de J. Mesa, 1853.

Dana, Richard Henry, Jr. *To Cuba and Back: A Vacation Voyage*. Boston: Ticknor and Fields, 1859. Reprint, edited by C. Harvey Gardiner. Carbondale, Ill.: Southern Illinois University Press, 1966.

[Davis, Oliver Wilson]. *Sketch of Frederic Fernández Cavada, a Native of Cuba*. Philadelphia: Privately printed, 1871.

De Armas y Céspedes, José. *Manifiesto de un cubano al Gobierno de España*. Paris: Librería Española, 1876.

———. *Position of the United States on the Cuban Question*. New York: N.p., 1872.

De Bona, Félix. *Cuba, Santo Domingo y Puerto Rico*. Madrid: M. Galiano, 1861.

[De Frías y Jacott, Francisco]. *Recuerdo de la despedida del Excmo. Sr. Teniente General don Domingo Dulce*. Havana: Mencey, 1866.

De Labra y Cadrana, Rafael María. *La abolición de la esclavitud en las Antillas Españolas*. Madrid: Morete, 1869.

———. *La brutalidad de los negros*. Reprint. Havana: Universidad de La Habana, 1961.

———. *La cuestión de ultramar*. Madrid: Nogueras, 1871.

De la Concha, José. *Memoria del Exmo. Sr. D. José de la Concha al actual Capitán General de la isla de Cuba sobre la hacienda pública de la misma*. Madrid: El Clamor Público, 1861.

———. *Reseña de lo ejecutado en la Capitanía General de la isla de Cuba en los dos períodos en que se ha desempeñado el teniente general D. José de la Concha*. Havana: N.p., 1859.

De la Gándara y Navarro, José. *La anexión y guerra de Santo Domingo*. 2 vols. Madrid: El Correo Militar, 1884.

De la Sagra, Ramón. *Cuba: 1860: Selección de artículos sobre agricultura cubana*. Havana: Comisión Nacional Cubana de la Unesco, 1963.

De la Torre, J. M. "Cuba." In *The Spanish West Indies: Cuba and Porto Rico*. Edited by Richard S. Fisher, 7–131. New York: J. H. Colton, 1861.

[Del Monte, Domingo]. "Memorial on the Present State of Cuba, Addressed to the Spanish Government by a Native of the Island." *United States Magazine and Democratic Review* 15, no. 77 (Nov. 1844): 475–83.

De Norzagaray, Fernando. "Diario del Gobernador Norzagaray." *Anales de Investigación Histórica* 6, nos. 1–2 (Jan.–Dec. 1979): 70–132. (Reprint.)

De Roches, V. *Cuba Under Spanish Rule*. New York: Great American Engraving and Printing, [1869?].

De Sedano, Carlos. *Cuba, estudios políticos*. Madrid: Manuel G. Hernández, 1872.

Editors of *La Verdad*. *Cuestión negrera de la isla de Cuba*. New York: La Verdad, 1851.

———. *A Series of Articles on the Cuban Question*. New York: La Verdad, 1849.

Ely, A. W. "Cuba: Its Present Condition—The Revenues—Taxes—Agricultural Industry, Etc., of the Island." *DeBow's Review* 18, no. 1 (Feb. 1855): 163–67.

———. "Cuba as It Is in 1854." *DeBow's Review* 17, no. 3 (Sept. 1854): 219–29.

Emigrado cubano, un. *Información sobre reformas en Cuba y Puerto Rico*. 2d ed. New York: Hallet and Green, 1877.

Erenchun, Félix. *Anales de la isla de Cuba*. Havana: Imprenta la Habanera, 1856.

España, Ministerio de Ultramar. *Cuba desde 1850 a 1873*. Compiled by Carlos de Sedano. Madrid: Imprenta Nacional, 1873.

Español americano, un. *Alerta a los cubanos*. New Orleans: La Patria, 1850.

Estorch, Miguel. *Apuntes para la historia sobre la administración del Marqués de la*

Pezuela en la isla de Cuba. Madrid: M. Galiano, 1856.

Estrada, Luis. *Las provincias ultramarinas y sus presupuestos*. Madrid: Imprenta La España, 1864.

Fabens, Joseph Warren. *Life in Santo Domingo, by a Settler*. 3d ed. New York: Carleton and Co., 1873.

Fisher, Richard S., ed. *The Spanish West Indies: Cuba and Porto Rico*. New York: J. H. Colton, 1861.

Fitzhugh, George. "Cuba: The March of Empire and the Course of Trade." *DeBow's Review* 30 (1861): 30–42.

———. "Destiny of the Slave States." *DeBow's Review* 17, no. 3 (Sept. 1854): 280–84.

García de Arboleya, José. *Manual de la isla de Cuba*. Havana: Imprenta del Tiempo, 1859.

Gibbes, Robert W. *Cuba for Invalids*. New York: W. A. Townsend and Co., 1860.

González, Ambrosio José. *Manifesto on Cuban Affairs Addressed to the People of the United States, September 1st, 1852*. New Orleans: Daily Delta Press, 1853.

González Ponce de Llorante, Antonio. *¿Qué es la anexión?: Consideraciones sobre la pretendida unión de la isla de Cuba a la república de los Estados Unidos de América*. 2d ed. Havana: A. M. Dávila, 1852.

Great Britain, Parliament, House of Commons. *British Parliamentary Papers [Slave Trade]*. 95 vols. Shannon, Ireland: Irish University Press, 1968–71.

Habanero, un. *Probable y definitivo porvenir de la isla de Cuba*. Key West, Fla., 1870.

Hacendado, un [Cristóbal F. Madan]. *Llamamiento de la isla de Cuba a la Nación Española*. New York: Hallet, 1854.

Hale, John P. *The Acquisition of Cuba. Speech of Hon. John P. Hale, of New Hampshire*. (U.S. Senate, Feb. 15, 1859). Washington, D.C.: Buell and Blanchard, 1859.

Hazard, Samuel. *Cuba with Pen and Pencil*. Hartford, Conn.: Hartford, 1871.

———. *Santo Domingo, Past and Present, with a Glance at Hayti*. London: Sampson, Low, Marston and Searle, 1873.

Hespel D'Harponville, Gustave. *La Reine des Antilles*. Paris: Gide et Baudry, 1850.

Howe, Samuel G. *Letters on the Proposed Annexation of Santo Domingo*. Boston: Wright and Potter, 1871.

Jones, Alexander. *Cuba in 1851*. New York: Stringer and Townsend, 1851.

Junta Cubana de Nueva York. *Exposición de la Junta Cubana al Pueblo de Cuba*. New York: Hallet, 1855.

———. *Facts About Cuba Published Under the Authority of the N.Y. Cuban Junta*. New York: Sun Job, 1870.

Just, Ramón. *Las aspiraciones de Cuba*. Paris: Mourgues, 1859.

Keim, DeBenneville Randolph. *Pen Pictures and Leaves of Travel, Romance and History, from the Portfolio of a Correspondent in the American Tropics*. Philadelphia: Claxton, Remsen and Haffelfinger, 1870.

[Kimball, Richard Burleigh]. *Cuba, and the Cubans: Comprising a History of the Island of Cuba, Its Present Social, Political, and Domestic Conditions . . .* New York: S. Hueston, 1850.

Leon, John A. *On Sugar Cultivation in Louisiana and Cuba*. 2 vols. London: Ollivier, 1848.

López de Letona, Antonio. *Isla de Cuba: Reflexiones sobre su estado social, político y económico*. Madrid: Ducazal, 1865.

Luperón, Gregorio. *Notas autobiográficas y apuntes históricos sobre la República Dominicana*. 3 vols. 2d ed. Santiago, Dominican Republic: Editorial El Diario, 1939.

[Madan, Cristóbal F.] *El trabajo libre y el liber-cambio en Cuba*. Paris: Bonaventure, 1864.

Madden, Richard Robert. *The Island of Cuba: Its Resources, Progress, and Prospects*. London: Partridge and Oakey, 1853.

Mallory, Stephen R. *Report of Mr. Mallory of Florida, on the Relations of the United States with Cuba*. Washington, D.C.: Towers, [1851].

Murray, Amelia Matilda. *Letters from the United States, Cuba and Canada*. New York, 1856; Negro Universities Press, 1969.

Murray, Henry Anthony. *Lands of the Slave and the Free; or, Cuba, the United States, and Canada*. 2 vols. London: J. W. Parker and Son, 1855.

Norton, Francis L. *Cuba*. New York: N.p., 1873.

O'Kelly, James J. *The Mambí-Land; or, Adventures of a Herald Correspondent in Cuba*. Philadelphia: J. B. Lippincott and Co., 1874.

O'Neil, J. T. "Porto Rico." In *The Spanish West Indies: Cuba and Porto Rico*. Edited by Richard S. Fisher, 132–90. New York: J. H. Colton, 1861.

Perry, John J. *The Filibuster Policy of the Sham Democracy*. (Speech in the U.S. Senate, May 23, 1860). Washington, D.C.: National Republican Committee, 1860.

Philalethes, Demoticus. *Yankee Travels Through the Island of Cuba; or, The Men and Government, the Laws and Customs of Cuba, as Seen by American Eyes*. New York: D. A. Appleton, 1856.

Phillippo, James Mursell. *The United States and Cuba*. London: Pewtress and Co., 1857.

Piñeyro y Barry, Enrique José Nemesio. *Morales Lemus y la revolución de Cuba*. New York: Zarzamendi, 1871; New York: Unión de Cubanos en el Exilio, 1970.

Quesada, Manuel. *Address of Cuba to the United States*. New York: N.p., 1873.
Quitman, John A. *Speech of John A. Quitman, of Mississippi, on the Subject of the Neutrality Laws: April 29, 1856*. Washington, D.C.: Union Office, 1856.
Rawson, James. *Cuba*. New York: Lane and Tippet, 1847.
Rebello, Carlos. *The Pith of the Sugar Question*. New York: McGowan and Slipper, 1879.
República Dominicana. *Colección de leyes, decretos y resoluciones*. 52 vols. to date. Santo Domingo: Publicaciones ONAP, 1982– .
[Rogers, Carlton H.]. *Incidents of Travel in the Southern States and Cuba*. New York: R. Craighead, 1862.
Ruiz Belvis, Segundo, José Julián Acosta, and Francisco Mariano Quiñones. *Proyecto para la abolición de la esclavitud*. Río Piedras: Editorial Edil, 1978.
[Saco, José Antonio]. *Algunas reformas en la isla de Cuba*. London: N.p., 1865.
Serra, José María. "Apuntes para la historia de los Trinitarios, fundadores de la República Dominicana." *Boletín del Archivo General de la Nación* 32–33 (Jan.–April 1944): 49–69.
Shufeldt, Robert W. "Secret History of the Slave Trade to Cuba." Edited by Frederick C. Drake. *Journal of Negro History* 55, no. 3 (July 1970): 218–35.
Special Committee of the Cuban League of the United States. *The Present Condition of Affairs in Cuba*. New York: Douglas Taylor, 1877.
Tacón, Miguel. *Correspondencia reservada del Capitán General don Miguel Tacón con el gobierno de Madrid, 1834–1836*. Edited by Juan Pérez de la Riva. Havana: Biblioteca Nacional José Martí, 1963.
Taylor, John G. *The United States and Cuba: Eight Years of Change and Travel*. London: Richard Bentley, 1851.
Taylor, Thomas E. *Running the Blockade: A Personal Narrative of Adventures, Risks, and Escapes During the American Civil War*. 4th ed. London: John Murray, 1912.
Thrasher, John S. "Cuba and the United States." *DeBow's Review* 17, no. 1 (July 1854): 43–49.
———. *A Preliminary Essay on the Purchase of Cuba*. New York: Derby and Jackson, 1859.
Torrente, Mariano. *Bosquejo económico político de la isla de Cuba*. 2 vols. Madrid: M. Pita-Barcina, 1852–53.
———. "Memoria del 28 de septiembre de 1852." In *Cuba desde 1850 a 1873*, 168–74. See España, Ministerio de Ultramar.
———. *Memoria sobre la esclavitud en la isla de Cuba*. London: Wood, 1853.
———. *Política ultramarina que abraza todos los puntos referentes a las relaciones de España con los Estados Unidos, con Inglaterra y las Antillas, y señaladamente con la isla de Santo Domingo*. Madrid: Compañía General de Impresos y Libros del Reino, 1854.

Tratado de Reconocimiento, Paz, Amistad, Comercio, Navegación y Extradicción entre S.M. la Reina de España y la República Dominicana. N.p., 1855.

Trollope, Anthony. *The West Indies and the Spanish Main*. Reprint. London: Frank Cass, 1968.

Turnbull, David. *Travels in the West: Cuba with Notices of Porto Rico and the Slave Trade*. London, 1840; New York: Negro Universities Press, 1969.

United States, Commission of Inquiry to Santo Domingo. *Report of the Commission of Inquiry*. Washington, D.C.: GPO, 1871.

United States, Congress, House. Congressman William W. Boyce of South Carolina speaking on the acquisition of Cuba. 33d Cong., 2d sess. *Congressional Globe*, Jan. 15, 1855, vol. 24, appendix, pp. 91–94.

———. *Duties at Porto Rico*. 23d Cong., 2d sess., 1834–35. H. Doc. 173.

———. *The World's Sugar Production and Consumption, 1800–1900*. 57th Cong., 1st sess., 1902. H. Doc. 15, pt. 7. Serial set 4314.

United States, Congress, Senate. *Report of the Secretary of the Treasury in Answer to a Resolution of the Senate, Calling for Statistics of Trade with Cuba for the Last Five Years (March 2, 1859)*. 35th Cong., 2d sess., 1859. S. Exec. Doc. 45. Serial set 984.

———. Senator George E. Pugh of Ohio speaking on the acquisition of Cuba. 35th Cong., 2d sess. *Congressional Globe*, Feb. 10, 1859, vol. 28, pt. 1, pp. 934–40.

———. Senator Stephen R. Mallory of Florida speaking on the acquisition of Cuba. 35th Cong., 2d sess. *Congressional Globe*, Feb. 25, 1859, vol. 28, pt. 2, pp. 1327–39.

———. Senator Zachariah Chandler of Michigan speaking on the acquisition of Cuba. 35th Cong., 2d sess. *Congressional Globe*, Feb. 17, 1859, vol. 28, pt. 2, pp. 1079–86.

United States, Department of State. *Correspondence on the Proposed Tripartite Convention Relative to Cuba*. Boston: Little, Brown and Co., 1853.

———. *Papers Relating to Foreign Affairs of the United States*. 1861–68. Washington, D.C.: GPO, 1861–68.

United States, Department of State, San Juan Consulate. *Despachos de los cónsules norteamericanos en Puerto Rico (1818–1868)*. Edited by Centro de Investigaciones Históricas. Río Piedras: Editorial Universitaria, 1982.

Uno de sus amigos [Cristóbal F. Madan]. *Contestación a un folleto titulado: "Ideas sobre la incorporación de Cuba en los Estados Unidos," por don José Antonio Saco*. New York: La Verdad, 1849.

Vicuña MacKenna, Benjamín. "La independencia de Cuba y Puerto Rico." *Revista Cubana* 3 (1935): 46–97, 316–62.

Watson, William. *Adventures of a Blockade Runner*. London: T. Fisher Unwin, 1892.

Wilkinson, J. *The Narrative of a Blockade-Runner*. New York: Sheldon and Co., 1877.

Williams, George W. *Sketches of Travel in the Old and New World*. Charleston: Walker, Evans and Cogswell, 1871.

Wilson, Thomas W. *An Authentic Narrative Upon the Political Descents Made Upon Cuba*. Havana, 1851.

———. *The Island of Cuba in 1850; Being a Description of the Island, Its Resources, Productions, Commerce & Co.* New Orleans: La Patria, 1850.

Wurderman, John George F. *Notes on Cuba*. Boston: J. Munro and Co., 1844; New York: Arno Press, 1971.

Zamora, José María. *Pronta contestación a "La memoria sobre el comercio de harinas" escrita por el señor don Manuel Gutiérrez*. Madrid: Imprenta del Amor de Dios, 1834.

Zaragoza, Justo. *Isla de Cuba, suspención de conventos y contribución extraordinaria de guerra*. Madrid: N.p., 1837.

Newspapers

La Crónica de Ambos Mundos (Madrid)
The Cuban Messenger
El Diario de la Marina (Havana)
El Dominicano (Santo Domingo)
La Española Libre (Santo Domingo)
La Gaceta de la Habana
La Gaceta de Puerto Rico
La Gaceta de Santo Domingo
Havana *Mercantile Weekly*
New York *Evening Post*
New York *Times*
New York *Tribune*
El Porvenir (Santo Domingo)
La República (Santo Domingo)
La Revolución (New York)
El Siglo (Havana)
El Triunfo (Havana)
La Verdad (New York)
La Voz de Cuba

Secondary Sources

Books and Articles

Aguirre, Sergio, ed. *Eco de caminos*. Havana: Editorial de Ciencias Sociales, 1974.

Alfau Durán, Vetilio, ed. *Controversia histórica: Polémica de Santana*. Santo Domingo: Editora Montalvo, 1968.

Archambault, Pedro María. *Historia de la Restauración*. Paris: Librerie Technique et Economique, 1938; Santo Domingo: Biblioteca Taller 20, 1973.

Bancroft, Frederic. "The Colonization of American Negroes, 1801–1865." In *Frederic Bancroft: Historian*, ed. Jacob E. Cooke. Norman: University of Oklahoma Press, 1957.

———. *The Life of William Seward*. 2 vols. New York: Harper and Brothers, 1900.

Barbier, Jaques A., and Allan J. Kuethe, eds. *The North American Role in the Spanish Imperial Economy, 1760–1819*. Manchester: Manchester University Press, 1984.

Bartlett, Christopher J. "British Reaction to the Cuban Insurrection of 1868–1878." *Hispanic American Historical Review* 37, no. 3 (Aug. 1957): 296–312.

Bécker, Jerónimo. *Historia de las relaciones exteriores de España durante el siglo xix*. 2 vols. Madrid: Voluntad, 1924–26.

Bemis, Samuel Flagg. *The Latin American Policy of the United States*. New York: Harcourt, Brace, and Co., 1943.

Bergad, Laird W. "Agrarian History of Puerto Rico, 1870–1930." *Latin American Research Review* 13, no. 3 (1978): 63–94.

———. *Coffee and the Growth of Agrarian Capitalism in Nineteenth-Century Puerto Rico*. Princeton, N.J.: Princeton University Press, 1983.

———. *Cuban Rural Society in the Nineteenth Century: The Social and Economic History of Monoculture in Matanzas*. Princeton, N.J.: Princeton University Press, 1990.

———. "¿Dos alas del mismo pájaro?: Notas sobre la historia socioeconómica comparativa de Cuba y Puerto Rico." *Historia y Sociedad* 1 (1988): 143–54.

———. "The Economic Viability of Sugar Production Based on Slave Labor in Cuba, 1859–1878." *Latin America Research Review* 24, no. 1 (1989): 95–113.

Betances, Ramón Emeterio. *Las Antillas para los antillanos*. Edited and translated by Carlos M. Rama. San Juan: Instituto de Cultura, 1975.

Bonafoux, Luis, ed. *Betances*. 3d ed. San Juan: Instituto de Cultura, 1987.

Bourne, Kenneth. *The Balance of Power in North America*. Berkeley: University of California Press, 1967.

———. "The Clayton-Bulwer Treaty and the Decline of British Opposition to the Territorial Expansion of the United States, 1857–1860." *Journal of Modern History* 33 (1961): 287–91.

———. *The Foreign Policy of Victorian England*. Oxford: Clarendon Press, 1970.

Bushnell, David, and Neil Macaulay. *The Emergence of Latin America in the Nineteenth Century*. New York: Oxford University Press, 1988.

Caldwell, Robert G. *The López Expeditions to Cuba, 1848–1851*. Princeton, N.J.: Princeton University Press, 1915.

Campbell, A. E., ed. *Expansion and Imperialism*. New York: Harper and Row, 1970.

Caro Costas, Aída, ed. *Ramón Power y Giralt*. San Juan: Privately printed, 1969.

Carr, Raymond. *España, 1808–1975*. Barcelona: Ariel, 1985.

Cassá, Roberto. *Historia social y económica de la República Dominicana*. 2 vols. 10th ed. Santo Domingo: Alfa y Omega, 1991.

Centro de Investigaciones Históricas, Universidad de Puerto Rico. *El proceso abolicionista en Puerto Rico: Documentos para su estudio*. 2 vols. San Juan: Centro de Investigaciones Históricas–Instituto de Cultura, 1974–78.

Cepero Bonilla, Raúl. *Azúcar y abolición*. 1948; Barcelona: Editorial Crítica, 1976.

———. *Obras históricas*. Havana: Instituto de Historia, 1963.

Coatsworth, John H. "American Trade with European Colonies in the Caribbean and South America, 1790–1812." *William and Mary Quarterly* 24 (1967): 243–61.

Cochran, Hamilton. *Blockade Runners of the Confederacy*. Indianapolis: Bobbs-Merrill Co., 1958.

Coll y Toste, Cayetano, ed. *Boletín histórico de Puerto Rico*. 14 vols. San Juan: Tipografía Cantero Fernández y Cía., 1914–27.

Corbitt, Duvon C. "The Junta de Fomento of Havana and the López Expeditions." *Hispanic American Historical Review* 17, no. 3 (Aug. 1937): 339–46.

———. "A Petition for the Continuation of O'Donnell as Captain General of Cuba." *Hispanic American Historical Review* 16, no. 4 (Nov. 1936): 537–43.

Corwin, Arthur F. *Spain and the Abolition of Slavery in Cuba, 1817–1886*. Austin: University of Texas Press, 1967.

Crawford, Martin. *The Anglo-American Crisis of the Mid–Nineteenth Century*. Athens: University of Georgia Press, 1987.

Cruz Monclova, Lidio. *Historia de Puerto Rico (siglo xix)*. 3 vols. Río Piedras: Editorial Universitaria, 1952–64.

Cuba, Instituto de Investigaciones Estadísticas. *Los censos de población y viviendas en Cuba*. Vol. 1. Havana: Instituto de Investigaciones Estadísticas, 1988.

Cubano Iguina, Ástrid. *El hilo en el laberinto: Claves de la lucha política en Puerto Rico (siglo xix)*. Río Piedras: Ediciones Huracán, 1990.

Curet, José A. "De la esclavitud a la abolición: Transiciones económicas en las haciendas azucareras de Ponce, 1845–1873." In *Azúcar y esclavitud*, ed. Andrés A. Ramos Mattei, 59–86. San Juan: Privately printed, 1982.

Current, Richard N. *The Lincoln Nobody Knows*. New York: Hill and Wang, 1984.

Curtin, Philip D. *The Atlantic Slave Trade: A Census*. Madison: University of Wisconsin Press, 1969.

De la Puente García, Esteban. "1861–1865: Anexión y abandono de Santo Domingo." *Revista de Indias* 22, nos. 89–90 (1962): 411–72.

Del Valle, Adrián. "Esclavitud y anexionismo en Cuba." *Revista Bimestre Cubana* 55, no. 1 (1945): 29–41.

Díaz Soler, Luis Manuel. *Historia de la esclavitud negra en Puerto Rico*. Río Piedras: Editorial Universitaria, 1967.

Domínguez, Jaime de Jesús. *La anexión de la República Dominicana a España*. Santo Domingo: Editora de la UASD, 1979.

———. *Economía y política: República Dominicana, 1844–1861*. Santo Domingo: Editora de la UASD, 1977.

———. *Notas económicas y políticas dominicanas sobre el período julio 1865–julio 1886*. 2 vols. Santo Domingo: Editora de la UASD, 1983–84.

Domínguez, Jorge. *Insurrection or Loyalty: The Breakdown of the Spanish American Empire*. Cambridge, Mass.: Harvard University Press, 1980.

Dos Santos, Theotonio. "La crisis de la teoría del desarrollo y las relaciones de dependencia en América Latina." *Boletín del Centro de Estudios Socioeconómicos* 3 (Oct. 1968): 2–40.

Eichner, Alfred S. *The Emergence of Oligopoly: Sugar Refining as a Case Study*. Baltimore: Johns Hopkins University Press, 1969.

Eltis, David. "The Nineteenth-Century Transatlantic Slave Trade: An Annual Time Series of Imports into the Americas Broken Down by Region." *Hispanic American Historical Review* 67, no. 1 (Feb. 1987): 109–38.

Ely, Roland T. *Cuando reinaba su majestad el azúcar: Estudio histórico-sociológico de una tragedia latinoamericana*. Buenos Aires: Editorial Sudamericana, 1963.

———. "The Old Cuba Trade: Highlights and Case Studies of Cuban American Interdependence During the Nineteenth Century." *Business History Review* 38, no. 4 (1964): 457–79.

Ettinger, Amos A. *The Mission to Spain of Pierre Soulé, 1835–1855*. New Haven, Conn.: Yale University Press, 1932.

Ferris, Nathan L. "The Relations of the United States with South America During the American Civil War." *Hispanic American Historical Review* 21, no. 1 (Feb. 1941): 51–78.

Figarola-Caneda, Domingo, ed. *Centón epistolario de Domingo del Monte*. 7 vols. Havana: Imprenta El Siglo XX, 1923–57.

Foner, Philip S. *A History of Cuba and Its Relations with the United States.* 2 vols. New York: International Publishers, 1962–63.

———. *The Spanish-Cuban-American War and the Birth of American Imperialism.* 2 vols. New York: Monthly Review Press, 1972.

Freire, Joaquín. *Presencia de Puerto Rico en la historia de Cuba.* San Juan: Instituto de Cultura, 1966.

Gates, Paul W. *Agriculture and the Civil War.* New York: Alfred A. Knopf, 1965.

Goizueta-Mimó, Félix. *Bitter Cuban Sugar: Monoculture and Economic Dependence from 1825 to 1899.* New York: Garland Publishing, 1987.

González, José Luis. *Nueva visita al cuarto piso.* Madrid: Exlesa, 1986.

González y Gutiérrez, Diego. *Historia documentada de los movimientos revolucionarios por la independencia de Cuba, de 1852 a 1867.* 2 vols. Havana: Imprenta El Siglo XX, 1939.

Goveia, Elsa V. *Slave Society in the British Leeward Islands at the End of the Eighteenth Century.* New Haven, Conn.: Yale University Press, 1965.

Great Britain, *British and Foreign State Papers.* (1816–17, 1834–35.) London: James Ridgway and Sons, 1838, 1852.

Grierson, Edward. *The Death of the Imperial Dream.* Garden City, N.Y.: Doubleday and Co., 1972.

Guerra y Sánchez, Ramiro. *Azúcar y población en las Antillas.* 3d ed. Havana: Cultural, S.A., 1944.

———. *Guerra de los Diez Años, 1868–1878.* 2 vols. Havana: Editorial de Ciencias Sociales, 1972.

———. *Manual de historia de Cuba.* Madrid: Editorial R., 1975.

Harris, Marvin. *Patterns of Race in the Americas.* New York: B. Walker and Co., 1964.

Hauch, Charles C. "Attitudes of Foreign Governments Towards the Spanish Reoccupation of the Dominican Republic." *Hispanic American Historical Review* 27, no. 2 (May 1947): 247–68.

Heitman, John Alfred. *The Modernization of the Louisiana Sugar Industry, 1830–1910.* Baton Rouge: Louisiana State University Press, 1987.

Henderson, Gavin B., ed. "Southern Designs on Cuba, 1854–1857, and Some European Opinions." *Journal of Southern History* 5 (Aug. 1939): 371–85.

Hoetink, H. *The Dominican People, 1850–1900.* Translated by Stephen K. Ault. Baltimore: Johns Hopkins University Press, 1982.

Iglesias García, Fe. "The Development of Capitalism in Cuban Sugar Production, 1860–1900." In *Between Slavery and Free Labor,* 54–76. See Moreno Fraginals, Manuel, Frank Moya Pons, and Stanley L. Engerman, eds.

Jenks, Leland H. *Our Cuban Colony: A Study in Sugar.* New York: Vanguard Press, 1928.

Jiménez de Wagenheim, Olga. *El Grito de Lares: Sus causas y sus hombres*. Río Piedras: Ediciones Huracán, 1984.

Johnson, John J. *A Hemisphere Apart: The Foundations of United States Policy Toward Latin America*. Baltimore: Johns Hopkins University Press, 1990.

Karras, William J. "Yankee Carpenter in Cuba, 1848." *Americas* 30, nos. 6–7 (1978): 17–23.

Kinsbruner, Jay. "Caste and Capitalism in the Caribbean: Residential Patterns and House Ownership Among the Free People of Color of San Juan, Puerto Rico, 1823–46." *Hispanic American Historical Review* 70, no. 3 (Aug. 1990): 433–61.

Kiple, Kenneth F. *The Caribbean Slave: A Biological History*. Cambridge: Cambridge University Press, 1981.

Klein, Herbert S. "Consideraciones sobre la viavilidad de la esclavitud y las causas de la abolición en la Cuba del siglo xix." *La Torre* 21 (July–Dec. 1973): 307–15.

Knight, Franklin W. *The Caribbean, the Genesis of a Fragmented Nationalism*. 1st and 2d eds. New York: Oxford University Press, 1978 and 1990.

———. "Origins of Wealth and the Sugar Revolution in Cuba, 1750–1850." *Hispanic American Historical Review* 57, no. 2 (May 1977): 231–53.

———. *Slave Society in Cuba During the Nineteenth Century*. Madison: University of Wisconsin Press, 1970.

Kuethe, Allan J. "Los Llorones Cubanos: The Sociomilitary Basis of Commercial Privilege in the American Trade Under Charles IV." In *The North American Role in the Spanish Imperial Economy*. Edited by Jaques A. Barbier and Allan J. Kuethe, 142–56. Manchester: Manchester University Press, 1984.

LaFeber, Walter. *The New Empire: An Interpretation of American Expansion, 1860–1898*. 1st and 7th eds. Ithaca, N.Y.: Cornell University Press, 1963 and 1984.

Langley, Lester D. *The Cuban Policy of the United States: A Brief History*. New York: John Wiley and Sons, 1968.

———. *Struggle for the American Mediterranean*. Athens: University of Georgia Press, 1976.

———. "The Whigs and the López Expeditions to Cuba, 1849–1851." *Revista de Historia de América* 71 (Jan.–June 1971): 9–22.

Lebroc, Reyneiro G. *Cuba: Iglesia y sociedad (1830–1860)*. Madrid: N.p., 1976.

Le Riverend, Julio. *Historia económica de Cuba*. Barcelona: Ariel, 1972.

Lewis, Gordon K. *Main Currents in Caribbean Thought: The Historical Evolution of Caribbean Society in Its Ideological Aspects, 1492–1900*. Baltimore: Johns Hopkins University Press, 1983.

Lockward, Alfonso, ed. *Documentos para la historia de las relaciones dominico americanas (1837–1860)*. Santo Domingo: Editora Corripio, 1987.

Lockward, George A. *El protestantismo en Dominicana*. 2d ed. Santo Domingo Universidad CETEC, 1982.

López Segrera, Francisco. *Cuba: Capitalismo dependiente y subdesarrollo (1510–1959)*. 2d ed. Mexico City: Editorial Diógenes, 1979.

Marrero, Leví. *Cuba: Economía y sociedad*. 14 vols. Madrid: Editorial Playor, 1971–88.

Marte, Roberto. *Cuba y la República Dominicana: Transición económica en el Caribe del siglo xix*. Santo Domingo: Universidad APEC, [1988?].

———. *Estadísticas y documentos históricos sobre Santo Domingo (1805–1890)*. Santo Domingo: Museo Nacional de Historia y Geografía, 1984.

Martínez, Rufino. *Hombres dominicanos*. Santiago, Dominican Republic: El Diario, 1943; Santo Domingo: Sociedad Dominicana de Bibliófilos, 1985.

May, Ernest E. *Imperial Democracy*. New York: Harcourt, Brace and World, 1961.

May, Robert E. "Lobbyists for Commercial Empire: Jane M. Cazneau, William Cazneau, and U.S. Caribbean Policy, 1846–1878." *Pacific Historical Review* 48, no. 3 (1979): 383–412.

———. "'Plenipotentiary in Petticoats': Jane M. Cazneau and American Foreign Policy in the Mid-Nineteenth Century." In *Women and American Foreign Policy*. Edited by Edward P. Crapol, 19–44. New York: Greenwood Press, 1987.

———. *The Southern Dream of a Caribbean Empire, 1854–1861*. Baton Rouge: Louisiana State University Press, 1973; Athens: University of Georgia Press, 1989.

Mintz, Sidney W. *Caribbean Transformations*. Chicago: Aldine Publishing Co., 1974.

———. *Sweetness and Power: The Place of Sugar in Modern History*. New York: Viking, 1985.

Monclús, Miguel Ángel. *El caudillismo en la República Dominicana*. 4th ed. Santo Domingo: Universidad CETEC, 1983.

Morales Carrión, Arturo. *Auge y decadencia de la trata negrera en Puerto Rico (1820–1860)*. San Juan: Instituto de Cultura, 1978.

———. "Los orígenes de las relaciones entre los Estados Unidos y Puerto Rico, 1700–1815." *Historia* 2, no. 1 (1952): 1–50.

Moreno Fraginals, Manuel. *El ingenio: El complejo económico social del azúcar*. 3 vols. Havana: Editorial de Ciencias Sociales, 1978.

———. "Plantations in the Caribbean: Cuba, Puerto Rico, and the Dominican Republic in the Late Nineteenth Century." In *Between Slavery and Free Labor*, 3–21. See Moreno Fraginals, Manuel, Frank Moya Pons, and Stanley L. Engerman, eds.

Moreno Fraginals, Manuel, Frank Moya Pons, and Stanley L. Engerman, eds.

Between Slavery and Free Labor: The Spanish-Speaking Caribbean in the Nineteenth Century. Baltimore: Johns Hopkins University Press, 1985.

Moya Pons, Frank. "La economía dominicana y el Partido Azul." *Eme Eme* 5, no. 28 (Jan.–Feb. 1977): 6–7.

———. "The Land Question in Haiti and Santo Domingo: The Sociopolitical Context of Transition from Slavery to Free Labor, 1801–1843." In *Between Slavery and Free Labor*, 181–214. See Moreno Fraginals, Manuel, Frank Moya Pons, and Stanley L. Engerman, eds.

———. *Manual de historia dominicana*. 8th ed. Santiago, Dominican Republic: Universidad Católica Madre y Maestra, 1984.

Murray, David. *Odious Commerce: Britain, Spain, and the Abolition of the Cuban Slave Trade*. Cambridge: Cambridge University Press, 1980.

Nelson, William J. *Almost a Territory: America's Attempt to Annex the Dominican Republic*. Newark, Del.: University of Delaware Press, 1990.

———. "The Haitian Political Situation and Its Effect on the Dominican Republic: 1849–1877." *Americas* 45, no. 2 (Oct. 1988): 227–35.

Nevins, Allan. *Hamilton Fish: The Inner History of the Grant Administration*. New York: Dodd, Mead and Co., 1936.

North, Douglass C. "The United States Balance of Payments, 1790–1860." In *Trends in the American Economy in the Nineteenth Century*, 573–628. Princeton, N.J.: National Bureau of Economic Research, 1960.

Oaks, James. *The Ruling Race: A History of American Slaveholders*. New York: Alfred A. Knopf, 1982.

Oostindie, Gert J. "La burguesía cubana y sus caminos de hierro, 1830–1868." *Boletín de Estudios Latinoamericanos y del Caribe* 37 (Dec. 1984): 99–115.

———. "Cuban Railroads, 1803–1868: Origins and Effects of Progressive Entrepreneurialism." *Caribbean Studies* 20, nos. 3–4 (1988): 24–45.

Ortiz, Altagracia. *Eighteenth-Century Reforms in the Caribbean*. Rutherford, N.J.: Fairleigh Dickinson University Press, 1981.

Ortiz Fernández, Fernando. *José Antonio Saco y sus ideas cubanas*. Havana: Universo, 1929.

Owsley, Frank Lawrence. *King Cotton Diplomacy: Foreign Relations of the Confederate States of America*. 2d rev. ed. Chicago: University of Chicago Press, 1959.

Pagán, Bolívar. *Procerato puertorriqueño del siglo xix*. San Juan: Librería Campos, 1961.

Paolino, Ernest N. *The Foundations of the American Empire*. Ithaca, N.Y.: Cornell University Press, 1973.

Paquette, Robert Louis. *Sugar Is Made with Blood: The Conspiracy of La Escalera and the Conflict Between Empires over Slavery in Cuba*. Middletown, Conn.: Wesleyan University Press, 1988.

Peguero, Valentina, and Danilo de los Santos. *Visión general de la historia domi-*

nicana. 10th ed. Santiago, Dominican Republic: Universidad Católica Madre y Maestra, 1986.

Pérez, Carlos F. *Historia diplomática de Santo Domingo (1492–1861)*. Santo Domingo: Escuela de Servicos Internacionales, Universidad Nacional Pedro Henríquez Ureña, 1973.

Pérez, Louis A., Jr. *Cuba: Between Reform and Revolution*. New York: Oxford University Press, 1988.

———. *Cuba and the United States: Ties of Singular Intimacy*. Athens: University of Georgia Press, 1990.

———. *Cuba between Empires, 1878–1902*. Pittsburgh: University of Pittsburgh Press, 1983.

Pérez de la Riva, Francisco. *El café: Historia de su cultivo y explotación en Cuba*. Havana: Jesús Montero, 1944.

Perkins, Dexter. *The Monroe Doctrine, 1826–1867*. Baltimore: Johns Hopkins University Press, 1933.

Peukert, Detlev Julio K. "Anhelo de dependencia: Las ofertas de anexión de la República Dominicana a los Estados Unidos en el siglo xix." *Jahrbuch für Geschichte von Staat, Wirtschaft and Gesellschaft Lateinamerikas* 23 (1986): 305–50.

Picó, Fernando. *1898: La guerra después de la guerra*. Río Piedras: Ediciones Huracán, 1987.

———. *Libertad y servidumbre en el Puerto Rico del siglo xix (los jornaleros utuadeños en vísperas del auge del café)*. 2d ed. Río Piedras: Ediciones Huracán, 1982.

Pinkett, Harold T. "Efforts to Annex Santo Domingo to the United States, 1866–1871." *Journal of Negro History* 26, no. 1 (Jan. 1941): 12–45.

Platt, D. C. M. *Latin America and British Trade, 1806–1914*. New York: Barnes and Noble, 1973.

Ponte Domínguez, Francisco J. *La masonería en la independencia de Cuba, 1809–1869*. Havana: Masonic World, 1944.

Portell Vilá, Herminio. *Historia de Cuba en sus relaciones con los Estados Unidos y España*. 4 vols. Havana: Montero, 1938–41.

———. *Narciso López y su época, 1848–1850*. 3 vols. Havana: Cultural, S.A., 1930–58.

Poyo, Gerald Eugene. *With All, and for the Good of All: The Emergence of Popular Nationalism in the Cuban Communities of the United States, 1848–1898*. Durham, N.C.: Duke University Press, 1989.

Pratt, Julius W. "The Ideology of American Expansion." In *Essays in Honor of William Dodd*. Edited by Avery Craven, 335–52. Chicago: University of Chicago Press, 1935.

Price, Marcus W. "Blockade Running as a Business in South Carolina During the War Between the States, 1861–1865." *American Neptune* 9 (1949): 31–62.

———. "Ships that Tested the Blockade of the Carolina Ports, 1861–1865." *American Neptune* 8 (1948): 196–241.

Prichard, Walter. "The Effects of the Civil War on the Louisiana Sugar Industry." *Journal of Southern History* 5, no. 3 (1939): 316–20.

Ramos, Marcos Antonio. *Panorama del protestantismo en Cuba*. San José, Costa Rica: Editorial Caribe, 1986.

Ramos Mattei, Andrés A. *Betances en el ciclo revolucionario antillano: 1867–1875*. San Juan: Instituto de Cultura, 1987.

———. *La hacienda azucarera: Su crecimiento y crisis en Puerto Rico (siglo xix)*. San Juan: CEREP, 1981.

———. "La importación de trabajadores contratados para la industria azucarera puertorriqueña: 1860–1880." In *Inmigración y clases sociales en el Puerto Rico del siglo xix*. Edited by Francisco A. Scarano, 125–42. Río Piedras: Ediciones Huracán, 1981.

———. "El liberto en el régimen de trabajo azucarero de Puerto Rico, 1870–1880." In *Azúcar y esclavitud*. See Ramos Mattei, Andrés A., ed.

Ramos Mattei, Andrés A., ed. *Azúcar y esclavitud*. San Juan: Privately printed, 1982.

Ramsdell, Charles W. "The Natural Limits of Slavery Expansion." *Mississippi Valley Historical Review* 16 (1929): 151–71.

Rauch, Basil. *American Interest in Cuba: 1848–1855*. New York: Columbia University Press, 1948.

Richardson, James D., ed. *A Compilation of the Messages and Papers of the Presidents, 1789–1897*. 10 vols. Washington, D.C.: GPO, 1896–99.

Robertson, William Spence. *Hispanic-American Relations with the United States*. New York: Oxford University Press, 1923.

Rodríguez, José Ignacio. *Estudio histórico sobre el origen, desenvolvimiento y manifestaciones de la idea de la anexión de la isla de Cuba a los Estados Unidos*. Havana: La Propaganda Política, 1900.

Rodríguez Demorizi, Emilio. "Antecedentes de la anexión." *Clio* 123 (Jan.–Aug. 1968): 36–43.

———. *Santana y los poetas de su tiempo*. Santo Domingo: Academia Dominicana de la Historia, 1966.

Rodríguez Demorizi, Emilio, ed. *Antecedentes de la anexión a España*. Santo Domingo: Academia Dominicana de la Historia, 1955.

———. *Correspondencia del consul de Francia en Santo Domingo, 1846–1850*. 2 vols. Santo Domingo: Editora Montalvo, 1944–47.

———. *Documentos para la historia de la República Dominicana*. 4 vols. Santo Domingo: Editora Montalvo–Academia Dominicana de la Historia, 1944–81.

———. *Papeles de Buenaventura Báez*. Santo Domingo: Editora Montalvo, 1955.

———. *Papeles de Pedro Bonó*. Santo Domingo: Editora del Caribe, 1964.

———. *Papeles de Santana*. Rome: Tipografía G. Menaglia, 1952.

———. *Proyecto para la incorporación de Santo Domingo a Norte América*. Santo Domingo: Editora Montalvo, 1945.

———. *Samaná, pasado y porvenir*. Santo Domingo: Editora Montalvo, 1945.

Roig de Leuchsenring, Emilio. "Cuba en 1840." *Revista Bimestre Cubana* 46, no. 2 (1940): 161–77.

———. *Cuba y los Estados Unidos, 1805–1898*. Havana: Sociedad Cubana de Estudios Históricos e Internacionales, 1949.

Rosario Natal, Carmelo. "Betances y los anexionistas, 1850–1870: Apuntes sobre un problema." *Revista de Historia* 1, no. 2 (1985): 113–30.

———. *Puerto Rico y la crisis de la Guerra Hispanoamericana*. Hato Rey, P.R.: Ramallo Printing, 1975.

Saco, José Antonio. *Contra la anexión*. Edited by Fernando Ortiz Fernández. Havana: Instituto Cubano del Libro, 1974.

Sang, Mu-Kien A. *Buenaventura Báez: El caudillo del sur (1844–1878)*. Santo Domingo: Ediciones Taller, 1991.

Santovenia y Echaide, Emeterio Santiago. *El presidente Polk y Cuba*. Havana: Academia de la Historia de Cuba, 1935.

Scarano, Francisco A., ed. *Inmigración y clases sociales en el Puerto Rico del siglo xix*. Río Piedras: Ediciones Huracán, 1981.

———. *Sugar and Slavery in Puerto Rico: The Plantation Economy of Ponce, 1800–1850*. Madison: University of Wisconsin Press, 1984.

Schroeder, Susan. *Cuba: A Handbook of Historical Statistics*. Boston: G. K. Hall, 1982.

Scott, Rebecca J. *Slave Emancipation in Cuba: The Transition to Free Labor, 1860–1899*. Princeton, N.J.: Princeton University Press, 1985.

Senior, Rafael. *Santana: Libertador, gobernante, anexionista*. Santo Domingo: La Información, 1938.

Sitterson, Joseph Carlyle. *Sugar Country: The Cane Sugar Industry in the South, 1753–1950*. Lexington: University Press of Kentucky, 1953.

Smith, Robert F., ed. *What Happened in Cuba? A Documentary History*. New York: Twayne Publishers, 1963.

Smith, Theodore Clarke. "Expansion After the Civil War, 1865–71." *Political Science Quarterly* 16, no. 3 (1901): 412–36.

Strode, Hudson. *The Pageant of Cuba*. New York: Random House, 1934.

Tansill, Charles C. *The United States and Santo Domingo, 1798–1873*. Baltimore: Johns Hopkins University Press, 1938.

Thomas, Emory. *The Confederate Nation, 1861–1865*. New York: Harper Torchbook, 1979.

United States, Department of Commerce, Bureau of the Census. *Historical Statistics of the United States*. 2 vols. Washington, D.C.: GPO, 1975.

———. *Historical Statistics of the United States, Colonial Times to 1957*. Washington, D.C.: GPO, 1960.

Urban, C. Stanley. "The Africanization of Cuba Scare, 1853–1855." *Hispanic American Historical Review* 37, no. 1 (Feb. 1957): 29–45.

———. "The Ideology of Southern Imperialism: New Orleans and the Caribbean, 1845–1860." *Louisiana Historical Quarterly* 34, no. 1 (1956): 48–73.

Van Alstyne, Richard W., ed. "Anglo-American Relations, 1853–57." *American Historical Review* 42 (1937): 491–500.

Vogt, Paul L. *The Sugar Refining Industry in the United States, Its Development and Present Condition*. Philadelphia: University of Pennsylvania Press, 1908.

Weinberg, Albert K. *Manifest Destiny: A Study of Nationalistic Expansion in American History*. Baltimore: Johns Hopkins University Press, 1935.

Welles, Sumner. *Naboth's Vineyard: The Dominican Republic, 1844–1924*. 2 vols. New York: Payson and Clarke, 1928.

Williams, Eric. *Capitalism and Slavery*. 7th ed. New York: Capricorn Books, 1966.

———. *From Columbus to Castro: The History of the Caribbean, 1492–1969*. New York: Vintage Books, 1984.

Williams, William Appleman. *The Roots of the Modern American Empire*. New York: Random House, 1969.

Williamson, James A. *A Short History of British Expansion*. 6th ed. New York: St. Martin's Press, 1967.

Wise, Stephen R. *Lifeline of the Confederacy: Blockade Running During the Civil War*. Columbia: University of South Carolina Press, 1988.

Yungling, David G., ed. *Highlights in the Debates in the Spanish Chamber of Deputies Relative to the Abandonment of Santo Domingo*. Washington, D.C.: Murray and Heister, 1941.

Unpublished Materials

Álvarez López, Luis. "Historia de la anexión de Santo Domingo a España, 1861–1863." M.A. thesis, Universidad de Puerto Rico, 1977.

Bunce, Kenneth W. "American Interests in the Caribbean Islands, 1783–1850." Ph.D. diss., Ohio State University, 1939.

Denslow, David A., Jr. "Sugar Production in Northeastern Brazil and Cuba, 1858–1908." Ph.D. diss., Yale University, 1974.

Leard, Robert B. "Bonds of Destiny: The United States and Cuba, 1848–1861." Ph.D. diss., University of California, Berkeley, 1953.

Poyo, Gerald Eugene. "Cuban Emigré Communities in the United States and the Independence of Their Homeland, 1852–1895." Ph.D. diss., University of Florida, 1983.

Ramos Mattei, Andrés A. "The Influence of Mechanization on the Puerto Rican System of Sugar Production, 1873–1898." Ph.D. diss., University of London, 1977.

Santana, Arturo. "The United States and Puerto Rico, 1797–1830." Ph.D. diss., University of Chicago, 1953.

Sonesson, Brigit. "Puerto Rico's Commerce, 1835–1865: From Regional to Worldwide Market Relations." Ph.D. diss., New York University, 1985.

Tirado Merced, Dulce María. "Las raíces sociales del liberalismo criollo: El Partido Liberal Reformista, 1870–1875." M.A. thesis, Universidad de Puerto Rico, 1981.

Vázquez Sotillo, Nelly. "La represión política en Puerto Rico durante la administración de Miguel López de Baños (1837–1840)." M.A. thesis, Universidad de Puerto Rico, 1983.

Watson, Hilbourne. "The United States and the Caribbean: Whose New World Order?" Paper presented at the seventeenth annual conference of the Caribbean Studies Association, St. George's, Grenada, May 26, 1992.

Wipfler, William L. "The Churches of the Dominican Republic in the Light of History." M.Div. thesis, Union Theological Seminary, 1964.

Index

www.ingramcontent.com/pod-product-compliance
Lightning Source LLC
LaVergne TN
LVHW030916080826
845145LV00013B/2924

* 9 7 8 0 8 2 0 3 4 1 6 5 1 *